FROM CAP ANSON TO ~~HITTING~~
DON MATTINGLY ... FROM THE BROOKLYN
EXCELSIORS TO THE NEW YORK *METS* ... THE
ULTIMATE BOOK FOR BASEBALL FANS!

- Do you know whose season and career home
  run records Babe Ruth broke?

- Do you know what current major league
  team was originally called the *Invaders*?

- Do you know who was the first player to get
  hits for two different teams in two different
  cities on the same day?

Test your memory and knowledge of America's
favorite pastime with the most comprehensive
sourcebook of every unusual, intriguing and
amazing baseball achievement—plus special
sections featuring the evolution of season and
career hitting, fielding and pitching records—
that everyone, from fan to fanatic, will devour.

DAVID NEMEC is a novelist and baseball historian.
He has written the historical sections of *The Ultimate
Baseball Book*, numerous baseball and memorabilia
books, and the franchise histories for major-league
team yearbooks.

GREAT BASEBALL FEATS, FACTS & FIRSTS

DAVID NEMEC

A SIGNET BOOK

NEW AMERICAN LIBRARY

PUBLISHED BY
PENGUIN BOOKS CANADA LIMITED

Copyright © 1989 by David Nemec

This book previously appeared in a Plume edition
published by New American Library.

First Signet Printing, April, 1989

2   3   4   5   6   7   8   9

SIGNET TRADEMARK REG. U.S. PAT. OFF. AND FOREIGN COUNTRIES
REGISTERED TRADEMARK — MARCA REGISTRADA
HECHO EN WINNIPEG. CANADA

SIGNET, SIGNET CLASSIC, MENTOR, ONYX, PLUME,
MERIDIAN and NAL BOOKS are published in Canada by Penguin
Books Canada Limited, 2801 John Street, Markham, Ontario,
L3R 1B4
PRINTED IN CANADA
COVER PRINTED IN U.S.A.

*To my father, Joseph Sylvester Nemec,
who was ahead of his time
but balanced matters by having a son
who is an anachronism in his.*

Contents

SECTION 3

SECTION 4

SECTION 5

SECTION 6

Acknowledgments

A book like this one is often the product of a single, highly skewed imagination, but usually there have been many minds along the way that have triggered, fostered and helped refine it.

Among those I especially wish to cite are: Philip Von Borries, baseball historian, whose favorite province is the old American Association and in particular Pete Browning; Bill Weiss, Pacific Coast League statistician, for providing me with copious material on the minor leagues; Dino Restelli for introducing me to many old players and fans in the San Francisco Bay area; Jill Grossman and Larry Zuckerman for their supportive and helpful editing; and Fran Collin for her representation of my interests in the publishing industry.

Foreword

It probably won't come as a surprise to those of you familiar with my other baseball history and memorabilia books to learn that I'm in a shrinking minority. I don't believe there is any way at the moment to compare George Brett's accomplishments to those, say, of Home Run Baker. Nor do I think anyone ever will devise a satisfactory method to do it. We are doomed to debate forever whether Babe Ruth would have out-homered Roger Maris if he too had been in his prime in 1961, or whether Cy Young would have won 500 games or just 400, or not even 300, if he had pitched under the same conditions and against the same batters that Dwight Gooden faces. Give me an argument if you like—I'm still open to being convinced that one or the other of our sabermetricians now on the case will discover a system to measure Reggie Jackson against Chuck Klein—but, meanwhile, it doesn't make me overly despondent not to know who was the greatest hitter or pitcher or shortstop of all time. Life—and baseball—are full of uncertainties. Differences of opinion are a large part of what makes them fun.

In the next breath, I'm going to haul off and say that I do have some suggestions that I think will help you make order out of the chaos that exists whenever baseball analysts gather to thrash out and attempt to settle once and for all the metaphysical issues of their profession. First off, many of them like to dismiss all records set before 1893 because the geometry of the playing field hadn't yet been properly established. This is a convenient way to dispose of a lot of unwieldly 50-win and 400-strikeout seasons, but ultimately it's an evasion of the problem. A record achieved in 1886 isn't any less meaningful because it happened when the pitcher's mound was only 50 feet from home plate. That it was accomplished by a pitcher who played left field between starting assignments or had a 6.90 ERA after the mound was moved to its present location is also beside the point. A record is a record regardless of when or under what circumstances it occurred. If five pitchers win 200 games in the course of a decade, but only one wins 250, then we all agree that one pitcher has the best mark for that particular 10-year-period. But if no pitchers win 200 games in the following decade, and only two win as many as 150, we'll all agree again that it doesn't necessarily mean those two pitchers aren't at least the equal of the five who won 200 a decade earlier and perhaps even as good as the 250-game winner. What it comes down to is that for us to grapple successfully with the many enormous disparities that exist between batting averages in the twenties and batting averages in the sixties, pitching strikeouts in 1906 and pitching strikeouts in 1986, shortstops' fielding averages in 1882 and shortstops' fielding averages in 1982, we can't simply call some of the figures unrepresentative and drop them from consideration. Instead, we have to set up a few ground rules. One that I've found helpful in winding my path through the record books is to divide the game into seven periods:

1. 1876, the year the National League began, through 1892
2. 1893, the first year the pitcher's mound was 60 feet six inches from the plate, through 1900
3. 1901, the American League's inaugural year as a major circuit, through 1919
4. 1920, the unofficial beginning of the lively ball era, through 1941
5. 1942, the first year World War II altered the game appreciably, through 1960
6. 1961, the first wave of expansion, through 1976
7. 1977, the third wave of expansion, through the present

To some extent these points of demarkation are arbitrary. Many, for example, feel that the seventh phase really began when the strike zone was redefined after the 1968 season and a second wave of expansion took place, or else when the American League adopted the designated hitter rule in 1973. If you want to side with either of those contentions, I have no quarrel. Neither will I be unhappy if you happen to think the National Association was a major league and the first phase should therefore begin with the 1871 season.

Almost every generalization that is made about baseball invites speculation, if not outright argument. Everybody is in accord that the game entered a new phase when the pitcher's mound was moved 10 feet farther away from the plate, because it altered the balance between batters and pitchers radically in favor of the former and immediately led to more hitting and scoring. But I have yet to unearth a good explanation for why batting averages and run production jumped in 1893, really took off for the stratosphere in 1894 and then returned for the next few years to about the level reached in 1893. What happened during the 1894 season? Why was it that hitters really feasted the second year—rather than the first year—after the mound was moved? I don't know the answer. I can't even make a reasonable guess why somebody like Hugh Duffy hit .438 in 1894, 75 points higher than he did in any other season. The record books are full of feats, facts and firsts that defy logic and leave us hungering for explanations. And the books themselves aren't always logical or consistent. Some claim Christy Mathewson won 374 games, others say 373, and there are still one or two around that credit him with only 372 victories. Which figure is the true one? For my purposes, I usually go with the Macmillan *Baseball Encyclopedia* when there is a conflict—but I haven't found the Macmillan so trustworthy that I'd be willing to stake my reputation on its data. What I've done when a serious dispute exists is attach an alert signal, letting you know that before you hold forth on Paul Hines, for one, at your favorite watering hole or the next SABR convention, you ought to be prepared for somebody to jump in and say, "Now wait a minute, ace. According to the *Sporting News*, the first triple Crown winner was . . ."

In any event, I think you'll have a good time looking through this book and seeing who holds a certain record and who held it before him. You'll also note how and why several dozen pitchers who were active before 1920 had career ERAs under 2.50 while only two pitchers who were active between 1920 and 1960 had career ERAs under 3.00. Maybe you already know who those two pitchers are. If so, you can still expect to find a fair amount you don't know, or haven't quite thought of in the same way I have, and will appreciate having it in a compact form. Enjoy yourself.

—*David Nemec*
San Francisco, California

The System for Evaluating Feats

In college, I had a coach who used to start out each season by telling us that baseball was essentially a simple game. Three strikes, three outs; nine players, nine innings. There was an inherent order to it, and when it was played right it worked like a mathematical equation. Listening to our coach, I always got a bad feeling in my stomach. He wasn't explaining baseball to us but reducing it. Seeing the game merely in terms of numbers and logic was deeply disturbing to me. It was so much more.

Yet, once I began to write about baseball, I realized that he had a point. It really is a game with a magic number, and that number beyond all doubt is three. Along with three strikes and three outs and a structure that is built on multiples of three, in the scheme of things 300 wins and 3000 hits have become the twin pinnacles that, when attained by a pitcher or a batter, assure him of eventual selection to the Hall of Fame. On a seasonal basis, a .300 or higher batting average for a hitter is almost exactly as likely to occur as a 3.00 or lower ERA for a pitcher, and in the utopian year there would be about 10 or 12 of each. To my knowledge that utopia has never been achieved in a season. Probably it never will be. One faction or the other will inevitably hold an edge, and in the ebb and flow of rule changes and developments in equipment and playing surfaces that edge will constantly swing back and forth like a pendulum. Arguably, the balance between hitters and pitchers is more even now than it's ever been. In the past 10 seasons we've had about the same number of .350 hitters and pitchers who have allowed fewer than two earned runs a game, and that, historically, has not always been the case. Indeed there have been times when virtually no pitchers could hold the opposition below three runs a game—forget two—and a .350

batting average just barely got its owner into the top 10 hitters. The 1930 season was like that. The 1968 season, however, in the American League especially, was the exact opposite. Was it because most of the great hitters were born around 1905 and somewhere in the early thirties something in the genes changed around and resulted in a lot of super pitching arms being hatched? Maybe, but there are several much more likely explanations. Wherever the truth lies, though, those two seasons and others like them created scads of records for batting zeniths and pitching nadirs or vice versa—records that in some instances are so skewed as to be all but unbreakable. Nobody in the past 40 years has come anywhere near to collecting 190 RBIs in a season or posting a 7.71 ERA in over 150 innings or rapping 67 doubles. What that means, to me, is that a straight fact and record book, while interesting, leaves something to be desired, namely a perspective that allows for other notable feats to receive their due. I've tried to provide that perspective, first by noting the all-time record and, where it's possible to do it without disrupting the continuity of the book, featuring it in the period in which it occurred, and then by tracing the evolution of the record and noting some of the significant high points and low points since it was set. In other words, touching on not only the major record but the records for each period as well.

It's not an altogether new approach, but what is unique, I think, is the manner in which it's been organized and served up to you. The main course is full of the staples that you rightfully want in a book of feats, facts and firsts, but it's spiced with flavors that ought to do some exciting things to your taste buds.

Introduction

The first section of this book, covering the years from 1846 through 1900, differs somewhat in design from the other sections. Though I'm not writing a history of baseball, I do feel both the obligation and the desire to offer up a backdrop—a setting of the stage, if you will.

In Section 1, along with the great feats and firsts that occurred in the last century, I'll introduce all of the various elements that are present in a typical day or night at a baseball game with the exception of the managers and the stadiums, which we'll meet in Section 2 when both subjects really began to come into their own. Tucked in amid the introductions are chapters on first basemen's records, some of the most interesting teams of the era and a few of the more intriguing bit players who flitted across the stage for only a moment or two but sometimes stole the show before disappearing into the wings. Some comments with regard to chapters on team and individual record holders: Although each for the most part is located in the section focusing on the era when the all-time record was set—i.e., Home Run Feats is found in Section 5, the period when Roger Maris and Hank Aaron set the single-season and career home run marks—all include the bulk of significant records established since 1901. Secondly, the seasons of 1918 and 1919, which were abbreviated due to World War I, and the strike-shortened 1981 season have been omitted from consideration except in cases when the number of games played had no bearing on the record figure. And finally, the names in capital letters designate the all-time record holders for the specified era or position, as distinguished from the names in regular case, which designate either league record holders or runners up to an all-time record.

SECTION 1

Famous Firsts:
1846–1900

The precise origins of many things about baseball that we take for granted are heavily shrouded by the almost impenetrable veils of the past. It would be wonderful to know who first thought of putting webbing in his glove or what pitcher was the first to pick a runner off base, but it is impossible even to pinpoint with any degree of certainty the moment of transition between ancient games like rounders and stoolball and to say this is how and where baseball began. There are still many people, some current major-league players among them, who believe that Abner Doubleday invented the game as we know it. The more tenable opinion for the past half-century has been that Alexander Cartwright was the inventor and that the first game under the Cartwright rules was played on June 19, 1846, at Elysian Fields in Hoboken, New Jersey, between the New York Nine and Cartwright's club, the Knickerbockers. There is no longer any serious dispute that this game took place; a complete record of it exists. We know that the final score was 23–1, and the game ended when the New York Nine scored their 21st run, then called an ace, in the fourth inning, added two more for safe measure, and then held the Knickerbockers scoreless in their last turn at bat. We even know that Cartwright, umpiring the game, levied a six-cent fine for swearing against a New York Nine player named Davis.

But was it really the first game? If so, how did the Knickerbockers, purportedly the first club ever to organize mainly for the purpose of playing baseball, manage to lose so egregiously? Who were the New York Nine? When and where did they assemble and start mastering the intricacies of the new sport? How sure are we that they didn't secretly play a slew of games to prepare for Cartwright's bunch and that those games weren't the first ones? Well, the unhappy truth is that we're not at all sure; nor, probably, will we ever be. Therefore be warned that some of the firsts you will encounter at the beginning of each section of this book may in fact have been seconds or thirds or, in some instances, no more than myths fashioned by the ageless pairing of a writer with space to fill and a player with an eye to posterity. But in any event, they are well worth sharing.

1849—The Knickerbockers adopt the first official club uniform, which consists of blue woolen pantaloons, a white flannel shirt and a straw hat; in 1855, a broad patent leather belt is added and the straw hat gives way to a mohair cap.

1857—The first league is formed and calls itself the National Association of Baseball Clubs. All games are played at the Fashion Race Course in Jamaica, New York, and spectators are assessed a 50¢ admission fee. The season runs from July to October because some clubs contend the weather is too hot before July.

1857—After the formation of the National Association, a nine-inning format replaces the first-team-to-score-21-runs-wins rule, with five innings constituting a legal contest.

1859—The Brooklyn Excelsiors become the first team to go on tour.

1859—The National Association of Baseball Players is formed, taking control of the game away from the Knickerbockers Club and giving it a national flavor to induce western clubs to participate. The Association also swiftly has the corollary effect of demolishing baseball's image as strictly a gentleman's game.

1862—Jim Creighton of the Brooklyn Excelsiors, highly paid pitcher and the first famous pro player, suffers a ruptured spleen while batting in a game and dies at his home. A large granite monument is erected over his grave in Brooklyn's Greenwood Cemetery. Carved on the granite and encircled by a wreath is a design featuring a pair of crossed bats, a scorebook, a base and a baseball cap. Above the granite design is the single scrolled word *Excelsior*, and balanced on the summit of the granite column rests a stone baseball.

1864—Second baseman Al Reach, later a sporting goods manufacturer and founder of the *Reach Baseball Guide*, becomes the first "revolver" when he jumps the Eckfords club to sign with the Philadelphia Athletics.

186?—Pitcher Candy Cummings discovers how to make a baseball curve . . . maybe. Cummings himself claims not to be the discoverer, but he nevertheless makes the Hall of Fame for it. In the years to come other pitchers will be credited with discovering various new types of deliveries, but it's open to speculation which of them did and which of them didn't. Elmer Stricklett is credited with discovering the spitball; or maybe it was Billy Hart, who claimed he first used it in 1896 after being taught how to throw it by Baltimore catcher Frank Bowerman; or maybe it was Frank Corridon. Nat Hudson is credited with the sinker; Dave Danforth, the shineball; Russ Ford, the emeryball, and maybe the knuckler too, or at least one of the first good ones; Christy Mathewson, the screwball, the first great one anyway, called a fadeaway; and Eddie Plank, the first great palmball.

187?—Nat Hicks of the Mutuals becomes the first catcher to play directly behind the bat; others claim it is Deacon White, who is almost definitely seen doing it in 1875, at any rate with runners on base.

1871—The National Association forms into an organized professional league and plays its first game on May 4, with Cleveland (Forest City) pitted against Fort Wayne (Kekionga). Bobby Mathews of Kekionga pitches a 2–0 shutout over Forest City's Uncle Al Pratt. Deacon White, catcher for Cleveland and the most famous player in the game, goes 3-for-4.

1871—Rynie Wolters, the first Dutch player, debuts with the New York Mutuals.

1871—Boston and Cleveland keep batting averages for all players, and the other National Association clubs soon do likewise. Previously only runs have been recorded.

1872—Oscar Bielaski, the first Polish player, debuts with the Washington Nationals.

1874—The Boston Red Caps and Philadelphia Athletics embark on the first overseas tour to promote baseball, traveling to England in July. While there, the two clubs play a series of exhibition baseball games as well as several cricket matches. The tour is neither a financial nor an artistic success as the British seem singularly uninterested in the new game.

1875—Fred Thayer of Harvard invents the first catcher's mask and shows it to classmate Jim Tyng, who tests it in a college game. Later Thayer is also credited by some with developing the first inflated chest protector.

1875—Joe Borden of the Philadelphias, aka Joe Josephs,

pitches the first recorded no-hitter on July 28 against the Chicago White Stockings.

1875—The Boston Red Caps turn a profit for the season of $2261.07, which is not lost on other National Association club owners and spurs them to begin thinking of forming a more tightly run league and getting rid of weak clubs, corrupt players and lackadaisical team officials.

1876—William Hulbert, taking the bit in his teeth, forms a new circuit and calls it the National League after getting Boston's four star players, Deacon White, Ross Barnes, Al Spalding and Cal McVey, to desert the Red Caps and sign with his Chicago club. Cynics contend Hulbert's motive in forming the National League isn't to provide a better-run operation but because he fears the National Association will expel the four players and his Chicago team in the bargain.

1876—The first National League game is played on April 22 at Philadelphia, with Joe Borden, now with Boston, beating Lon Knight of the Athletics 6–5. Boston's Jim O'Rourke gets the first National League hit, a single in the top of the first inning. Third baseman Ezra Sutton of the A's has the distinction of having also played in the first National Association game, five years earlier, with Cleveland.

1876—Al Spalding appears on the field wearing a black kid glove with layers of padding to reduce the sting of a thrown or hit ball. (If you prefer another player of the time, feel free to substitute his name for Spalding's. Literally dozens are credited with having been the first to use a glove.)

1876—Philadelphia and New York are booted out of the new circuit for failing to complete their last western road trips. Not until 1883 will the two largest cities in the country again be permitted to have franchises in the National League.

1877—The first uniform playing schedule is adopted so that fans in all cities will know in advance which dates their club will be playing at home and can plan accordingly.

1877—The National League starts its second season with a new rule, which states that for a batted ball to be fair it must stay within the foul lines until it passes a base or else is fielded. The rule is put in to curb Ross Barnes, Davy Force and other batsmen who are adept at slicing hits that land in fair territory and then carom foul, forcing infielders to play outside the boundaries when they come to bat. Other players who will force rules to be changed in the years ahead are George Wright and Dickey Pearce, specialists at trapping pop flies before the infield fly rule is created; Will White and Jack Schappert, deft at hitting and intimidating batters without penalty until it occurs to somebody that maybe these wounded batsmen should be awarded first base; King Kelly, who is credited perhaps falsely, with instigating a rule that prevents him from hopping off the bench when a foul fly heads his way and announcing himself into the game as a substitute in order to catch it; Roy Thomas, so skilled at fouling off pitches that the National League finally, in 1901, decides to start counting foul balls as strikes; and Germany Schaefer, whose crowd-catching device of setting out from second base to steal first causes a rule to be written that the bases can no longer be run backward.

1878—For the first time a commercial league, the National, plays all its scheduled games. Always before at least one team has failed to finish the season.

1879—Boston owner Arthur Soden devises the reserve clause. At first it protects only five players on each team, but with time it's expanded to include the whole roster.

1879—The Providence Grays build the first wire screen behind home plate and across the grandstand in their park to protect spectators from foul tips in a seating area that has become known as the "Slaughter Pens." That same year or maybe a year earlier the Grays are also, some say, the first team to install a turnstile in their park.

1880—Rules are put in to declare a runner out if hit by a batted ball and to award a base on balls on eight balls instead of nine.

1880—The *Chicago Tribune* begins reporting RBIs, but RBI records are not consistently kept until 1907 and then are not officially recognized until 1920.

1881—The pitcher's box is moved to 50 feet from home plate instead of 45 feet.

1882—Denny McKnight of Pittsburgh and Justus Thorner of Cincinnati create the American Association as a competitor to the National League. The AA puts teams in cities dropped by the NL, charges 25¢ admission instead of 50¢, says it's okay to play games on Sunday where the blue laws allow and to sell liquor at them, and outfits its players in gorgeous silk uniforms. Best of all, as far as the players are concerned, it chooses not to honor the NL's blacklist and to go after all players not bound to the NL by the reserve clause. The NL reacts to the threat by trying to ignore it.

1882—The number of balls needed to get a walk is knocked down to seven.

1882—Providence centerfielder Paul Hines trots out to his position wearing sunglasses. Fred Clarke is later credited with being the first player to wear pull-down sunglasses attached to his cap.

1882—Pete Browning of the Louisville Eclipse club wins the American Association batting title with a .388 average, 40 points higher than the runner-up, as only four players in the new league break the .300 mark. Two years later Browning will have the first modern baseball bat made for him by J. A. "Bud" Hillerich, an accidental occurrence that leads to the formation of Hillerich and Bradsby, the world's most famous batmaker. (A century later players credited with inventing curveballs and shin guards will be immortalized on bronze plaques in the Baseball Hall of Fame. Browning, the owner of a .343 career batting average, the first player to have his bats custom made and one of the most colorful and controversial characters in a league replete with them, will not.)

1883—The term *fan* is coined by St. Louis Browns manager Ted Sullivan when team owner Christ Von der Ahe calls the club's followers fanatics. Heretofore the popular word for a baseball fan has been *krank*, and kranks have already been analyzed in depth by Thomas Lawson in his book *The Krank: His Language and What It Means*, which contains a lexicon that includes many phrases that will still be in vogue 100 years later—to wit, the umpire as a 10th man or a robber, a bat as a willow or an ash, outstanding fielding plays as circus catches. The first great krank emerges around the time Sullivan thinks up a shorter word for him. His name is Arthur Dixwell, and he lives in Boston. Independently wealthy, he lavishes rewards on Beaneater players who do something unexpectedly fine and boosts the minor leagues in the New England area with his award of the coveted Dixwell trophy. When excited, Dixwell is heard to scream, "Hi! Hi!" and hence becomes known as Hi! Hi! Dixwell.

1884—Pitchers are allowed to employ shoulder-high deliveries instead of being restricted to those in which their hands must pass below their hips. As a sop to hitters, who now must face overhand fastballs from only 50 feet away, the number of balls needed for a walk is cut to six. In 1886, when observers feel that games are cluttered with too many walks, the figure is again hiked to seven.

1884—Henry Lucas, a young real estate scion who had been operating a minor league called the Union Association, grows convinced that baseball players are little more than chattels and vows to build his minor league into a powerful new major league that will not have the reserve clause. Lucas pilfers many good players from the American Association and National League, but his circuit fails when he stacks his own team, the St. Louis Maroons, with most of the good players and places competing UA teams in such thriving metropolises as Wilmington and Altoona.

188?—Harry Stevens, the "Scorecard Man," aka "Hustling Harry," comes out of the woodwork. By 1900 Harry has nailed down the scorecard and food concessions at most major-league parks, a distinction that his heirs still carry on in 1987. His sales prompt fans to beg owners to put numbers on players' uniforms so that better use can be made of the scorecards; some owners actually oblige their fans for a week or two, but the players resist, not liking the idea of wearing a number. Meanwhile, Stevens is so flush from his commissions that by 1910 he has sent his son to Yale Law School.

1886—The New York Giants set a record when 20,709 attend a Memorial Day game at the Polo Grounds. Later in the season the Giants get nearly 30,000 to a game.

1886—Cincinnati owner Aaron Stern observes that women swarm to the Reds ball park on days that handsome Tony Mullane is scheduled to pitch. Shrewdly, Stern begins designating games that Mullane will work against weak teams that normally draw poorly as special "Ladies Day" events. Mullane becomes known as "The Apollo of the Box" and receives credit from many historians for starting Ladies Days, but further research turns up Ladies Day games as far back as 1876. Whatever the truth of the matter is, Ladies Day games mushroom in the 1880s, and clubs like Brooklyn begin making every day except holidays Ladies Day in the belief that women add a certain tone to the crowd and curtail rowdyism and drunkenness. Brooklyn owner Charles Byrne also points out to his fellow moguls that it's a lot cheaper than hiring special police.

1887—Batters are no longer permitted to call for high or low pitches, and the strike zone is now defined as the area between the tops of the shoulders and the bottoms of the knees rather than above or below the waist. Also in 1887, the NL belatedly goes along with the Association and gives a batter first base if hit by a pitch. To further complicate things for umpires, a base on balls is reduced to five balls, and a strikeout requires four strikes instead of three. Major-league rulers, still not content, next decide to count walks as base hits. After all this, Tip O'Neill and Pete Browning post astronomical batting averages in the Association, which are discounted because they were compiled by men who got four strikes and received many walks. (Years later, after statisticians have removed the walks from their hit totals, their averages remain well over .400 and are still viewed as flukes.)

1887—Before the season, Chicago peddles King Kelly to Boston for $10,000, a record transaction. Two years earlier the Detroit Wolverines had shelled out only $7000 to obtain four players nearly as good as Kelly from Buffalo.

1887—Cap Anson takes his champion Chicago White Stockings to Hot Springs, Arkansas, to prepare for a preseason series with the defending AA champion St. Louis Browns and is credited with originating the concept of spring training.

1887—Browns first baseman Charlie Comiskey touts Menell's Penetrating Oil as a panacea, the first player endorsement of a product, some say, although players have already begun appearing on cigarette and chewing tobacco cards.

1887—Henry Chadwick decides it's time to revise won-lost records for pitchers. Previously a pitcher who worked the most innings in a game was credited with the decision regardless of the score when he departed. Chadwick, called "the father of the game," was born in England in 1824 and became a sportswriter in 1848. By 1887 he has long since invented the box score, begun editing *Spalding's Official Baseball Guide*, authored the first rule book and originated the scoring system still in use today.

188?—Third baseman Arlie Latham of the St. Louis Browns takes it upon himself to start coaching his teammates when they're on base. A torrential heckler and ace sign stealer, Latham soon becomes so popular with fans that it's feared efforts to control his antics may cut attendance. In 1907, John McGraw pays Latham to do nothing more than act as a base coach for the Giants, making him the first contracted coach.

1888—Detroit begins issuing rainchecks, which state, "In case rain interrupts the game before three innings are played this check will admit the bearer to grounds for the next league game only." Other clubs also adopt the practice, and the next-league-game rule will remain the custom for a long while.

1888—Pitcher Tim Keefe of the New York Giants designs and sells to his team their tight-fitting all-black uniforms with white raised letters that spell NEW YORK across the chest. Called "Funeral" uniforms at first, their color will soon catch on. The 1889 Baltimore Orioles, for one, play in black pants with white side stripes, white shirts and maroon stockings, and black-and-white-striped caps.

1888—Officials finally have it all figured out: Batters should get only three strikes, and that's it. The following year four balls, for the first time, constitute a walk.

188?—Philadelphia manager Harry Wright introduces pregame batting practice and also starts fungoing fly balls to his outfielders before games.

1889—For the first time in major-league history a pennant race is decided on the last day of the season. On October 5, New York beats Cleveland while lowly Pittsburgh is downing Boston's ace pitcher John Clarkson. Had the Beaneaters won, they, and not the Giants, would have claimed the NL flag.

1889—Indianapolis owner John T. "Tooth" Brush waits until Monte Ward, organizer of the first major league players union, goes on a world tour and then sneaks through a classification rule wherein players are graded from A to E, with A players limited to salaries of $2500 and E players able to earn no more than $1500—Ward explodes when he comes home and learns that salaries have been capped.

1890—Ward, Ned Hanlon and several other angry players get Cleveland street railway magnate Albert Johnson to influence other capitalists to loan money to players so that they can build parks in eight cities and start a new league. By the spring of 1890, the Players League has corraled most of the top players in the AA and NL and is a reality. Six months later the Players League concludes its first and only season of play, and Ward and its other leaders are unaware that the AA and NL are near collapse. In their ignorance, the players agree to return to the fold, after getting a few concessions from the owners that are quickly reneged on when the AA ceases operation in the fall of 1891 and the NL absorbs its four strongest franchises, leaving the players with only one major league to which to sell their talents and no recourse but retirement or the minors if they don't like what they're offered.

1890—Harry Decker perfects the "Decker Safety Catching Mitt"—a forerunner of modern mitts. Previously, catchers used heavily padded mittens. Buck Ewing, the first to use Decker's mitt, enthusiastically endorses it.

1891—The substitution rule is liberalized, allowing a player to enter a game at any time and at any position, the only restriction being that the player for which he is substituted cannot reenter the game.

1891—Pittsburgh fines outfielder Pete Browning for not wearing spikes on his shoes. Spikes have been in general use for several years and by now are mandatory equipment.

1892—The new 12-team National League for the first time plays a 154-game schedule, clubs meeting each of their rivals 14 times. (The longer schedule is tried again later in the decade, then reduced to 140 games, where it remains until 1904.)

1892—On June 2, Benjamin Harrison becomes the first president to attend a game while in office, when he watches the Reds beat Washington 7–4 in 11 innings.

1893—The pitcher's mound is moved from 50 feet to 60 feet 6 inches from home plate, and a rule is added that bats must be completely round, eliminating all the bats that are flat on one side or sawed off at the end. It puzzles officials at first why those extra six inches were tacked onto the new mound distance, until they learn that a surveyor misread the blueprint, which correctly read 60 feet 0 inches.

1893—Clifford Spencer proposes that, in conjunction with increasing the mound distance, the field should be made pentagonal with four bases for better balance, fewer foul balls, more stealing and higher status for second basemen. Many are intrigued by the idea, but it's shelved for the moment because the lengthened mound distance immediately leads to more scoring and revitalizes fan interest.

1894—To curb pesky hitters like Willie Keeler who stick out their bats and deliberately poke pitches foul until they get one to their liking, a batter for the first time is charged with a strike for hitting a foul bunt.

1894—Players on the Baltimore Orioles conspire with groundskeeper Tom Murphy to landscape the baselines in their home park in order to prevent their bunts from rolling foul while at the same time leaving the outfield grass high to hide illegal balls that can be put into play at propitious moments. Murphy also loosens the dirt in front of the pitcher's mound to stymie rival hurlers like Cy Young and Amos Rusie and reduce them to a par with Baltimore's moundsmen, who are among the worst in the league.

1895—The infield fly rule is adopted, and a strike is now assessed a batter on a foul tip—but not as yet on a foul ball. Umpires are left to judge between a tipped ball and a fouled one.

1896—A Princeton professor named Hinton invents the first mechanical pitching machine, a smoothbored breechloading cannon mounted on two wheels and fitted with curved prongs attached to the sides of the muzzle in order to curve a ball.

1897—Eddie Abbaticchio, the first Italian player of note, debuts with Philadelphia.

1897—Oliver Perry Caylor dies. Although never himself a major league player, Caylor helped to found the American Association, managed the Cincinnati Reds and the New York Metropolitans for two seasons and part of a third, subsequently edited *Reach's Official Baseball Guide* and then became baseball editor of the *New York Herald* and official scorer for the Giants. His witty, cutting style and iconoclastic viewpoint are sorely missed in the next decade.

1898—The first modern balk rule is put in the book; also the modern rule for recognizing stolen bases, making it forever impossible to compare Ty Cobb, Lou Brock and Rickey Henderson to Harry Stovey, Billy Hamilton and other early base thieves.

1899—Bob Stafford plays his last major-league game. By 1987 Stafford will have begun to seem, to some, the most enigmatic player in history in that he played 10 seasons, several of them as a regular, for teams in cities like New York and Boston and at a time when the media had already made players a focus of detailed analysis—and yet he managed to depart without a single firm piece of biographical information being recorded about him; where he was born, when, what year he died, which way he batted and threw.

1900—A pentagon-shaped home plate is unveiled, replacing the old diamond-shaped one.

1900—At the conclusion of the season, the infield fly rule is modified so that it's in effect with none out as well as with one out. The National League also decides to start calling foul balls strikes in 1901, unable to care less that the upstart

Western League, which has changed its name to the American League and began billing itself as a major circuit, doesn't want to go along with the foul-strike rule and will not conform until 1903.

Season Record Holders Prior to 1901

It would take an entire book to chronicle the rules that were used to determine batting and pitching records in the 19th century, the exceptions that were made to them, the numerous seasons in which incomplete statistics were kept and the many disputes that are still raging over whether a certain batter hit .492 one year or only .435 and whether a certain pitcher struck out 513 batters another year or only 505. Suffice to say these are the consensus records of an era that was not as yet consumed by the mystique of records and the devotion to minutiae needed to keep them accurately.

The record holders prior to 1893 played when the pitcher's mound was either 45 feet or 50 feet from home plate. The record holders between 1893 and 1900 played under present rules for the most part but in a period when there was only one 12-team league, no meaningful postseason play, and a batter was still allowed to hit an unlimited number of foul balls without a strike being charged against him.

1876 THROUGH 1892

Batting

Department	National League	American Association
Batting Average	.404, Ross Barnes, Chicago, 1876	.435, TIP O'NEILL, St. Louis, 1887
Slugging Average	.581, Dan Brouthers, Detroit, 1886	.691, TIP O'NEILL, St. Louis, 1887
Home Runs	20, SAM THOMPSON, Philadelphia, 1889	19, Harry Stovey, Philadelphia, 1889
		19, Bug Holliday, Cincinnati, 1889

Department	National League	American Association
RBIs	166, SAM THOMPSON, Detroit, 1887	199, Harry Stovey, Philadelphia, 1889
Runs	153, Dan Brouthers, Detroit, 1887	177, TOM BROWN, Boston, 1891
Hits	205, Jack Glasscock, Indianapolis, 1889	225, TIP O'NEILL, St. Louis, 1887
Doubles	49, Ned Williamson, Chicago, 1883	52, TIP O'NEILL, St. Louis, 1887
Triples	26, John Reilly, Cincinnati, 1890	31, DAVE ORR, New York, 1886
Total Bases	311, Sam Thompson, Detroit, 1887	357, TIP O'NEILL, St. Louis, 1887
Bases on Balls	136, JOHN CROOKS, St. Louis, 1892	119, Dummy Hoy, St. Louis, 1891
Stolen Bases	115, Billy Hamilton, Philadelphia, 1891	138, HUGH NICOL, Cincinnati, 1887

Note: Ned Williamson of the Chicago White Stockings hit 27 home runs in 1884, most of them over a fence so close to the plate that in every other season but 1884 his hits would have been ground-rule doubles—as were the majority of his two-baggers in 1883.

Pitching

Department	National League	American Association
Wins	60, HOSS RADBOURN, Providence, 1884	52, Guy Hecker, Louisville, 1884
Losses	48, JOHN COLEMAN, Philadelphia, 1883	41, Larry McKeon, Indianapolis, 1884
Innings Pitched	680, WILL WHITE, Cincinnati, 1879	671, Guy Hecker, Louisville, 1884
Strikeouts	441, Hoss Radbourn, Providence, 1884	513, MATTY KILROY, Baltimore 1886
Complete Games	75, WILL WHITE, Cincinnati, 1879	72, Guy Hecker, Louisville, 1884
Shutouts	16, GEORGE BRADLEY, St. Louis, 1876	12, Ed Morris, Pittsburgh, 1886
ERA	1.23, George Bradley, St. Louis, 1876	1.21, DENNY DRISCOLL, Pittsburgh, 1882

Batting

Department	Record Holder	Runner-up
Batting Average	.438, HUGH DUFFY, Boston, 1894	432, Willie Keeler, Baltimore, 1897
Slugging Average	.679, HUGH DUFFY, Boston, 1894	670, Sam Thompson, Philadelphia, 1894
Home Runs	25, BUCK FREEMAN, Washington, 1899	19, Ed Delahanty, Philadelphia, 1893
RBIs	165, SAM THOMPSON, Philadelphia, 1895	146, Ed Delahanty, Philadelphia, 1893
Runs	196, BILLY HAMILTON, Philadelphia, 1894	167, Joe Kelley, Baltimore, 1894
Hits	243, WILLIE KEELER, Baltimore, 1894	240, Jesse Burkett, Cleveland, 1896
Doubles	56, ED DELAHANTY, Philadelphia, 1899	50, Hugh Duffy, Boston, 1894
Triples	31, HEINIE REITZ, Baltimore, 1894	29, Perry Werden, St. Louis, 1893*
Total Bases	366, HUGH DUFFY, Boston, 1894	352, Sam Thompson, Philadelphia, 1895
Bases on Balls	126, BILLY HAMILTON, Philadelphia, 1894	124, John McGraw, Baltimore, 1899
Stolen Bases	99, BILLY HAMILTON, Philadelphia, 1894	95, Billy Hamilton, Philadelphia, 1895

Note: *The Macmillan Baseball Encyclopedia credits Werden with 29 triples in 1893, but other sources give him 33.

Pitching

Department	Record Holder	Runner-up
Wins	36, JOUETT MEEKIN, New York, 1894 36, AMOS RUSIE, New York, 1894	35, Cy Young, Cleveland, 1895
Losses	33, RED DONAHUE, St. Louis, 1897	30, Jim Hughey, Cleveland, 1899
Innings Pitched	482, AMOS RUSIE New York, 1893	447, Ted Breitenstein, St. Louis, 1894

Department	Record Holder	Runner-up
Strikeouts	244, CY SEYMOUR, New York, 1898	208, Amos Rusie, New York, 1893
Complete Games	50, AMOS RUSIE, New York, 1893	46, Ted Breitenstein, St. Louis, 1894, 1897
Shutouts	6, WILEY PIATT, Philadelphia, 1898 6, JACK POWELL, Cleveland, 1898	5, done by six different pitchers
ERA	1.88, CLARK GRIFFITH, Chicago, 1898	2.10, Al Maul, Baltimore, 1898

TEAM SEASON RECORD HOLDERS

1876 through 1892

Highest	National League	American Association
Batting Average	.337, CHICAGO, 1876	.307, St. Louis, 1887
Slugging Average	.446, CHICAGO, 1884	.413, St. Louis, 1887
Winning Pct.	.788, CHICAGO, 1880 (67–17)	.705, St. Louis, 1885 (79–33)
Lowest		
Batting Average	.208, Washington, 1888	.204, BALTIMORE, 1886
Slugging Average	.261, New York, 1876	.254, BALTIMORE, 1882
Winning Pct.	.138, CINCINNATI, 1876 (9–56)	.196, Louisville, 1889 (27–111)

1893 through 1900

	Highest	Lowest
Batting Average	.349, Philadelphia, 1894	.247, St. Louis, 1898
Slugging Average	.484, Boston, 1894	.305, St. Louis, 1898 .305, Cleveland, 1899
Winning Pct.	.705, Boston, 1897 (93–39)	.130, Cleveland, 1899 (20–134)

The Four Most
Interesting Teams Before 1901

1884 PROVIDENCE GRAYS
W-84 L-28
Manager: Frank Bancroft

Regular Lineup—1B, Joe Start; 2B, Jack Farrell; SS, Arthur Irwin; 3B, Jerry Denny; RF, Paul Radford; CF, Paul Hines; LF, Cliff Carroll; C, Barney Gilligan: P, Hoss Radbourn; P, Charlie Sweeney.

Fourth in the National League in batting and fifth in runs scored, the Grays nonetheless won the pennant by 10½ games. Their lineup had just one .300 hitter, Hines, and Radford hit only .197, one of the poorest averages ever for a regular outfielder. The Grays had finished third in 1883 and seemed destined to drop out of contention altogether when Sweeney jumped the club midway in the 1884 season and signed with St. Louis in the Union Association. Sweeney reportedly had the best fastball in the game at the time and was, moreover, an excellent hitter—good enough to play the outfield on the days Radbourn pitched. After Sweeney's defection, manager Bancroft tried to find a replacement for him, but there were three major leagues in 1884, and experienced pitchers were scarce. Finally Bancroft in desperation struck a bargain with Radbourn, who had been under suspension for drunkenness when Sweeney left. Radbourn offered to pitch every game for the rest of the season if in return Providence released him from his contract. Then he proceeded to fulfill his part of the deal by posting an all-time record 60 wins. Radbourn didn't literally pitch every game down the stretch—other Providence players, Radford among them, took a turn on the mound now and then to spell him—but he did work far more often than necessary considering the Grays' runaway win, and it took its toll on his arm. After 1884 he was only an average pitcher and was out of baseball entirely eight years later.

Upon leaving the game, Radbourn opened a billiard parlor and spent his days there, drinking and schmoozing with patrons until he suffered an injury that left his face partially paralyzed. Self-conscious, he retired to a back room, where he sat most of the time in dim light, which concealed his disfigurement. He died of paresis in 1897.

His team fared no better. The smallest city in the National League, Providence, despite winning the pennant, could not draw enough fans to meet its payroll and withdrew from the majors after the 1885 season, never to return.

1882 CINCINNATI REDS
W-55 L-25
Manager: Pop Snyder

Regular Lineup—1B, Dan Stearns; 2B, Bid McPhee; SS, Chick Fulmer; 3B, Hick Carpenter; RF, Harry Wheeler; CF, Jimmy Macullar; LF, Joe Sommer; C, Pop Snyder; P, Will White.

Expelled from the National League after the 1880 season for playing games on Sunday and selling beer in its park, the Cincinnati franchise was quick to regroup when the American Association formed in time to begin the 1882 season. The Reds signed White, Sommer, Carpenter and Wheeler, all members of the 1880 team who were either released or left unprotected by National League clubs, and then snatched catcher Snyder away from the Boston Red Stockings to serve as player-manager. These five players became the nucleus of the only Cincinnati club to win a pennant before 1919. Joining with them were 22-year-old second baseman McPhee, getting his first opportunity to play in the majors, and shortstop Fulmer, who had been blacklisted by the National League early in the 1880 season. In the Association's inaugural year, the Reds were easily the class of the league, romping home 11½ games ahead of Philadelphia. Whether they were as good as Chicago, the NL champ in 1882, was never settled—a postseason series between the

two teams ended in controversy after each had won a game—
but they were undoubtedly the best Cincinnati nine since
the legendary Red Stockings. The club remained strong for
several more years but was never again able to mount a
serious pennant bid as the St. Louis Browns emerged as the
league's powerhouse team.

1894 PHILADELPHIA PHILLIES
W-71 L-57
Manager: Arthur Irwin

Regular Lineup—1B, Jack Boyle; 2B, Bill Hallman; SS,
Joe Sullivan; 3B, Lave Cross; RF, Sam Thompson; CF, Billy
Hamilton: LF, Ed Delahanty; C, Jack Clements; P, Jack
Taylor; P, Kid Carsey; P, Gus Weyhing; util., Tuck Turner.

The Phillies had an all-time record team batting average
of .349, averaged over nine runs a game and featured three
.400 hitters. But the club could do no better than finish a
distant fourth, 10 games behind third-place Boston. At a
glance, the reason would seem to be inadequate pitching—
the Phillies mound staff had an aggregate 5.63 ERA in
1894—but every team except the New York Giants had the
same problem that year. With the mound now 60 feet 6 inches
from the plate, hitters in 1894 were so far ahead of pitchers
that the league batting average was .309, and five teams
scored over 1000 runs.

The better explanation for the Phillies' failure to challenge for the pennant probably lay in manager Irwin. Boston, New York and Baltimore, the three clubs that finished
ahead of Philadelphia, were piloted by Frank Selee, Monte
Ward and Ned Hanlon, three of the best minds in the game,
and I have a hunch that Irwin found himself on the wrong end
of a lot of 10–9 and 10–8 scores when he came up against them.

1899 CLEVELAND SPIDERS
W-20 L-134
Managers: Lave Cross and Joe Quinn

Regular Lineup—1B, Tommy Tucker; 2B, Joe Quinn;
SS, Harry Lockhead; 3B, Suter Sullivan; RF, Sport McAllister;
CF, Tommy Dowd; LF, Dick Harley; C, Joe Snyder;

P, Jim Hughey; P, Charlie Knepper; P, Frank Bates; P, Crazy Schmidt.

One of the National League's best clubs earlier in the decade, the Spiders were disemboweled by their owners, the Robison brothers, after they bought the St. Louis franchise and gauged that its fans would be more supportive of a good team. Syndicate ownership was outlawed shortly thereafter—but too late to save the Spiders. The Robisons shipped every single regular from the 1898 club to St. Louis, leaving manager Cross with only three quality players—himself, Quinn and Dowd—plus aging Tommy Tucker, talked out of retirement to play one more season. After the club lost 30 of its first 38 games, Cross was mercifully transferred to St. Louis, which needed a third baseman, and the reins were handed to Quinn. Under Quinn, the Spiders had a 12–104 record and were so inept that they no longer dared to show their wares in front of a Cleveland crowd. After June, the club played out the season on the road, where it lost 102 of 113 games and became known as the Wanderers. The leading pitcher, Knepper, had a .154 win percentage, and no hurler won more than four games. Amid all this, Tommy Dowd hit a respectable .278 in 147 games. Dowd, in his 10-year career, had the unpleasant distinction of playing on just about every rotten team in the period. Ironically, he began with the pennant-winning 1891 Boston AA team but played only four games with them before being swapped to Washington, which finished in the cellar. There is a theory that Lave Cross, whose career stats are better than many contemporary players who made the Hall of Fame, never got in because he played for and managed—albeit for only a few weeks—the 1899 Spiders, the worst team in history.

Wild Men
On the Mound

Bases-on-balls statistics prior to 1893 require that anyone interested in interpreting them read a rule book for each season. As an illustration, in 1883 Pud Galvin of Buffalo walked only 50 batters in 656 innings; seven years later he walked 62 in 247 innings. What happened to Galvin's control? Nothing—the fact is it probably got better. But in 1883 a batter had to receive seven balls before he drew a walk. By 1889 the number of balls needed for a walk had dropped to four, and the following year Amos Rusie of the Giants set an all-time record when he granted 289 free passes. In 1893 the mound was moved 10 feet 6 inches farther from the plate, but by that time most pitchers, Rusie included, had adapted, at least partially, to the less liberal margin for errant tosses, and pitchers on the whole issued fewer walks at the longer distance.

MOST BASES ON BALLS, SEASON

		Team	League	Year	
1893–1900	Amos Rusie (R)	New York	National	1893	218[1]
	Cy Seymour (L)	New York	National	1898	213
1901–19	Bob Harmon (R)	St. Louis	National	1911	181
	Nap Rucker (L)	Brooklyn	National	1908	125
1920–41	Bob Feller (R)	Cleveland	American	1938	208[2]
	Ken Chase (L)	Washington	American	1941	143
1942–60	Sam Jones (R)	Chicago	National	1955	185[3]

[1] Probably the wildest pitcher in history, Rusie got better as his career went along. By 1897 his control had improved so much that he gave up only 87 walks in 322 innings.
[2] Both the 20th-century record and the American League record.
[3] The 20th-century National League record.

		Team	League	Year	
	Tommy Byrne (L)	New York	American	1949	179[4]
162-Game	Nolan Ryan (R)	California	American	1977	204[5]
Schedule	Sam McDowell (L)	Cleveland	American	1971	153

[4]The 20th-century record for a left-hander.
[5]Walked 202 in 1974 and is the only pitcher in the 20th century to issue 200 or more walks in a season twice.

Most Seasons League Leader in Bases on Balls
AL—6—Nolan Ryan, last in 1978; Ryan also led the NL in 1980 and 1982.
NL—5—Amos Rusie, 1890–94 consecutive
NL since 1901—4—Jimmy Ring, 1922–25 consecutive
Bob Veale, last in 1968

Most Intentional Walks, Season
23—Mike Garman, 1975, St. Louis, NL
Dale Murray, 1978, Cincinnati, NL
Ken Tekulve, 1982, Pittsburgh, NL

Most Hit Batsmen, Season, Since 1893
NL—41—Joe McGinnity, 1900, Brooklyn
AL—31—Chick Fraser, 1901, Philadelphia

Fewest Bases on Balls, Season, by League Leader in Bases on Balls
NL—92—Sheriff Blake, Chicago, 1926
AL—97—Jimmy Dygert, Philadelphia, 1908

Most Bases on Balls, Game, Nine Innings
NL—16—Bill George, New York Giants, May 30, 1887, versus the Chicago White Stockings. George, a 22-year-old rookie left-hander, set the record in a season when five balls were still needed for a walk. Some sources contend that in 1887 White Stockings rookie George Van Haltren also gave up 16 walks in a game.

NL since 1893—14—Henry Mathewson, New York, October 5, 1906, versus Boston. Christy's younger brother, Mathewson set the modern NL record while making his only major-league start.

AL—16—Bruno Haas, Philadelphia, June 23, 1915, versus New York. In 1915 A's pitchers issued an all-time record

827 walks—only 28 of them by Haas, who was released soon after his record-shattering performance. Six years later, however, he resurfaced as a halfback in the newly formed National Football League.

Most Consecutive Bases on Balls, Game

7—Dolly Gray, Washington, AL, August 28, 1909. Gray walked eight batters altogether in the course of the inning, also a record. But it must have been only a momentary lapse, for he walked just 77 batters in 218 innings that season.

Co-Winners of the "Why Let a Few Walks Bother You" Award

Yankees Hall of Famer Lefty Gomez pitched a shutout on August 1, 1941, despite giving up 11 walks. On May 21, 1970, Mel Stottlemyre of the Yankees was relieved with one out in the ninth inning after surrendering 11 walks in a game that also ended as a shutout.

MOST BASES ON BALLS, CAREER, TOP 10

		Years Active	BB
1.	Nolan Ryan	1966–	2268
2.	Early Wynn	1939–63	1775
3.	Bob Feller	1936–56	1764
4.	Phil Niekro	1964–	1749
5.	Steve Carlton	1965–	1742[1]
6.	Bobo Newsom	1929–53	1732
7.	Amos Rusie	1889–1900	1704
8.	Gus Weyhing	1887–1901	1566[2]
9.	Red Ruffing	1924–47	1541
10.	Bump Hadley	1926–41	1442[3]

[1]The lefty career record.

[2]Like Rusie, his control began to improve dramatically after the mound distance was increased.

[3]The only member of the top 10 with fewer career strikeouts than walks, Hadley was one of the most notorious wild men in the thirties. It was he who beaned Mickey Cochrane in 1936, ending Cochrane's career.

Most Hit Batsmen, Career

206—Walter Johnson, 1907–27. Johnson also shares with Earl Wilson and Nolan Ryan the AL record for most wild pitches in a season—21. The NL record since 1901 is held by Red Ames of the Giants, who let 30 pitches get away from him in 1905.

The Amos Rusie Award for the Most Consistent Lack of Control

Left-hander—Tommy Byrne, 1943–57. Byrne spent most of his career with the Yankees, but in 1951, while pitching for the St. Louis Browns, he walked 16 Washington Senators in a 13-inning game. Over his career, he gave up 1037 bases on balls in only 1362 innings.

Right-hander—Dick Weik, active between 1948 and 1954 with the Senators, Indians and Tigers. Weik made only 26 starts but four times walked 10 or more batters in a game. In 1949 he issued 103 walks in only 95 innings, and if his control improved after that his stats didn't show it. Lifetime, he had a 6–22 won-lost record and 237 walks in 214 innings. Despite it all the Indians liked him enough to trade Mickey Vernon for him in 1950. Three years later Vernon won his second AL batting crown while Weik had a 13.97 ERA in 12 games.

Weik's control problems were equally manifest in the minors. In his very first pro game, with Charlotte in the Tri-State League in 1946, he walked 15 men. Two years later he led the Southern Association in bases on balls, issuing 173 in just 132 innings.

Owners

George Steinbrenner, August Busch, Ted Turner and Calvin Griffith are poles apart in their philosophies on operating a major-league baseball franchise, and each may seem like one of a kind. But the truth is that each of them has had numerous prototypes throughout the game's history. Here are fourteen of my favorite owners; by no means the most famous fourteen, nor the most influential, nor the wackiest—just a representative selection from the legion of fascinating men and women who have had a hand in shaping events.

The First Steinbrenner

Aaron Champion became president of the Cincinnati Red Stockings baseball club in 1867 and immediately embarked on a no-holds-barred commercial expansion program. He pushed through an $11,000 stock issue so that the Red Stockings could refurbish their home grounds, Union Field, and then set out with manager Harry Wright to obtain the best players available regardless of the price. The Red Stockings were not, as some historians have written, the first professional team. Rather, they were the first nationally successful one by dint of being the first all-salaried team, a device to hold players to full-season contracts and prevent them from "revolving," or jumping to rival teams. For more about the Red Stockings see "Team Records," but let's look for a moment at the salaries of the 1869 Red Stockings as a point of comparison to, say, what Yankees regulars got in 1986.

Harry Wright, CF	$1800
George Wright, SS	$1800
Asa Brainard, P	$800
Charlie Gould, 1B	$800

Fred Waterman, 3B	$800
Charlie Sweazy, 2B	$700
Doug Allison, C	$700
Andy Leonard, LF	$700
Cal McVey, RF	$700
Dick Hurley, Sub	$600
Total salaries:	$9400

The First Calvin Griffith

Arthur Soden was principal owner and team president of the Boston Beaneaters from 1877 through 1906. To stop revolving, Soden instituted the reserve clause and later was a leader in the movement to limit players' salaries. Tightfisted, intransigent, Soden was nevertheless highly successful —Boston was the National League's strongest team as late as 1898—until the American League arrived on the scene. Refusing to match the huge sums of money dangled in front of his stars by AL clubs, Soden had lost virtually every player of merit by the time the two leagues reached a peace settlement in 1903. Boston deservedly finished deep in the cellar in 1906—his last season as its owner.

The First August Busch/Charlie Finley/Ted Turner

Chris Von der Ahe was owner and sometimes manager of the St. Louis Browns in the American Association. Von der Ahe was just one of several brewery magnates who helped start the Association in 1882, but by the middle of the decade he stood alone. Outfitting his players in elegant multicolored silk uniforms, bickering with umpires and rival owners, getting more press than all the other club officials combined, Von der Ahe at the same time gave Browns fans high-quality baseball. Sadly, the game swiftly passed him by when the Association folded after the 1891 season, and he died nearly broke.

The Biggest Reason the American Association Failed

The Metropolitan Exhibition Company owned both the American Association New York Metropolitans and the National League New York Giants in the mid-1880s. Convinced that the NL would survive the civil war between the two circuits, company officials stocked the Giants with many of the Mets' best players after the club won the 1884 Association pennant and even included in the package the Mets manager, Jim Mutrie. When the Pittsburgh Alleghenies switched to the National League after the 1886 season, the Association was left without any strong owners except Von der Ahe. The Metropolitan Exhibition Company's machinations were a forerunner of the syndicate ownership practices of the Robison brothers and the von der Horsts, which nearly ruined the National League too in the late 1890s.

Big City Versus Little City I
When Fredrick Stearns bought the Detroit National League franchise in the mid-1880s, the automobile was still only a fantasy, and Detroit was one of the smallest cities to have a major-league team. The Buffalo franchise, likewise serving a small city, was on the verge of collapsing, and Stearns, thinking he saw a quick way to enliven his franchise, purchased Buffalo's four best players—Deacon White, Dan Brouthers, Jack Rowe and Hardy Richardson—at the close of the 1885 season. With the addition of the "Buffalo Four," Detroit became an instant contender in 1886 and won the NL pennant the following year, but Stearns was thwarted from reaping the benefits he had anticipated. His plan, since Detroit had too small a population to draw many fans regardless of the quality of the team, was to make the Wolverines the top road attraction in the game and earn the bulk of his money on visits to Chicago, Boston, Philadelphia and New York. But team owners in these cities abruptly changed the rules governing the sharing of gate receipts when they fathomed Stearn's strategy, and by 1889 Detroit had folded and would be without major-league baseball again until 1901.

Big City Versus Little City II
Andrew Freedman, the New York Giants owner in the late 1890s, believed that having possession of the team in the largest population center in the country entitled him to run it any way he pleased, and for eight years he did. Even more penurious than Arthur Soden and far and away the most loathed baseball mogul in his day, Freedman aborted the career of his star pitcher Amos Rusie by forcing Rusie to hold out one entire season. By the end of the decade the Giants had sunk to last place and seemed destined to stay there unless Freedman was removed. After a bitter struggle, he sold out to a group headed by John Brush, and within a few months Brush had induced John McGraw to desert the American league for the Giants managerial post, and the

franchise was on its way to becoming once again the most financially successful in the game.

Big City Versus Little City III

Horace Fogel was part of the new regime that Brush brought with him when he took over the Giants—Fogel even managed the club for a while in 1902—but by 1912 he had switched allegiance to Philadelphia and bought a chunk of the moribund Phillies. He was forced to divest himself of his stock and barred from the game when he allegedly charged that St. Louis manager Roger Bresnahan had allowed the Giants to beat the Cardinals in a crucial series near the end of the 1912 season so that Bresnahan's crony John McGraw would be assured of winning the pennant. The accusation had really emanated not from Fogel and the Phillies camp but from Cubs owner Charles Murphy, who headed the one NL franchise that was on a par at the time with New York's and was thus too powerful to oust. Interestingly, the only other owner ever banned was another Phillies mogul, Billy Cox, who was given the gate by Commissioner Judge Landis early in World War II for betting on his own team. Cox departed meekly and sold the club to the Carpenters, who installed their youngest son, Bob, as team president.

The First Marge Schott

Helen Britton assumed control of the St. Louis Cardinals in 1911 after her uncle, Stanley Robison, died, and she ran them through 1916 when her marriage came apart and she sold the team. After Britton and her husband separated, she took over his post as club president for the 1916 season, making her the first woman ever to act in that capacity on a major league level.

The Federal League Legacy I

In 1915 Harry Sinclair bought a controlling interest in the Newark Federal League franchise and quickly found a way to recoup his losses—and then some—after the Feds closed up shop. As part of the peace settlement with organized baseball, Sinclair was allowed to take over the contracts of many Federal League players and sell them to major-league clubs, earning himself a sizable piece of change and in the process becoming a broker of players and the greatest trader in human merchandise since the abolition of slavery. If the name seems to ring a bell, you're right—it's the same Harry Sinclair who was later implicated in the Teapot Dome Scandal.

The Federal League Legacy II

Another stipulation of the peace settlement with the Federal League granted Fed moguls Phil Ball and Charles Weegham the privilege of purchasing the St. Louis Browns and the Chicago Cubs respectively. Ball did little to improve the Browns plight, but Weegham provided a sharp contrast to former Cubs owner Charles Murphy and indeed to most major-league magnates of his time. In 1916 Weegham began the groundwork that would soon make Wrigley Field a national treasure. Among his many innovations was to build concession booths in back of the stands so that fans weren't continually being disturbed by hawkers peddling scorecards and refreshments.

The Braves Have That History

Atlanta owner Ted Turner decided in 1977 that he could manage his team better than anyone else and handled the Braves for one game before Commissioner Bowie Kuhn, probably fearing that George Steinbrenner, Ray Kroc and Charlie Finley would soon get the same brainstorm, ordered Turner to cut out the nonsense. Back in 1929, however, Commissioner Landis sat quietly by while Braves owner Judge Fuchs ran the club. Manager Fuchs, the last mogul foolish enough to station himself in his team's dugout for a full season, finished a dreary last, thanks largely to the assistance he'd received from owner Fuchs, who sent Rogers Hornsby to the Cubs prior to the season for a packet of cash, a pocketful of minor leaguers and second baseman Freddie Maguire, whom Hornsby outhit in 1929 by a mere 128 points.

The Greatest Innovator Prior to World War II

Many would vote for Branch Rickey, who brought Jackie Robinson to the majors and was the first major-league mogul to operate a minor-league "farm" system to develop young players, but equally high marks should go to Larry MacPhail. As owner of the Cincinnati Reds in 1935, MacPhail introduced night baseball to the majors and later brought it to Brooklyn and the Yankees when he took over those clubs. Furthermore, he orchestrated the first televised World Series in 1947 and the first official old-timers' game, also in

1947, to commemorate Babe Ruth, ill with throat cancer, Ruth's Foundation for Boys receiving the entire proceeds. But perhaps his most significant act of all was to bring Red Barber with him when he moved from Cincinnati to Brooklyn. Try, if you can, to summon back a vision of Ebbets Field in the forties and fifties without hearing Barber's voice as a counterpoint to it.

The Greatest Innovator Since World War II

Bill Veeck—and there's no one else even close. Over and above the countless zany and delightful spectacles he gave his fans, Veeck owned the last Cleveland team to win a World Championship, the last Chicago team to win a pennant and the last team, in 1953, to play under a name that will always be among the most tradition-laden in history—the St. Louis Browns.

The Greatest Innovator Since Veeck

Charlie Finley has been with us too recently to get into perspective. We laughed when he adorned his Kansas City A's in green, white and gold uniforms in the fifties, and we groaned when he scheduled weekday World Series games exclusively at night, but history, I think we're going to find, will be very generous to him.

Famous Brother Acts

After the Cincinnati Red Stockings broke up, Harry Wright and his brother George signed with the Boston Red Caps in the newly formed National Association. In 1876 they were joined on the Boston club, now in the National League, by a third brother, Sam, for a short time. Hence the Wrights were not only the first brothers to play in the major leagues, they were also the first trio of brothers. In 1877 a second set of brothers arrived on the scene in Boston when Deacon White was joined on the Red Caps by his younger brother Will. The following season both White brothers jumped to the Cincinnati club and formed the first sibling battery in the National League, with Deacon catching and Will pitching. They stayed together through the 1880 season; when the Cincinnati franchise folded, Deacon caught on with Buffalo while Will was cast adrift until the American Association was organized two years later.

First Brother Battery in the American League

Homer and Tommy Thompson with the 1912 Yankees. You might have missed seeing them since Tommy pitched only 33 innings and Homer didn't even catch one entire game.

Second Brother Battery in the American League

Milt and Alex Gaston with the 1929 Red Sox. Both played several seasons in the AL but were together only in 1929.

First Brother Battery in the National League after 1900

Jack and Mike O'Neill with the 1902–3 Cardinals. Mike, the pitching half, also served as the Cardinals' main pinch hitter—on June 30, 1902, he hit the first pinch grand slam in history, off Togie Pittinger of the Braves. A few years later, two younger brothers, Steve and Jim, arrived in the majors. Steve, who managed the 1945 Tigers to a World Championship, is the lone O'Neill remembered today, but all four brothers made a dent.

Most Successful Brother Battery
AL—Rich and Wes Ferrell played together from 1934 through 1938 with the Red Sox and Senators. Rick is in the Hall of Fame, and Wes not only won nearly 200 games but was perhaps the best hitting pitcher ever. In 1948, seven years after leaving the majors, he led the Western Carolina League with a .425 average while serving as a player-manager for Marion.

NL—Mort and Walker Cooper helped power the Cardinals to three pennants in the early forties. Mort won 20 games three years in a row, and Walker was voted to several All-Star squads.

Oldest Player to Act as His Brother's Batterymate
Johnny Riddle, nearly 43 years old, caught his brother Elmer for the 1948 Pirates.

First Brothers to Oppose Each Other as Starting Pitchers
Jesse and Virgil Barnes on May 3, 1927; pitching for the Dodgers, Jesse beat Virgil and the Giants 7–6. Earlier in the decade the two had both been with the Giants and formed the first brother starter-reliever combo, Virgil acting the part of savior.

Second Brothers to Oppose Each Other as Starting Pitchers
Joe Niekro, then with the Cubs, faced his brother Phil on July 5, 1967, the first of what would be many duels between them, Phil and the Braves winning 8–3.

Only Pitcher to Start Against His Brother in His First Major-League Game
By special arrangement, Pat Underwood of the Tigers faced his brother Tom of the Blue Jays in his major-league debut on May 31, 1979.

First Brothers Each to Win 20 Games in a Season
Harry and Stan Coveleski. Harry first collected 20 wins with the 1914 Tigers, Stan with the 1918 Indians. The Coveleskis played for rival teams in the AL for several years

but made a pact not to pitch against each other and never did.

Only Brothers to Win a Combined 40 Games in a Season as Teammates
Dizzy Dean won 30 games and brother Paul won 19 for the 1934 Cardinals.

Only Brothers to Pitch a Combined Shutout
Rick and Paul Reuschel of the Cubs on August 21, 1975, 7–0 over the Dodgers.

Brothers with the Best Combined Career Winning Percentage, Each Winning at Least One Game
The famous Hovlik brothers. Ed was 2–1 with the 1918–19 Senators, and Joe was 3–0 with the 1911 White Sox, giving them a family winning percentage of .833

Only Brothers Born in the Same Year Who Were Not Twins
The Durhams, Jimmy and Bull, were both born in 1881, Jimmy in Douglass, Kansas, and Bull in Bolivar, New York.

First Twins to Play in the Major Leagues
John and Phil Reccius with the 1882–83 Louisville Eclipse club in the American Association. For a time the Louisville manager was their older brother Bill.

Only Twins in the 20th Century to Play Beside Each Other
Johnny and Eddie O'Brien formed a keystone combination for the 1953 Pirates; later they both also pitched for the Pirates.

First Brothers to Play Beside Each Other in the Outfield
Jim and John O'Rourke of the 1880 Boston Red Stockings.

First Brothers to Play Beside Each Other in the Infield
Bill and Jack Gleason of the 1881 St. Louis Browns, Bill at shortstop and Jack at third base.

First Brothers to Oppose Each Other in a World Series
Doc and Jimmy Johnston in 1920, Doc with Cleveland and Jimmy with Brooklyn. The second pair of brothers to face each other in the Series were the Meusels in 1921, Bob

with the Yankees and Emil with the Giants. In 1908 the Clarke brothers, Fred and Josh, narrowly missed becoming the first brothers to play against each other in a Series when Fred's Pirates lost the NL pennant on the last day of the season and Josh's Indians finished ½ game behind the victorious Tigers.

First Black Siblings to Play in the Major Leagues
Fleet and Welday Walker, in 1884, with Toledo in the American Association.

First Black Siblings to Play in the Major Leagues in the 20th Century
Sammy and Solly Drake, Solly with the 1956 Cubs and Sammy four years later, also with the Cubs.

Only Brothers to Have 100 or More RBIs, Season, in the Same League
Bob and Roy Johnson, Bob with the Philadelphia A's and Roy with the Red Sox. Two other sets of brothers—the Meusels and Joe and Vince DiMaggio—also had 100 RBI seasons but in different leagues.

Most Home Runs, Season, by Brothers Who Were Teammates
54—Tony Conigliaro (36) and Billy Conigliaro (18), 1970 Red Sox.

Brothers With the Highest Combined Career Batting Average
The Sherlocks. Monk hit .324 for the 1930 Phillies, and Vince hit .462 for the 1935 Dodgers; their combined career average is .335.

Brothers With the Highest Combined Season Batting Average
The Waners. Playing side by side in the outfield for the 1927 Pirates, they hit a combined .367, Paul leading the NL with a .380 average and Lloyd hitting .355—between them they also had a brother-record 460 hits.

Only Brothers Who Celebrated Their Major-League Debuts More Than 25 Years Apart
Jesse and Art Fowler. Born in 1898, Jesse broke in with the 1924 Cardinals. Art, 24 years younger, first appeared with the 1954 Reds.

Only Brothers Who Both Played and Managed Against Each Other

Jake and Chick Stahl. In 1906 Jake was the Senators player-manager, and Chick served the same role for the Red Sox. Jake later switched to the Red Sox and managed them to the 1912 World Championship. Note, though, that it isn't universally accepted that the Stahls were brothers.

Player With the Most Brothers Who Preceded Him in the Major Leagues

Joe Delahanty. By the time he broke in with the 1907 Cardinals, four of his brothers—Ed, Tom, Jim and Frank— had paved the way for him. Hall of Famer Ed, who drowned in 1903 after falling from a railroad trestle over Niagara Falls, was the best of the Delahantys, and Tom was the only one never a big-league regular.

Last Trio of Brothers to Play in the Same League

AL—Bob, Ted and Ed Sadowski; all were active in the AL in 1962.

NL—Technically, the Cruzes—Jose, Hector and Cirilio— but Cirilio played only a few innings. Felipe, Matty and Jesus Alou were the last trio of brothers in the NL who were all quality players.

TOP 10 BROTHERS, CAREER HITS*

1.	Paul and Lloyd Waner	5611
2.	Felipe, Matty and Jesus Alou	5094
3.	Joe, Dom and Vince DiMaggio	4853
4.	Ed, Jim, Frank, Joe and Tom Delahanty	4211
5.	Hank and Tommy Aaron	3987
6.	Joe and Luke Sewell	3619
7.	Ken, Clete and Cloyd Boyer	3559
8.	Honus and Butts Wagner	3489
9.	Bob and Roy Johnson	3343
10.	Emil and Bob Meusel	3214

*Including only brothers who contributed to the family's total figure. For example, Cloyd Boyer had 20 hits but no home runs; Tommy Sewell was hitless in one at bat; and the Mathewsons, Whites and Galvins were omitted from the pitchers' list because in each case one brother failed to win a game.

BROTHERS WITH 1,725 OR MORE CAREER RBIS

1. Joe, Dom and Vince DiMaggio — 2739
2. Hank and Tommy Aaron — 2396
3. Ed, Jim, Frank, Joe and Tom Delahanty — 2153
4. Paul and Lloyd Waner — 1907
5. Bob and Emil Meusel — 1885
6. Bob and Roy Johnson — 1839
7. Lee and Carlos May — 1780
8. Honus and Butts Wagner — 1766
9. Joe and Luke Sewell — 1747

BROTHERS WITH 300 OR MORE CAREER HOME RUNS

1. Hank and Tommy Aaron — 768
2. Joe, Vince and Dom DiMaggio — 573
3. Lee and Carlos May — 444
   Ken and Clete Boyer — 444
5. Graig and Jim Nettles — 400
6. Dick, Hank and Ron Allen — 358
7. Bob and Roy Johnson — 346

BROTHERS WITH 1,800 OR MORE CAREER RUNS

1. Joe, Dom and Vince DiMaggio — 2927
2. Paul and Lloyd Waner — 2867
3. Ed, Jim, Frank, Joe and Tom Delahanty — 2309
4. Hank and Tommy Aaron — 2276
5. Felipe, Matty and Jesus Alou — 2209
6. Bob and Roy Johnson — 1956
7. Joe and Luke Sewell — 1834

BROTHERS WITH 200 OR MORE CAREER WINS

1. Gaylord and Jim Perry — 529
2. Phil and Joe Niekro — 527
3. John, Dad and Walter Clarkson — 386
4. Hoss and George Radbourn — 309
5. Stan and Harry Coveleski — 297
6. Gus and John Weyhing — 267
7. Bob and Ken Forsch — 257
8. Jesse and Virgil Barnes — 214
9. Dizzy and Paul Dean — 200

Invisible Men:
Umpires

Don Denkinger achieved a unique distinction in 1985—he became the first umpire ever to be the most memorable performer in a World Series. Years from now, long after it has grown misty whose pinch single finally won Game Six, his controversial safe call on Jorge Orta's seeming ground-out will still seem vivid. But whether Denkinger himself will become a major figure in the umpires' pantheon remains to be determined. If he does, he'll have a lot of company.

The First Famous Umpire

In the early days umpires were required to be consum-mate gentlemen, and the man appointed to umpire a game was generally deemed to be both the most honorable and the most knowledgeable club member. But when baseball became a business and players were no longer necessarily of the gentleman class, a new breed of umpire appeared. The first such man was probably Bill McLean, an ex-prizefighter. Officiating in the National Association in the early 1870s, McLean earned the nickname "King of Umpires" because of the vigorous manner in which he took charge of games. McLean later umpired in the National League through the 1884 season. Living in Boston, he customarily walked from his home to work an afternoon game in Providence, rising at 4:00 A.M.

First to Make Umpiring a Full-Time Profession

Nobody knows for sure, but a good guess would be "Hon-est" John Gaffney, who joined the National League in 1884 and introduced the style of working behind the catcher with no runners on base. By 1888 Gaffney was paid $2500 plus expenses for a season's work, more than most players re-ceived. Only a few years earlier umpires had earned just $5 a game, paid by the visiting team while the home team absorbed all other expenses.

First League to Put Its Umpires on a Regular Salary

In 1883 the American Association paid its umpires $140 a month and $3 per diem for travel expenses. Accordingly, the AA had a better overall caliber of umpiring than the National League in the early eighties. The AA's most highly esteemed umpire was probably Ben Young, who pioneered in forming a code of ethics for umpires before he was killed in a railway accident en route to an assigned game. Before his death, Young was also instrumental in getting the AA to hire a full-time staff of umpires by 1888, issue them blue coats and caps and have three umpires working each game. The NL regarded the three-umpire system as a needless extravagance and preferred to leave each game in the hands of one man like Gaffney or Bob Ferguson, a former NL player and manager, whose philosophy after becoming an umpire was "Never change a decision, never stop to talk to a player—make 'em play ball and keep their mouths shut and never fear but the people will be on your side and you'll be called the king of umpires." As late as 1908, in fact, both the National and the American League had a staff of only six umpires, one of whom served as an alternate, meaning that three umpires each day worked a game entirely alone.

Most Difficult Call for an Umpire Prior to 1884

Whether or not a pitch was legally delivered. Until 1884 pitchers were restricted to below-the-waist deliveries, much like fast-pitch softball pitchers. Umpires in the early days often consulted with players and sometimes even with fans before rendering a decision on a play or a pitch.

Only Umpire Banned for Rigging Games

Dick Higham, a former National League player and a good one. Higham was suspected of throwing games while playing, which makes you wonder what the NL expected when he was hired in 1882 to umpire. His downfall came midway in the season while he was umpiring a string of games that involved Detroit and kept making questionable calls against the Wolverines. Detroit officials were finally led to inspect his mail, much of which was in code and not a particulary sophisticated one. From it, they were easily able to deduce that Higham was in collusion with gamblers who were making a nifty sum, thanks to his help, by betting against Detroit.

First Former Player to Have a Lengthy Career as an Umpire
Bob Emslie joined the National League umpiring staff in 1891 after pitching for three seasons with Baltimore in the American Association and remained an umpire until 1924. Emslie was working the bases in the famous "Merkle Game" between the Giants and the Cubs in 1908, and it was actually his responsibility to decide whether Giants rookie Fred Merkle touched second base after Al Bridwell singled home the apparent winning run. But when Emslie claimed not to have seen the play, the onus fell on home plate umpire Hank O'Day, himself a former National League pitcher. O'Day ruled that Merkle was out, and pandemonium reigned at the Polo Grounds, making it impossible for O'Day and Emslie to clear the field and resume the game. Instead it had to be replayed at the end of the season when the Giants and Cubs wound up in a dead heat. The Cubs won the makeup game and the pennant and then went on to win their second and—to date—last World Championship in the Series that fall against the Tigers. Hence Emslie and O'Day are well remembered by both Giants and Cubs fans for their role in the Merkle game, and the game itself was pivotal for major league baseball as a whole in that it, along with several other controversial games in that same period, eventually forced officials to realize that more umpires were needed.

First World Series Game to Have More Than Two Umpires
The fourth game of the 1909 Series between the Pirates and the Tigers found Bill Klem behind the plate, Billy Evans working the bases and Silk O'Loughlin and Jimmy Johnstone on the foul lines after a bitter dispute in Game Three over whether a batted ball had been fair or foul.

Umpire with Most Seasons of Service
NL—Bill Klem. In 1909 Klem was in the fifth season of what would be a record 37-year career. He also officiated in a record 18 World Series, the last in 1940.

AL—Tommy Connolly served 31 years, from 1901 through 1931, and umpired in eight World Series. He, Klem, Hank O'Day, Cy Rigler, Billy Evans and Jocko Conlon are the only umpires to work more than five Series.

Active Umpire with Most Seasons of Service
AL—Larry Barnett and Don Denkinger, 18 seasons
NL—Doug Harvey, 25 seasons

Umpire Who Started the Custom of Raising His Right Arm to Signal a Strike
Cy Rigler. He reputedly initiated it so that Dummy Hoy, a deaf-mute, could keep track of the count while on base or playing in the outfield. The problem with this story is that Rigler first raised his arm to call a strike around 1905, by which time Hoy had already been out of the game for several years.

Only Hall of Fame Player Later to Umpire
Jake Beckley. But many outstanding players became umpires after their playing careers ended. Among them were the aforementioned O'Day and Emslie, plus George Moriarty, Babe Pinelli, Lon Warneke, George Pipgras, Al Orth, Sherry Magee, Charlie Berry, Bob Caruthers, Firpo Marberry, Ed Rommel, Mal Eason, Butch Henline, Bill Dinneen, Lip Pike, Chief Zimmer and Ed Swartwood.

Men Who Both Played and Umpired in a World Series
Dineen, Warneke, Rommel, Pipgras and Frank Secory, a substitute with the 1945 Cubs. Former umpires Ken Burkhart and Bill Kunkel were also members of World Series teams, but neither got into a game.

The "Right Man for the Job" Award
The home plate umpire for the famous double no-hit game on May 2, 1917, between Fred Toney of the Reds and Hippo Vaughn of the Cubs was former pitcher Al Orth. In 1908 Orth and Vaughn had been teammates on the Yankees for a brief while.

The "Lou Gehrig in Blue" Award
Bill McGowan, who worked in the American League from 1925 through 1954, umpired a record 2541 consecutive games over a 16½ year period without missing a single inning. Born in 1896, McGowan began his umpiring career in the Tri-State League in 1913 at age 17.

The "Going Out with a Bang" Award
Babe Pinelli served as a home plate umpire for the final

time in his long career on October 8, 1956. His last official action that day was to signal a called third strike on Dodgers pinch hitter Dale Mitchell and thus ring down the curtain on Don Larsen's perfect World Series game.

The "Umpires' Best Friend" Award
Tom Lynch, former National League umpire, became the NL president after Harry Pulliam committed suicide in 1909. Lynch was the first official to back umpires to the hilt in their war to reduce player rowdyism. He was so successful that he became despised by owners and players alike and was soon fired.

First Umpire to Wear Glasses on the Field
Ed Rommel on April 18, 1956, at Washington in a game between the Senators and Yankees. Larry Goetz was the first National League umpire to do it.

The "Longest Day" Award
On October 2, 1920, the Pirates and Reds played the last major-league tripleheader. Peter Harrison worked behind the plate in all three games—until darkness began to descend over Forbes Field in the sixth inning of the finale, with the Pirates ahead 6–0, and he was at last able to call a halt to the marathon without argument.

First Basemen's Records

Prior to 1900 most of the dominant hitters in the major
leagues were first basemen. Then as now size and batting
prowess were the key qualities sought by managers when
testing players at the position. Four first sackers of the
game's first phase—Dan Brouthers, Roger Connor, Cap
Anson and Dave Orr—hold most of the pre-1900 career
batting records. Others, like Harry Stovey, Long John Reilly,
Tommy Tucker, and Jake Beckley, also ranked consistently
among the leading hitters and sluggers. Connor, Anson,
Beckley, and Brouthers are in the Hall of Fame, and several
more of their contemporary gateway guardians probably
should be. Achieved during a time when the season schedule called for far fewer games than are played today, the
bulk of their season and career marks have long since been
eclipsed. So too have the fielding standards that were set by
men, like Joe Start and Charlie Comiskey, who used rudi-
mentary gloves and in some cases none at all. In fact, only
one first baseman's season record that was established before 1900 is still on the books—for most triples.

SEASON BATTING RECORDS

Department	National League	American League
Batting Average	.401, Bill Terry, New York, 1930	.420, GEORGE SISLER, St. Louis, 1922
Slugging Average	.656, Willie McCovey, San Francisco, 1969	.765, LOU GEHRIG, New York, 1927
Home Runs	51, Johnny Mize, New York, 1947	58, HANK GREENBERG, Detroit, 1938
RBIs	143, Don Hurst, Philadelphia, 1932	184, LOU GEHRIG, New York, 1931

Department	National League	American League
Runs	139, Bill Terry, New York, 1930	167, LOU GEHRIG, New York, 1936
Hits	254, Bill Terry, New York, 1930	257, GEORGE SISLER, St. Louis, 1920
Doubles	48, Keith Hernandez, St. Louis, 1979	64, GEORGE BURNS, Cleveland, 1926
Triples	29, PERRY WERDEN, St. Louis, 1893 22, Jake Daubert, Cincinnati, 1922*	20, Lou Gehrig, New York, 1926
Total Bases	392, Bill Terry, New York, 1930	447, LOU GEHRIG, New York, 1927
Stolen Bases	67, FRANK CHANCE, Chicago, 1903	52, Frank Isbell, Chicago, 1901
Bases on Balls	137, WILLIE MCCOVEY, San Francisco, 1969	137, ROY CULLENBINE, Detroit, 1947
Strikeouts	163, Don Clendenon, Pittsburgh, 1968	166, STEVE BALBONI, Kansas City, 1985
Fewest Strikeouts (Minimum 500 ABs)	6, Stuffy McInnis, Boston, 1924	5, STUFFY MCINNIS, Cleveland, 1922

*Record since 1901. Records are otherwise since 1893 for NL players and 1901 for AL players with the all-time holder's name in caps.

Note: Some sources credit Werden with 33 triples in 1893; if his total of 29 is accepted, then the all-time record holder is Dave Orr, who had 31 triples in 1886 for the American Association New York Mets. In 1932 Jimmie Foxx hit 58 homers for the Philadelphia A's but played 13 games at third base; similarly, Stan Musial of the Cardinals had 50 doubles in 1946 but played 42 games in the outfield. Hence both Foxx and Musial are not recognized as record holders here because a significant portion of their accomplishments occurred while they were playing other positions.

Most Games, Career, at First Base
2377—Jake Beckley, 1888–1907

Most Consecutive Games at First Base
885—Lou Gehrig, New York Yankees, June 6, 1925, through September 27, 1930

EVOLUTION OF SEASON RECORD FOR BEST FIELDING AVERAGE

	Team	League	Year	Average
Joe Start	New York	National	1876	.964[1]
Joe Start	Hartford	National	1877	.964
Chubb Sullivan	Cincinnati	National	1878	.975
Cap Anson	Chicago	National	1879	.975
Cap Anson	Chicago	National	1880	.977
Joe Start	Providence	National	1884	.980
Dave Orr	New York	Amer. Assoc.	1886	.981
Roger Connor	New York	National	1887	.993
Patsy Tebeau	Cleveland	National	1897	.994
Dan McGann	New York	National	1906	.995
Ed Konetchy	St. Louis	National	1913	.995[2]
Ed Konetchy	Pittsburgh	National	1914	.995
Stuffy McInnis	Philadelphia	American	1914	.995
Fritz Mollwitz	Cincinnati	National	1915	.996
Chick Gandil	Chicago	American	1919	.997[3]
Stuffy McInnis	Boston	American	1921	.999[4]
Frank McCormick	Philadelphia	National	1946	.999
Wes Parker	Los Angeles	National	1968	.999
Jim Spencer	Texas	American	1973	.999
Steve Garvey	Los Angeles	National	1981	.999
Eddie Murray	Baltimore	American	1981	.999
Steve Garvey	San Diego	National	1984	1.000

[1] Several sources credit him with being the first first sacker to play off the bag with the bases empty.

[2] Among the better first basemen in his time, but hidden away on bad teams until late in his career.

[3] He and Hal Chase were two of the *enfants terribles* in the teens. Chase got all the raves for his glove, but Gandil got the stats—he led the AL in fielding four consecutive years, 1916–19, whereas Chase, ironically, was never a fielding leader.

[4] For a player who was never considered among the greats, even in his time, McInnis holds an awful lot of records. His .999 average was better than any of the .999 FAs that followed in that he handled more chances.

Best Career Fielding Average, Minimum 1,000 Games
.996—Steve Garvey, 1969 through 1986

Most Seasons League Leader in Fielding Average
NL—9—Charlie Grimm, last in 1933
AL—6—Joe Judge, last in 1930

Most Consecutive Errorless Games
193—Steve Garvey, San Diego Padres, June 26, 1983, through April 14, 1985

Most Consecutive Errorless Chance
1700—Stuffy McInnis, Boston Red Sox and Cleveland Indians, May 31, 1921, through June 2, 1922

Most Chances Accepted, Career
25,505—Jake Beckley, 1888–1907

Most Chances Accepted, Season
1986—Jiggs Donahue, Chicago White Sox, 1907

Most Chances Accepted, Game, Nine Innings
NL—22—Ernie Banks, Chicago, May 9, 1963 (22 putouts)
AL—22—Tom Jones, St. Louis, May 11, 1906 (22 putouts)
          Hal Chase, New York, September 21, 1906 (22 putouts)

Most Assists, Season
184—Bill Buckner, Boston Red Sox, 1985: breaking his old record of 161, set in 1983 with the Cubs, which in turn had broken his 1982 mark of 159. The current NL mark is 166, set in 1986 by Sid Bream of Pittsburgh.

Most Seasons League Leader in Assists
NL—8—Fred Tenney, last in 1907
AL—6—George Sisler, last in 1927
        Vic Power, last in 1962

Most Double Plays, Season
194—Ferris Fain, Philadelphia A's, 1949. That year the A's turned 217 double plays, an all-time team record, and then topped 200 again in 1950 and 1951.

Best Glove Man Ever at First Base
Hal Chase had the rep, Vic Power was compared to him, and George Scott won the most Gold Gloves—eight—but don't overlook Paul Campbell. In 1941, playing with Montreal in the International League, Campbell set an all-time record for first basemen by starting 26 double plays; the major league record is 18. Furthermore, Campbell tied a major-league single-game mark on May 14, 1949, when he performed two unassisted double plays for the Tigers.

Under the Lights

If you thought night baseball was a comparatively recent innovation, you might be surprised to learn that the first night game was played on September 2, 1880, between Jordan Marsh & Company and R. H. White & Company, two Boston department stores. The two company nines battled to a 16–16 tie at Nantasket Bay near Hull, Massachusetts, as part of a series of lighting displays put on by the Northern Electric Company of Boston to prove the far-reaching value of the incandescent lamp, invented by Thomas Edison only the year before.

There were other night games during the latter part of the 19th century, but few had the foresight to envision that night baseball would ever be anything more than a novelty. One who did was sportswriter O. P. Caylor. In 1893 Caylor wrote:

> Should the time ever come when by some system of illumination base ball could be played as well at night as in the daytime the possibilities of the game's earnings could hardly be estimated. . . . But the chances are that the time will never come when base ball at night will be possible. . . . However, it is a subject which will be worth consideration. If any one ever does discover a system of out-of-door lighting sufficiently good for base ball playing in the open air at night he will at once take ranks with the millionaires of the land.

Caylor's remarks are quite prescient in all, but his last statement makes me wince each time I read it. George Cahill, the man who first discovered a way of economically staging night games, never made anything close to a million from his invention and indeed is largely forgotten today.

By 1910 Cahill had devised a portable lighting system good enough to get the grudging permission of Charlie Comiskey to stage a game under artificial glare at the new White Sox park. Some 20,000 fans watched two local amateur teams play a full nine innings under the gleam of twenty 137,000-candlepower arc lights and from all accounts thoroughly enjoyed the proceedings. But Comiskey and other major-league owners saw no future in night baseball, and it would be another 25 years before Cahill realized his dream.

The first major-league night game did not take place until 1935. On May 24, at Crosley Field, Paul Derringer of the Reds beat the Phillies 2–1 after President Franklin Roosevelt turned on the lights by pushing a button in the White House. The first to bat under artificial light in a major-league game was Phillies outfielder Lou Chiozza. Among the 20,422 in attendance, though no great ceremony was made of it, was the man who had the largest hand in making it all possible, George Cahill.

Although the first major-league team to install lights, the Reds were far from being the first team in organized baseball to do so. On April 28, 1930, Independence, Kansas, of the Class C Western Association staged the first offical pro night game, losing 13–3 to Muskogee, and by 1935 many other minor-league clubs had already begun playing under the lights.

Second Major-League Team to Install Lights

The Dodgers, and they could not have had a better sense of timing. Their guests on June 15, 1938, for the inaugural night game at Ebbets Field, were the Reds. Four days earlier the Reds scheduled starting pitcher, left-hander Johnny Vander Meer, had pitched a no-hitter against the Braves, and in case you don't know what he did to the Dodgers in front of the first crowd in the New York area to witness a major-league game under the lights, see "No-hitters and Perfect Games."

First American League Team to Install Lights

The Indians, but the Athletics were the first team actually to play at home under the lights. A complete list follows of the opening night games for the 16 franchises that were around when it all started.

Stadium	Date	Result
At Crosley Field	May 24, 1935	Reds 2, Phillies 1
At Ebbets Field	June 15, 1938	Reds 6, Dodgers 0
At Shibe Park	May 16, 1939	Indians 8, A's 3, 10 innings
At Shibe Park (Phillies)	June 1, 1939	Pirates 5, Phillies 2
At Cleveland Stadium	June 27, 1939	Indians 5, Tigers 0
At Comiskey Park	August 14, 1939	White Sox 5, Browns 2
At Polo Grounds	May 24, 1940	Giants 8, Braves 1
At Sportsman's Park	May 24, 1940	Indians 3, Browns 2
At Sportsman's Park (Cards)	June 4, 1940	Dodgers 10, Cardinals 1
At Forbes Field	June 4, 1940	Pirates 14, Braves 2
At Griffith Stadium	May 28, 1941	Yankees 6, Senators 5
At Braves Field	May 11, 1946	Giants 5, Braves 1
At Yankee Stadium	May 28, 1946	Senators 2, Yankees 1
At Fenway Park	June 13, 1947	Red Sox 5 White Sox 3
At Briggs Stadium	June 15, 1948	Tigers 4, A's 1

First Night All-Star Game
June 13, 1943, at Shibe Park, won by the American League 5–4. However, the last part of the 1942 game, at the Polo Grounds, was played under the lights when darkness began to set in after a lengthy rain delay.

First Night World Series Game
October 13, 1971, at Three Rivers Stadium, when the Pirates beat the Orioles 4–3 to even the Series at two games apiece.

Players We Wish We'd Seen More of: 19th Century

Now that there are 26 teams and baseball is no longer the only professional sport to attract the nation's top athletes, there is enough room in the major leagues to accommodate just about every player who has the talent and the desire to make the game a career. But prior to expansion, free agency and changes in the minor league draft rules, every era had its share of shooting stars, players who crossed our line of vision for only a few short moments, just long enough to light up the sky brightly—in some instances brilliantly—before they were inexplicably sent back to the minors or otherwise allowed to fade off, often disappearing so completely that nothing at all is known about them today. Here are my top seven choices from the 19th century.

1. Jocko Flynn. As a 22-year-old rookie with the 1886 Chicago White Stockings, he won 24 games and led the National League in winning percentage. Used also on occasion in the outfield, he played part of one game there in 1887 and then was gone.

2. George Nicol. A pitcher-outfielder, Nicol threw a seven-inning no-hitter for the St. Louis Browns as a rookie in 1890, beating Philadelphia 21–2. It was by far his best mound effort, but before departing at age 23 in 1894, he hit .362 with 25 RBIs and 51 hits in 141 at bats, the second-highest career average in history among players with over 100 at bats.

3. Harry Moore. Playing left field for the Washington Union Association team in 1884, he hit .336 in 111 games, the third-best average in the league, but then departed so precipitously that not a single morsel of biographical information is known about him.

4. Levi Meyerle. One of the game's first great stars, he led all National Association batters in 1871 with a .492 average, the highest in major-league history if you're among those who consider the NA a major league. Meyerle hit .346 with Philadelphia in 1876, the National League's inaugural season, and then was mysteriously blacklisted by Cincinnati the following season, at age 28, despite carrying a .327 average after 27 games.

5. Walter Thornton. A pitcher-outfielder, Thornton broke in with Chicago in 1895 at age 20 and exited in 1898 with a 23–18 career pitching record and a .312 career batting average in 154 games.

6. Jack Rothfuss and Jesse Hoffmeister. For years Pittsburgh was plagued with first base problems, and they may have begun in 1897 when the Pirates cut Rothfuss after he hit .313 in 35 games and showed good power, knocking home 18 runs in 115 at bats. In 1897 the Pirates also had a gaping hole at third base where Jim Donely, the incumbent, hit only .193. They tried Hoffmeister for 48 games, and he hit .309 and had 36 RBIs but fielded only .792 with 31 errors. His glove convinced the Pirates to drop him in 1898 and go with Bill Grey, who hit a robust .229 and made 59 errors.

7. Herb Goodall and Charlie Hamburg. After finishing deep in the American Association cellar in 1889, Louisville won the pennant the following year, mostly because manager Jack Chapman lost fewer players than the other AA clubs to the Players League. But among the key regulars who did jump to the PL were leftfielder Pete Browning, two-time AA batting champ, and pitcher John Ewing, brother of Hall of Fame catcher Buck Ewing. They were replaced by two rookies, Hamburg and Goodall. In 133 games Hamburg hit .272 and scored 93 runs while Goodall won eight games, led the AA with four saves and batted a phenomenal .422 with 19 hits in 45 at bats. Despite their large contributions to the team's revival, both were dropped from the roster in the 1891 season, and without them Louisville fell all the way to seventh place.

World Series Play: 1876–1900

FRANCHISE SUMMARY

Team	League	WS Record	Years in Series
New York Giants	National	2–0–0	1888, 1889
Providence Grays	National	1–0–0	1884
Detroit Wolverines	National	1–0–0	1887
Louisville Eclipse	Association	0–0–1	1890
Cincinnati Red Stockings	Association	0–0–1	1882
St. Louis Browns	Association	1–2–1	1885, 1886; 1887 1888
Chicago White Stockings	National	0–1–2	1882, 1885, 1886
Brooklyn Bridegrooms	Both	0–1–1	1889, 1890
New York Metropolitans	Association	0–1–0	1884

Yearly Highlights

1882—Cincinnati (AA) and Chicago (NL) tied 1 game to 1

At the conclusion of the American Association's first season as a major league, the pennant winners in the AA and the National League played a "World Series" to settle which circuit was superior. But the Series ended abortively after two games when AA president Denny McKnight wired the Red Stockings that they would be expelled if they continued play. Cincinnati was prepared to defy McKnight, but Chicago manager Cap Anson withdrew his White Stockings from the Series in what he believed was the best interest of both teams.

1884—Providence (NL) defeated New York (AA) 3 games
to 0

Responding to a challenge from New York manager Jim
Mutrie, Providence manager Frank Bancroft brought his
Grays to the Mets' home park, the original Polo Grounds,
for a three-game World Series. The first contest was played
on October 23, 1884, before a crowd of 2500 in blustery
conditions and under Association rules, which called for hit
batsmen to be given first base. As a result, both Providence
leadoff batter Paul Hines and second batter Cliff Carroll
reached base after being hit by the Mets' Tim Keefe. Hines
scored the first run on a wild pitch and a passed ball, and
the Grays won 6–0 behind their 60-game winner Hoss
Radbourn. The following day Radbourn won 3–1 on a three-
run homer by Jerry Denny and then closed out the Series
with 11–2 win in even rawer conditions, which caused the
third game to be terminated after six innings. The Grays
played all three games without using a single substitute.

1885—St. Louis (AA) and Chicago (NL) tied 3 games to 3

The Browns and White Stockings played seven games and
wound up deadlocked at three-all, with one contest a tie, in
what was now called "The World Championship Series," so
named by Alfred Spink, the creator of the *Sporting News*.
Players did not take the games seriously because the owners, in their greed, were more concerned with attracting
spectators than making for good baseball, and the crowds
at times overran the field. Neither team's players received a
penny for participating in this Series, which was sloppily
played and ineptly umpired.

1886—St. Louis (AA) defeated Chicago (NL) 4 games to 1

The first best-four-of-seven Series played to a conclusion.
After splitting the first two games in Chicago, the teams
moved to St. Louis, where the Browns won three straight,
the finale in the 10th inning when Curt Welch scored from
third base on a wild pitch that sailed over the head of
Chicago catcher King Kelly. Welch was the first Series hero
to be immortalized for a feat that was largely fiction. His
"$15,000 Slide," which was made to seem the tail end of a
brazen dash for the plate, wasn't even necessary—he could
have jogged home and scored standing up.

1887—Detroit (NL) defeated St. Louis (AA) 8 games to 3

Frederick Stearns, eager to take full advantage of his slugging Wolverines, challenged Browns owner Chris Von der Ahe to a 15-game Series, with the two teams traveling in a special train of parlor cars and playing in all major cities as well as St. Louis and Detroit. Von der Ahe further agreed to hiking admission prices to one dollar and to Stearns's suggestion that two umpires be used, "Honest John" Kelly and "Honest John" Gaffney. In search of a way to plug her acting career, Helen Dauvray, wife of New York Giants shortstop Monte Ward, hit upon the notion of awarding a cup in her name to the winning team. Detroit won the first Dauvray Cup, which has disappeared over the years, by taking 8 of the first 11 games, but the teams played the last four anyway.

1888—New York (NL) defeated St. Louis (AA) 6 games to 2

Jim Mutrie, having switched his loyalty to the NL in 1885, became the first man to manage Series teams in two leagues. His war cry to herald his Giants was "We are the people!" Nobody quite knew what it meant, least of all Mutrie, but it sounded good and a song went with it. A 10-game Series was arranged and played out even though the Giants won six of the first eight games. Von der Ahe, supported by his players and in particular Arlie Latham, a notorious rabble-rouser, blamed the umpires for his club's defeat, even accusing umpires Kelly and Gaffney of betting on the Giants. This Series also had the first goat, Browns shortstop Bill White, who had replaced the popular Bill Gleason after Gleason was traded to Philadelphia. White was unfairly chastised—his fielding cost St. Louis one game at most—and never again played in the majors. The Dauvray Cup came to Helen's husband and his Giants, to be kept by them pending the results of the following year's Series.

1889—New York (NL) defeated Brooklyn (AA) 6 games to 3

The Giants played the Bridegrooms in what would have been the first subway Series if there had been subways in 1889—at the time New York and Brooklyn were still separate cities. The Giants won in nine games, making the 10th game unnecessary, and now had two legs up on the three Series wins required to take permanent possession of the Dauvray Cup.

1890—Louisville (AA) tied Brooklyn (NL) 3 games to 3

It was the last Dauvray Cup World Series, as the war between the two leagues in 1891 made postseason play between their pennant winners out of the question. The Bridegrooms, after switching to the NL intact with no key players lost to Players League raids, beat Louisville three of the first four games. But Louisville won the next two, in Brooklyn no less, evening the Series. The weather was so dreadful for the deciding seventh game that only 300 fans showed up and the contest was called off, the Series ending, as it had begun eight years earlier, in a tie.

Postscript

In 1892 the National League, now inflated to 12 teams after absorbing 4 clubs from the defunct Association, played a split schedule for the first and only time in major-league history, the Cleveland Spiders winning the first half season and the Boston Beaneaters the second. After the first game of the postseason series ended in a tie, Boston swept five in a row and terminated proceedings. No championship was played in 1893, but William Temple, president of the Pittsburgh Pirates, which unexpectedly finished second to Boston that year, felt cheated of a crack at the Beaneaters and proposed a plan whereby the second-place team at the end of each season would challenge the first-place team to a best four-of-seven series and win by default if the first place team refused the challenge. He then ordered a cup in his name for $800 from New York jeweler A. E. Thrall and stipulated that, like the Dauvray Cup, permanent possession of the Temple Cup would go to the first team to win it three times. To Temple's chagrin, the Baltimore Orioles won easily in 1894, and the Giants finished second while his Pirates plummeted to seventh place. To the chagrin of all club owners in the league, the Orioles merely went through the motions in their series with the Giants and dropped four straight games. When the same lack of player enthusiasm persisted the next three years, the Temple Cup series was scrapped, owners citing low motivation and secret agreements between teams to split the take fifty-fifty regardless of the result. The irony was that the Orioles, after dismal performances in the 1894 and 1895 series, had revved up their act and taken the next two series in a row, putting them on the brink of seizing permanent ownership of the Temple Cup, which now resides, instead, in the Hall of Fame.

SECTION 2

SECTION 2

Famous Firsts:
1901–19

1901—The American League opens its first season as a major league on April 24 but runs into bad luck—three of the four scheduled lid-lifters are rained out. Hence the honor of playing the first AL game falls exclusively to Chicago and Cleveland, which meet at the Chicago Cricket Club in front of 14,000 or so. Chicago, behind rookie right-hander Roy Patterson, wins 8–2. Bill Hoffer, himself a record-shattering rookie 30-game winner in the National League only six years earlier, goes all the way for Cleveland in defeat but is released a few weeks later with a 3–7 record. Cleveland outfielder Ollie Pickering earns the distinction of being the first player to bat in an AL game while his teammate, second baseman Erv Beck, goes 2-for-2 and gets the game's only extra-base hit, a double. The following day Beck hits the first AL home run.

1902—Tom Rice of the *Brooklyn Eagle* begins campaigning for scoreboards and other fan conveniences like having teams announce lineup changes; his efforts lead, among other things, to announcers with megaphones strolling about the grounds and calling out starting lineups and substitutions.

1903—The first moving picture of a baseball game is made, featuring Nap Lajoie and Harry Bay of Cleveland during a post-season series with Cincinnati. In 1910 the National Commission receives $500 for World Series movie rights; the figure climbs to the gigantic sum of $3500 in 1911. Four years later Harry Aitken of the Mutual Film Corporation talks John McGraw of the Giants into becoming the first manager to film his players during spring training for instructional purposes.

1905—Roger Bresnahan experiments with a batting helmet—called a "pneumatic head protector"—after being beaned. In 1907 Bresnahan catches the opening game of the season for the Giants wearing shin guards. The game winds up being forfeited to the Phillies when the Polo Grounds crowd gets unruly, but Bresnahan nonetheless makes the Hall of Fame, in part for his experimentation with headgear and shin guards. Nig Clarke, a rookie catcher for Cleveland who regularly wore soccer guards under his socks in 1905, becomes a footnote in the shin guard story.

1907—Albert Spalding creates a commission to unearth the origins of baseball and names A. G. Mills to head it. Mills, a former National League president, after some months of digging attributes the game's invention to his old friend Gen. Abner Doubleday, who purportedly concocted it one afternoon in 1839 in Cooperstown, New York, while still a West Point cadet. Mills's report is nine-tenths fiction and one-tenth the vague testimony of Abner Graves, a boyhood friend of Doubleday's who claimed to have seen the first game. On the basis of Mills's findings, the Hall of Fame and National Baseball Museum are placed in Cooperstown, and a centennial celebration of the game's birth is planned for 1939. Long before 1939 all the historical material accumulated by Mills is reportedly destroyed in a fire, making verification of it impossible. But the hoopla attending the centennial celebration is so vast that it reaches all the way to Hawaii, where Bruce Cartwright, grandson of a man named Alexander Cartwright, writes a letter in 1938 and encloses supporting evidence that touches off an investigation that seems to prove beyond all doubt that the Mills Commission's findings were phony and Alexander Cartwright was the true inventor of baseball. Hall of Fame committee members, upon deliberation, buy grandson Bruce's evidence, and Doubleday, the man responsible for the shrine's placement in Cooperstown, is himself never enshrined.

1908—George Baird of Chicago invents an electric scoreboard that instantly records balls, strikes, runs, etc.

1908—In July the Giants stun the baseball world by paying $11,000 for Rube Marquard, an unproven minor-league pitcher.

1908—On August 4 the Cardinals and Dodgers play a full game at Brooklyn's Washingtion Park using only one ball. There is nothing to attest that this was the last time it was done, only that it was still something that happened as late as 1908.

1909—On July 18 Cleveland shortstop Neal Ball, in a game against the Red Sox, performs the first unassisted triple play. The previous year, while playing for the Yankees, Ball led the majors with 80 errors and fielded .898.

1910—President Taft throws out the first ball at the Senators' opener on April 14, then watches Walter Johnson pitch a one-hit 3–0 shutout over the Athletics. Taft likes the experience so much that he decides to make it an annual event.

1911—It becomes mandatory for home teams to wear white uniforms and visiting teams dark uniforms. The Giants and the Phillies are the first to start doing this as a way for both fans and players to distinguish one team from the other.

1911—A cork-and-rubber-center ball replaces the dead-as-duck-feathers rubber-core ball; Ty Cobb hits .420, Wildfire Schulte of the Cubs cracks 21 homers, and batting averages as a whole in the American League skyrocket 30 points.

1912—Ty Cobb is suspended by AL president Ban Johnson for going into the Hilltop Park stands on May 15 and fighting with Yankees fan Claude Lueker. The Tigers react to Cobb's suspension by going on strike before their game on May 18 against the Athletics, forcing Detroit manager Hugh Jennings to use Philadelphia seminary student Aloysius Travers, later a priest, on the mound, local amateurs at other positions, and 48-year-old coach Deacon McGuire behind the bat. Travers pitches a complete-game 26-hitter, losing 24–2, while McGuire singles and scores a run, and 30-year-old third baseman Ed Irvin, playing his only major-league game, raps two triples in three at bats, giving him a record 2.000 career slugging average. Late in the game, Jennings inserts himself as a pinch hitter and avoids getting hit by a pitch, thereupon failing in his last big-league at bat to increase his all-time career record for being hit 260 times by pitches.

1914—The Federal League opens its first of two seasons as a major circuit after luring many major-league players into its camp. The first to jump ship is St. Louis Browns first baseman George Stovall. Joe Tinker is the first star to join the Feds. Walter Johnson signs a Fed contract, then recants when Washington owner Clark Griffith gives him a raise, plus a healthy bonus, which is subsidized by other American League owners to keep him out of the Feds' clutches.

1915—The Tigers, the last team to wear collars on their uniforms, finally abandon them. The Yankees, meanwhile, wear pinstriped uniforms for the first time.

1915—The National League makes it a rule that all clubs must have canvases to cover their fields in the event of rain so that play can resume when it stops without resorting to the ancient method of burning wood and spreading oil and sawdust.

1915—The American League starts the policy of giving each player two passes, good for any park in the league.

1915—Cardinals officials, convinced that St. Louis can't support two major-league teams and the Browns are the stronger franchise, attempt to move the team to Baltimore when Federal League owners of the Baltimore club express an interest in buying the Cardinals and transfering them, but other National League owners block the move. Thirty-nine years later the Browns move to Baltimore.

1916—Cubs owner Charles Weegham comes up with the revolutionary idea of allowing fans to keep balls hit into the stands, seemingly bringing to an end the warfare between park policemen and fans trying to obtain souvenir balls. But as late as 1923 a Philadelphia boy is arrested and housed overnight in the slammer for keeping a ball hit into the Baker Bowl bleachers, and in 1937 a Yankees fan is vigorously pummeled by ushers when he attempts to retrieve a ball lodged in the home plate screen. His suit against the Yankees, in which he wins $7,500, results in a sort of truce between club officials and fans on the issue.

1917—The Cardinals establish the first "Knothole Gang" for kids. The brainchild of St. Louis insurance man W. E. Bilheimer to combat juvenile delinquency, it is so successful that in 1920 the Cardinals admit an estimated 64,000 boys to their games for free.

1917—On June 27 Braves catcher Hank Gowdy becomes the first major leaguer to enter the military service in World War I. In October of the following year, former Phillies third baseman Eddie Grant becomes the first major-leaguer player ever to be killed in combat.

1919—The Cardinals pay $10,000 to Kansas City for pitcher Jesse Haines. Haines is the last minor leaguer to be purchased by the Cardinals until World War II, as their farm system, for the next quarter of a century, supplies them with all the talent they need.

A Short History
of Team Names

Unlike the Kansas City Royals and several other expansion teams whose names were chosen logically and systematically by their fans, most of the 16 teams that constituted the major leagues from 1901 through 1960 had a number of names before settling on the one now in vogue. To eliminate confusion, all references to teams for the remainder of the book will use their current names.

American League
California Angels (1961)—Originally the Los Angeles Angels, the name of the Pacific Coast League team in the "City of Angels," they became the California Angels when the franchise moved to its new stadium in Anaheim.

Baltimore Orioles (1901)—During the 1901 season the franchise was located in Milwaukee. Moving to St. Louis in 1902, the team became known as the Browns because of the brown trim on its uniforms, a carryover from the old St. Louis Browns in the American Association. When the franchise shifted to Baltimore in 1954, team officials and fans were eager to rid the club of all association with the losing Browns and revive the old Orioles tradition. All Baltimore major league teams since 1882, with the exception of the Federal League Terrapins, had been called the Orioles, as had the International League franchise, the city's lone link to organized baseball from 1916 through 1953.

Boston Red Sox (1901)—Called the Pilgrims or the Puritans in the early years of the American League, and also for a time the Somersets—after owner Charles Somers—they became the Red Sox when new owner John Taylor decided the club needed a zippier name. For a time the club was labeled the Red Stockings, the name of the original Boston

National League team, but sportswriters soon shortened it to Red Sox, and in later years, to BoSox.

Chicago White Sox (1901)—Called the Invaders at first when the American League "invaded" Chicago before the opening of the 1900 season, the club then assumed the name White Stockings, which had been discarded by its National League counterpart in the late 1890s, but the sobriquet was immediately abbreviated to fit into sports page headlines. Within a few years it began being shortened, still more, to ChiSox. Also called the Pale Hose, as opposed to the Red Sox, who are known as the Crimson Hose.

Cleveland Indians (1901)—Known as the Broncos in 1901, then the Blues because of their uniforms, and then the Naps when Nap Lajoie became the team's player-manager, the Indians didn't settle finally on a name until 1915. From 1912 through 1914 they were called the Mollie McGuires since many of their players were Irish, but when they finished last in 1914, it seemed time for a completely fresh start. Some believe the name Indians was chosen to commemorate Louis Sockalexis, the ill-fated Penobscot Indian who played with the Cleveland Spiders in the 1890s. Also called the Tribe.

Detroit Tigers (1901)—The team began as the Wolverines, after the Detroit National League entry which had adopted the name of the state animal, but sportswriter Phil Reid of the *Detroit Free Press* noticed that the blue-and-orange-striped stockings worn by the 1901 club resembled Princeton's colors and started calling them the Tigers. Also known as the Bengals.

Kansas City Royals (1969)—The name was chosen by the team's fans.

Milwaukee Brewers (1970)—The name of the first National League team representing Milwaukee in 1878; also the name of the first American League team in 1901 and the minor-league American Association team.

Minnesota Twins (1901)—Named for the twin cities of Minneapolis and St. Paul. From 1901 through 1960, the team was known as both the Senators and the Nationals, sometimes abbreviated to Nats, because its home was the nation's capital.

New York Yankees (1901)—Began in 1901 as the Baltimore Orioles. Shifted to New York in 1903, the team was called the Highlanders because its home ground, Hilltop Park, was so high and also because its first president was Joseph Gordon, whose name suggested the Gordon Highlanders, at the time a crack regiment in the British army. Around 1914 Jim Price of the *New York Press* coined the current name. Also called the Bronx Bombers.

Oakland Athletics (1901)—Began in 1901 as the Philadelphia Athletics; moved to Kansas City in 1955 and then to Oakland in 1968. The name has a long and rich history that both Kansas City and Oakland officials fortunately chose to preserve. In 1871 the Philadelphia Athletics won the first National Association pennant. Also called the A's.

Seattle Mariners (1977)—The name was adopted to honor the nautical tradition of the Pacific Northwest. The first major-league team in Seattle survived only one season—1969—before moving to Milwaukee, and was called the Pilots. There was some sentiment to name the team the Rainiers, after the Seattle club in the Pacific Coast League, but Mariners was a more popular choice.

Texas Rangers (1961)—Upon leaving Washington after the 1971 season, the franchise assumed the name of the state's traditional lawmen and took the example of the Minnesota team by coupling it with Texas so as not to slight either Dallas or Forth Worth.

Toronto Blue Jays (1977)—Name chosen in a fan contest.

National League

Atlanta Braves (1876)—The team moved from Boston to Milwaukee in 1953—the first franchise since 1903—then abandoned Milwaukee for Atlanta after the 1965 season. While in the National Association the team was dubbed the Red Caps. The red hosiery they sported led to their being called the Red Stockings after they joined the National League, but by the 1890s they were more commonly known as the Beaneaters. The name Braves came into existence in 1912 because owner Jim Gaffney was a Tammany Hall chieftain. Prior to that they had also been known as the Doves, while the team president was George Dovey, and the Pilgrims after the Red Sox dropped that name. A horrible season in 1935 spurred team officials and fans to call the club the Bees from 1936 to 1940, but the name never really caught on.

Chicago Cubs (1876)—Originally the White Stockings, the team became known as the Colts after player-manager Cap Anson appeared on stage in a play called *Runaway Colt* in the mid-1890s. When Anson left the club after being denied the share of the franchise he'd been promised, people began calling them the Orphans. For several years they were also known as the Cowboys and the Broncos, but in 1901 Chicago sportswriters George Rice and Fred Hayner began referring to them as the Cubs because their roster was stocked with so many young players after American League raids had depleted it. Also known as the Bruins.

Cincinnati Reds (1890)—Short for Red Stockings, the name of the great Cincinnati team in the late 1860s. Briefly called the Red Legs in the 1940s when *reds* was an evil word in America.

Houston Astros (1962)—First called the Colt 45s. Became the Astros when the Astrodome was opened in 1965.

Los Angeles Dodgers (1890)—Based in Brooklyn until 1958, the club shrewdly kept the Dodgers name after moving to the West Coast, thereby retaining the loyalty of its East Coast fans and also appealing to the many transplanted New Yorkers in the L.A. area. In 1889, while the franchise was still in the American Association, the team acquired the name Bridegrooms after three players got married in the off-season. When Ned Hanlon became manager in 1899, the team was called the Superbas because there was a popular vaudeville troupe at the time known as "Hanlon's Superbas." The club was also called the Atlantics—after the old Brooklyn National Association team—and later the Robins when Wilbert Robinson became manager, but by World War I the Dodgers name had taken hold. It had its roots in "Trolley Dodgers," the pejorative sobriquet given turn-of-the-century Brooklynites by New Yorkers.

Montreal Expos (1969)—Named after Expo '67, the World's Fair exposition.

New York Mets (1962)—Short for Metropolitans, a revival of the name borne by the New York American Association franchise in the 1880s.

Philadelphia Phillies (1883)—The original name of the Philadelphia team in the National League, it was spelled Fillies at first, as in female horses. Also briefly called the Quakers and later the Bluejays when the Carpenters bought the team during World War II and tried to create a new image, but neither name stuck.

Pittsburgh Pirates (1887)—The team was called the Alleghenies while it was in the American Association and then, facetiously, the Innocents after the franchise traitorously deserted the AA and switched to the National League. Became the Pirates in 1891 when the club "pirated" Lou Bierbauer and Harry Stovey, two star players the Philadelphia American Association team neglected to protect after they jumped to the Players League. Also called the Bucs or the Corsairs.

St. Louis Cardinals (1892)—Originally the St. Louis Browns American Association franchise, accepted into the National League when the AA folded after the 1891 season. Also known in the 1890s as the Maroons and the Perfectos. In 1899 the Robison brothers, who owned both the Cleveland and the St. Louis franchises, not only stocked St. Louis with all of Cleveland's best players but also brought along the Spiders' uniforms. St. Louis sportswriter Willie McHale, observing the red trim, coined the name Cardinals.

San Diego Padres (1969)—Assumed the nickname of the old Pacific Coast League team whose place they took in town.

San Francisco Giants (1883)—Like the Dodgers, the Giants retained their name when they moved from New York to the West Coast in 1958. But though the Dodgers also successfully kept their identity, the Giants failed. It is doubtful that very many San Francisco fans know much about the franchise's history, let alone that the team name was originated in 1885 by manager Jim Mutrie, who called his charges "My boys, my Giants!" Before Mutrie came along the club was known as the Green Stockings or the Gothams.

Team Records since 1901

On September 7, 1916, the New York Giants embarked on a 26-game winning streak, the longest victory skein since the National League was formed in 1876, by beating the Dodgers 4–1 at the Polo Grounds. All 26 victories came in their home park, giving them a second record for the most consecutive wins at home. In the course of the streak the Giants beat every National League rival at least once. The only blemish on their record was a 1–1 tie with the Pirates on September 18 in the second of three straight doubleheaders that postponements forced the two clubs to play.

Earlier in the 1916 season the Giants had rattled off 17 straight victories away from the Polo Grounds, the last coming on May 29 when Christy Mathewson beat the Braves 3–0 and registered the final shutout of his career. On the strength of Mathewson's arm, the Giants broke the previous record for most consecutive road wins—16, set by the Washington Senators between May 30 and June 15, 1912. The two long streaks gave the Giants 43 wins without a loss; their record when they weren't on a tear also included 43 wins—but against 66 losses. Overall, the club finished with an 86–66 mark, good only for fourth place.

Most Consecutive Wins without a Tie

NL—21—Chicago, 1935. The 1881 Chicago White Stockings also won 21 in a row, but tied a game with Providence.

AL—19—New York, 1947. In 1906 the White Sox also won 19 straight but had one tie.

Most Consecutive Wins Prior to 1876

The National Association Boston Red Caps won 26 straight in 1875. If you recognize the NA as a major league—and many do—then the 1875 Red Caps share the all-time major-league record with the 1916 Giants. The record for the most consecutive wins by a professional team was set by the 1869–70 Cincinnati Red Stockings, who won 130 straight games with one tie before losing 8–7 to the Brooklyn Atlantics on June 14, 1870, in 11 innings. After scoring two runs in the top of the 11th to go ahead 7–5, the Red Stockings let the game slip away when second baseman Charlie Sweazy muffed a throw from shortstop George Wright, who was trying for a double play on a ground ball with runners on first and second. Bob Ferguson, the lead runner, scored the winning run on the error. Ironically, at the end of the nine innings the Red Stockings had refused the Atlantics' offer of a tie and insisted on playing to a decision.

Most Consecutive Doubleheaders Won
5—New York Yankees, 1906; the last one on September 4 when they beat the Red Sox 7–0 and 1–0

Most Consecutive Wins, Start of Season
NL—13—Atlanta, April 6 to April 21, 1982
AL—11—Oakland, April 9 to April 19, 1981

Most Consecutive Wins, Start of Season, before 1901
20—St. Louis Maroons, Union Association, April 20 to May 22, 1884. The runaway UA pennant winners didn't suffer their first loss until May 24, when they were beaten 8–1 by Boston's Tommy Bond.

Most Consecutive Losses
NL—23—Philadelphia, 1961; the streak ended on August 20 when the Phils beat the Braves in the second game of a doubleheader
AL—20—Boston, 1906; Philadelphia, 1916 and 1943

Most Consecutive Losses Prior to 1901
26—Louisville Eclipse, American Association, May 22 to June 22, 1889. Louisville finished in the cellar with a 27–111 record. In 1890 the club won 61 more games, the largest improvement in major-league history, and became the only major-league team to vault from last place to a pennant the following season.

Most Consecutive Losses, Expansion Team
NL—20—Montreal, 1969
AL—15—Texas, 1972

Most Consecutive Losses on the Road
NL—22—New York Mets, June 16 through July 28, 1963. The Mets played some home games, which they won, in the midst of their road losing streak, but the Pittsburgh Innocents, co-holders of the all-time record, in 1890 dropped 22 straight, all on the road.

AL—19—Philadelphia, July 25 through August 8, 1916; in the process the A's also set an all-time record for the most losses—19—in a two-week span.

Most Consecutive Losses at Home
AL—20—St. Louis, June 3 through July 7, 1953
NL—14—Boston, May 8 through May 24, 1911

Most Consecutive Doubleheaders Lost
In 1929 weather postponements forced the Boston Braves to play a record nine doubleheaders in a row from September 4 through September 15; at one point in their travails they lost five consecutive twin bills, one at Philadelphia and four straight to the Giants in Boston.

Most Consecutive Losses, Start of the Season
AL—13—Washington, 1904; Detroit, 1920
NL—9—Brooklyn, 1918; Boston, 1919; New York Mets, 1962

Special Mention
In 1899 the Cleveland Spiders, playing their final season in the National League, had losing streaks of 24 games, 16 games and 14 games.

Highest Batting Average, Season
NL—.319—New York Giants, 1930
AL—.316—Detroit, 1921

Lowest Batting Average, Season
AL—.212—Chicago, 1910
NL—.213—Brooklyn, 1908

Highest Slugging Average, Season
AL—.489—New York, 1927
NL—.481—Chicago, 1930

Lowest Slugging Average, Season
   AL—.261—Chicago, 1910. Patsy Dougherty led the club
with a .300 slugging average, 85 points below Ty Cobb's
batting average that season.
   NL—.274—Boston, 1909

Most Runs, Season
   AL—1067—New York, 1931
   NL—1004—St. Louis, 1930

Fewest Runs, Season
   NL—372—St. Louis, 1908; only three fewer than Brook-
lyn scored that year
   AL—380—Washington, 1909

Most Home Runs, Season
   AL—240—New York, 1961, including a record 128 on the
road
   NL—221—New York Giants, 1947; Cincinnati, 1956

Fewest Home Runs, Season
   AL—3—Chicago, 1908; pitcher Ed Walsh tied for the
club lead with one homer.
   NL—7—Pittsburgh, 1917

Most Pennants
   AL—33—New York, last in 1981
   NL—17—Brooklyn-Los Angeles, last in 1981

Fewest Pennants
   AL—0—Seattle; Toronto; Washington-Texas; Los Angeles-
California
   NL—0—Houston; Montreal

Most Consecutive Pennants
   AL—5—New York, 1949–53; 1960–64
   NL—4—New York Giants, 1921–24

Most Consecutive Seasons without Winning a Pennant
   AL—42—St. Louis, 1902–43
   NL—41—Chicago, 1946–86

Most Seasons Finishing in Last Place
   NL—24—Philadelphia, last in 1971
   AL—24—Philadelphia-Kansas City-Oakland, last in 1967

Most Consecutive Seasons Finishing in Last Place
    AL—7—Philadelphia, 1915–21
    NL—5—Philadelphia, 1938–42

Most Consecutive Seasons Avoiding a Last-Place Finish
    NL—81—Brooklyn-Los Angeles, 1906–86
    AL—54—Cleveland, 1915–68

Highest Winning Percentage, Season
    NL—.763, Chicago, 1906 (116–36)
    AL—.721, Cleveland, 1954 (111–43)

Highest Winning Percentage, Season, 162 Games
    AL—.673—New York, 1961 (109–53); Baltimore, 1969
(109–53)
    NL—.667—Cincinnati, 1975 (108–54)
      New York Mets, 1986 (108–54)

Lowest Winning Percentage, Season
    AL—.235—Philadelphia, 1916 (36–117)
    NL—.248—Boston, 1935 (38–115)

Lowest Winning Percentage, Season, 162 Games
    NL—.250—New York Mets, 1962 (40–120)
    AL—.327—Toronto, 1979 (53–109)

Lowest Winning Percentage, Pennant Winner
    NL—.509—New York Mets, 1973 (82–79)
    AL—.556—Oakland, 1974 (90–72)

Highest Winning Percentage, Non-Pennant Winner
    NL—.680—Chicago, 1909 (104-49)
    AL—.669—New York, 1954 (103-51)

Fewest Games Needed to Clinch Pennant, 154-Game Schedule
    AL—136—New York, 1941
    NL—137—New York, 1904

Fewest Games Needed to Clinch Pennant of Division, 162-Game Schedule
    NL—142—Cincinnati, 1975
    AL—146—Baltimore, 1969

Largest Margin of Victory by Pennant Winner
    NL—27½ games—Pittsburgh, 1902
    AL—19½ games—New York, 1936. (In 1983 Chicago
won the Western Division by 20 games but lost the League
Championship Series for the pennant.)

Most Games Finishing behind Pennant Winner
    NL—66½—Boston, 1906
    AL—64½—St. Louis, 1939

**Fewest Games Finishing behind Pennant Winner, Last Place
Team, Prior to 1969**
    NL—21—New York Giants, 1915
    AL—25—Washington, 1944

**Largest Improvement by Pennant Winner over Previous
Season's Record**
    AL—33 games—Boston, 1946
    NL—27 games—New York Mets, 1969

Most Consecutive Years Finishing in First Division
    39—New York Yankees, 1926–64

Most Consecutive Years Finishing in Second Division
    20—Chicago Cubs, 1947–66

Best Home Record, Season
    AL—.805—New York, 1932 (62–15)
    NL—.789—Pittsburgh, 1902 (56–15)

Worst Home Record, Season
    AL—.234—St. Louis, 1939 (18–59)
    NL—.260—Boston, 1911 (19–54)

Best Road Record, Season
    NL—.800—Chicago, 1906 (60–15)
    AL—.730—New York, 1939 (54–20)

Worst Road Record, Season
    NL—.167—Boston, 1935 (13–65)
    AL—.169—Philadelphia, 1916 (13–64)

Most Consecutive Games Won from One Club
    AL—23—Baltimore from Kansas City Royals, May 10,
1969, through August 12, 1970

NL—20—Pittsburgh from Cincinnati, last 17 in 1937, first 3 in 1938

Most Games Won from One Club, Season
AL—21—New York from St. Louis, 1927

NL—21—Chicago from Cincinnati, 1945; Chicago from Boston, 1909. In 1909 the Braves also lost 20 of 21 games to Pittsburgh, giving them a 2–41 record against the NL's top two teams that year.

Where the Games Are Played

During the period between 1909 and 1915 more than half the teams then in the major leagues either built new stadiums or made massive renovations in the parks they were using. There were several reasons for the feverish construction, not the least of which were the ever-present threat of fire in the old wood parks and the many lawsuits the Phillies faced when a section of the rickety Baker Bowl grandstand collapsed in 1903, killing several spectators.

The first ballpark on record was built in 1862 when William Cammeyer, the owner of the Union Club's grounds in Brooklyn, conceived the notion of enclosing his field and charging admission to games. Cammeyer's park did not survive long, nor did the majority of other parks that were built in the last century—the lifespan for most was only a few years—but Sulphur Dell, built in 1866, was the home of the Southern Association Nashville Volunteers until 1963 and set an all-time park longevity record of 97 years. The longest-enduring major-league park still in use is Comiskey, home of the White Sox, which opened in 1910. To keep you abreast of who is playing where at the moment, and how long they have been there, here is a list—which includes facts about some former major-league stadiums, now long gone, that, if you're like me, you wish you'd seen.

AMERICAN LEAGUE
Memorial Stadium, Baltimore Orioles
First game—April 15, 1954; Baltimore 3, Chicago 0.
Seating capacity—54,076. Natural surface.
Used by the Orioles ever since the franchise transferred from St. Louis. Built in 1949 and inherited from the Baltimore International League team. Although nearly 40 years old, it's still one of the most appealing all-around parks in the game.

Fenway Park, Boston Red Sox
First game—April 20, 1912; Boston 7, New York 6, 11 innings.
Seating capacity—33,583. Natural surface.

Considered the ultimate in parks when it was built, but within a year the Red Sox already had a sneaking suspicion it was too small and that its left-field wall would always be both a boon and a burden.

Anaheim Stadium, California Angels
First game—April 19, 1966; Chicago 3, California 1.
Seating Capacity—64, 573. Natural surface.

Clean, efficient, yet spacious and without a single major flaw. The Angels first played in tiny Wrigley Field, which they inherited from the Los Angeles franchise in the Pacific Coast League, and then, for several years, shared Chavez Ravine with the Dodgers while waiting for their own new park to be completed.

Comiskey Park, Chicago White Sox
First game—July 1, 1910; St. Louis 2, Chicago 0.
Seating capacity—44,087. Natural surface.

Has been remodeled several times and undergone major contour changes since it first opened. Before moving to Comiskey, the White Sox played in South Side Park, so huge that in some seasons not a single home run was hit into the stands.

Cleveland Stadium, Cleveland Indians
First game—July 31, 1932; Philadelphia 1, Cleveland 0.
Seating capacity—74,208. Natural surface.

The inaugural game drew 80,284, the largest crowd ever for a major-league stadium opening. Formerly called Municipal Stadium, it was the last of the cavernous stadiums to be built. So mammoth that until the late forties the Indians continued to use smaller, cozier League Park, their former home, except on weekends and holidays.

Tiger Stadium, Detroit Tigers
First game—April 20, 1912; Detroit 6, Cleveland 5, 11 innings.
Seating capacity—52,806. Natural surface.

Probably the most esthetically pleasing of the still-extant old stadiums and definitely the favorite park for power hitters. Formerly called Briggs Stadium and prior to that Navin Field. Before it was built, the Tigers played in Bennett Park, named after Charlie Bennett, a catcher with the Detroit Wolverines who lost both legs in a railway accident.

Bennett Park seated only 8500 and was the smallest park in the majors when it closed.

Royals Stadium, Kansas City Royals
First game—April 10, 1973; Kansas City 12, Texas 1.
Seating capacity—40,625. Artificial surface.

Features a 322-foot-wide water spectacular with a fountain and a 10-foot waterfall from the upper cascade plus two lower pools that empty into five more 10-foot falls. The Royals played in Municipal Stadium, with a seating capacity of 30,611, until their new park was finished.

County Stadium, Milwaukee Brewers
First game—April 14, 1953; Milwaukee 3, St. Louis 2, 10 innings.
First AL game—April 7, 1970; California 12, Milwaukee 0.
Seating capacity—53,192. Natural surface.

Used by the Milwaukee Braves in the National League through 1965, then sat idle until the Seattle Pilots franchise shifted to Milwaukee in 1970 except for some "home" games played there by the White Sox. At one time had a seating capacity of only 46,625.

The Metrodome, Minnesota Twins
First game—April 6, 1982; Seattle 11, Minnesota 7.
Seating capacity—55,244. Artificial surface and sky.

The Twins' home from 1961 until 1982 was Metropolitan Stadium.

Yankee Stadium
First game—April 18, 1923; New York 4, Boston 1.
Seating capacity—57,545. Natural surface.

Closed for two years in the middle seventies, the Yankees sharing Shea Stadium with the Mets during the hiatus. Before it was built the Yankees shared Polo Grounds with the Giants from 1912 through 1922 after forsaking Hilltop Park, their original home field. Yankee Stadium took 284 days to build—the renovation took more than twice that long and reduced the capacity by some 13,000 seats.

Oakland Coliseum, Oakland Athletics
First game—April 17, 1968; Baltimore 4, Oakland 1.
Seating capacity—50,219. Natural surface.

The park was there waiting for the A's when they moved from Kansas City, where they used Municipal Stadium. While the franchise was based in Philadelphia, the A's played in Columbia Park, located at Twenty-ninth and Columbia Avenue, until 1909 when Shibe Park was completed. Shibe was the first all concrete-and-steel stadium in the majors.

The Kingdome, Seattle Mariners
First game—April 6, 1977; California 7, Seattle 0.
Seating capacity—59,438. Artificial surface and sky.

The only home the Mariners have known. Their predecessors in Seattle, the Pilots, in 1969 were forced to use Sicks Stadium, former home of the Seattle Pacific Coast League team, which seated only 25,000, and moved to Milwaukee partly because their home facility was so inadequate.

Arlington Stadium, Texas Rangers
First game—April 21, 1972; Texas 7, California 6.
Seating capacity—43,508. Natural surface.

A former minor-league stadium, upgraded to major-league capacity. During the franchise's last years in Washington, RFK Stadium was its home, but Griffith Stadium was where the original Senators played before moving to Minnesota. Decrepit, archaic, it was the second-oldest park in the majors when it closed and seated only 29,731.

Exhibition Stadium, Toronto Blue Jays
First game—April 7, 1977; Toronto 9, Chicago 5.
Seating capacity—43,737. Artificial surface.

The stadium was built in 1975, primarily for the Toronto team in the Canadian Football League, with whom the Blue Jays presently share it.

NATIONAL LEAGUE
Fulton County Stadium, Atlanta Braves
First game—April 12, 1966; Pittsburgh 4, Atlanta 3, 13 innings.
Seating capacity—52,006. Natural surface.

Also used by the Atlanta Falcons in the NFL, finished in 1965 in preparation for the Braves' move from Milwaukee. Before transferring to Milwaukee from Boston, the team played in Braves Field, which opened in 1915, replacing South End Grounds, the oldest park in the majors, home to the Boston Red Caps in the National Association as far back as 1873.

Wrigley Field, Chicago Cubs
First game—April 23, 1914; Chicago Whales 9, Kansas City Packers 1.
First NL game—April 20, 1916; Chicago 7, Cincinnati 6, 11 innings.
Seating capacity—38,040. Natural surface, natural everything.

Called North Side Park originally, it was taken over by the Cubs from the Whales when the Federal League folded.

The Cubs had previously played in West Side Park at Polk and Lincoln. Plans to install lights in time for the opening of the 1942 season had to be put on hold after Pearl Harbor because electrical equipment was needed for defense purposes—and stayed on hold for 46 years.

Riverfront Stadium, Cincinnati Reds
First game—June 30, 1970; Atlanta 8, Cincinnati 2.
Seating capacity—52,392. Artificial surface.

Until 1970 the Reds played in Crosley Field which held fewer than 30,000, making it the smallest park in the majors. Called Redland Field when it opened in 1912, it also had the distinction of having the first "artificial" surface—in 1937, when the Reds dyed the sun-burned outfield grass green.

The Astrodome, Houston Astros
First game—April 12, 1965; Philadelphia 2, Houston 0.
Seating capacity—45,011. Artificial surface and sky.

The Astrodome cost $31,600,000 to construct and was first used on April 9, 1965, for an exhibition game between the Astros and Yankees. Prior to 1965 the Astros played in Colts Stadium, built in 1962 for the new Houston National League team.

Dodger Stadium, Los Angeles Dodgers
First game—April 10, 1962; Cincinnati 6, Los Angeles 3.
Seating capacity—56,000. Natural surface.

Their first four seasons in L.A., the Dodgers played in Memorial Coliseum where they set an all-time attendance record on May 7, 1959, when they drew 93,103 for an exhibition game against the Yankees, honoring Roy Campanella. They also set an Opening Day attendance record of 78,672 in their first game in the Coliseum on April 18, 1958, against the Giants. In Dodger Stadium, also known as Chavez Ravine, they set an all-time single-season attendance record in 1982. Before transferring to Los Angeles from Brooklyn, the team played at Ebbets Field, which held only 32,111; nevertheless the Dodgers attracted 1,807,526 fans in 1947, at the time a National League record. Long since torn down and replaced by an apartment complex, Ebbets Field opened in 1913 in an area called "Pigtown" between what was the then-fashionable Bedford section and suburban Flatbush. In the last major-league game played at Ebbets Field, Danny McDevitt of the Dodgers shut out the Pirates 3–0.

Olympic Stadium, Montreal Expos
First game—April 15, 1977; Philadelphia 7, Montreal 2.
Seating capacity—59,149. Artificial surface.

The Expos originally played in Jarry Park, home of the minor-league Montreal Royals. The last games in Jarry Park were on September 26, 1976, when the Phillies won a divison-clinching doubleheader from the Expos, their first title of any sort in 26 years.

Shea Stadium, New York Mets
First game—April 17, 1964; Pittsburgh 4, New York 3.
Seating capacity—55,601. Natural surface.

Windy, too close to the airport, a tough place to spend an evening in the fall or early spring—unless you're a pitcher. While waiting for Shea to be built, the Mets played their first two seasons in the Polo Grounds.

Veterans Stadium, Philadelphia Phillies
First game—April 10, 1971; Philadelphia 4, Montreal 1.
Seating capacity—66,271. Artificial surface.

Features a monstrous TV screen and probably the fastest turf in the majors. The Phillies played in Shibe Park from July 4, 1938, through 1970. Prior to switching to Shibe and sharing it with the A's, the club had called Baker Bowl home for over half a century. Refurbished a number of times, especially after the 1903 disaster, the Baker Bowl seated just 18,000 and hosted its first game on April 30, 1887, the Phils beating the Giants 15-9.

Three Rivers Stadium, Pittsburgh Pirates
First game—July 16, 1970; Cincinnati 3, Pittsburgh 2.
Seating capacity—58,438. Artificial surface.

When Three Rivers took longer to complete than expected, the Pirates had to open the 1970 season in Forbes Field, giving baseball fans a last opportunity to attend a game in the oldest concrete-and-steel stadium still extant. The first fully modern park in the majors when it opened in 1909, Forbes had triple-decker stands, elevators, electric lights, telephones, inclined ramps instead of stairs and maids in the ladies' restrooms. Moreover, it shared with Shibe Park the distinction of having the first visitors' dressing room, ending the custom of visiting teams dressing at their hotels and then riding to the park in open horse-drawn buses.

Busch Stadium, St. Louis Cardinals
First game—May 16, 1966; St. Louis 4, Atlanta 3, 12 innings.
Seating capacity—50,222. Artificial surface.

Before 1966 the Cardinals played in Sportsman's Park, a relic that dated back to 1876 when it was used by the first St. Louis team in the National League. The park was later taken over by Chris Von der Ahe's American Association Browns and then renovated by the St. Louis Browns American League team and used by them until they moved to Baltimore. Until 1920 the Cardinals played in Robison Field, built by the St. Louis Maroons for their 1884 season in the Union Association. The final game played at Robison Field, the last wood park in the majors, was on July 6, 1920.

Jack Murphy Stadium, San Diego Padres
First game—April 8, 1969; San Diego 2, Houston 1.
Seating capacity—58,433. Natural surface.

Underrated, in some ways the best all-around facility in the majors. The last major-league park to be built without a carpet.

Candlestick Park, San Francisco Giants
First game—April 12, 1960; San Francisco 3, St. Louis 1.
Seating capacity—58,000. Natural surface.

The Giants had a carpet for a while but wisely removed it. While waiting for Candlestick to be finished, the team played in Seals Stadium, which was built in 1931 exclusively for baseball and was still one of the finest parks in the country when it went the way of all abandoned inner-city sports facilities. Before moving to the Bay Area, the Giants called the Polo Grounds home. The original Polo Grounds was a polo field, located at 110th Street and Fifth Avenue in Manhattan and owned by James Bennett of the *New York Herald.* The Giants moved to the new Polo Grounds in Coogan's Hollow at Eighth Avenue, between 155th and 157th Streets, in 1889 and remained there without any further changes until a fire destroyed most of the park. Rebuilt in 1911, the "modern" Polo Grounds was an illustration of how the shape of baseball parks was often determined by the contours of real estate available in the inner city, making fields widely varied in size and often awkwardly proportioned. Polo Grounds was famed for 250-foot home runs and 450-foot outs. Candlestick is famed for being the only major-league park where a pitcher—Stu Miller, in the 1961 All-Star Game—committed a balk when he was blown off the mound.

Managers' Records

Connie Mack took over the Pittsburgh manager's job late in the 1894 season, lasted through 1896 and then was replaced by Patsy Donovan. He had to wait until 1901 to get a second opportunity to manage in the majors. John McGraw had a similar experience, guiding the Baltimore Orioles to an unexpectedly high fourth-place finish in 1899 and then having to endure a one-year hiatus in St. Louis as a player only before Baltimore was granted an American League franchise and he was given the reins in 1901. By the time Mack and McGraw were done managing, they held almost every dugout longevity record.

Most Years as Manager, League
    AL—50—Connie Mack, Philadelphia, 1901 through 1950
    NL—32—John McGraw, Baltimore, 1899; New York Giants, 1902 through 1932

Most Games Won as Manager, League
    AL—3776—Connie Mack, Philadelphia. Mack also holds the AL record for most losses, 4025.
    NL—2744—John McGraw, Baltimore and New York Giants. McGraw also suffered the most losses in the NL, 1885.

Most Pennants Won as Manager, League
    AL—10—Casey Stengel, New York, last in 1960
    NL—10—John McGraw, New York, last in 1924

Most World Series Won as Manager, League
    AL—7—Joe McCarthy, New York, last in 1943; Casey Stengel, New York, last in 1958
    NL—4—Walter Alston, Brooklyn-Los Angeles, last in 1965

Most Consecutive Pennants Won as Manager, League
    AL—5—Casey Stengel, New York, 1949–53
    NL—4—John McGraw, New York, 1921–24
    AA—4—Charlie Comiskey, St. Louis, 1885–88

Most Clubs Managed
    7—Frank Bancroft, Worcester, NL; Detroit, NL; Cleveland, NL; Providence, NL; Philadelphia, AA; Indianapolis, NL; Cincinnati, NL. Bancroft managed less than nine full seasons and had just one pennant winner, the 1884 Providence Grays, but he spread his work over a 22-year period and was the only man to manage in the NL before the American Association came into existence and after the American League replaced the Association as the NL's rival. One of the game's first great promoters and missionaries, Bancroft took a team to Cuba in 1879, the first such expedition in history, and later staged a wedding at home plate. He spent the last 30 years of his life as the Cincinnati Reds business manager and traveling secretary.

Most Clubs Managed, since 1901
    6—Jimmy Dykes, Chicago AL; Philadelphia, AL; Baltimore, AL; Cincinnati, NL; Detroit, AL; Cleveland, AL. Dykes also used to hold the record for most years as a manager without winning a pennant and still shares with Joe Gordon the distinction of being the only two managers ever traded for each other in midseason—1960, when Frank "Trader" Lane, looking for a way to shake up the Indians, found the Tigers in search of a way to shed Dykes.

Most Clubs Managed to Pennants
    3—Bill McKechnie, Pittsburgh, NL; St. Louis, NL; Cincinnati, NL
    Dick Williams, Boston, AL; Oakland, AL; San Diego, NL

Most Clubs Managed to Division Titles
    4—Billy Martin, Minnesota, AL; Detroit, AL; New York, AL; Oakland, AL

Only Manager to Lead Same Club to Consecutive Pennants in Two Different Leagues
Bill McGunnigle steered Brooklyn to the American Association flag in 1889, then repeated in 1890 after the Bridegrooms transferred to the National League.

First Manager to Pilot Two Clubs to Pennants, Same League, since 1901
   NL—Pat Moran, Philadelphia, 1915; Cincinnati, 1919
   AL—Joe Cronin, Washington, 1933; Boston, 1946

First Manager to Pilot Pennant Winners in Two Leagues, since 1901
   Joe McCarthy, Chicago, NL, 1929; New York, AL, 1932

Most Years Managed Without Winning a Pennant
   25—Gene Mauch, Philadelphia, NL, 1960 into 1968; Montreal, NL, 1969 through 1975; Minnesota, AL, 1976 into 1980; California, AL, 1981 through 1982, 1985 through 1986

Only Man to Win a Pennant in His Lone Season as a Manager
   George Wright, Providence, NL, 1879

First Man to Win a World Championship in His First Full Season as Manager
   AL—Tris Speaker, Cleveland, 1920
   NL—Rogers Hornsby, St. Louis, 1926

First Manager to Pilot Club in World Series without Managing It for Full Season
   NL—Charlie Grimm, Chicago, 1932
   AL—Bob Lemon, New York, 1978. Lemon piloted the Yankees in two Series—1978 and 1981—without ever managing the club a full season.

Only Manager to Win Four Pennants since 1901 and Not Make the Hall of Fame
   Billy Southworth, St. Louis, NL, 1942, 1943, 1944; Boston, NL, 1948

Only Manager to Win Back-to-Back World Championships and Not Make the Hall of Fame
   Bill Carrigan, Boston, AL, 1915 and 1916. Carrigan retired after the 1916 triumph but in the late twenties was coaxed into returning to manage a string of awful Red Sox teams, tarnishing his reputation as a great manager.

Last Manager to Win Three Consecutive Pennants
Earl Weaver, Baltimore, AL, 1969–71. The last NL manager to win three flags in a row was Billy Southworth with the 1942–44 Cardinals.

Highest Career Winning Percentage as Manager
.614—Joe McCarthy, 24 seasons, 2126 wins and 1335 losses

Lowest Career Winning Percentage as Manager, Minimum 1000 Games
.401—Jimmy Wilson, nine seasons, 493 wins and 735 losses. Wilson's best team was the 1943 Cubs, who finished fifth.

Lowest Career Winning Percentage as Manager, Minimum 500 Games
.312—John McCloskey, five seasons, 197 wins and 434 losses. McCloskey, who helped found the Texas League, skippered the 1908 Cardinals, probably the National League's most dismal team in the deadball era.

First Great Manager Who Was Never a Major-League Player
Frank Selee. After managing the Boston Beaneaters to five pennants in the 1890s, Selee moved to the lackluster Chicago Cubs in 1902. Within a year he had the Cubs in contention and was just putting the finishing touches on a club that would win three consecutive pennants (1906–8) when failing health forced him to step down in 1905 and turn the reins over to Frank Chance, his personal choice as his replacement.

First Manager to Win 1000 Games
Cap Anson of the Chicago White Stockings and Harry Wright, then in his last season as the Philadelphia Phils skipper, both went over the 1000 mark in 1893.

Youngest Manager to Win 1000 Games
Fred Clarke, who became player-manager of the Louisville Colonels in 1897 when he was only 24 years old, collected his 1000th win at age 35 in 1908 while at the helm of the Pittsburgh Pirates. Only 42 when he stepped down at the end of the 1915 season, Clarke departed with 1602 wins, the most by any manager in history to that point.

Oldest Rookie Manager

Tom Sheehan was 66 years old when he took over the San Francisco Giants in June 1960 and steered them to a 46–50 record for the remainder of the season before giving way to Al Dark.

Youngest Rookie Manager, since 1901

Roger Peckinpaugh was only 23 years old when he served as the Yankees player-manager for the last 17 games of the 1914 season.

Youngest Player-Manager to Lead Club for Full Season, since 1901

Lou Boudreau bid for and was given the Cleveland manager's post at age 24 in 1942. Six years later he became the last player-manager to steer his club to a pennant.

Last Player-Manager to Win a National League Pennant

Technically, Leo Durocher, who played a few games for his Brooklyn Dodgers in 1941. The last to do it while still a full-time player was Gabby Hartnett with the 1938 Chicago Cubs.

Last Year Both Teams in World Series Were Led by Player-Managers

1934—Frankie Frisch, St. Louis Cardinals, and Mickey Cochrane, Detroit Tigers. The Tigers repeated in 1935 under Cochrane and played the Cubs, led by Charlie Grimm, who'd played two games during the regular season but didn't appear at all in the Series.

First Year Both Teams in World Series Were Led by Player-Managers

1903—Jimmy Collins, Boston Red Sox, and Fred Clarke, Pittsburgh Pirates. Player-managers were so common then that the 1905 World Series, when McGraw's Giants played Mack's A's, was the only one until 1911 in which neither team was led by a manager who was also a full-time player.

Only Pitchers to Win a Pennant as Player-Managers

NL—Al Spalding, Chicago, 1876
AL—Clark Griffith, Chicago, 1901

Only American League Manager to Win Two Pennants between 1936 and 1968 for Teams Other Than the Yankees
Al Lopez, Cleveland, 1954; Chicago, 1959

Winners of the "Might Have Been Another Casey Stengel" Award

Burt Shotton. Fired by the Phillies in 1933 after managing a string of rotten teams, he lucked into the Dodgers' managerial post in 1947 when Leo Durocher was suspended for the season, won a pennant and then won again in 1949 as Durocher's replacement after Durocher was axed. In 1950 Shotton lost the NL pennant to the Phillies in the last game of the season when he failed to replace slow-footed Cal Abrams with a pinch runner and saw Abrams thrown out at the plate trying to bring home the run that would have tied the Dodgers with the Phillies and forced a pennant playoff. That lapse as much as anything else caused the Dodgers to can him. Over the next six seasons Brooklyn won four pennants under Chuck Dressen and Walter Alston with basically the same team that Shotton had in 1950. If Shotton had stayed with the club, we can only wonder now what might have happened—but it's a fairly strong possibility that fans in the 1950s would have had the treat of watching two eccentric senior citizens trying to outmaneuver one another each fall.

The Three Most Interesting Teams Between 1901 and 1919

1908 PITTSBURGH PIRATES
W-98 L-56
Manager: Fred Clarke

Regular Lineup—1B, None; 2B, Eddie Abbatichio; 3B, Tommy Leach; SS, Honus Wagner. RF, Owen Wilson; CF, Roy Thomas; LF, Fred Clarke; C, George Gibson; P, Vic Willis; P, Nick Maddox; P, Howie Camnitz; P, Lefty Leifield; P, Sam Leever.

Led by Wagner **and** player-manager Clarke, this team finished only one game shy of the pennant and in so doing immortalized Fred Merkle and the Cubs infield of Tinker, Evers and Chance. Merkle's "boner" probably would have been overlooked amid the welter of strange occurrences in 1908 if the Pirates had won their final game of the season, against the Cubs, clinching the pennant and making it unnecessary for the Cubs and Giants to replay the game in which Merkle neglected to touch second base. As it is, the Pirates' own boner that year has been largely overlooked. The club played all season without a decent first baseman after cutting Jim Nealon, who had an off year in 1907 after leading the National League in RBIs as a rookie in 1906. In preference to Nealon, the Pirates alternated Harry Swacina, Jim Kane and Al Storke, none of whom could do the job. The following year the Pirates picked up Bill Abstein, won the pennant and then released him after he had a poor World Series. Without Abstein, the club once again had a gaping hole at first base that would go unplugged until 1920, when Charlie Grimm emerged.

1913 WASHINGTON SENATORS
W-90 L-64
Manager: Clark Griffith

Regular Lineup—1B, Chick Gandil; 2B, Ray Morgan; 3B, Eddie Foster; SS, George McBride; RF, Danny Moeller; CF, Clyde Milan; LF, Howard Shanks; C, John Henry and Eddie Ainsmith; P, Walter Johnson; P, Joe Boehling; P, Bob Groom.

After finishing second to the Red Sox in 1912, the Senators seemed ready to provide Washington fans with their first major-league pennant, especially when rookie left-hander Boehling looked sharp in spring training. Boehling continued to shine when the season started—he finished with a 17–7 record, combining with Johnson to post 54 wins and only 14 losses. But the rest of the mound staff had a dismal 37–50 record, and the Senators again could do no better than second place. Griffith, in his search for supporting moundsmen, tried 23 pitchers all told in 1913, ranging from his own 43-year-old arm to that of 18-year-old Jack Bentley. It was a shame none of them worked out because Johnson had an incredible season. In 1913 he won 36 games, lost only 7 and had a 1.14 ERA and an .837 win percentage. All of his stats towered over those of the second-best pitcher in the league, Cleveland's Cy Falkenberg, who had a 23–10 record. The following year Boehling slumped to only 12 wins, and the Senators slipped to third place and did not seriously contend again until a decade later.

1916 PHILADELPHIA ATHLETICS
W-36 L-117
Manager: Connie Mack

Regular Lineup—1B, Stuffy McInnis; 2B, Nap Lajoie; 3B, Charlie Pick; SS, Whitey Witt; RF, Jimmy Walsh; CF, Amos Strunk; LF, Rube Oldring; C, Wally Schang; P, Elmer Myers; P, Joe Bush; P, Jack Nabors; P, Tom Sheehan.

The A's had the worst team in this century only two years after they won their fourth pennant in five seasons. Mack blamed Federal League defections and his having to sell stars like Home Run Baker, who wanted more money than he could pay, but his explanation didn't quite wash then, and history has made it look even lamer. After the Federal League folded, there were a number of good players floating loose whom Mack could have gotten cheaply, but they weren't his kind of people, and he played out the season instead with the few members of the 1914 crew who'd remained loyal to him, plus 41-year-old Lajoie and a pack of rejects from other clubs. Myers and Bush, two quality pitchers, had a combined 29–45 record, but the rest of the staff lost 72 games and won only 7. A truly embarrassing operation, from 1915 through 1921 the A's finished in the cellar a record seven straight years.

ERA Records

The National League didn't officially begin keeping earned run averages until 1912, and the American League didn't follow suit until the following year. As a result, many of the ERA records that were set before 1912 have been unearthed only after today's standards were applied to what, in some cases, were previously uncalculated statistics.

Lowest ERA, Season, 1901 through 1919
 AL—1.01—Dutch Leonard, Boston, 1914; the all-time season record
 NL—1.04—Three Finger Brown, Chicago, 1906; the all-time National League record

Lowest ERA, Season, 1920 through 1941
 NL—1.66—Carl Hubbell, New York Giants, 1933
 AL—2.05—Lefty Grove, Philadelphia, 1931

Lowest ERA, Season, 1942 through 1960
 AL—1.64—Spud Chandler, New York, 1943
 NL—1.75—Howie Pollett, St. Louis, 1943

Lowest ERA, Season, 1961 through 1976
 NL—1.12—Bob Gibson, St. Louis, 1968
 AL—1.65—Dean Chance, Los Angeles, 1964

Lowest ERA, Season, since 1977
 NL—1.53—Dwight Gooden, New York, 1985
 AL—1.74—Ron Guirdy, New York, 1978

Only Pitcher to Lead League in ERA Both before and after 1893
 Billy Rhines, Cincinnati, led the NL in 1890 and again in 1896.

Most Seasons League Leader in ERA
    AL—9—Lefty Grove, last in 1939
    NL—5—Pete Alexander, last in 1920; Sandy Koufax, 1962–66 consecutive

Lowest ERA, Season, Team, since 1901
    NL—1.73—Chicago, 1907
    AL—1.79—Philadelphia, 1910

Last Team with an ERA below 2.25, Season
    NL—Chicago, 1919 (2.21); Cincinnati, 1919 (2.23)
    AL—Washington, 1918 (2.14)

Last Team with an ERA below 2.50, Season
    NL—St. Louis, 1968 (2.49)
    AL—Chicago, 1967 (2.45); the best ERA by any team since 1919

Lowest Team ERA, Season, since 1968
    AL—Baltimore, 1972 (2.54)
    NL—Houston, 1981 (2.66)

TOP 10 IN ERA, CAREER, SINCE 1893
(Minimum 1500 innings)

		Years Active	ERA
1.	Ed Walsh	1904–17	1.82
2.	Addie Joss	1902–10	1.88
3.	Joe Wood	1908–20	2.03
4.	Three Finger Brown	1903–16	2.06
5.	Christy Mathewson	1900–16	2.13
6.	Rube Waddell	1897–1910	2.16[1]
7.	Walter Johnson	1907–27	2.17[2]
8.	Orval Overall	1905–13	2.24
9.	Ed Reulbach	1905–17	2.28
10.	Jim Scott	1907–17	2.32

[1]Lefty record holder.
[2]Only member of the career top 10 who pitched in the lively ball era.

Lowest Career ERA, Pitcher Active Exclusively after 1910
    2.43—Jeff Tesreau, 1912–18

Lowest Career ERA, Pitcher Active Exclusively between 1920 and 1945

2.97—Carl Hubbell, 1928-43. Hubbell is the only pitcher in that period who had an ERA under 3.00 in over 1500 innings.

Lowest Career ERA, Pitcher Active Exclusively between 1940 and 1960

2.92—Harry Brecheen, 1940–53. Brecheen and Hubbell are the only two pitchers active between 1920 and 1960 who had career ERAs under 3.00.

TOP 10 IN ERA, CAREER, SINCE 1920
(Minimum 1500 innings)

		Years Active	ERA
1.	Whitey Ford	1950–67	2.75
2.	Sandy Koufax	1955–66	2.76
3.	Jim Palmer	1965–84	2.86
4.	Andy Messersmith	1968–79	2.86
5.	Juan Marichal	1960–75	2.89
6.	Rollie Fingers	1968–75	2.90
7.	Bob Gibson	1959–75	2.91
8.	Harry Brecheen	1940–53	2.92
9.	Dean Chance	1961–71	2.92
10.	Don Drysdale	1956–69	2.95

Only Pitcher since 1901 with Career 0.00 ERA, Minimum Nine Innings

Tim Jones, Pittsburgh, 1977, in 10 innings had a 1–0 record and 0.00 ERA.

On the Black

Which pitcher had the best control? It all depends on what standard you use to measure control and whether you accept that different eras require different standards. Cy Young gave up 103 bases on balls in 423 innings in 1893 and walked just 37 batters in 342 innings 10 years later. Had Young's control really improved that much by 1903, or were other factors operating? On the evidence Young definitely got sharper as his career progressed—he may even have had the best control of any pitcher in history—but it's also true that he was playing in a time that was extremely forgiving of pitchers who disdained nibbling at the corners of the plate and elected simply to come in with the ball. A very dead ball it was, scuffed up, dirt-stained and often laden with other foreign substances as well—a ball that was usually kept in play for several innings and sometimes even for an entire game. In any event, virtually all the career and season records for control were set in the early part of the 20th century.

Best Control, Career, since 1893, Minimum 2500 Innings
Deacon Phillippe issued 363 walks in 2607 innings, an average of 1.25 walks per nine innings. Phillippe pitched in the National League, mostly with the Pirates, from 1899 to 1911. In 1910 he walked only nine batters in 123 innings, a National League record low among pitchers in over 100 innings. Phillipe won 185 games, plus three more in the 1903 World Series when he started five games, completed them all, and relieved in two others. Almost as remarkable as his iron-man Series effort was the fact that he gave up only four walks in 50 innings.

Best Control, Career, since 1920, Minimum 2500 Innings
Red Lucas, 455 walks in 2542 innings. Active in the

National League between 1923 and 1938, Lucas only once gave up more than 50 walks in a season. See "Pinch-Hitting Feats," page 254, for more about Lucas.

Best Control, Career, since 1893, Left-hander
Noodles Hahn, 379 walks in 2012 innings, an average of 1.70 walks per nine innings. Hahn, a 22-game winner for the Reds in 1901, is also the only lefty in this century besides Steve Carlton to win 20 games for a last-place team.

Best Control, Career, since 1920, Left-hander
Fritz Peterson, 426 walks in 2218 innings, and never more than 49 in a season

Best Control, Career, 300-Game Winner
Cy Young, hands down. With 1217 walks in 7356 innings —an average of only 1.49 walked per nine innings—Young begs that anyone seriously interested in determining who was the best pitcher ever examine his overall record carefully.

Best Control, Career, 1920 through 1941, Minimum 3000 Innings
First Prize—Carl Hubbell, 724 walks in 3589 innings
Second Prize—Paul Derringer, 761 walks in 3645 innings

Best Control, Career, 1942 through 1960, Minimum 3000 Innings
First Prize—Robin Roberts, 902 walks in 4689 innings
Second Prize—Lew Burdette, 628 walks in 3068 innings

Best Control, Career, since 1961, Minimum 3000 Innings
First Prize—Juan Marichal, 709 walks in 3509 innings
Second Prize—Fergie Jenkins, 967 walks in 4499 innings. Jenkins is also the only pitcher to record more than 3000 K's and fewer than 1000 walks.

Best Control, Season, Minimum 250 Innings
AL—Cy Young, Boston, 1904, 29 walks in 380 innings
NL—Babe Adams, Pittsburgh, 1920, 18 walks in 263 innings. Adams also set an NL record in 1913 when he worked 314 innings without hitting a batter. The major-league record for kindness to hitters is held by Al Crowder, who pitched 327 innings for Washington in 1932 without incurring a single hit batsman. That same season, Crowder set a

second all-time record when he went the entire year without uncorking a wild pitch. Crowder's remarkable control exhibition helped him to end the season with 15 straight wins.

Most Consecutive Innings without Giving up a Base on Balls

AL—84⅓—Bill Fischer, Kansas City A's, 1962. Largely because of his long skein, Fischer also set an AL season record in 1962 for pitchers in over 100 innings, walking only eight batters in 128 innings.

NL—68—Christy Mathewson, New York Giants, 1913; Randy Jones, San Diego, 1976

Second Basemen's Records

Three names head almost everyone's list of the greatest second basemen, and all three were active between 1901 and 1919. In the new century's first decade the dominant player in the American League was Nap Lajoie. By the end of the century's second decade Rogers Hornsby was emerging as the best player in the N. L. Between their periods of dominance was Eddie Collins, viewed by many as the finest second basemen ever.

SEASON BATTING RECORDS

Department	National League	American League
Batting Average	.424, ROGERS HORNSBY, St. Louis, 1924	.422, Nap Lajoie, Philadelphia, 1901
Slugging Average	.756, ROGERS HORNSBY, St. Louis, 1925	.630, Nap Lajoie, Philadelphia, 1901
Home Runs	42, ROGERS HORNSBY, St. Louis, 1922 / 42, DAVE JOHNSON, Atlanta, 1973	32, Joe Gordon, Cleveland, 1948
RBIs	152, ROGERS HORNSBY, St. Louis, 1922	125, Nap Lajoie, Philadelphia, 1901
Runs	156, ROGERS HORNSBY, Chicago, 1929	144, Charlie Gehringer, Detroit, 1930, 1936
Hits	250, ROGERS HORNSBY, St. Louis, 1922	229, Nap Lajoie, Philadelphia, 1901
Doubles	57, Billy Herman, Chicago, 1935, 1936	60, CHARLIE GEHRINGER, Detroit, 1936
Triples	31, HEINIE REITZ, Balt., 1894 / 25, Larry Doyle, N.Y. Giants, 1911[1]	22, Snuffy Stirnweiss, New York, 1945

Department	National League	American League
Total Bases	450, ROGERS HORNSBY, St. Louis, 1922	356, Charlie Gehringer, Detroit, 1936
Bases on Balls	148, EDDIE STANKY, Brooklyn, 1945	128, Max Bishop, Philadelphia, 1929, 1930
Stolen Bases	77, Davey Lopes, L.A., 1975	81, EDDIE COLLINS, Philadelphia, 1910
Strikeouts	168, JUAN SAMUEL, Philadelphia, 1984	144, Bobby Knoop, California, 1966
Fewest Strikeouts (Minimum) 500 ABS)	8, EMIL VERBAN, Philadelphia, 1947	8, Eddie Collins, Chicago, 1923 *Record since 1901.

Note: Dave Johnson also had one home run as a pinch hitter, giving him a total of 43 in 1973.

Most Games, Career, at Second Base
2650—Eddie Collins, 1906–30

Most Consecutive Games at Second Base
798—Nellie Fox, Chicago White Sox, August 7, 1955, through September 3, 1960.

EVOLUTION OF SEASON RECORD FOR BEST FIELDING AVERAGE

	Team	League	Year	Average
Ross Barnes	Chicago	National	1876	.910
Jack Burdock	Boston	National	1878	.918
Joe Quest	Chicago	National	1879	.925
Davy Force	Buffalo	National	1880	.939[1]
Charlie Bastian	Philadelphia	National	1886	.945[2]
Fred Dunlap	Pittsburgh	National	1889	.950
Charlie Bassett	New York	National	1890	.952
John Crooks	Columbus	Amer. Assoc.	1891	.957[3]
Lou Bierbauer	Pittsburgh	National	1893	.959
Heinie Reitz	Baltimore	National	1894	.968
Bid McPhee	Cincinnati	National	1896	.978[4]
Gus Dundon	Chicago	American	1905	.978
George Cutshaw	Pittsburgh	National	1919	.980
Aaron Ward	New York	American	1923	.980
Sparky Adams	Chicago	National	1925	.983

	Team	League	Year	Average
Max Bishop	Philadelphia	American	1926	.987[5]
Max Bishop	Philadelphia	American	1932	.988
Ski Melillo	St. Louis	American	1933	.991
Snuffy Stirnweiss	New York	American	1948	.993[6]
Al Schoendienst	St. Louis-New York	National	1956	.993
Jerry Adair	Baltimore	American	1964	.994
Bobby Grich	Baltimore	American	1973	.995
Rob Wilfong	Minnesota	American	1980	.995[7]
Bobby Grich	California	American	1985	.997

[1]Force also played a slew of games at shortstop, a more error-prone position, in 1880, and his average combines his work at both spots. A weak hitter, if not the weakest ever, he relied heavily on his fielding to keep him in the league.

[2]Another extraordinarily inept hitter who got by on his fielding.

[3]The American Association consistently had poorer fielding averages than the National League during its decade as a major circuit, leading to the surmise that either the NL had better fielders—unlikely since the two leagues were about equal in every other respect—or else scorers were tougher in the AA. If the latter was the case, and I tend to think it probably was, Crooks must have been quite a good fielder.

[4]The record crept up a point or two every couple of years until Reitz and McPhee came along. McPhee had actually been around a good while by 1896 but didn't start using a glove until late in his career. Considering that his record stood for 23 years, you have to wonder if he wouldn't have been close to perfect with one of today's models.

[5]A good ballplayer whose skills weren't the sort that were highly regarded in his time. Comparable to Johnny Evers, who's in the Hall of Fame, and Nellie Fox, who one day will be.

[6]Bobby Doerr also fielded .993 in 1948, but Stirnweiss won the fielding crown that year and also became the record holder, because his average was a shade higher.

[7]Wilfong's 1980 average was .99481 in 120 games; Grich's 1973 average was .99471 in 162 games. In 1970 Ken Boswell of the Mets fielded .9956 but wasn't in enough games to qualify as the fielding leader.

Best Career Fielding Average
.984—Bobby Grich, 1970–86

Most Seasons League Leader in Fielding Average
AL—9—Eddie Collins, last in 1924
NL—7—Red Schoendienst, last in 1958

Most Consecutive Errorless Games
91—Joe Morgan, Cincinnati Reds, July 6, 1977, through April 22, 1978

Most Consecutive Errorless Chances Accepted
479—Manny Trillo, Philadelphia Phillies, April 8 (part) through July 31 (part), 1982

Most Chances Accepted, Career
14,156—Eddie Collins, 1906–30

Most Chances Accepted, Season
1059—Frankie Frisch, St. Louis Cardinals, 1927; Frisch also set an all-time record that season when he had 641 assists.

Most Chances Accepted, Game, Nine Innings
NL—18—Terry Harmon, Philadelphia, June 12, 1971

AL—18—Julio Cruz, Seattle, June 7, 1981, first nine innings of an 11-inning game; he handled 19 chances altogether before the game was over.

Most Gold Glove Awards
8—Bill Mazeroski, 1955–72. Generally recognized as the best fielding second baseman ever, Mazeroski holds virtually all the career and season records for double plays. In 1966 he fielded a near-record .992 while taking part in an all-time record 161 twin kills.

Triples Records

After a little more juice was added to the ball prior to the 1911 season, the scale on the hitters' side once again began to rise—but not so markedly that it can account for Owen Wilson's staggering all-time record achievement. In 1912 Wilson clubbed 36 triples, easily the most by any player in this century and 22 more than Wilson himself collected in his second-best season. There has never been a satisfactory explanation for how he did it. True, Joe Jackson of Cleveland hit 26 triples that same season, the American League record, and Detroit's Sam Crawford tied Jackson's mark just two years later, a lusty sign that the period was probably the most sanguine one in history for triples. True also that Wilson played in Forbes Field, which for many years was sculpted in such a way that balls hit between outfielders frequently grew into triples, helping the Pirates to total 110 or more three-baggers in a season seven times between 1902 and 1930, something that all the other 15 teams combined were able to do only five times. But that still doesn't begin to tell us why it was Wilson who set the record and not Honus Wagner or Fred Clarke or Tommy Leach or Max Carey, four teammates of his who were all much more prolific triples hitters over their careers than he was. To understand why, you had to be in Forbes Field that year, evidently, and even then it might not have come clear. In all likelihood, Wilson's record is just one of the many inexplicable feats that we call a fluke for the lack of a more adequate word.

Most Career Triples by Player Active Exclusively since 1941
177—Stan Musial, 1941–63

Most Career Triples by Player Active since Musial Retired
166—Roberto Clemente, 1955–72

TOP 10 IN CAREER TRIPLES

		Years Active	Triples
1.	Sam Crawford	1899–1917	312
2.	Ty Cobb	1905–28	297
3.	Honus Wagner	1897–1917	252
4.	Jake Beckley	1888–1907	244[1]
5.	Roger Connor	1880–97	233[2]
6.	Fred Clarke	1894–1915	224[3]
7.	Tris Speaker	1907–28	223
8.	Dan Brouthers	1879–1904	206
9.	Joe Kelley	1891–1908	194
10.	Paul Waner	1926–45	190[4]

[1]Held the career record before Crawford broke it in 1912.

[2]Held the career record before Beckley broke it in 1904. Prior to Connor, the record belonged to Harry Stovey with 185 career triples.

[3]Clarke's career total is disputed, as are the totals of everyone on the list who played before 1900.

[4]The most career triples by a player active exclusively since 1920.

Most Career Triples by Player Active since 1977
135—Pete Rose, 1963–86

Most Seasons League Leader in Triples
AL—5—Sam Crawford, last in 1915. He also led the National League in 1902.

NL—5—Stan Musial, last in 1951

Most Consecutive Seasons League Leader in Triples
AL—3—Sam Crawford, 1913–15; Elmer Flick, 1905–07

NL—3—Garry Templeton, 1977–79

Most Triples, Season, 1920 through 1941
NL—26—Kiki Cuyler, Pittsburgh, 1925

AL—23—Earle Combs, New York, 1927

Most Triples, Season, 1942 through 1960
AL—23—Dale Mitchell, Cleveland, 1949

NL—20—Stan Musial, St. Louis, 1946; Willie Mays, New York Giants, 1957

Most Triples, Season, 1961 through 1977
NL—17—Ralph Garr, Atlanta, 1974

AL—15—Gino Cimoli, Kansas City A's, 1962

Most Triples, Season, since 1977
AL—21—Willie Wilson, Kansas City Royals, 1985
NL—19—Garry Templeton, St. Louis, 1979; Juan Samuel, Philadelphia, 1984; Ryne Sandberg, Chicago, 1984

Fewest Triples, Season, League Leader in Triples
AL—8—Del Unser, Washington, 1969
NL—10—Johnny Callison, Philadelphia, 1962; Willie Davis, Los Angeles, 1962; Maury Wills, Los Angeles, 1962; Dickie Thon, Houston, 1982

Fewest Triples, Season, 600 or More at Bats
NL—0—Cookie Rojas, Philadelphia, 1968, 621 at bats
AL—0—Jim Morrison, Chicago, 1980, 604 at bats

Only Catchers Ever to Lead League in Triples
NL—Tim McCarver, St. Louis, 1966, led with 13 triples.
AL—Carlton Fisk, Boston, 1972, tied Joe Rudi, Oakland, for the lead with nine triples.

Last First Baseman to Lead League in Triples
NL—Stan Musial, St. Louis, 1946, led with 20 triples.
AL—Vic Power, Kansas City A's and Cleveland, 1958, led with 10 triples.

Last Team to Hit 100 Triples in a Season
NL—Pittsburgh, 1930, 119 triples
AL—Washington, 1932, 100 triples

Last Team to Hit More Triples Than Home Runs
AL—Chicago, 1949, 66 triples and 43 home runs
NL—Houston, 1979, 52 triples and 49 home runs

Only Player to Lead League in RBIs Two Years in a Row Without Hitting a Triple
Jackie Jensen, Boston Red Sox, 1958–59. Ironically, just two years earlier, in 1956, Jensen had led the American League in triples with 11.

Pitching Records for Most Wins

Among the many records Jack Chesbro established in 1904, probably the most significant occurred when he achieved his 41st victory. Only one other pitcher in major-league history, Ed Walsh in 1908, has had a 40-win season since the mound was moved to its present 60-foot-6-inch distance from the plate. Ironically, both Chesbro and Walsh fell just short of bringing pennants to their teams by losing games on the last day of the season.

TOP 10 IN SEASON WINS SINCE 1901

		Team	League	Year	Wins
1.	Jack Chesbro	New York	American	1904	41
2.	Ed Walsh	Chicago	American	1908	40[1]
3.	Christy Mathewson	New York	National	1908	37[2]
4.	Walter Johnson	Washington	American	1913	36
5.	Joe McGinnity	New York	National	1904	35
6.	Joe Wood	Boston	American	1912	34
7.	Cy Young	Boston	American	1901	33
	Christy Mathewson	New York	National	1904	33
	Pete Alexander	Philadelphia	National	1916	33
10.	Cy Young	Boston	American	1902	32
	Walter Johnson	Washington	American	1913	32

[1]Disputed. Some sources say he had only 39 wins.
[2]20th-century National League record.

TOP 10 IN SEASON WINS SINCE 1920

	Team	League	Year	Wins
1. Jim Bagby	Cleveland	American	1920	31
2. Lefty Grove	Philadelphia	American	1930	31[1]
3. Denny McLain	Detroit	American	1968	31
4. Dizzy Dean	St. Louis	National	1934	30[2]
5. Hal Newhouser	Detroit	American	1944	29
6. Dazzy Vance	Brooklyn	National	1924	28
Dizzy Dean	St. Louis	National	1935	28
Lefty Grove	Philadelphia	American	1930	28
Robin Roberts	Philadelphia	National	1952	28

10. 11 pitchers with 27 wins, last done by Steve Carlton, Philadelphia Phils, 1972.

[1]20th-century lefty record.
[2]One of Dean's wins in 1934 is disputed. On June 27 he was credited with a victory in relief over the Giants that even by the scoring rules of that time should have gone to Jim Mooney.

TEAM MILESTONE PITCHERS (SINCE 1893)

National League

Team	Last 30-Game Winner	Last 25-Game Winner	Last 20-Game Winner
Astros	None	None	Joe Niekro, 21 (1980)
Braves	Kid Nichols, 30 (1897)	Dick Rudolph, 27 (1914) Bill James, 26 (1914)	Phil Niekro, 21 (1979)
Cardinals	Dizzy Dean, 30 (1934)	Dizzy Dean, 28 (1935)	John Tudor, 21 (1985) Joaquin Andujar, 21 (1985)
Cubs	None	Charlie Root, 26 (1927)	Rick Reuschel, 20 (1977)
Dodgers	None	Sandy Koufax, 27 (1966)	Fernando Valenzuela, 21 (1986)
Expos	None	None	Ross Grimsley, 20 (1978)
Giants	Christy Mathewson, 37 (1908)	Juan Marichal, 26 (1968)	Mike Krukow, 20 (1986)

Team	Last 30-Game Winner	Last 25-Game Winner	Last 20-Game Winner
Mets	None	Tom Seaver, 25 (1969)	Dwight Gooden, 24 (1985)
Padres	None	None	Gaylord Perry, 21 (1978)
Phillies	Pete Alexander, 30 (1917)	Steve Carlton, 27 (1972)	Steve Carlton, 23 (1982)
Pirates	Pink Hawley, 32 (1895)	Burleigh Grimes, 25 (1928)	John Candelaria, 20 (1977)
Reds	None	Bucky Walters, 27 (1939)	Tom Browning, 20 (1985)

American League

Team	Last 30-Game Winner	Last 25-Game Winner	Last 20-Game Winner
A's	Lefty Grove, 31 (1913)	Catfish Hunter, 25 (1974)	Mike Norris, 20 (1980)
Angels	None	None	Nolan Ryan, 22
Blue Jays	None	None	None
Brewers	None	None	Ted Higuera, 20 (1986)
Indians	Jim Bagby, 31 (1920)	Bob Feller, 26 (1946)	Gaylord Perry, 21 (1974)
Mariners	None	None	None
Orioles	None	Steve Stone, 25 (1980)	Mike Boddicker, 20 (1984)
Rangers	None	Fergie Jenkins, 25 (1974)	Fergie Jenkins, 25 (1974)
Red Sox	Joe Wood, 34 (1912)	Mel Parnell, 25 (1949)	Roger Clemens, 24 (1986)
Royals	None	None	Bret Saberhagen, 20 (1985)
Tigers	Denny McLain, 31 (1968)	Mickey Lolich, 25 (1971)	Jack Morris, 21 (1986)
Twins	Walter Johnson, 36 (1913)	Jim Kaat, 25 (1966)	Jerry Koosman, 20 (1979)
White Sox	Ed Walsh, 40 (1908)	Red Faber, 25 (1921)	LaMarr Hoyt, 24 (1983)
Yankees	Jack Chesbro, 41 (1904)	Ron Guidry, 25 (1978)	Ron Guidry, 22 (1985)

Last Pitcher to Win 30 or More Games Three Years in a Row

Pete Alexander, 1915–17. Christy Mathewson, 1903–5, is the only other pitcher to do it since 1901.

Last Pitcher to Win 25 or More Games Three Years in a Row
Hal Newhouser, 1944–46 .

Most Seasons League Leader in Wins
NL—9—Warren Spahn, last in 1961
AL—6—Walter Johnson, last in 1924; Bob Feller, last in 1951

Most Seasons 30 or More Wins
Right-hander—7—Kid Nichols, 1891–97 consecutive
Left-hander—1—Lefty Grove, 1931

Most Seasons 20 or More Wins
Right-hander—16—Cy Young, last in 1908
Left-hander—13—Warren Spahn, last in 1963

Most Wins, Season, Against One Team
9—Ed Walsh, Chicago White Sox, 1908, was a perfect 9–0 versus the Red Sox and 9–1 versus the Yankees. His record when he opposed the other five AL clubs was "only" 22–14. Also in 1908, Ed Reulbach of the Cubs beat Brooklyn nine times.

Best Pitching Duo, Season, since 1901
NL—Joe McGinnity (35) and Christy Mathewson (33) won 68 games between them for the 1904 Giants.
AL—Jack Chesbro (41) and Jack Powell (23) won 64 games between them for the 1904 Yankees.

Best Pitching Duo, Season, since 1920
AL—Hal Newhouser (29) and Dizzy Trout (27) won 56 games between them for the 1944 Tigers.
NL—Bucky Walters (27) and Paul Derringer (25), 52 wins between them for the 1939 Reds

Best Pitching Duo, Season, since 1961
NL—Sandy Koufax (26) and Don Drysdale (23), 49 wins between them for the 1965 Dodgers
AL—Denny McLain (31) and Micky Lolich (17), 48 wins between them for the 1968 Tigers; Mike Cuellar (24) and Dave McNally (24), 48 wins between them for the 1970 Orioles

Best Pitching Trio, Season, since 1901
Joe McGinnity (35), Christy Mathewson (33) and Dummy Taylor (21), 89 wins among them for the 1904 New York Giants

Best Pitching Trio, Season, since 1920
Jim Bagby (31), Stan Coveleski (24) and Ray Caldwell (20), 75 wins among them for the 1920 Cleveland Indians

Best Pitching Trio, Season, since 1961
Mike Cuellar (24), Dave McNally (24) and Jim Palmer (20), 68 wins among them for the 1970 Baltimore Orioles

Best Pitching Quartet, Season, since 1901
Joe McGinnity (35), Christy Mathewson (33), Dummy Taylor (21) and Hooks Wiltse (13), 102 wins among them for the 1904 New York Giants

Best Pitching Quartet, Season, since 1920
Red Faber (23), Lefty Williams (22), Eddie Cicotte (21) and Dickie Kerr (21), 87 wins among them for the 1920 Chicago White Sox

Best Pitching Quartet, Season, since 1961
Dave McNally (21), Mike Cuellar (20), Pat Dobson (20) and Jim Palmer (20), 81 wins among them for the 1971 Baltimore Orioles

Fewest Wins, Club Leader in Wins, World Championship Team
NL—14—John Candelaria, Pittsburgh, 1979
AL—15—Lefty Gomez and Red Ruffing, New York, 1941

First League Champion without a 20-Game Winner
AL—Philadelphia, 1914, led by Chief Bender and Joe Bush with 17 wins each
NL—New York, 1922, led by Art Nehf with 19 wins. The Giants also won in 1923 and again in 1924 without a 20-game winner.

First Season Neither World Series Team Had a 20-Game Winner
1975—Rick Wise led the Red Sox with 19 wins, and Gary Nolan, Jack Billingham and Don Gullett led the Reds with only 15 wins.

First Pitcher to Win 20 Games in a Season Divided Between Two Leagues, since 1901

Joe McGinnity, 1902, 13 wins for Baltimore in the AL and then 8 more in the NL, for a total of 21, after jumping to the Giants. Pat Flaherty with the White Sox and Pirates in 1904, Hank Borowy with the Yankees and Cubs in 1945, and Rick Sutcliffe with the Indians and Cubs in 1984 have also done it.

Most Wins by Pitcher on a Last-Place Team

NL—27—Steve Carlton, Philadelphia, 1972; NL record .459 percent of team's wins

AL—22—Nolan Ryan, California, 1974

Most Career Wins, Relief Pitcher

124—Hoyt Wilhelm, 1952–72

Most Games Won, Career, From One Team

NL—70—Pete Alexander, 1911–30, from Cincinnati

AL—66—Walter Johnson, 1907–27, from Detroit

300-GAME WINNERS

		Years Active	*Wins*
1.	Cy Young	1890–1911	511
2.	Walter Johnson	1907–27	416
3.	Pete Alexander	1911–30	373
4.	Christy Mathewson	1900–1916	373
5.	Warren Sphan	1942–65	363
6.	Pud Galvin	1879–92	361
7.	Kid Nichols	1890–1906	360
8.	Tim Keefe	1880–93	344
9.	John Clarkson	1882–94	328
10.	Eddie Plank	1901–17	327
11.	Steve Carlton	1965–	323
12.	Gaylord Perry	1962–83	314
13.	Mickey Welch	1880–92	311
	Tom Seaver	1967–	311
	Phil Niekro	1964–	311
16.	Don Sutton	1966–	310
17.	Hoss Radbourn	1881–91	308
18.	Early Wynn	1939–63	300
	Lefty Grove	1925–41	300

Pitchers Who Won 100 or More Games in Each League (In Order Accomplished)

1. Cy Young
2. Jim Bunning
3. Gaylord Perry
4. Fergie Jenkins
5. Nolan Ryan

Fewest Full Seasons Needed to Win 200 Games, since 1901

Pete Alexander had 190 wins after his first seven seasons, won two more in 1918 before he was inducted into the army, then had 16 wins in 1919 after he was discharged, giving him 208 wins in his first eight full seasons. Christy Mathewson had a 0–3 record in 1900, won 174 games in his first seven full seasons and had 211 wins after his eighth. Hence Mathewson achieved more wins in his first eight full seasons, but Alexander had more after his first seven seasons and probably would have had more after his eighth season, too, if his career hadn't been interrupted by military service.

Fewest Full Seasons Needed to Win 300 Games, since 1901

12—Christy Mathewson; he had 312 wins at the end of his 12th full season

Fewest Wins at Age 30, 300-Game Winner

31—Phil Niekro. The record was formerly held by Gaylord Perry, who had only 76 wins on his 30th birthday. Early Wynn, with 83 wins when he turned 30, was the record-holder before Perry. Niekro also holds the record for the fewest wins at age 40—he had only 197—by a future 300-game winner.

Pitching Records
for Most Starts
and Complete Games

In 1904 Jack Chesbro of the Yankees set a post-1893 record when he started 52 games. The modern National League record holder is the Giants' Joe McGinnity, who made 48 starts in 1903. McGinnity's record is in some ways the more remarkable because it came in the last major-league season that the schedule called for only 140 games.

Most Games Started, Career
816—Cy Young, 1890 through 1911. Young made 30 or more starts in 19 consecutive seasons (1891–1909), another all-time record.

Most Games Started, League, Career
AL—666—Walter Johnson, 1907 through 1927
NL—665—Warren Spahn, 1942 through 1965

Most Seasons League Leader in Starts
NL—6—Robin Roberts, 1950–55. consecutive
AL—5—Bob Feller, last in 1948; Early Wynn, last in 1959

Most Games Started, Season, 1920 through 1941
AL—44—George Uhle, Cleveland, 1923
NL—40—Pete Alexander, Chicago, 1920

Most Games Started, Season, 1942 through 1960
AL—42—Bob Feller, Cleveland, 1946
NL—42—Bob Friend, Pittsburgh, 1956

Most Games Started, Season, 1961 through 1976
AL—49—Wilbur Wood, Chicago, 1972. Wood also made 48 starts in 1973, as did Mickey Lolich of the Tigers in 1971.

Wood's 49 starts in 1972 were the most by any pitcher since Ed Walsh made 49 for the 1908 White Sox.

NL—42—Fergie Jenkins, Chicago, 1969; Don Drysdale, Los Angeles, 1963 and 1965; Jack Sanford, San Francisco, 1963

Most Games Started, Season, Since 1977
NL—44—Phil Niekro, Atlanta, 1979; the most by an NL pitcher since Alexander made 44 starts in 1917
AL—40—Mike Flanagan, Baltimore, 1978; Dennis Leonard, Kansas City, 1978; Jim Clancy, Toronto, 1982

Most Consecutive Starting Assignments, No Relief Appearances
NL—534—Steve Carlton, May 15, 1971, through August 5, 1986
AL—272—Mel Stottlemyre, April 10, 1967, through June 11, 1974

Most Opening Day Starting Assignments
AL—14—Walter Johnson, all of them with Washington
NL—14—Steve Carlton, 13 with Philadelphia and one with St. Louis

Most Consecutive Opening Day Starting Assignments
16—Tom Seaver, 13 in the National League and three in the American League

Chesbro also set a modern record when he completed 48 games in 1904. Two years earlier Vic Willis of the Boston Braves set the National League record when he went the route 45 times in his 46 starts.

Most Complete Games, Season, 1920 through 1941
NL—33—Pete Alexander, Chicago, 1920; Burleigh Grimes, Brooklyn, 1923
AL—32—Red Faber, Chicago, 1922; George Uhle, Cleveland, 1926

Most Complete Games, Season, 1942 through 1960
AL—36—Bob Feller, Cleveland, 1946
NL—33—Robin Roberts, Philadelphia, 1953

Most Complete Games, Season, 1961 through 1976
AL—30—Catfish Hunter, New York, 1975

NL—30—Steve Carlton, Philadelphia, 1972; Fergie Jenkins, Chicago, 1971; Juan Marichal, San Francisco, 1968

Most Complete Games, Season, since 1977
AL—28—Rick Langford, Oakland, 1980
NL—23—Phil Niekro, Atlanta, 1979

Most Complete Games, Season, since 1901, Left-hander
NL—41—Noodles Hahn, Cincinnati, 1901
AL—39—Rube Waddell, Philadelphia, 1904

Last Team with Three Pitchers Who Completed 20 or More games
The 1980 Oakland A's registered 94 complete games, led by Rick Langford with 28, Mike Norris with 24 and Matt Keough with 20.

Most Consecutive Complete Games
188—Jack Taylor, St. Louis Cardinals and Chicago Cubs, June 20, 1901, through August 9, 1906. On August 13, 1906, Taylor was knocked out in the third inning by the Dodgers, ending a record string of 1,727 consecutive innings without being relieved; altogether, he threw the last pitch for his team in 203 straight games in which he appeared.

Most Seasons League Leader in Complete Games
NL—9—Warren Spahn, last in 1963
AL—6—Walter Johnson, last in 1916

First Season League Leader Had Fewer Than 30 Complete Games
NL—1910—Three Finger Brown of the Cubs, Nap Rucker of the Dodgers and Christy Mathewson of the Giants all tied for the lead with 27 complete games.
AL—1923—George Uhle of Cleveland led with 29 complete games.

Last Season League Leader Had Fewer Than 20 Complete Games
AL—1955—Whitey Ford of the Yankees led with only 18.
NL—1957—Warren Spahn of the Milwaukee Braves led with 18; 1957 was also the first season that neither league had a pitcher who completed 20 games.

Fewest Complete Games, League Leader in Complete Games
    NL—13—Mario Soto, Cincinnati, 1984
    AL—15—Frank Lary, Detroit, 1960; Dean Chance, Los Angeles, 1964

Most Starts, Season, without Completing a Game
    NL—37—Steve Bedrosian, Atlanta, 1985. Shipped to the Phillies in 1986, Bedrosian was sent to the bullpen and proceeded to notch 29 saves, a club record.
    AL—33—Milt Wilcox, Detroit, 1983

Most Starts, Career, without Completing a Game
    36—Ken Clay, 1977 through 1981;
    Jamie Easterly, 1974 through 1986

Most Complete Games, League, Career
    AL—531—Walter Johnson, 1907 through 1927
    NL—437—Pete Alexander, 1911 through 1930

Most Complete Games, League, Career, Since 1920
    NL—382—Warren Spahn, 1942 through 1965
    AL—356—Ted Lyons, 1923 through 1946

TOP TEN IN COMPLETE GAMES, CAREER, SINCE 1893

		Years active	*CG*
1.	Cy Young	1890–1911	643[1]
2.	Walter Johnson	1907–27	532
3.	Christy Mathewson	1900–1916	439
4.	Pete Alexander	1911–30	439
5.	Jack Powell	1897–1912	424
6.	Eddie Plank	1901–17	412[2]
7.	Kid Nichols	1890–1906	391[3]
8.	Vic Willis	1898–1910	388
9.	Warren Spahn	1942–65	382
10.	Ted Lyons	1923–46	356

[1]Had 108 CGs prior to 1893.
[2]The most by a left-hander.
[3]Had 142 CGs prior to 1893.

Players We Wish We'd Seen More of: 1901–19

The deadball era was loaded with ephemeral performers. Some, like Judge McCreedie and Ham Iburg, simply preferred life on the Pacific Coast to life in the eastern major-league cities. Others, like Bill Keister, never found a team that could tolerate their abundant talents. Keister hit with power, scored a goodly number of runs, stole plenty of bases and compiled a .312 career batting average in seven seasons. Yet no team kept him for longer than a year, and he was permanently jettisoned from the majors after the 1903 season in which he led the Phillies in slugging average, homers and RBIs despite playing in only 100 games. Here are some of the many other fine players in the early part of the century who appeared on the major-league stage all too briefly.

1. Erv Beck. Cleveland's regular second baseman as a rookie in 1901, he not only hit the American League's first home run, but at the end of the season he had a .289 batting average and 79 RBIs. Beck lost his job when Cleveland obtained Nap Lajoie from Philadelphia and was sent to Cincinnati. In 1902, split between the Reds and Detroit, he hit .301 and finished the season as the Tigers' starting first baseman. Notwithstanding his two fine years, he never again played in the majors.

2. Irv Waldron. In 1901, his one and only major-league season, he started out with Milwaukee, then was shipped to Washington, where he hit .322. Overall, Waldron had a .311 batting average in 141 games, scored 102 runs and led the American League in at bats.

3. Pop Foster. Another who dropped from view after the 1901 American League season, split between Washington and Chicago. In his finale he cracked seven homers and had a .422 slugging average. Despite his nickname, Foster was only 23 when he left the majors.

4. Dave Rowan. Aside from Terry Foster, he has the record for the highest career batting average among players with 50 or more at bats. Rowan hit .385 for the 1911 St. Louis Browns in an 18-game trial and collected 11 RBIs in only 65 at bats, but wasn't invited back in 1912.

5. Tacks Neuer. Threw a shutout in his first start for the 1907 Yankees and was 4–2 with a 2.17 ERA and three shutouts in six career starts. Neuer died at 86 in 1966 leaving no record with which arm he threw, let alone why that arm got such short shrift in the majors.

6. Horace Milan. Most younger brothers of star players get lengthy trials if they show any promise at all. Clyde Milan's brother was the rare exception; despite hitting .320 and swiping six bases, he got into only 42 games with the Senators in the mid-teens.

7. Henry Schmidt. See "Red-Hot Rookies," page 375, for more about Schmidt. Suffice to say here that if you're into baseball history and you haven't discovered him yet, you've missed one.

8. Elmer Stricklett. The distinction of being the first spitballer may or may not have been his, but what indisputably belongs to him are three solid major-league seasons, all of them unfortunately with Brooklyn. In the last one, 1907, he completed 25 of 26 starts and racked up four shutouts and a 2.27 ERA—yet had only a 12–14 record. With a contender he might have became a star; like so many pitchers of that era who labored for Brooklyn, he just became disenchanted.

9. Erwin Harvey. Called "Zaza" and used as a pitcher by the White Sox for most of the 1901 season, he had a mediocre mound record, but his bat was so good that the Sox tried him in the outfield. He hit .333 in 1901 and then .348 with Cleveland the following year, but after a few weeks the Indians mysteriously cut him. For his career, Harvey hit .332 and stole 17 bases in only 76 games.

10. Bud Ryan. Came to the majors with Cleveland in 1912 after he hit .339 for Portland in the Pacific Coast League, but was sent back to the minors after stroking .296 in 1913. The following year, without him, Cleveland plummeted to the American League cellar and had only one player, Joe Jackson, whose batting average was higher than Ryan's career .282.

11. The Federal League Four. Supposedly all the players

who jumped to the Federal League were welcomed back to the majors when the Feds folded after the 1915 season, but don't you believe it. If there wasn't an unwritten blacklist in operation, how else can what happened to Steve Evans, Vin Campbell, Rebel Oakes and Ted Easterly be explained? The Cardinals' best outfielder in the early teens, Evans in 1915 led the Federal League in doubles and hit .308 after topping the Feds in slugging average and triples on a .348 average in 1914. Campbell led the National League in batting much of the 1910 season, yet was reduced by the Pirates to a part-time outfielder in 1911. Sent to the Braves the following year, he hit .296 and led the NL in at bats—then was cut. Two .300-plus seasons in the Federal League gave him, at age 27, a .310 career batting average. Oakes, a teammate of Evans's on the Cardinals, became the player-manager of the Pittsburgh Rebels after joining the Feds in 1914 and nearly spearheaded the Rebels to the 1915 FL pennant. One of the best-hitting catchers in the deadball era and an outstanding pinch hitter, Easterly was just 29 after the 1915 season and boasted a .300 career batting average, second at the time among catchers only to Chief Meyers. Evans, Campbell, Oakes and Easterly were all top-notch players, all seemingly with several years of good play left in them, and yet all four were left without a home in the majors after the 1915 season ended.

The Great Scandals

In 1920 eight members of the Chicago White Sox were barred for life from organized baseball for their part in throwing the 1919 World Series. The eight players were Chick Gandil, Eddie Cicotte, Swede Risberg, Lefty Williams, Happy Felsch, Fred McMullin, Joe Jackson and Buck Weaver, and the order in which they are listed may also reflect their degree of guilt. Gandil, the ringleader, quit after the 1919 season and never attempted to deny or mitigate his actions. The next five players acknowledged their complicity but offered extenuating circumstances to explain their lapse from grace. Jackson admitted he took money but claimed he played his best in the Series. Weaver admitted only that he knew the fix was on and that he chose not to betray his teammates by informing on them. Although brought to trial, none of the eight players was ever convicted in court of the slightest wrongdoing. Because of testimony he gave at their trial, St. Louis Browns second baseman Joe Gedeon was also barred from the game, as were a host of former players and hangers-on. Gedeon and the Chicago Eight were neither the first nor the last players banished from the game, however. Nor were they necessarily the worst offenders. Here is a partial list of baseball's top malefactors.

The First Great Scandal

In 1865 three players with the New York Mutuals, Thomas Devyr, Edward Duffy and William Wamsley, were accused of conspiring with gamblers to lose a game to the Brooklyn Eckfords. All three players admitted their guilt and were expelled by the Mutuals, only to be reinstated a few months later without further penalty.

The Louisville Four

Major-league baseball in its infancy was rife with gamblers and players suspected of dumping games. One reason the National Association collapsed was its inability to police itself, and there is ample evidence that the National League, which replaced it, improved matters only slightly. At the close of the 1877 season, NL President William Hulbert was faced with a situation he could not ignore when evidence was given to him that four Louisville players, Jim Devlin, George Hall, Al Nichols and Bill Craver, had thrown games on the team's final eastern road trip. Devlin had reputedly been approached by a gambler named McLeod and Hall simultaneously approached by his own brother-in-law. Both were urged to see to it that Louisville found a way to blow its 3½-game lead with 12 contests to play and swing the pennant to Boston. Nichols was made part of the plot and led to its unraveling when Louisville team officials, noting the deluge of telegrams he suddenly began receiving, examined their contents and discovered they were from gamblers informing him which games to lose. A case has been made that Craver wasn't one of the conspirators and was banned solely because he stood on his constitutional right not to have his mail opened without his permission.

In any event, the Louisville Four were probably not the only dishonest players in 1877—they were merely the most flagrant. In subsequent years, players under suspicion were blacklisted rather than barred, a practice that soon included not only the game's shady characters but also those who exhibited rebellious tendencies. In 1881 a formal blacklist was drawn up; on it were nine players: Mike Dorgan, Buttercup Dickerson, Emil Gross, Lipman Pike, Sadie Houck, Edward "The Only" Nolan, Bill Crowley, John Fox and Blower Brown. All except Nolan and Pike were later reinstated without undue disruption to their careers. Pike, who had first been blacklisted back in 1878 for an unrecorded offense, was 36 years old in 1881 and near the end anyway, while Nolan, who had also been blacklisted in 1878 for lying to the owner of his Indianapolis team, in disgust dropped down to the minor leagues, where he starred for years.

The Scots Verdict

In 1904, St. Louis Cardinals pitcher Jack Taylor fell under suspicion of throwing games. Testimony was heard for and against him, and he received what sources in the period called a "Scots Verdict," meaning there was good reason to believe him to be guilty but insufficient evidence to convict him.

The Corkscrew Brain

It belonged, Fred Lieb wrote, to Hal Chase, quite possibly the greatest fielding first baseman ever and a fine all-around player—when he wanted to be. Much has been written about Chase in recent years, all of it condemnatory and perhaps justly so, but too many sources would have you believe that Chase all by himself undermined the fabric of baseball and created the climate for the Black Sox scandal. This is ludicrous. Chase was first and foremost an opportunist. As a rookie with the Yankees in 1905, he found himself on a team that had lost the pennant the previous year on a ninth-inning wild pitch on the last day of the season, an occurrence that did not seem to overly depress team owners Frank Farrell and Big Bill Devery. Both men were gamblers by occupation and surrounded themselves with others of their breed, a combination that Chase no doubt viewed as license to do his thing. In support of this are the numerous instances when Yankees managers begged Farrell to get rid of Chase and found themselves axed instead, plus the fact that Chase was himself named manager of the club while supposedly under clouds of suspicion.

How far up into the front office and how wide on the field Chase's chicanery extended can only be guesswork now, but it is intriguing that despite his reputation for wrecking the morale of every team he played for, John McGraw hired him in 1919 and gave him the Giants first-base job. True, McGraw released him at the end of the season, along with Heinie Zimmerman and Jean Dubuc, two other questionable figures of the era, and none of the three ever played in the majors again—but where had McGraw's head been back in the spring? Did he discredit all the rumors about Chase? Had he seen Chase as still capable of being reformed? Or does the full story, for some reason, remain buried?

The Douglas Incident

Subsequent to the Black Sox scandal, a number of players found themselves outside the barred gates of organized baseball. Among them were Gene Paulette of the Phillies, who was banned for betting on games and being foolish enough to admit it, pitchers Paul Carter and Claude Hendrix of the

Cubs, who were never formally banished but were rather declared personae non grata, and Benny Kauff, expelled in 1920 by Commissioner Landis after he was accused of being part of a stolen car ring. Three ex-big leaguers, Bill Rumler, Gene Dale and Harl Maggert, were also dismissed by Landis in 1920 for dumping Pacific Coast League games, and pitcher Ray Fisher incurred Landis's wrath when he refused to sign the contract the Reds tendered him and instead took a coaching job at the University of Michigan. When Fisher applied for reinstatement at the close of the college season, Landis refused to grant it, and Fisher, unfairly, found himself on the same list with all the crooked players who had been booted from the game in the massive effort to clean it up and restore its image. The effort seemed at an end in 1922, until pitcher Phil Douglas jumped the league-leading Giants and then sent a letter to Cardinals outfielder Les Bell, offering to make himself scarce for the rest of the season if the Cardinals would send him a little travel money. Bell, one of the most strait-laced players in the twenties, instead turned the letter over to team officials, it soon wound up on Landis's desk, and Douglas found himself out of the game.

A Double Standard?

Rube Benton, another ex-Giants pitcher, was let go by McGraw in 1921 after admitting he bet on games. When Benton had an outstanding season with St. Paul in the American Association in 1922, the Reds tried to bring him back to the majors, but McGraw blocked the move, claiming Benton had been blacklisted. Forced by the Reds to decide the issue, Landis ruled that since Benton had never been officially expelled he was eligible to pitch for any team that would have him. So Benton, a self-confessed friend to gamblers, returned to the majors with the Reds in 1923 while Ray Fisher, whose only crime had been to reject a contract he considered to be inadequate, was left permanently outside the walls.

The Last Major-League Player to Be Barred

In the final days of the 1924 season, with the Giants rolling to their fourth straight pennant, Giants outfielder Jimmy O'Connell sidled up to Phillies shortstop Heinie Sand before a game and offered him $500 to go easy on the Giants that day. Sand reported the bribe attempt to his manager, and the machinery was quickly set into motion that would expel both O'Connell and Giants coach Cozy Dolan, who had allegedly put O'Connell up to approaching Sand. But few at the time believed that O'Connell, a Santa Clara graduate, had been either the instigator of the bribe offer or Dolan's unwitting dupe. There was testimony from O'Connell that several other Giants players had a hand in it and statements from them that it had all been meant as a joke. In any event, O'Connell went down alone, and Dolan, after bitterly shouting that the real story had yet to be told, then decided he wasn't going to be the one to tell it and remained mum until his death. What really happened that September afternoon in 1924? Probably no one will ever know, but, for whatever it means, it was the last scandal involving a New York Giants player, and 1924 was the last season that a club managed by John McGraw won a pennant.

Cobb and Speaker Dodge a Bullet

In 1926 an event that threatened for a time to eclipse even the Black Sox scandal erupted when former Tigers pitcher Dutch Leonard let it be known that he had certain incriminating letters from Smokey Joe Wood regarding bets that Leonard, Wood, Tris Speaker and Ty Cobb had made on a 1919 game between the Tigers and Indians. According to Leonard, the bet was an added thought after Speaker agreed to let the Tigers win the game so that they could beat the Yankees out of second-place money. Speaker and Cobb were at first persuaded to retire in exchange for having the matter left unexplored; then they reconsidered and decided to fight the charge. When Leonard refused to appear publicly to confront them, Landis let the issue die—although neither Speaker nor Cobb, both player-managers at the time, was ever offered a manager's job again—and the popular theory was that Leonard was merely trying to retaliate against Cobb for releasing him during the 1926 season and against Speaker for not giving him a chance to catch on with the Indians. Yet the possibility is strong that if Leonard's letters had come to light a few years earlier, when Landis was mercilessly striving to rid baseball of even the smallest hint of corruption, the game might have been shorn of its two greatest stars as it was about to enter its golden era.

Player Takes on Commissioner and Wins

In 1946 Jorge Pasquel, a wealthy customs broker in Mexico who had a financial interest in the Mexican professional league, after a chance meeting with Giants outfielder Danny Gardella at Al Roon's gymnasium in Manhattan seized upon the notion of spiriting major-league players south of the border. Soon thereafter, Gardella and several dozen other players had been induced to play in Mexico, and alarmed major-league owners looked to newly appointed commissioner Happy Chandler for help. Chandler ruled that all players who did not leave Mexico by his deadline were automatically barred from organized baseball for five years. The ban stuck until 1949 when a flurry of legal suits, most of them initiated by Gardella, made Chandler recant and take wayward players back into the fold. Gardella, a mediocre player, benefited little himself from his besting Chandler and was released after a few games. But Sal Maglie, another Mexican League renegade, became one of the National League's top pitchers.

Most Recent Player Suspended for Gambling

Pitcher Denny McLain of the Tigers was made to sit out much of the 1970 season by Commissioner Bowie Kuhn after being implicated in a bookmaking operation. In recent years several players have been suspended for parts of a season upon being convicted of using and/or trafficking in drugs, but no one has been suspected of allowing his drug involvement to affect the honesty with which he approached the game. To date, even those who served prison sentences or incurred fines have managed to suffer nothing more serious than a momentary interruption of their careers.

World Series Play: 1901–19

FRANCHISE SUMMARY

Team	League	WS Record	Years in Series
Boston	American	5–0	1903, 1912, 1915, 1916, 1918
Cincinnati	National	1–0	1919
Boston	National	1–0	1914
Chicago	American	2–1	1906, 1917, 1919
Philadelphia	American	3–2	1905, 1910, 1911, 1912, 1914
Pittsburgh	National	1–1	1903, 1909
Chicago	National	2–3	1906, 1907, 1908, 1910, 1918
New York	National	1–4	1905, 1911, 1912, 1913, 1917
Philadelphia	National	0–1	1915
Brooklyn	National	0–1	1916
Detroit	American	0–3	1907, 1908, 1909

Yearly Highlights

1903—Boston (AL) defeated Pittsburgh (NL) 5 games to 3

The first "World Series" since 1890 and the first between the NL and the AL was a five-of-nine affair, Boston winning despite yeoman's work by the Pirates' Deacon Phillippe, who pitched five complete games and had three wins. Boston was led by Bill Dinneen, who won three of his four starts. Phillippe was called on so often because Sam Leever had injured his shoulder in a trapshooting tournament prior to the Series, and another Pirates pitcher, Ed Doheny, was committed to a mental hospital. Jimmy Sebring of the Pirates was the batting star, starting a Series tradition wherein lightly regarded players were often the ones to shine most brilliantly. The teams hit a record 25 triples between them due to a ground rule that any ball going into the overflow crowds that ringed the outfield rated three bases. Members of the Pirates received a larger Series share than the winning

Red Sox because Pittsburgh owner Barney Dreyfuss gave all of the club's take to his players while Boston owner Henry Killilea pocketed his portion and then sold the team to John Taylor, son of the owner of the *Boston Globe*.

1905—New York (NL) defeated Philadelphia (AL) 4 games to 1

There was no World Series in 1904, largely because Giants manager John McGraw and team owner John Brush feared the Yankees would win the AL pennant and were loath to risk their supremacy against a rival New York team. The Giants made this decision in July while the Yankees were leading the AL and then were stuck with it when Yankees ace Jack Chesbro, on the last day of the season, wild-pitched home the run that handed Boston the game and the pennant. In October of 1904, Brush issued an announcement that if the Giants won again in 1905 they would play the AL champ, regardless of who it was. When the Giants repeated, Christy Mathewson, their star pitcher and a Bucknell graduate, found himself pitted against the A's Eddie Plank of Gettysburg College. It was the first time two college grads faced each other in a Series, and the Giants prevailed easily, with all five contests ending in shutouts, three of them pitched by Mathewson.

1906—Chicago (AL) defeated Chicago (NL) 4 games to 2

The Cubs were 26–3 in August and 24–5 down the stretch to finish with a 50–8 surge that gave them a record 116 victories. Against their vaunted pitching staff, the White Sox, known at "The Hitless Wonders," seemed hopelessly overmatched. But after holding the Sox to 6 runs in the first four games, Cubs pitchers gave up 16 runs in the last two contests. Ed Walsh of the triumphant Sox struck out 12 batters in Game Three, a Series nine-inning record that stood until 1929.

1907—Chicago (NL) defeated Detroit (AL) 4 games to 0

The first game ended in a 12-inning deadlock after the Cubs scored the tying run in the ninth on a passed ball. The Cubs then swept the next four games.

1908—Chicago (NL) defeated Detroit (AL) 4 games to 1

In the first Series that matched repeat pennant winners, the Cubs again won easily as Orval Overall and Three

Finger Brown each won two games and allowed only two earned runs between them.

1909—Pittsburgh (NL) defeated Detroit (AL) 4 games to 3

It was the first Series to go the distance. In his third and final try to win a World Championship, Ty Cobb of the Tigers once again came up on the short end. Pirates rookie Babe Adams became the second pitcher to win three games in a seven-game Series, and Pittsburgh stole 18 bases, tying the Series record set in 1906 by the Cubs.

1910—Philadelphia (AL) defeated Chicago (NL) 4 games to 1

Jack Coombs of the A's won three games and hit .385. The Cubs won Game Four after a last-ditch ninth inning rally to avert a Series sweep.

1911—Philadelphia (AL) defeated New York (NL) 4 games to 2

Home Run Baker earned his nickname by hitting two key four-baggers in the Series. Giants second baseman Larry Doyle, carrying the winning run in Game Five, missed home plate on his slide, but none of the A's noticed, and home plate umpire Bill Klem rightfully held silent. The A's lapse became unimportant when they won Game Six 13–2.

1912—Boston (AL) defeated New York (NL) 4 games to 3

The first Series played in Fenway Park and the first truly great one. Art Irwin, who played with Providence in the 1884 World Series, attended the opener and lamented that he'd been born too soon when he saw the size of the crowd. The Series was decided in the bottom of the 10th inning of the seventh game when the Red Sox, trailing 2–1, scored two runs after Giants outfielder Red Snodgrass muffed a fly ball, Christy Mathewson issued an uncharacteristic walk to weak-hitting Steve Yerkes, Tris Speaker singled home the tying run after Fred Merkle and Chief Meyers of the Giants let his pop foul drop between them, Duffy Lewis was intentionally walked, and Larry Gardner then brought Yerkes home with the Series-ending run on a sacrifice fly. The overall hitting star was Buck Herzog of the Giants with 12 hits, while Joe Wood, who won three games for the Red Sox, topped all pitchers.

1913—Philadelphia (AL) defeated New York (NL) 4 games to 1

Home Run Baker was again the hitting star, rapping his third Series four-bagger. Chief Bender of the A's won two complete games despite being hit hard while Christy Mathewson, in his final Series, lost the last game 3–1 to Eddie Plank.

1914—Boston (NL) defeated Philadelphia (AL) 4 games to 0

The only team to win a pennant after being in last place on July 4, the Braves were accorded little chance in the Series. But they swept the A's behind pitchers Bill James and Dick Rudolph, who won two games apiece and allowed only one earned run between them. The Braves, who played in decrepit South End Grounds, borrowed Fenway Park for the Series. A year later the Red Sox borrowed brand-new Braves Field, which was larger than Fenway.

1915—Boston (AL) defeated Philadelphia (NL) 4 games to 1

Babe Ruth made his first Series appearance, as a pinch hitter, in Baker Bowl, where 400 extra seats were put in right field, reducing the park's dimensions and enabling Red Sox outfielder Harry Hooper to bounce two balls into the temporary seats in Game Five—hits that now would be ground-rule doubles that then counted as home runs. The Phils, in a sense, were the victims of their own greed, losing their fourth Series game in a row by one run when Hooper's second park-created homer came in the ninth inning.

1916—Boston (AL) defeated Brooklyn (NL) 4 games to 1

In the longest Series game in history—Game Two on October 2—it took Babe Ruth 14 innings to beat Sherry Smith of the Dodgers 2–1. The following day Jack Coombs edged Carl Mays, 4–3, to give Brooklyn its only win.

1917—Chicago (AL) defeated New York (NL) 4 games to 2

In Game Four, Benny Kauff became the first National Leaguer to hit two homers in a Series game; Patsy Dougherty of Boston had been the first American Leaguer, in 1903. Heinie Zimmerman of the Giants was tagged the Series goat when Eddie Collins was trapped off third base in the fourth inning of the sixth game but darted past Giants catcher Bill Rariden, leaving Zimmerman to chase Collins helplessly across the plate when neither pitcher Rube Benton nor first baseman Walter Holke covered home. Red Faber of the White Sox won three games and lost one, making him the only pitcher ever to post four decisions in a seven-game Series.

1918—Boston (AL) defeated Chicago (NL) 4 games to 2

In anticipation of big crowds that never materialized, the Cubs borrowed Comiskey Park from the White Sox. George Whiteman of the Red Sox hit .250 and knocked in only one run but is still remembered as one of the Series heroes, whereas Cubs second baseman Charlie Pick, who, like Whiteman, came up from the minors in midseason and played only because his team was short-handed, isn't remembered at all despite batting .389 and leading both clubs with seven hits. The Red Sox scored only nine runs in the Series and hit just .186 but won because Carl Mays and Babe Ruth held the Cubs to only four runs and won two games each.

1919—Cincinnati (NL) defeated Chicago (AL) 5 games to 3

Aiming for increased gate receipts to make up for the short—140-game—regular-season schedule, the National Commission, comprising the two league presidents, Ban Johnson and John Heydler, plus Gary Herrmann, president of the Reds, expanded the Series to a best-five-of-nine format but could have halted proceedings after the first game because the verdict was already self-evident to many in attendance. The signal that the Series was fixed came in the bottom of the first inning when Eddie Cicotte of the White Sox deliberately plunked Reds leadoff hitter Morrie Rath in the back. Joe Jackson, one of the fixers, led all batters with 12 hits and a .375 average, giving credence to his lifelong contention that he promised his worst to gamblers but played his best.

SECTION 3

Famous Firsts:
1920–41

1920—The pall that hangs over baseball after the 1919 World Series leads officials to abolish the spitball and all other pitches that involve applying foreign substances to the ball in an effort to sanitize the game and increase hitting. A select few pitchers are exempted from the abolition and allowed to continue throwing spitters until their careers are over.

1920—The Bill Doak fielder's glove is introduced by the Rawlings Sporting Goods Company of St. Louis. In contrast to the old pancake glove, it has a natural pocket whose size can be adjusted by leather laces.

1920—Cleveland shortstop Ray Chapman becomes the first player to die as a result of an injury incurred in a major-league game when he succumbs after Carl Mays of the Yankees beans him with a submarine pitch on August 16 in a game at the Polo Grounds.

1921—On August 25, Harold Arlen, the voice of radio station KDKA in Pittsburgh, broadcasts the first baseball game over the air, from Philadelphia, the Pirates winning 8–5 over the Phillies. In the fall of that year KDKA installs a wire between Pittsburgh and New York, which Grantland Rice uses to issue sporadic reports from the Polo Grounds, where the World Series is being played between the Yankees and Giants. Another radio station, WJZ in Newark, New Jersey, is even more ambitious and manages to broadcast the Series in its entirety by relay as Sandy Hunt of the *Newark Sunday Call* reports play-by-play action from his seat in the Polo Grounds to the WJZ radio shack, where Tommy Cowan then repeats Hunt's account to station listeners.

1921—American League pitcher Al Sothoron sets a post-deadball era record when he works the entire season—178 innings—without surrendering a home run.

1921—Eppa Rixey of the Reds gives up only one homer in 301 innings—an NL post-deadball record.

1922—The Williams shift is introduced—not to frustrate Ted Williams, who's only about four years old at the moment, but rather to combat lefty pull-hitters Ken Williams of the Browns and Cy Williams of the Phillies.

1922—George Uhle of the Indians wins 22 games with a 4.07 ERA, the first pitcher since 1901 to achieve 20 victories despite allowing over four runs a game.

1922—White Sox owner Charlie Comiskey, anxious to shed his miserly image, forks over $125,000 to the San Francisco Seals for the contract of third baseman Willie Kamm, the first $100,000 purchase of a minor leaguer.

1923—The Giants buy pitcher/first baseman Jack Bentley from the Baltimore club in the International League for $65,000, but Bentley refuses to report unless he's given a piece of his sale price. The first minor leaguer to demand a cut of the action, Bentley finally relents—but the suspicion will always linger that the Giants secretly gave him signing money after extracting a pledge from him to deny it.

1923—Graham McNamee, the first famous baseball announcer, begins his career. Although not terribly knowledgeable about baseball McNamee has personality—or what in later years is called "charisma." By profession a singer, McNamee obtains his first radio job on a lunch break while serving on jury duty and shortly thereafter is heard for the first time over the air on WEAF in New York, a forerunner of WNBC. From the start it is obvious that McNamee's enthusiastic cultivated delivery gives his audience the feeling that it is part of whatever he is describing, and he is the natural choice to handle the microphone when WEAF decides to broadcast the 1923 World Series.

1924—WMAQ of Chicago broadcasts the home games of both the Cubs and the White Sox, with Hal Totten the voice. Totten is later joined by Pat Flaherty.

1925—The American League permits resin bags to counteract somewhat the ruinous effect that banning foreign substances has had on pitchers.

1929—The Indians and the Yankees become the first teams to put numbers on the backs of their uniforms and leave them there. On May 13, at League Park in Cleveland, fans for the first time are treated to the sight of two teams wearing numbered uniforms and get an additional charge when Willis Hudlin beats the Yankees 4–3. Two years later the American League makes numbered uniforms mandatory for all teams.

1929—On July 5, the Giants use the first public address system in a major-league park for a game against Pittsburgh.

1929—Cincinnati's Harry Hartman becomes the first radio announcer to say "Going, going, gone," whenever a fair-hit ball is headed over the wall.

1932—Jack Graney, former Cleveland outfielder and the first major league player to hit a home run off Babe Ruth, in 1914, starts as the voice of the Indians, a job he will hold until his retirement after the 1954 World Series. Since announcers in the early days of radio don't travel with teams, Graney becomes a master at re-creating road games, play-by-play reports of which he receives by wire. (In the late 1950s, long after most other teams have begun putting their announcers on the scene, Waite Hoyt and Les Keiter, the twin voices of the Cincinnati Reds, will still be re-creating away games.) To Graney falls the honor of being the first ex–major-leaguer to become a play-by-play announcer, with Hoyt not far behind him—but the first future Hall of Famer to hold down the job is Harry Heilmann, the longtime voice of the Detroit Tigers.

1932—The Kessler brothers provide a harbinger of what fans in Philadelphia will be like in another few decades when they heap so much abuse on A's third baseman Jimmy Dykes that manager-owner Connie Mack finally gives Dykes a break and sells him to the White Sox.

1933—Washington deals first baseman Joe Judge to Brooklyn, ending the record 18 consecutive years that Judge and Senators outfielder Sam Rice have been road roommates.

1934—On Sunday, April 29, the Pirates entertain the Reds in Forbes Field and beat them 9–5 as Pittsburgh becomes the last major-league city to lift its blue laws and host a Sunday game.

1934—Burleigh Grimes wins his 270th and final victory in relief for the Cardinals on May 1, beating the Reds 3–2 in 11 innings. Grimes's win is the last in major-league history by a pitcher legally permitted to throw a spitball.

1934—A few members of the Cincinnati Reds fly to a game in Chicago, the first major-league team to travel together by air.

1935—William Wrigley of the Cubs becomes the first owner to allow all his team's games to be broadcast.

1935—Augie Galan of the Cubs sets a major-league record when he becomes the first player to play an entire 154-game season without grounding into a double play.

1938—The Giants, Dodgers and Yankees for the first time allow their home games to be broadcast on a regular basis. The Yankees hire Mel Allen and team him with Arch McDonald.

1938—Ernie Lombardi of the Reds grounds into 30 double plays, a National League record.

1939—The *Reach Baseball Guide* merges with the *Spalding Baseball Guide*. The two publish under the *Spalding-Reach Baseball Guide* name through 1941, then both bow out after over half a century in the business as the *Sporting News* takes over the publication of the annual guide.

1939—The 25-player limit, reduced to 23 in the depression, is restored and, with the exception of the 1946 season when teams are allowed to carry more players to accommodate returning service vets, remains unchanged until 1986 when the owners, locked in a power struggle with the players' union, cut back to 24-man rosters.

1939—On May 17, W2XBS of New York televises a college contest between Princeton and Columbia, the first baseball game ever to appear on the new video device. On August 26 of that same year, also over W2XBS, the first major-league game is telecast when a TV camera is lugged into Ebbets Field, where the Dodgers are hosting the Reds.

1939—Lou Gehrig becomes the first player to have his uniform number retired. By 1986 the Yankees will have permanently removed 11 numbers from circulation.

1940—Ernest Thayer dies without revealing what player was his real-life model for the 52-line poem he published in 1888. Former Philadelphia Phillies pitcher Dan Casey and his three children contend that he was the inspiration for Thayer's "Casey at the Bat," while others believe that it was his brother Dennis, an outfielder with the Baltimore Orioles in the mid-1880s. But there is no evidence that Thayer ever saw either of the Casey brothers play, and, moreover, neither Philadelphia nor Baltimore particularly wants the honor of being Mudville, the city in the poem.

1941—The Dodgers become the first team to wear plastic batting helmets after Pee Wee Reese and Peter Reiser are idled by beanings.

1941—The Tigers give $52,000 to University of Michigan student Dick Wakefield, making him the first big "bonus baby."

1941—On March 8, Phillies pitcher Hugh Mulcahy becomes the first major-leaguer to be drafted in the prelude to World War II; Tigers outfielder Hank Greenberg becomes the second after playing 19 games. Within two years over 100 major leaguers are involved in the war effort, but only two, Elmer Gedeon and Harry O'Neill, are killed in action.

RBI Records

The official tabulation of RBIs was not adopted by both major leagues until 1920 when all slugging statistics suddenly took on an increased importance with Babe Ruth's emergence as the game's greatest home run hitter and the accompanying surge in attendance. Prior to 1920 RBI statistics were kept unofficially, and there were many seasons, especially in the 1880s, when some team scorers noted how runs were brought home and others didn't. As a result it is now impossible to reconstruct who led the American Association in RBIs in 1885, for example, or how many career RBIs Pete Browning, Dave Orr, Deacon White and many other early-day stars had.

EVOLUTION OF THE SEASON RBI RECORD

	Year	Team	League	RBIs
1. Sam Thompson	1887	Detroit	National	166[1]
2. Babe Ruth	1921	New York	American	171
3. Lou Gehrig	1927	New York	American	175[2]
4. Hack Wilson	1930	Chicago	National	190[3]

[1] Some purists prefer to start with the 1888 season when both the National League and the American Association began keeping reasonably accurate RBI data. Even if you align yourself with their thinking, Thompson remains the pre-Ruth record holder, with 165 RBIs for the 1895 Philadelphia Phillies. In addition, Thompson was the most prolific player ever at knocking in runs—.921 per game. Lou Gehrig ranks second with .919 per game; Hank Greenberg is third with .915 per game.

[2] In 1931 Gehrig set an American League record, which still stands, when he had 184 RBIs; six years later Hank Greenberg of Detroit had 183.

[3] In 1930 Gehrig led the AL with 174 RBIs, and Chuck Klein of the Phillies had 170 RBIs; the season was so skewed that Bill Terry's RBI total of 129, good for only fifth place in 1930, would have led the NL the following year.

Most RBIs, Season, 1901 through 1919
  AL—144—Ty Cobb, Detroit, 1911; although some sources
credit him with only 127 RBIs that season
  NL—128—Gavvy Cravath, Philadelphia, 1913

Most RBIs, Season, 1941 through 1960
  AL—159—Vern Stephens and Ted Williams, Boston, 1949
  NL—143—Ernie Banks, Chicago, 1959

Most RBIs, Season, 1961 through 1977
  NL—153—Tommy Davis, Los Angeles, 1962
  AL—142—Roger Maris, New York, 1961

Most RBIs, Season, since 1977
  NL—149—George Foster, Cincinnati, 1977
  AL—145—Don Mattingly, New York, 1985

Most Seasons League Leader in RBIs
  AL—6—Babe Ruth, last in 1928 when he tied with Gehrig
  NL—5—Honus Wagner, last in 1912

Fewest RBIs, Season, League Leader in RBIs, since 1920
  AL—105—Al Rosen, Cleveland, 1952
  NL—105—Gary Carter, Montreal, and Mike Schmidt,
Philadelphia, 1984

Fewest RBIs, Season, League Leader in RBIs, Prior to 1920
  NL—80—Bill Dahlen, New York Giants, 1904
  AL—83—Harry Davis, Philadelphia, 1905

Most RBIs, Game
  NL—12—Jim Bottomley, St. Louis, September 16, 1924
  AL—11—Tony Lazzeri, New York, May 24, 1936

Most RBIs, Game, Pitcher
  9—Harry Staley, Boston Beaneaters, June 1, 1893, against
the Louisville Colonels

Most RBIs, Doubleheader
  NL—13—Nate Colbert, San Diego, August 1, 1972, against
Atlanta as the Padres won 9–0 and 11–7
  AL—No American League player has ever collected more
than 11 RBIs in a twin bill, the number Lazzeri amassed in a
single game.

Fewest RBIs, Season, Outfielder, Minimum 400 at Bats
  12—Goat Anderson, Pittsburgh Pirates, 1907, 413 at bats

Fewest RBIs, Season, First Baseman, Minimum 400 at Bats
  20—Ivy Griffin, Philadelphia A's, 1920, 467 at bats

Fewest RBIs, Season, Third Baseman, Minimum 400 at Bats
  14—Bobby Byrne, St. Louis Cardinals, 1908, 439 at bats

Fewest RBIs, Season, Minimum 500 at Bats
  12—Enzo Hernandez, San Diego Padres, 1971, 549 at bats

Fewest RBIs, Season, Minimum 150 Games
  20—Richie Ashburn, Philadelphia Phillies, 1959, 153 games

Fewest RBIs, Season, Minimum 100 Games and 300 at Bats
  6—Dick Howser, Cleveland Indians, 1965, 307 at bats

Largest Differential, Season, Between Runs and RBIs
  106—Lloyd Waner, Pittsburgh Pirates, 1927, scored 133 runs and had only 27 RBIs. The only other player with a differential of over 100 is Roy Thomas, who scored 134 runs and had 33 RBIs for the 1900 Philadelphia Phillies.

Most Home Runs, Season, with Fewer Than 100 RBIs
  45—Harmon Killebrew, Minnesota Twins, 1963

PLAYERS WHO HAD 40 HOMERS AND FEWER THAN 100 RBIS IN A SEASON

	Year	Team	League	Homers	RBIs
Duke Snider	1957	Brooklyn	National	40	92
Mickey Mantle	1958	New York	American	42	97
Mickey Mantle	1960	New York	American	40	94
Harmon Killebrew	1963	Minnesota	American	45	96
Hank Aaron	1969	Atlanta	National	44	97
Rico Petrocelli	1969	Boston	American	40	97
Hank Aaron	1973	Atlanta	National	40	96
Davy Johnson	1973	Atlanta	National	43	99
Darrell Evans	1985	Detroit	American	40	94

Most RBIs, Season, with Fewer Than 10 Home Runs
    AL—144—Ty Cobb, Detroit, 1911, 8 home runs
    NL—128—Pie Traynor, Pittsburgh, 1928, 3 home runs

Most Seasons with 100 or More RBIs and Fewer Than 10 Home Runs
    7—Honus Wagner, last in 1912

Last Player to Collect 100 or More RBIs and Fewer Than 10 Home Runs
    Tommy Herr, St. Louis Cardinals, 1985; 8 home runs and 110 RBIs. Herr was the first player to do it since George Kell of the Tigers in 1950.

Most RBIs, Season, With No Home Runs
    121—Hugh Jennings, Baltimore Orioles, 1896

Last Player to Lead League in RBIs with Fewer Than 10 Home Runs
    Dixie Walker, Brooklyn, led the National League in 1945 with 124 RBIs despite hitting only eight homers.

Special Mention
    In 1979 Jim Rice of the Boston Red Sox became the first player ever to string together three successive seasons in which he had, at minimum, 110 RBIs, 35 home runs and 200 hits.

Most Seasons 150 or More RBIs
    7—Lou Gehrig, last in 1937

Most Consecutive Seasons 100 or More RBIs
    13—Lou Gehrig, 1926–38; Jimmie Foxx, 1929–41

Most RBIs Per Each Home Run, Career
    1.77—Lou Gehrig, 873 RBIs on 493 home runs

TOP TEN IN CAREER RBIS

		Years Active	RBIs
1.	Hank Aaron	1954–76	2297[4]
2.	Babe Ruth	1914–35	2204[3]
3.	Lou Gehrig	1923–39	1990
4.	Ty Cobb	1905–28	1959[2]
5.	Stan Musial	1941–63	1951
6.	Jimmie Foxx	1925–45	1921
7.	Willie Mays	1951–73	1903[5]
8.	Cap Anson	1876–97	1879[1]
9.	Mel Ott	1926–47	1860
10.	Carl Yastrzemski	1961–83	1844

[1]The first player to accumulate 1,000 RBIs.
[2]Broke Anson's career RBI record in 1927.
[3]Broke Cobb's career mark in 1931.
[4]Broke Ruth's career mark in 1975 while serving as a DH for the Milwaukee Brewers.
[5]Although seventh on the all-time list, Mays never led the National League in RBIs.

TOP 10 IN CAREER RBIS, PLAYERS ACTIVE THROUGH 1986 SEASON

		First Year	RBIs
1.	Reggie Jackson	1967	1659
2.	Tony Perez	1964	1648
3.	Mike Schmidt	1973	1392
4.	Ted Simmons	1968	1348
5.	Pete Rose	1963	1314[1]
6.	Steve Garvey	1969	1299
7.	Jim Rice	1974	1289[2]
8.	Graig Nettles	1967	1257
9.	Dave Winfield	1973	1234
10.	Dave Kingman	1971	1210

[1]Quite a number of players have collected over 1000 RBIs in their careers without ever having a 100 RBI season. Rose heads the list with 1314 RBIs and is also the only player on it who never had as many as 90 RBIs in a season: His top total was 82 in 1969.
[2]Rice and Winfield are probably the only two on the list who have a realistic shot at cracking the all-time top 10.

Total Bases Records

In 1921 Babe Ruth set an all-time major-league record when he collected 457 total bases. The following year Rogers Hornsby amassed 450 total bases, setting the National League mark. Since 1930 no player has seriously threatened either record.

TOP 10 IN TOTAL BASES, SEASON

	Year	Team	League	Total Bases
1. Babe Ruth	1921	New York	American	457
2. Rogers Hornsby	1922	St. Louis	National	450
3. Lou Gehrig	1927	New York	American	447
4. Chuck Klein	1930	Philadelphia	National	445
5. Jimmie Foxx	1938	Boston	American	438
6. Stan Musial	1948	St. Louis	National	429[1]
7. Hack Wilson	1930	Chicago	National	423
8. Chuck Klein	1932	Philadelphia	National	420[2]
9. Lou Gehrig	1930	New York	American	419
10. Joe DiMaggio	1937	New York	American	418

[1]The only player on the list who didn't do it in a season between 1920 and 1941.

[2]The only player to have two seasons with 420 or more total bases.

Most Total Bases, Season, 1901 through 1919
    AL—367—Ty Cobb, Detroit, 1911
    NL—325—Cy Seymour, Cincinnati, 1905

Most Total Bases, Season, 1942 through 1960
    NL—429—Stan Musial, St. Louis, 1948
    AL—368—Ted Williams, Boston, 1949

Most Total Bases, Season, 1961 through 1976
  NL—382—Willie Mays, San Francisco, 1962
  AL—374—Tony Oliva, Minnesota, 1964

Most Total Bases, Season, since 1977
  AL—406—Jim Rice, Boston, 1978
  NL—388—George Foster, Cincinnati, 1977

Fewest Total Bases, Season, League Leader in Total Bases
  NL—237—Honus Wagner, Pittsburgh, 1906
  AL—260—George Stone, St. Louis, 1905

Most Seasons 400 or More Total Bases
  AL—5—Lou Gehrig, last in 1936
  NL—3—Chuck Klein, last in 1932

Most Seasons 300 or More Total Bases
  NL—15—Hank Aaron, last in 1971
  AL—13—Lou Gehrig, 1926 through 1938 consecutive

TOP 10 IN TOTAL BASES, CAREER

	Years Active	Total Bases
1. Hank Aaron	1954–76	6856[3]
2. Stan Musial	1941–63	6134[2]
3. Willie Mays	1951–73	6066
4. Ty Cobb	1905–28	5860[1]
5. Babe Ruth	1914–35	5793
6. Pete Rose	1963–	5752[4]
7. Carl Yastrzemski	1961–83	5539
8. Frank Robinson	1956–76	5373
9. Tris Speaker	1907–28	5105
10. Lou Gehrig	1923–39	5059

[1]The first player to collect 5000 total bases.
[2]Broke Cobb's career total bases record in 1962.
[3]Broke Musial's career total bases record in 1972.
[4]The only player on the top 10 list who never had a season in which he was a league leader in total bases.

Fewest Total Bases, Season, Minimum 500 Plate Appearances
    NL—119—Sparky Anderson, Philadelphia, 1959
    AL—127—Jim Levey, St. Louis, 1933. After batting .209 as a rookie shortstop in 1931, Levey became a switch-hitter the following year and batted .280. But in 1933 the bottom fell out on him as he hit only .195.

Most Total Bases, Game
    NL—18—Joe Adcock, Milwaukee Braves, July 31, 1954, against Brooklyn in Ebbets Field; four home runs and a double
    AL—16—Held by several players. The first to do it was Ty Cobb, who hit three home runs, two singles and a double in six at bats against the St. Louis Browns in Sportsman's Park on May 5, 1925. The next day Cobb hit two more homers, making him the first player since Cap Anson in 1884 to hit five home runs in two games.

Record Slugging Averages

Once again we find the same two names at the head of the class. In 1920 Babe Ruth compiled an all-time record .847 slugging average when he clubbed 54 home runs in only 458 at bats. Five years later Rogers Hornsby slugged at a .756 clip to set the National League record.

Highest Slugging Average, Season, 1901 through 1919
    AL—.657—Babe Ruth, Boston, 1919
    NL—.571—Heinie Zimmerman, Chicago, 1912

Highest Slugging Average, Season, 1941 through 1960
    AL—.731—Ted Williams, Boston, 1957; the last player to slug .700
    NL—.702—Stan Musial, St. Louis, 1948

Highest Slugging Average, Season, 1961 through 1976
    AL—.687—Mickey Mantle, New York, 1961
    NL—.669—Hank Aaron, Atlanta, 1971

Highest Slugging Average, Season, since 1977
    AL—.664—George Brett, Kansas City Royals, 1980
    NL—.644—Mike Schmidt, Philadelphia, 1981

Most Seasons League Leader in Slugging Average
    AL—13—Babe Ruth, last in 1931
    NL—9—Rogers Hornsby, last in 1929

Highest Slugging Average, Season, by Runner-up to League Leader
    AL—.765—Lou Gehrig, New York, 1927; second to Babe Ruth who slugged .777
    NL—.687—Chuck Klein, Philadelphia, 1930; second to Hack Wilson, Chicago, who slugged .723

All-time Highest Slugging Average, Season, by Player Who Hit No Home Runs
.484—Hugh Jennings, Baltimore, 1896

Lowest Slugging Average, Season, League Leader in Slugging Average
NL—.436—Hy Myers, Brooklyn, 1919
AL—.466—Elmer Flick, Cleveland, 1905

Lowest Slugging Average, Season, since 1920, League Leader in Slugging Average
AL—.476—Snuffy Stirnweiss, New York, 1945
NL—.521—Johnny Mize, New York Giants, 1942

Lowest Slugging Average, Season, since 1961, League Leader in Slugging Average
AL—.502—Reggie Jackson, Baltimore, 1976
NL—.540—Dale Murphy, Atlanta, 1983

Lowest Slugging Average, Season, since 1901, Minimum 400 at Bats
NL—.206—Pete Childs, Philadelphia, 1902; 403 at bats and 83 total bases
AL—.228—Billy Sullivan, Chicago, 1908; 430 at bats and 98 total bases

Lowest Slugging Average, Season, since 1901, Minimum 500 at Bats
AL—.240—Jim Levey, St. Louis, 1933; 529 at bats and 127 total bases
NL—.242—Al Bridwell, Boston, 1907; 509 at bats and 123 total bases

Smallest Differential between Slugging Average and Batting Average, Season, since 1901, Mininum 500 at Bats
NL—19 points—Spike Shannon, St. Louis and New York Giants, 1906; .256 batting average and .275 slugging average
AL—36 points— Ed Hahn, New York and Chicago, 1906; .221 batting average and .257 slugging average

Special Mention
Only one player in major-league history, Roger Metzger, was a league leader more than once in an extra-base hit department and yet retired with a career slugging average

that was under .300. Metzger tied for the National League lead in triples in 1972, then led alone in 1974 before an amputated finger forced him to quit in 1980 with a .231 career batting average and a .293 career slugging average.

THE 10 HIGHEST CAREER SLUGGING AVERAGES

	Years Active	SA
1. Babe Ruth	1914–35	.690
2. Ted Williams	1939–60	.634
3. Lou Gehrig	1923–39	.632
4. Jimmie Foxx	1925–45	.609
5. Hank Greenberg	1930–47	.605
6. Joe DiMaggio	1938–51	.579
7. Rogers Hornsby	1915–37	.577
8. Johnny Mize	1936–53	.562
9. Stan Musial	1941–63	.559
10. Willie Mays	1951–73	.557

Highest Career Slugging Average, Player Active Primarily between 1901 and 1919
.518—Joe Jackson, 1908–20

Highest Career Slugging Average, Player Active Primarily between 1942 and 1960
.559—Stan Musial, 1941–63

Highest Career Slugging Average, Player Active Primarily after 1961
.557—Willie Mays, 1951–73

Highest Career Slugging Average, Player with under .300 Career Batting Average
First Place—.557—Mickey Mantle, 1951–68; .298 batting average. Mantle ranks 11th on the career list, a fraction below Mays.
Second Place—.548—Ralph Kiner, 1946–55; .279 batting average

Lowest Career Slugging Average, Player with .300 Career Batting Average
.355—Patsy Donovan, 1890–1907; .301 batting average.

Among players with 2,000 hits, Donovan also has the second-fewest extra-base hits. Of his 2,256 hits, .867 percent of them were singles. Maury Wills, with a single percentage of .874, ranks first in fewest extra-base hits.

ACTIVE PLAYERS WITH CAREER SLUGGING AVERAGES OVER .500
(Minimum 2000 at bats)

		First Year	SA
1.	Don Mattingly	1982	.538
2.	Mike Schmidt	1972	.536
3.	Jim Rice	1974	.518
4.	Pedro Guerrero	1978	.514
5.	George Brett	1973	.505
6.	Bob Horner	1978	.505
7.	Eddie Murray	1977	.505
8.	Jesse Barfield	1981	.502

Among officers with 2500 hits. Dimaggio also hit the second
lowest point-base price for his .325 slug. NY, however, of
then were Amigone Marty Marie, with a single percentage of
.906, thanks to et in fewer at-bat base hits.

Long Day's Journey

The 1920 season was less than a month old when a reminder
was served that even though the deadball era was over a
whiff of it still lingered. On May 1, in Boston, the Brooklyn
Dodgers hooked up in a 26-inning 1–1 tie with the Braves
that will probably always stand as both the longest game in
major-league history and the longest game not played to a
decision. What made the game most seem like a throwback
to an earlier time, however, was not its extraordinary length
but the fact that both starting pitchers, Leon Cadore of the
Dodgers and Joe Oeschger of the Braves, went all the way.
The following day the Dodgers played 13 innings against the
Phillies and then went into overtime again on May 3 against
the Braves, losing to them 2–1 in 19 innings. Brooklyn's
three-game total of 58 innings played—the equivalent of six
and a half games—is a record that has never been even
remotely challenged.

Longest Game Played to a Decision
   NL—25 innings—St. Louis 4, New York Mets 3, September 11, 1974; also the longest night game in major-league
history
   AL—24 innings—Philadelphia 4, Boston 1, September 1,
1906. Both Jack Coombs of the A's and Joe Harris of the
Red Sox went all the way. Harris, rarely the recipient of any
support from his teammates, had a dreadful 3–21 record in
1906, tying him with Don Larsen (3–21 in 1954 with Baltimore) for the worst record since 1901 among 20-game
losers.

Longest 1–0 Game, since 1901
   24 innings—Houston 1, New York Mets 0, April 15,
1968

Most Innings without Scoring, One Day
27—St. Louis Cardinals, July 2, 1933, lost the first game of a double-header 1–0 to Carl Hubbell and the New York Giants in 18 innings, then were blanked 1–0 again in the nightcap by Roy Parmalee.

Longest Day's Work to No Avail
On May 31, 1964, the New York Mets lost a double-header to San Francisco that consumed an all-time record 10½ hours; the nightcap, in addition, lasted 23 innings.

Longest Game in Organized Baseball History
33 innings—Pawtucket 3, Rochester 2, International League, April 19, 1981. The game was suspended at 4:07 A.M. after 32 innings with the score 2–2, then completed that night, with Pawtucket pushing across the winning run almost as soon as the game was resumed. The longest game that was not interrupted by suspension was played on June 14, 1966, between Miami and St. Petersburg of the Class A Florida State League, Miami, managed by Billy DeMars, winning 4–3 in 29 innings over Sparky Anderson's St. Pete Club.

Last Team to Play Two Opponents in One Day
Rainouts in 1951 forced the Cardinals into a situation whereby they had to entertain the pennant-bound New York Giants on the afternoon of September 13 in a makeup game at Sportsman's Park, then shower, change uniforms and return to the field that night for a regularly scheduled game against the Boston Braves.

Most Days in a Row, since 1901, Playing No Opponents
10—Philadelphia Phillies, 1909. On August 19 a prolonged spell of poor weather in the East resulted in the Phillies being rained out for the 10th straight day.

Only Tripleheader in Which All Three Games Went the Full Nine Innings
September 1, 1890—Brooklyn Bridegrooms (NL) versus Pittsburgh Innocents (NL). The Bridegrooms swept the triple bill—10–9, 3–2, and 8–4—and went on to win the National League pennant that season. Not surprisingly, Pittsburgh finished in the cellar, 66 ½ games behind Brooklyn.

Shortest Day's Work by Pitcher Hurling Complete Game
Red Barrett of the Boston Braves pitched a 2–0 shutout against Cincinnati on August 10, 1944, in which he threw only 58 pitches—an average of 6.4 pitches per inning.

Iron-Man Pitchers

On June 19, 1927, Jack Scott of the Phillies pitched both ends of a double-header against the Reds, winning the first game 3–1 and then losing the nightcap 3–0. Thirty-five at the time, Scott became the oldest major-league player ever to pitch two complete games in one day. No one realized then that he would also be the last major-league player to do it.

First Pitcher to Win Two Complete Games in One Day
Candy Cummings, Hartford, beat Cincinnati 14–4 and 8–4 on September 9, 1876.

First Pitcher to Win Two Complete Games in One day, Mound at Its Present Distance
Cy Seymour of the New York Giants, while beating Louisville 11–1 and 4–3 on May 30, 1898, became the first pitcher to win a doubleheader after the mound was moved to 60 feet 6 inches from the plate. The second game was called after seven innings.

First Pitcher to Pitch Two Complete Games in One Day, since 1901
Joe McGinnity of the Baltimore Orioles worked both ends of a doubleheader twice in 1901, splitting on each occasion. On August 1, 1903, McGinnity became the first pitcher in this century to win both ends of a doubleheader. With the Giants by then, he won two more complete-game doubleheaders before the month was out, the last on August 31.

Only Pitcher since 1901, Besides McGinnity, to Win Two Complete Games in One Day More Than Once
Pete Alexander of the Phillies in 1916 and again in 1917

Only Pitcher since 1901, Besides McGinnity, to Pitch More Than Two Complete-Game Doubleheaders
Mule Watson did it twice with the Philadelphia A's in 1918 and a third time in 1921 with the Boston Braves. His record for the six games was three wins, two losses and one tie.

Only Pitcher to Hurl Two Complete-Game Shutouts in One Day
Ed Reulbach of the Cubs, in the thick of the 1908 pennant race, beat Brooklyn 5–0 and 3–0 on September 26.

Only Pitcher to Be Involved in Two Complete-Game 1–0 Decisions in One Day
On July 31, 1915, Dave Davenport, pitching for the St. Louis Terriers in the Federal League, beat Buffalo 1–0 and then lost the second game of the twin bill 1–0. Davenport gave up only five hits that day—and just one in the game he lost.

Last Pitcher to Win Two Complete Games in One Day
Emil Levsen, Cleveland, beat the Boston Red Sox 6–1 and 5–1 on August 28, 1926. Levsen did it without striking out a batter in either game. Johnny "Stud" Stuart of the St. Louis Cardinals also pitched a double-header win against the Boston Braves in 1923 without registering a single strike-out that day. Stuart's performance enabled rookie Harry McCurdy, who caught both games, to set a major-league mark when he completed the twin bill without handling a single chance.

First Pitcher to Lose Two Complete Games in One Day
Dave Anderson of Pittsburgh lost two of the three games the Innocents dropped in their tripleheader loss to the Brooklyn Bridegrooms on September 1, 1890.

Only Pitcher in This Century to Lose Two Complete Games in One Day
Wiley Piatt, Boston Braves, lost 1–0 and 5–3 to Pittsburgh on June 25, 1903.

Closest Any Pitcher Has Come since 1927 to Hurling Two Complete Games in One Day
On September 6, 1950, Don Newcombe of the Brooklyn

Dodgers started both ends of a doubleheader against the league-leading Phillies. Newcombe shut out the Phils 2–0 in the opener but left in the sixth inning of the nightcap, trailing 2–0.

Last Pitcher to Start Both Ends of a Doubleheader
Wilbur Wood, Chicago White Sox, on July 20, 1973, against the Yankees. He was knocked out in both games and wound up with two losses that day.

No-Hitters and
Perfect Games

On April 30, 1922, Charlie Robertson of the White Sox became the first pitcher in major-league history to hurl a perfect game on the road when he beat Detroit 2–0 at Navin Field. It was the fourth perfect game in the American League since 1904, but after Robertson's masterpiece there was a 34-year drought before Don Larsen of the Yankees pitched a perfect game in the 1956 World Series.

CHRONOLOGY OF FULL-LENGTH PERFECT GAMES

June 12, 1880	Lee Richmond; Worcester defeated Cleveland (NL) 1–0.
June 17, 1880	Monte Ward; Providence defeated Buffalo (NL) 5–0.[1]
May 5, 1904	Cy Young; Boston defeated Philadelphia (AL) 1–0.
October 2, 1908	Addie Joss; Cleveland defeated Chicago (AL) 1–0.[2]
June 23, 1917	Ernie Shore; Boston defeated Washington (AL) 4–0.[3]
April 30, 1922	Charlie Robertson; Chicago defeated Detroit (AL) 2–0.
October 8, 1956	Don Larsen; New York (AL) defeated Brooklyn (NL) 2–0.[4]
May 29, 1959	Harvey Haddix; Pittsburgh lost to Milwaukee (NL) 1–0 in 13 innings.[5]
June 21, 1964	Jim Bunning; Philadelphia defeated New York Mets (NL) 6–0.
September 9, 1965	Sandy Koufax; Los Angeles defeated Chicago (NL) 1–0.[6]

May 8, 1968	Catfish Hunter; Oakland defeated Minnesota (AL) 4–0.
May 15, 1981	Len Barker; Cleveland defeated Toronto (AL) 3–0.
September 30, 1984	Mike Witt; California defeated Texas (AL) 1–0.

[1]Richmond's and Ward's perfect games, even though they came only five days apart, attracted little attention at the time. Some newspaper accounts didn't even note that Richmond and Ward had allowed no opposition base runners, let alone that theirs were the first such pitching feats in history. Richmond was a left-hander, the only one besides Koufax and Haddix to pitch a perfect game.

[2]Probably the greatest clutch pitching job ever. Cleveland and Chicago were locked, along with Detroit, in the closest pennant race in American League history when Joss took the mound that day; his opponent was 40-game winner Ed Walsh. The final score alone attests to how valiantly Joss had to pitch.

[3]See "Relievers' Records" for details of Shore's game.

[4]Larsen beat Sal Maglie in his perfect game; the last batter he faced, pinch hitter Dale Mitchell, took a called third strike on a 3–2 count. Three days earlier, in Game Two of the Series, Larsen had been knocked out by the Dodgers in the second inning.

[5]The final score should have been 3–0, but Joe Adcock of the Braves, who homered with two on, was declared out for passing Hank Aaron on the base paths.

[6]Koufax's opponent, Bob Hendley, pitched a one-hitter.

Close But No Cigar Award

On the closing day of the 1986 season Curt Young of the A's lost his bid to become the first southpaw in American League history to hurl a perfect game when Royals rookie Kevin Seitzer beat out an infield hit in the seventh inning to become Kansas City's lone baserunner, but many other hurlers have come even closer to achieving immortality.

First Prize—Tom Seaver. In 1969 Seaver missed a perfect game when Jim Qualls of the Cubs rapped a pinch double with one out in the ninth inning. Six years later Joe Wallis of the Cubs singled with two out in the ninth inning to break up a no-hit bid by Seaver.

Second Prize—Milt Pappas. On September 2, 1972, Pappas, working for the Cubs, was one pitch away from a perfect game when he walked San Diego pinch hitter Larry Stahl on a 3–2 count.

Third Prize—In 1958 Billy Pierce of the White Sox had a 1–0 lead over Washington and was one out away from a perfect game, the first by an American League left-hander, when pinch hitter Ed Fitzgerald stroked an opposite-field double.

Fourth Prize—Tommy Bridges of the Tigers shut out Washington 13–0 on August 15, 1932, but lost a perfect game with two out in the ninth inning when pinch hitter Dave Harris hit a bloop single.

Fifth Prize—In 1983 another Tigers pitcher, Milt Wilcox, saw his try for a perfect game slip away when Jerry Hairston of the White Sox singled with two out in the ninth inning.

On June 15, 1938, in the initial night game played at Ebbets Field, Johnny Vander Meer of the Reds no-hit the Dodgers 6–0 four days after he'd held the Braves hitless. Vander Meer's back-to-back gems were the first no-hitters in the National League since 1934 and made him the first player to pitch consecutive no-hitters as well as the first to throw two in the same season. Fifteen years earlier an American League pitcher, Howard Ehmke with the last-place Red Sox, narrowly missed earning the dual distinction that fell to Vander Meer. Ehmke no-hit the Athletics on September 7, 1923, and then lost his chance at a second straight no-hitter four days later when the official scorer called a ground ball that was misplayed by the Red Sox third baseman a single. The muffed grounder turned out to be the only hit off Ehmke, but the scorer might have only been trying to even up the breaks. While Ehmke had a valid argument that he'd been cheated out of a second no-hitter, he could not deny that his first one was a gift from Athletics pitcher Slim Harriss, who doubled off the right-field wall early in the game but was called out for missing first base.

Pitcher Who Came the Closest After 1938 to Equaling Vander Meer's Feat

Ewell Blackwell of the Reds no-hit the Braves 6–0 on June 18, 1947. Following the same pattern as Vander Meer, he started against the Dodgers four days later and was working on a second consecutive no-hitter when Eddie Stanky singled with one out in the ninth inning.

Second Pitcher to Throw Two No-Hitters in a Season

Allie Reynolds, New York Yankees, 1951. Three other pitchers have also done it—Virgil Trucks, Detroit Tigers, 1952; Jim Maloney, Cincinnati Reds, 1965; and Nolan Ryan, California Angels, 1973. Trucks, who had only a 5–19 record for the season, won both his no-hitters by a 1–0 score and also hurled a 1–0 one-hit victory over Washington that year that was marred only by leadoff batter Eddie Yost's single on the first pitch of the game.

First Pitcher to Hurl Three Career No-Hitters
Larry Corcoran, Chicago White Stockings, 1880, 1882 and 1884

First Pitcher to Hurl Four Career No-Hitters
Sandy Koufax, Los Angeles Dodgers, threw no-hitters in four consecutive seasons (1962–65), the last one a perfect game.

First Pitcher to Hurl Five Career No-Hitters
Nolan Ryan, California Angels, 1973 (2), 1974, 1975, and Houston Astros, 1981

First Pitcher to Hurl Two No-Hitters after 1901
Christy Mathewson, New York Giants, 1901 and 1905

First Pitcher to Hurl Three No-Hitters after 1901
Bob Feller, Cleveland Indians, 1940, 1946 and 1951. Feller won all three of his no-hitters by one run and also pitched a record 12 complete-game one-hitters.

First Major-League No-Hitter
It depends on what you believe was the first major league. On July 28, 1875, a couple of months before the National Association concluded its final season, Philadelphia's Joe Borden, aka Joe Josephs, no-hit Chicago 4–0. The following year, in the National League's first season, George Bradley of St. Louis no-hit Hartford 2–0 on July 28.

Only Pitcher since 1893 to Hurl a No-Hitter in His First Start
Bobo Holloman, St. Louis Browns, held the Philadelphia A's hitless on May 6, 1953; it was his only complete game in the majors. Before the mound was moved to its present distance from the plate, Ted Breitenstein of the American Association St. Louis Browns, in 1891, and Bumpus Jones of the Cincinnati Reds, in 1892, also threw no-hitters in their first starts. On April 14, 1967, Red Sox rookie Bill Rohr, pitching in his first major-league game, saw his no-hit

bid in Yankee Stadium disappear when Elston Howard of the Yankees singled with two out in the ninth inning. Similarly, Padres yearling Jimmy Jones lost a no-hitter in his first major-league game on September 22, 1986, when Bob Knepper of the Astros, Jones's mound opponent, tripled for the lone hit the rookie surrendered in his 5–0 win.

Most Famous No-Hit Game

A close call among several possible choices, but most pitching afficionados vote for the double no-hit duel on May 2, 1917, between the Reds' Fred Toney and Hippo Vaughn of the Cubs, won 1–0 by Toney in the 10th inning when Jim Thorpe drove in the winning run. The only other double no-hit game in organized baseball history occurred on August 20, 1952, when Frank Etchberger of Bradford edged Batavia's Jim Mitchell 1–0 in a Pony League game that was decided on an eighth-inning error by shortstop George Genovese, Batavia's player-manager.

First American League No-Hitter

On May 9, 1901, Cleveland's Earl Moore no-hit the White Sox for nine innings but lost 4–2 in the 10th, making him also the first pitcher in this century to lose a no-hit game.

First Pitcher to Hurl a No-Hitter In Each League

Tom Hughes, Boston Braves, pitched a no-hitter against Pittsburgh in 1916 six years after he'd pitched a nine-inning no-hitter for the Yankees before losing 5–0 to Cleveland in the 11th. Jim Bunning was the second pitcher to throw a no-hitter in each league; Nolan Ryan was the third and last to do it.

Only Teammates to Pitch No-Hitters on Consecutive Days

In 1917 two St. Louis Browns pitchers, Ernie Koob and Bob Groom, no-hit that year's World Champion, the White Sox, on consecutive days—May 5 and May 6—but not in consecutive games; Groom's no-hitter came in the second half of a double-header. Less than a month earlier, on April 14, 1917, Eddie Cicotte of the White Sox had no-hit the Browns 11–0. After May, the White Sox went the rest of the year without being involved in any more hitless games, but they still remain the only World Champion to be victimized twice in a season by no-hitters.

Only No-Hitters Lost in Nine Innings

NL—On April 23, 1964, Ken Johnson of Houston became the only pitcher ever to lose a complete-game no-hitter in nine innings when he was beaten 1–0 by the Reds.

AL—On April 30, 1967, Steve Barber of the Orioles carried a no-hitter into the ninth inning against the Tigers, then was relieved by Stu Miller, who lost the game 2–1 on an error by shortstop Mark Belanger.

Only Fans to See Their Team No-Hit Twice in Three Years and Yet Win Both Games

On May 26, 1956, Milwaukee fans watched Johnny Klippstein, Hersh Freeman and Joe Black of the Reds combine to no-hit the Braves through nine innings before losing in the tenth. Exactly three years later, on May 26, 1959, County Stadium hosted another no-hitter—indeed, the first perfect game in the National League since 1880—when the Pirates' Harvey Haddix held the Braves without a base runner for 12 innings before losing 1–0 in the 13th.

Only Opening Day No-Hitters

NL—Red Ames, New York Giants, lost 3–0 to the Dodgers in 13 innings on April 15, 1909, after holding them hitless until the 10th inning.

AL—Bob Feller, Cleveland, defeated Chicago 1–0 on April 16, 1940.

First Independence Day No-Hitters

NL—Hooks Wiltse, New York Giants, defeated Philadelphia 1–0 in 10 innings on July 4, 1908.

AL—George Mullin, Detroit, defeated St. Louis 7–0 on July 4, 1912, which also happened to be his 32nd birthday.

Only No-Hitters to Clinch Titles

AL—Allie Reynolds, New York, 8–0 over Boston on September 28, 1951.

NL—Mike Scott, Houston, 2–0 over San Francisco on September 25, 1986.

Pitcher Receiving the most Support While Throwing a No-Hitter

Frank Smith, Chicago White Sox, defeated Detroit 15–0 on September 6, 1905. Twenty years later, on September 19, 1925, Ted Lyons of the White Sox, about to put the final touch on a 17–0 no-hitter against Washington, instead became the first of many pitchers to fall prey to a Senators pinch hitter when Bobby Veach singled with two out in the ninth inning.

First No-Hitter by Pitcher With Expansion Team

AL—Bo Belinsky, Los Angeles, defeated Baltimore 2–0 on May 5, 1962.

AL—Don Nottebart, Houston, defeated Philadelphia 4–1 on May 17, 1963.

FIRST NO-HITTER FOR EACH TEAM AFTER 1900
(Present Franchise Location Only)
National League

Team	Pitcher	Date	Opponent	Score
Atlanta	Phil Niekro	August 7, 1973	San Diego	9–0[1]
Chicago	Bob Wicker	June 11, 1904	New York	1–0, 12 innings
Cincinnati	Fred Toney	May 2, 1917	Chicago	1–0, 10 innings
Houston	Don Nottebart	May 17, 1963	Philadelphia	4–1
Los Angeles	Sandy Koufax	June 30, 1962	New York	5–0[2]
Montreal	Bill Stoneman	April 17, 1969	Philadelphia	7–0
New York	None			
Philadelphia	Chick Fraser	September 18, 1903	Chicago	10–0
Pittsburgh	Nick Maddox	September 20, 1907	Brooklyn	2–1[3]
St. Louis	Jesse Haines	July 17, 1924	Boston	5–0[4]
San Diego	None			
San Francisco	Juan Marichal	June 15, 1963	Houston	1–0[5]

[1]Frank Pfeffer pitched the first Boston Braves no-hitter, beating Cincinnati 6–0 on May 8, 1907; Jim Wilson pitched the first Milwaukee Braves no-hitter, beating Philadelphia 2–0 on June 12, 1954.

[2]Mal Eason pitched the first Brooklyn Dodgers no-hitter, beating St. Louis 2–0 on July 20, 1906.

[3]Maddox's no-hitter was the last by a Pittsburgh pitcher at home until John Candaleria no-hit Los Angeles 2–0 on August 9, 1976, at Three Rivers Stadium. No Pirate ever pitched a no-hitter at Forbes Field 1909–70)—nor, for that matter, did any pitcher for a visiting team.

[4]The last team to register a no-hitter in this century. Moreover, Haines's no-hitter was the first by a pitcher on a St. Louis National League team since 1876.

[5]Christy Mathewson pitched the first New York Giants no-hitter, beating St. Louis 5–0 on July 15, 1901.

Most One-Hitters, Season
    4—Pete Alexander, Philadelphia, 1915. Alexander never pitched a no-hitter.

Special Mention
    Jim Barr also never pitched a no-hitter, but he once did something far more extraordinary. With the Giants in 1972, he retired a record 41 batters in a row over the course of two games before surrendering a double to Bernie Carbo of the Cardinals.

American League

Team	Pitcher	Date	Opponent	Score
Baltimore	Hoyt Wilhelm	September 2, 1958	New York	1–0[1]
Boston	Cy Young	May 5, 1904	Philadelphia	3–0[2]
California	Bo Belinsky	May 5, 1962	Baltimore	2–0
Chicago	Nixey Callahan	September 20, 1902	Detroit	3–0
Cleveland	Earl Moore	May 9, 1901	Chicago	2–4, 10 innings
Detroit	George Mullin	July 4, 1912	St. Louis	7–0
Kansas City	Steve Busby	April 27, 1973	Detroit	3–0
Milwaukee	None			
Minnesota	Jack Kralick	August 26, 1963	Kansas City	1–0[3]
New York	Tom Hughes	August 30, 1910	Cleveland	0–5, 11 innings
Oakland	Catfish Hunter	May 8, 1968	Minnesota	4–0[4]
Seattle	None			
Texas	Jim Bibby	July 7, 1973	Oakland	6–0[5]
Toronto	None			

[1] Earl Hamilton pitched the first St. Louis Browns no-hitter, beating Detroit 5–1 on August 30, 1912.
[2] Perfect game. Young's mound opponent that day was Rube Waddell.
[3] Walter Johnson pitched the first Washington Senators no-hitter, beating Boston 1–0 on July 1, 1920.
[4] Perfect game. Weldon Henley pitched the first Philadelphia A's no-hitter, beating St. Louis 6–0 on July 22, 1905. No A's pitcher threw a no-hitter while the franchise was in Kansas City.
[5] The franchise's first no-hitter. No member of the expansion Washington Senators ever threw one.

Record-breaking Scorers

In 1939 third baseman Red Rolfe of the New York Yankees set a 20th-century record when he scored at least one run in 18 consecutive games; the all-time record is held by Billy Hamilton of the Philadelphia Phillies, who scored in 24 straight games in 1894. Rolfe was typical of a kind of player who flourished in the 1930s when runs were scored at a record rate, especially by the Yankees, but would have been only a footnote in any other era. Between 1934 and 1941 Rolfe scored 846 runs—an average of 105.8 per year—without ever having more than 14 home runs, 90 walks or 80 RBIs in a season. Moreover, his batting average during that span was under .300.

Most Runs, Season, since 1901
AL—177—Babe Ruth, New York, 1921
NL—158—Chuck Klein, Philadelphia, 1930

Most Runs, Season, 1901 through 1919
AL—147—Ty Cobb, Detroit, 1911
NL—139—Jesse Burkett, St. Louis, 1901

Most Runs, Season, 1942 through 1960
AL—150—Ted Williams, Boston, 1949
NL—137—Johnny Mize, New York Giants, 1947

Most Runs, Season, 1961 through 1976
NL—137—Billy Williams, Chicago, 1970
AL—132—Mickey Mantle and Roger Maris, New York, 1961

Most Runs, Season, since 1977
AL—146—Rickey Henderson, New York, 1985
NL—133—Tim Raines, Montreal, 1983

Most Years League Leader in Runs
   AL—8—Babe Ruth, last in 1928
   NL—5—George Burns, last in 1920; Rogers Hornsby, last in 1929; Stan Musial, last in 1954

Most Years 150 or More Runs, since 1901
   AL—6—Babe Ruth, last in 1930
   NL—2—Chuck Klein, last in 1932

Only Player to Score Six Runs in a Game Twice
   Mel Ott, New York Giants, August 4, 1934, and again on April 30, 1944. The all-time record for the most runs scored in a game is seven, on August 15, 1886, by Guy Hecker of the Louisville Eclipse team in the American Association.

Highest Percentage of Team's Runs Scored, Season
   AL—.199—Burt Shotton, St. Louis, 1913, scored 105 of the Browns' 528 runs.
   NL—.196—Tim Raines, Montreal, 1983, scored 133 of the Expos' 677 runs.

Fewest Runs, Season, League Leader in Runs
   NL—89—Gavvy Cravath, Philadelphia, 1915
   AL—92—Harry Davis, Philadelphia, 1905

CAREER TOP 10 IN RUNS

		Years Active	*Runs*
1.	Ty Cobb	1905–28	2245
2.	Babe Ruth	1914–35	2174
	Hank Aaron	1954–76	2174
4.	Pete Rose	1963–	2165
5.	Willie Mays	1951–73	2062
6.	Stan Musial	1941–63	1949
7.	Lou Gehrig	1923–39	1888[1]
8.	Tris Speaker	1907–28	1881[2]
9.	Mel Ott	1926–47	1859
10.	Frank Robinson	1956–76	1829

[1]In the 14 full seasons he played—1925–38—Gehrig *averaged* 134 runs per year.
   [2]Eighth on the career list, although he was never a league leader in runs.

The Three Most Interesting Teams between 1920 and 1941

1921 NEW YORK YANKEES
W-98 L-55
Manager: Miller Huggins

Regular Lineup—1B, Wally Pipp; 2B, Aaron Ward; 3B, Home Run Baker; SS, Roger Peckinpaugh; RF, Bob Meusel; CF, Elmer Miller; LF, Babe Ruth; C, Wally Schang; P, Carl Mays; P, Waite Hoyt; P, Bob Shawkey.

The first Yankees team to win a pennant and the first club in the 20th century to post a slugging average above .450, they also had the league's best pitching staff and could even run when necessary. Ruth, Meusel and Pipp, the three top RBI men, all tied for the club lead in stolen bases with 17, not a bad figure in 1921—only three players in the AL had as many as 25. Yankees pitchers led the AL with a 3.79 ERA and 481 strikeouts, the first number reflecting the sudden surge in run production, the latter number indicating that even with the increase in scoring batters weren't as yet swinging from the heels. Mays topped the AL with 27 wins a year after the Chapman tragedy. On the club also was Shotgun Rogers, who had killed John Dodge, a former major-league infielder, with a pitch in a 1916 Southern Association game.

1930 PHILADELPHIA PHILLIES
W-52 L-102
Manager: Burt Shotton

Regular Lineup—1B, Don Hurst; 2B, Freco Thompson; 3B, Pinky Whitney; SS, Tommy Thevenow; RF, Chuck Klein; CF, Denny Sothern; LF, Lefty O'Doul; C, Spud Davis; P, Phil Collins; P, Ray Benge; P, Les Sweetland; P, Claude Willoughby; P, Hap Collard; P, Hal Elliott.

Spearheaded by Klein and O'Doul, the Phils scored 944 runs and had a .315 batting average. Yet they finished last, attributable mostly to their grisly pitching staff, which was the worst in this century. Collins posted a fine 16–11 record and Benge finished at 11–15, but the rest of the Phillies hurlers had a combined 25–76 mark and surrendered over 7.5 runs a game. Sweetland, Willoughby and Elliott were the leading culprits (see "Astronomical ERAs" for more about them), but Collard was only a notch better. Dead last in every pitching department except strikeouts, the 1930 Phillies allowed 1199 enemy base runners to cross the plate, a record that will almost surely never be broken. A year later the Phils still had the poorest pitching in the league but improved to sixth place when some of the rabbit was siphoned from the ball, reducing the number of runs they surrendered to 828. Twenty years later Shotton repaid Phillies fans for their patience with his efforts in 1930 by mismanaging a Brooklyn Dodgers team that lost the pennant to the Phils on the last day of the season.

1936 CLEVELAND INDIANS
W-80 L-74
Manager: Steve O'Neill

Regular Lineup—1B, Hal Trosky; 2B, Roy Hughes; 3B, Bad News Hale; SS, Bill Knickerbocker; RF, Roy Weatherly; CF, Earl Averill, LF, Joe Vosmik; C, Billy Sullivan; P, Johnny Allen; P, Mel Harder; P, Oral Hildebrand; P, Denny Galehouse; P, Lloyd Brown.

The Indians led the AL with a .304 batting average, had the league's RBI leader in Trosky, got a .351 season from catcher Sullivan, a .378 season from Averill, and 20 wins from Allen—yet finished in fifth place, albeit one game short of the all-time best record for a second division team. The reasons they faltered were obvious; Harder, who posted 223 career wins, had an off year with a 15–15 record and a 5.16 ERA, and Joe Vosmik, after losing the 1935 batting crown on his last at bat of the season, sagged to a .287 mark. Apart from Harder and Vosmik, the team got good numbers from all its regulars and seemed only to be waiting on the development of a 17-year-old rookie phenom Bob Feller to make its move. By 1938 Feller was ready, but the Indians, it turned out, had peaked two years too early. They would not contend until 1940 and then only for that one season before once again falling back into the pack.

Doubles Records

Owen Wilson's 36 triples in 1912, the most improbable feat in the deadball era, had its counterpart in the lively ball era when Earl Webb of the Boston Red Sox socked an all-time major-league record 67 doubles in 1931, shattering George Burns's mark of 64 two-baggers, set five years earlier. In 1931 Webb also led American League outfielders in errors, a stat that was probably more indicative of his talent. The 1931 season was the only one in which Webb collected more than 30 doubles. In contrast, Joe Medwick, who set the National League record when he rapped 64 doubles in 1936, had 40 or more doubles seven years in a row.

Most Doubles, Season, 1901 through 1919
AL—53—Tris Speaker, Boston, 1912
NL—44—Honus Wagner, Pittsburgh, 1904

Most Doubles, Season, 1942 through 1960
AL—56—George Kell, Detroit, 1950
NL—53—Stan Musial, St. Louis, 1953

Most Doubles, Season, 1961 through 1976
NL—51—Frank Robinson, Cincinnati, 1962
AL—47—Fred Lynn, Boston, 1975

Most Doubles, Season, since 1977
AL—54—Hal McRae, Kansas City Royals, 1978
NL—51—Pete Rose, Cincinnati, 1978

Most Seasons League Leader in Doubles, since 1901
AL—8—Tris Speaker, last in 1923
NL—8—Stan Musial, last in 1954

Most Seasons 50 or More Doubles
    AL—5—Tris Speaker, last in 1926
    NL—3—Paul Waner, last in 1936; Stan Musial, last in
1953

Most Doubles, Season, All-time Organized Baseball Record
    100—Lyman Lamb, Tulsa (Western League), 1924. The
St. Louis Browns gave Lamb short trials in 1920 and again
in 1921, mostly at third base, and he did well enough to
make one wonder whether the Browns, lacking a third baseman in 1922 when they missed the pennant by one game,
would have won if he'd been given a full shot at the job.

Most Doubles, Season, Team
    373—St. Louis Cardinals, 1930; eight players had 32 or
more doubles.

Most Doubles, Season, Team, since 1942
    310—Boston Red Sox, 1979

Fewest Doubles, Season, League Leader in Doubles
    AL—32—Sal Bando, Oakland, and Pedro Garcia, Mil-
waukee, 1972
    NL—32—Sam Mertes, New York Giants, Harry Steinfeldt,
Cincinnati, and Fred Clarke, Pittsburgh, 1902

Fewest Doubles, Season, since 1901, Minimum 500 at Bats
    NL—4—Roy Thomas, Philadelphia, 1902; 531 at bats
    AL—6—Billy Purtell, Chicago-Boston, 1910; 536 at bats

TOP 10 IN CAREER DOUBLES

		Years Active	*Doubles*
1.	Tris Speaker	1907–28	793
2.	Pete Rose	1963–	746
3.	Stan Musial	1941–63	725
4.	Ty Cobb	1905–28	724
5.	Nap Lajoie	1896–1916	652
6.	Honus Wagner	1897–1917	651
7.	Carl Yastrzemski	1961–83	646
8.	Hank Aaron	1954–76	624
9.	Paul Waner	1926–45	603
10.	Charlie Gehringer	1924–42	574

Fewest Doubles, Career, Minimum 5000 at Bats
100—Roy Thomas, 1899–1911. Thomas also has the fewest extra-base hits—160—among players with over 1500 career hits.

MVP Award Winners

Between 1911 and 1914 the Chalmers Award, in the form of a new car, was given each season to the most valuable players in both leagues but was stopped largely because the rules stipulated that no player could win it twice. From 1922 through 1928 the American League gave a most valuable player award, with the voting limited to eight players, one from each team, and the National League followed suit, beginning in 1924 and continuing through 1929. But the league awards never quite managed to capture public fancy, and the concept of choosing a most valuable player was shelved until 1931 when the Baseball Writers Association of America revived it. They have selected two Most Valuable Players, one in each league, ever since.

First BWAA Most Valuable Player Award Winners
   AL—Lefty Grove, Philadelphia
   NL—Frankie Frisch, St. Louis

First Player to Win Two MVP Awards
   AL—Jimmie Foxx, Philadelphia, 1932 and 1933; also the first to win consecutive MVP Awards
   NL—Carl Hubbell, New York Giants, 1933 and 1936

First Player to Win Three MVP Awards
   AL—Jimmie Foxx, Philadelphia, Boston, 1932, 1933 and 1938
   NL—Stan Musial, St. Louis, 1943, 1946 and 1948

Other Three-time MVP Award Winners
   AL—Joe DiMaggio, New York, 1939, 1941 and 1947; Yogi Berra, New York, 1951, 1954 and 1955; Mickey Mantle, New York, 1956, 1957 and 1962

NL—Roy Campanella, Brooklyn, 1951, 1953 and 1955;
Mike Schmidt, Philadelphia, 1980, 1981, and 1986

**First Player on a Second-Division Team to Win an MVP
Award**
   NL—Hank Sauer, Chicago, 1952; the Cubs finished fifth.
   AL—None

**First Player to Win MVP Award and Cy Young Award in
Same Season**
   NL—Don Newcombe, Brooklyn, 1956
   AL—Denny McLain, Detroit, 1968

Youngest Player to Win MVP Award
   NL—Johnny Bench, Cincinnati, 1980; 22 years old; just
16 days younger than Stan Musial was when he finished his
award-winning 1943 season.
   AL—Jeff Burroughs, Texas, 1974; 23 years old

Oldest Player to Win MVP Award
   NL—Willie Stargell, Pittsburgh; 39 years old
   AL—Spud Chandler, New York, 1943; 36 years old

First Catcher to Win MVP Award
   AL—Mickey Cochrane, Detroit, 1934
   NL—Gabby Hartnett, Chicago, 1935

First Shortstop to Win MVP Award
   NL—Marty Marion, St. Louis, 1944
   AL—Lou Boudreau, Cleveland, 1948

First Third Baseman to Win MVP Award
   NL—Bob Elliott, Boston, 1947
   AL—Al Rosen, Cleveland, 1953

First Relief Pitcher to Win MVP Award
   NL—Jim Konstanty, Philadelphia, 1950
   AL—Rollie Fingers, Milwaukee, 1981

Only Second Baseman to Win Two MVP Awards
   Joe Morgan, Cincinnati, 1975 and 1976

Only Third Baseman to Win Two or More MVP Awards
   Mike Schmidt, Philadelphia Phillies, (3) 1980, 1981 and
1986.

Only Shortstop to Win Two MVP Awards
    Ernie Banks, Chicago Cubs, 1958 and 1959

Only Player to Win MVP Awards in Both Leagues
    Frank Robinson, Cincinnati (NL), 1961; Baltimore (AL), 1966.

Only Pitcher to Win Consecutive MVP Awards
    Hal Newhouser, Detroit, 1944 and 1945. Newhouser and Roger Maris are also the only two-time MVP Award winners who are eligible for the Hall of Fame but haven't been selected.

Only Rookie to Win MVP Award
    Fred Lynn, Boston Red Sox, 1975

First Unanimous Selection for MVP Award
    AL—Hank Greenberg, Detroit, 1938
    NL—Orlando Cepeda, St. Louis, 1967

Teams That Have Never Had an MVP Award Winner
    NL—New York Mets, Houston, Montreal and San Diego
    AL—Toronto and Seattle. No St. Louis Browns player ever won an MVP Award before the franchise moved to Baltimore, nor did any player on either the original or the expansion Washington Senators.

Teams with the Most MVP Winners
    AL—19—New York; but only two—Thurman Munson in 1976 and Don Mattingly in 1985—since 1963
    NL—14—St. Louis

Players We Wish We'd Seen More of: 1920-41

The list of players in the 1920s and 1930s who were blocked either because they were on the wrong team or played the wrong position is a long one, and only some perverse streak in me, I suppose, caused me to limit it to a luckless 13.

1. Charlie Dorman. Like Ty Cobb, Dorman had a .367 career batting average in the major leagues, and also like Cobb, his last season came in 1928. But there the similarity ends. An outfielder, he was dropped by Cleveland after hitting .364 in 25 games.

2. Suds Sutherland. Won six games and lost only two as a rookie with the 1921 Tigers. But it wasn't good enough to earn him an encore—not even when coupled with a .407 batting average.

3. Herm Merritt. A 20-year-old shortstop, he hit .370 in 20 games for the 1921 Tigers but suffered the same fate as Sutherland.

4. Tripp Sigman. Had a .326 batting average and a .519 slugging average for the 1929-30 Phillies, but room couldn't be found for him in an outfield that featured Chuck Klein and Lefty O'Doul, and he got into only 62 games before being given a pink slip.

5. Pete Scott. Another outfielder in the late 1920s whose path was blocked by players like the Waner brothers and Hack Wilson. After three half-time seasons with the Cubs and Pirates, he departed in 1928 with a .303 career batting average and 88 RBIs in 522 at bats.

6. Jack Cummings. Had a .341 career batting average, showed good power and was an excellent pinch hitter, yet played in only 89 games between 1926 and 1929 with the Giants and Braves. A catcher, he hit .363 in 1927 and had 14 RBIs in 80 at bats, but was only rarely used by McGraw to spell Zack Taylor, who hit .233.

7. Babe Twombley. A singles hitter who was sent packing by the Cubs after he batted .377 in 1921, including a remarkable 15-for-38 as a pinch hitter.

8. Chicken Hawkes. Unlike Twombley, Hawkes had some power, but not enough to impress the Phillies, who dumped him after he hit .322 in 105 games in 1925. The following season they gave his first base job to Jack Bentley, who hit .258.

9. Tom Hughes. An outfielder with the 1930 Tigers, he hit .373 in 17 games but never got another crack at a major-league job.

10. Johnnie "Ty Ty" Tyler. Hit .340 and slugged .553 in 47 at bats with the 1935 Boston Braves, one of the most dismal teams ever, but was nevertheless let go.

11. Ben Paschal. Hit .357 for the 1920 Red Sox in a brief look but then bounced around the minors until the Yankees purchased him to serve as a backup outfielder to Babe Ruth, Earle Combs and Bob Meusel. Played six years with the Yankees without ever getting a shot at a full-time job even though he hit .360 in 1925 while filling in for an ailing Ruth. Apart from Buzz Arlett and Ike Boone, Paschal was probably the best player in this era who never got a full opportunity to showcase his talent in the majors.

12. Roy Carlyle. Another outfielder who wound up, to his detriment, with the Yankees. Released after hitting .377 for the 1926 team. Career batting average of .318 in 174 games and a fine 18-for-47 as a pinch hitter.

13. Merv Connors. Unable to wrest the White Sox first-base job away from Zeke Bonura and Joe Kuhel, Connors spent most of his career in the minors even though he hit .355 in his second and last big-league trial in 1938 and became the first White Sox player to hit three homers in a game at Comiskey Park. For more about Connors, Buzz Arlett, Ike Boone and other stars of the period who were denied major-league exposure, see "Minor League Feats and Firsts," page 229.

All-Star Game Feats

In 1933 Arch Ward of the *Chicago Tribune* hit upon the notion of holding a major-league all-star game as an adjunct to the World's Fair in Chicago that year, and it has been an annual event ever since with the exception of 1945, the final year of World War II.

First All-Star Game Home Run
AL—Babe Ruth, New York, in the very first game, July 6, 1933, at Comiskey Park
NL—Frankie Frisch, St. Louis, also in the inaugural game

First All-Star Game Won, League
AL—1933 at Comiskey Park, by a 4–2 score
NL—1936 at Braves Field, by a 4–3 score. A record-low crowd of 25,556 attended after a story was circulated around Boston that the game was sold out when in fact there were still plenty of seats available.

First Pitcher to Win Two All-Star Games
AL—Lefty Gomez, New York, 1933 and 1935. Gomez won a record third game in 1937 and then was the losing pitcher the following year, giving him an additional record of four decisions in All-Star play.
NL—Bob Friend, Pittsburgh, 1956 and 1960 (first game)

First Player to Hit Two Home Runs in All-Star Competition
NL—Frankie Frisch, St. Louis, 1933 and 1934
AL—Lou Gehrig, New York, 1936 and 1937

First Player to Hit Two Home Runs in One Game
Arky Vaughan, Pittsburgh, 1941 at Briggs Stadium, Detroit

First Player to Get Four Hits in One Game
Joe Medwick, St. Louis Cardinals, 1937 at Griffith Stadium, Washington

Longest Pitching Stint in an All-Star Game
Lefty Gomez of the Yankees went six innings as the starting pitcher for the American League in 1935, at Cleveland, as the AL won 4–1. The rules then did not limit pitchers to three innings.

Most Memorable Single Feat in All-Star Play
Probably Carl Hubbell's five consecutive strikeouts at the Polo Grounds in 1934. Hubbell opened the game by giving up a single to Charlie Gehringer and a walk to Heinie Manush. Then he fanned Babe Ruth, Lou Gehrig and Jimmie Foxx to end the first inning and began the second inning by whiffing Al Simmons and Joe Cronin. Hubbell's record for consecutive strikeouts in an All-Star Game was tied in 1986 by Fernando Valenzuela, who fanned Don Mattingly, Cal Ripken, Jesse Barfield, Lou Whitaker and Ted Higuera in order.

Most Serious Injury in All-Star Play
NL—Dizzy Dean's broken toe, suffered when Earl Averill of Cleveland hit a line drive off Dean's foot in the first inning of the 1937 game. Dean pitched three innings before giving in to the injury, then tried to come back from it too soon, hurt his arm and was never the same pitcher.
AL—Ted Williams's broken elbow, sustained when he crashed into the left-field wall in the first inning of the 1950 game at Comiskey Park. The injury koayed Williams for the season, and without him the Red Sox lost the pennant by four games.

Most Exciting All-Star Game
The 1950 game gets my vote for several reasons. Not only was it the first extra-inning game and the first one televised, but when Red Schoendienst homered in the top of the 14th inning to win 4–3 for the NL, it seemed to have an odd impact on the American League that has lasted ever since. Prior to 1950, the AL held a 12–4 lead in games; by 1964 the NL had caught up. A year later the NL took the lead for the first time in games won and is now ahead 36 to 19 with 1 tie.

Second Most Exciting Game
The 1957 game at Sportsman's Park, won by the AL 6–5. After scoring three runs in the top of the ninth inning, the AL led 6–2, but the NL came back with three runs in the bottom half and had the tying run on base when Minnie Minoso speared Gil Hodges's line drive to end the game.

Highest-Scoring Game
The 1954 game at Cleveland Stadium won by the AL 11–9. You won't get much of an argument from my corner if you vote this also the most exciting game.

Most Lop-sided Game
The 1946 game at Fenway Park, won by the AL 12–0 as Ted Williams hit two home runs, compiled a record 10 total bases and five RBIs, also a record, later tied by Al Rosen in the 1954 game.

Last Time the American League Won Two Games in a Row
In 1958 at Baltimore. The following year two games were played, an experiment that lasted until 1962; in that four-year span the NL won seven of the eight games with one a tie, in 1961 at Fenway Park, when rain began falling after the ninth inning with the score knotted 1–1.

First Indoor Game
In 1968 at the Astrodome. It was also the first 1–0 game and the only game in which no player had an RBI. The NL's winning run scored in the bottom of the first inning as Willie McCovey of the Giants hit into a double play.

First Game Played Outside the United States
In 1982 at Montreal, won by the NL 4–1.

Last of the 16 Teams that Existed in 1933 to Host a Game
The Philadelphia Phillies. The 1943 game was played in Shibe Park, their home ground, but the Athletics were the hosts. By the time the Phillies finally got the honor in 1952 both the White Sox and Tigers had hosted two games. To add to the grief of Phillies fans, who'd waited nearly 20 years to see their club in the host's role, rain forced the game to be called after five innings.

Best Pitcher in All-Star Play
AL—Mel Harder, Cleveland, appeared in four games, a total of 13 innings, without allowing an earned run.

NL—Juan Marichal, San Francisco, in 18 innings of All-Star Play gave up only one earned run.

Most Career Strikeouts by Pitcher in All-Star Play
19—Don Drysdale, Los Angeles. But his record probably won't last much longer now that Gooden and Valenzuela are on the scene.

Most All-Star Appearances
24—Stan Musial, Willie Mays and Hank Aaron

Most Career Hits in All-Star Play
23—Willie Mays

Most Career Home Runs in All-Stay Play
6—Stan Musial

Most Career Total Bases in All-Star Play
40—Stan Musial and Willie Mays

Most Career RBIs in All-Star Play
12—Ted Williams

First Player to Win Two All-Star Game MVP Awards
Willie Mays, 1963 and 1968

Most Recent Player to Win Two All-Star Game MVP Awards
Gary Carter, 1981 and 1984

Most Recent Player to Win All-Star Game MVP Award Playing for Losing Team
Carl Yastrzemski, 1970, when the AL lost 5–4 in 12 innings. Altogether there have been seven extra-inning All-Star Games, and the NL has won all seven.

Shortstops' Records

I'm probably going to make myself even more unpopular with sabermetricians when I say that there is no way we are ever going to be able to gauge which shortstop had the greatest range, the best arm or the surest glove. Statistics alone can't give us any of these answers, and no one has had the fortune to see all of the contenders for the title of best-ever play, let alone play under conditions similar enough to allow meaningful comparisons to be made. But statistics do tell us that two of the top-hitting shortstops of all time were Luke Appling and Arky Vaughan, and that both were active in the 1930s. Appling and Vaughan were not just offensive standouts, however. Both were also among the best glovemen of the era, and Vaughan regularly led the NL in double plays and assists. By the time World War II began they had been joined by five outstanding young shortstops— Lou Boudreau, Marty Marion, Pee Wee Reese, Eddie Miller and Phil Rizzuto—perhaps the most massive gathering of fielding talent at the position in history. These five men would sweep the vast majority of fielding honors in both leagues during the 1940s, and three of them would win Most Valuable Player Awards.

SEASON BATTING RECORDS

Department	National League	American League
Batting Average	.398, HUGHIE JENNINGS, Baltimore, 1896 .385, Arky Vaughan, Pittsburgh, 1935*	.388, Luke Appling, Chicago, 1936
Slugging Average	.614, ERNIE BANKS, Chicago, 1958	.578, Robin Yount, Milwaukee, 1982

Department	National League	American League
Home Runs	47, ERNIE BANKS, Chicago, 1958	40, Rico Petrocelli, Boston, 1969
RBIs	143, Ernie Banks, Chicago, 1959	159, VERN STEPHENS, Boston, 1949
Runs	159, HUGHIE JENNINGS, Baltimore, 1896 132, Pee Wee Reese, Brooklyn, 1949*	137, Frank Crosetti, New York, 1936
Hits	211, Garry Templeton, St. Louis, 1978	213, TONY FERNANDEZ, Toronto, 1986
Doubles	48, Dick Bartell, Philadelphia, 1932	51, JOE CRONIN, Boston, 1938
Triples	24, ED MCKEAN, Cleveland, 1894 20, Honus Wagner, Pittsburgh, 1912*	21, Bill Keister, Baltimore, 1901
Total Bases	379, ERNIE BANKS, Chicago, 1958	367, Robin Yount, Milwaukee, 1982
Stolen Bases	104, MAURY WILLS, Los Angeles, 1962	62, Bert Campaneris, Oakland, 1968
Bases on Balls	118, Arky Vaughan, Pittsburgh, 1936	149, EDDIE JOOST, Philadelphia, 1949
Strikeouts	114, Roy Smalley, Chicago, 1950 114, Bill Almon, San Diego, 1977 114, Shawon Dunston, Chicago, 1986	122, ZOILO VERSALLES, Minnesota, 1965
Fewest Strikeouts	5, Charlie Hollocher, Chicago, 1922	4, JOE SEWELL, Cleveland, 1925

*Record since 1901
Note: Cecil Travis of Washington had 218 hits in 1941, but a number of them came while he was playing third base.

Most Games, Career, at Shortstop
2581—Luis Aparicio, 1956–73

Most Consecutive Games at Shortstop
1307—Everett Scott, Boston Red Sox and New York Yankees, June 20, 1916, through May 5, 1925

Best Career Fielding Average
.980—Larry Bowa, 1970–85

EVOLUTION OF SEASON RECORD FOR BEST FIELDING AVERAGE

	Team	League	Year	Average
Johnny Peters	Chicago	National	1876	.932
George Wright	Boston	National	1878	.947[1]
George Davis	Chicago	American	1902	.951[2]
Tommy Corcoran	Cincinnati	National	1905	.952
Terry Turner	Cleveland	American	1906	.960
Terry Turner	Cleveland	American	1910	.973[3]
Everett Scott	Boston	American	1919	.976[4]
Eddie Miller	Boston	National	1942	.981
Buddy Kerr	New York	National	1946	.982
Lou Boudreau	Cleveland	American	1947	.982[5]
Phil Rizzuto	New York	American	1950	.982
Ernie Banks	Chicago	National	1959	.985
Larry Bowa	Philadelphia	National	1971	.987
Ed Brinkman	Detroit	American	1972	.990
Larry Bowa	Philadelphia	National	1979	.991

[1]Through documented, many of the relatively high fielding averages in the National League's early years are suspect, Wright's among them. Official scorers of that period were notoriously uneven. Testimony to this is that despite continuous improvements in gloves and overall playing conditions Wright's mark stood unchallenged, even by Wright himself, until 1895 when Hughie Jennings of Baltimore became only the second shortstop to field .940 or better.

[2]Seldom mentioned anymore by historians, Davis was not only a fine fielder but also at one time held the record for most career hits by a switch hitter.

[3]Turner's 1910 mark is disputable because it includes many games he played at other infield positions. Even so, he was undoubtedly one of the top fielders of his era. How good, exactly? Good enough to play regularly also at third and second and to be the only player ever to hold simultaneously a season record for the best fielding average at two different positions—shortstop and third base.

[4]Scott's record, long forgotten, can now be seen to have been a quantum leap; he also fielded just a hair lower in 1918.

[5]Boudreau fielded .983 in 1944, but injuries kept him from playing in enough games to qualify as a record breaker. His 1947 mark is actually a shade higher than Rizzuto's .982 average four years later; though both made the same number of errors, Boudreau handled 27 more chances.

Most Seasons League Leader in Fielding Average

AL—8—Everett Scott, 1916 through 1923 consecutive; Lou Boudreau, last in 1948; Luis Aparicio, 1959 through 1966 consecutive.

NL—6—Larry Bowa, last in 1983

Most Consecutive Errorless Games
    72—Ed Brinkman, Detroit Tigers, May 21, 1972, through
August 4, 1972

Most Consecutive Errorless Chances
    383—Buddy Kerr, New York Giants, July 28, 1946, through
May 25, 1947

Most Chances Accepted, Career
    12,564—Luis Aparicio, 1956–73

Most Chances Accepted, Season
    984—Dave Bancroft, New York Giants, 1922

Most Chances Accepted, Game, Nine Innings, since 1902
    19—Eddie Joost, Cincinnati Reds, May 7, 1941

Most Consecutive Games, No Chances Accepted
    3—Tommy Tresh, New York Yankees, August 30, August 31 and September 1, 1968

Most Assists, Season
    621—Ozzie Smith, San Diego Padres, 1980

Most Assists, Game, Nine Innings, since 1901
    14—Tommy Corcoran, Cincinnati Reds, August 7, 1903

Most Seasons League Leader in Assists
    AL—7—Luke Appling, last in 1946
    Luis Aparicio, last in 1968
    NL—5—Mickey Doolan, last in 1913
    Ozzie Smith, last in 1985

Most Double Plays, Season
    AL—147—Rick Burleson, Boston, 1980
    NL—137—Bobby Wine, Montreal, 1970

Most Years League Leader in Double Plays
    AL—6—George McBride, last in 1914
    NL—5—Mickey Doolan, last in 1913
    Dick Groat, last in 1964

Most Gold Glove Awards
    8—Louis Aparicio, 1956–73
    Mark Belanger, 1965–82

Astronomical ERAs

The law that for every action there is an equal and opposite reaction applies not only in physics but also in baseball. While slugging statistics and scoring totals were soaring in the 1920s and 1930s so were pitchers' ERAs. In 1930 Remy Kremer of the Pirates became the first pitcher in major-league history to win 20 games despite allowing over five earned runs (5.02) per each nine innings he worked. Before the decade was out Bobo Newsom had won 20 games with an even higher ERA, and Roxie Lawson of the Tigers had somehow managed to achieve an 18–7 record and a dazzling .720 winning percentage in 1937 on a 5.27 ERA. But Kremer, Newsom and Lawson were stingy with enemy batters compared to three other pitchers in the 1930s who posted the three worst season ERAs in history among hurlers in 150 or more innings.

The Terrible Trio
First Prize—Les Sweetland, Philadelphia Phillies, 1930; 7.71 ERA in 167 innings
Second Prize—Claude Willoughby, Philadelphia Phillies, 1930; 7.59 ERA in 153 innings
Third Prize—Jim Walkup, St. Louis Browns, 1937; 7.36 ERA in 150 innings

Highest ERA, Season, since 1942, Minimum 100 Innings
First Prize—Troy Herriage, Kansas City A's, 1956; 6.64 ERA in 103 innings
Second Prize—Bob Wiesler, Washington Senators, 1956; 6.44 ERA in 123 innings

Highest ERA, Season, 1901 through 1919, Minimum 150 Innings
5.30—Orlie Weaver, Chicago Cubs and Boston Braves, 1911; 165 innings

Highest ERA, Season, Prior to 1901, Minimum 10 Starts
  10.32—Charlie Stecher, Philadelphia, American Association, 1890

Highest ERA, Season, since 1901, Minimum 10 Starts
  9.85—Steve Blass, Pittsburgh Pirates, 1973. After a 19–8 season in 1972, Blass suffered a mysterious loss of control the following season and gave up 84 walks and 109 hits in 89 innings. A career .172 hitter, he ironically discovered the secret of hitting while forgetting everything he knew about pitching and rapped .417 (10-for-24) in 1973.

Highest ERA, Season, League Leader in ERA
  AL—3.20—Early Wynn, Cleveland, 1950
  NL—3.08—Bill Walker, New York Giants, 1929

Highest ERA, Season, 20-Game Winner
  1893–1900—4.92—Kid Carsey (24–16), Philadelphia, 1895
                    Brickyard Kennedy (22–19), Brooklyn, 1894, Clark Griffith (21–11), Chicago, 1894
  1901–19—3.83—Henry Schmidt (21–13), Brooklyn, 1903
  1920–41—5.08—Bobo Newsom (20–16), St. Louis Browns, 1938
  1942–60—4.07—Lew Burdette (21–15), Milwaukee Braves, 1959
  1961–76—3.98—Paul Splittorff (20–11), Kansas City Royals, 1973
  1977–86—3.79—Dennis Leonard (20–11), Kansas City Royals, 1980

Highest Career ERA, 300-Game Winner
  3.54—Early Wynn, 1939–63

HALL OF FAME PITCHERS WITH THE HIGHEST CAREER ERAS

		Years Active	*Wins*	*ERA*
1.	Red Ruffing	1924–47	273	3.80
2.	Ted Lyons	1923–46	260	3.67
3.	Jesse Haines	1918–37	210	3.64
4.	Herb Pennock	1912–34	241	3.61
5.	Waite Hoyt	1918–38	237	3.59

Highest Career ERA, 200-Game Winner
4.36—Earl Whitehill, 1923–39. Lew Burdette has never revealed whom he chose as his model when he was learning to pitch, but Whitehill would be a good guess. In 3566 innings he gave up 3917 hits and 1431 walks while striking out only 1350 batters. Yet he won 218 games and lost only 185.

Winner of the "Where Did He Go Wrong?" Award
Russ Van Atta. As a rookie with the 1933 Yankees, Van Atta pitched a shutout in his first major-league start and finished with a 12–4 record. Traded to the Browns in 1935, he twice led the American League in mound appearances and lasted until 1939 solely, it would seem, in the hope that he'd recover his early form. But Van Atta only got worse and worse. By the time he retired he'd absorbed so many fearful shellings that he had a 5.60 career ERA, the third highest in history among pitchers in over 700 innings. Whatever the Browns' strategy was in those years, it apparently didn't include molding a decent pitching staff. While they were clinging to Van Atta and Jim Walkup, they cut people like Fay Thomas, who won seven games in 1935 on a respectable (for the Browns) 4.78 ERA and all during the 1930s was regarded as one of the top pitchers in the minors.

Winner of the "Team That Never Learned How to Pick Them" Award
The Browns. In their 52-year history they never had a single ERA leader, and in 1951 they contrived to put together a mound staff that for a time had on it possibly the two worst pitchers ever—Sid Schacht and Irv Medlinger. Schacht, mainly a relief pitcher, worked in 19 games in 1950–51, gave up 44 hits and 21 walks in 22 innings and left with a 14.34 ERA, the all-time highest among pitchers in more than 20 innings. Medlinger, who had a 13.83 ERA in 14 innings, is fifth on the all-time list among pitchers who worked more than 10 innings.

The All-Time Worst Career ERAs
100 Innings—8.30—John McDougal, 123 innings (1895–96)
           7.60—Bill Rhodes, 153 innings, (1893)
           7.20—Jake Boyd, 136 innings (1894–96)
100 Innings—since 1901—7.19—Chet Nichols, 123 innings
                    (1926–32)

                    7.06—Lauren Pepper, 110 innings
                            (1954–57)
                    6.97—Herman Besse, 243 innings
                            (1940–46)
                    6.95—Carl Boyle, 223 innings
                            (1935–40)
250 Innings—6.99—Bill Kissinger, 319 innings (1895–97)
             6.95—Hal Elliott, 322 innings (1929–32)
400 Innings—6.74—Jim Walkup, 462 innings (1934–39)
             6.06—Lefty Mills, 435 innings (1934–40)
700 Innings—6.10—Les Sweetland, 741 innings (1927–31)
             5.84—Claude Willoughby, 841 innings (1925–
                    31)
1000 Innings—5.11—Mike Sullivan, 1123 innings (1889–99)
              5.02—Chief Hogsett, 1222 innings (1929–44)
              5.01—Roy Mahaffey, 1056 innings (1926–36)
              4.97—Jack Knott, 1557 innings (1933–46)
              4.95—Kid Carsey, 2222 innings (1891–1901)
              4.94—Buck Ross, 1365 innings (1936–45)
              4.91—Alex Ferguson, 1236 innings (1918–29)

The Hall of Fame

In the mid-1930s Ford Frick, then the National League president, was the prime mover behind the sentiment that a Hall of Fame to commemorate the game's greatest players should be opened in 1939, marking the centennial season for those who believed the Mills Commission's report that Abner Doubleday invented baseball. Acting on Frick's lead, Henry Edwards, secretary of the American League Service Bureau, polled the 226 members of the Baseball Writers Association of America for their choices from a list of 33 players. Two-thirds of the ballots cast were needed for selection. Ty Cobb led with 222 votes, Babe Ruth and Honus Wagner both had 215, Christy Mathewson had 205, and Walter Johnson received 189 votes. Before 1939 two more pollings were done, resulting in the selection of Nap Lajoie, Tris Speaker, Eddie Collins, George Sisler, Cy Young, Willie Keeler, Peter Alexander and Lou Gehrig (by special election) as well as 13 pre-1900 figures chosen by the Centennial Commission and the Committee on Old-Timers. These 26 immortals had their plaques installed in the Hall of Fame in a special induction ceremony in 1939 and have been joined in the years since by a long list. Although exceptions have been made in special cases, the three original criteria for selection have remained constant. A player must be active at least 10 seasons, must be retired at least 5 and must receive at least 75 percent of the vote.

In 1971 a Special Negro League Committee was formed to select players from the defunct Negro Leagues. Names followed by (NL) designate Negro League players who never played in the majors. Starred names belong to figures who were selected to the Hall of Fame as non-players.

Members of the Hall of Fame

1936 Ty Cobb, Honus Wagner, Babe Ruth, Christy Mathewson, Walter Johnson

1937 Nap Lajoie, Tris Speaker, Cy Young, Morgan Buckley,* Ban Johnson,* Connie Mack, John McGraw, George Wright.

1938 Pete Alexander, Alexander Cartwright,* Henry Chadwick*

1939 George Sisler, Eddie Collins, Willie Keeler, Lou Gehrig, Cap Anson, Charlie Comiskey, Candy Cummings, Buck Ewing, Hoss Radbourn, Al Spalding

1942 Rogers Hornsby

1944 Judge K. M. Landis*

1945 Roger Bresnahan, Dan Brouthers, Fred Clarke, Jimmy Collins, Ed Delahanty, Hugh Duffy, Hughie Jennings, Mike Kelly, Jim O'Rourke, Wilbert Robinson

1946 Jesse Burkett, Frank Chance, Jack Chesbro, Johnny Evers, Clark Griffith, Tom McCarthy, Joe McGinnity, Eddie Plank, Joe Tinker, Rube Waddell, Ed Walsh

1947 Carl Hubbell, Frank Frisch, Mickey Cochrane, Lefty Grove

1948 Herb Pennock, Pie Traynor

1949 Charlie Gehringer, Three Finger Brown, Kid Nichols

1951 Mel Ott, Jimmie Foxx

1952 Harry Heilmann, Paul Waner

1953 Dizzy Dean, Al Simmons, Ed Barrow,* Chief Bender, Tom Connolly,* Bell Klem,* Bobby Wallace, Harry Wright*

1954 Rabbit Maranville, Bill Dickey, Bill Terry

1955 Joe DiMaggio, Ted Lyons, Dazzy Vance, Gabby Hartnett, Frank Baker, Ray Schalk

1956 Hank Greenberg, Joe Cronin

1957 Sam Crawford, Joe McCarthy*

1959 Zack Wheat

1961 Max Carey, Billy Hamilton

1962 Bob Feller, Jackie Robinson, Bill McKechnie,* Edd Roush

1963 John Clarkson, Elmer Flick, Sam Rice, Eppa Rixey

1964 Luke Appling, Red Faber, Burleigh Grimes, Miller Huggins, Tim Keefe, Heinie Manush, John Ward

1965 Pud Galvin

1966 Ted Williams, Casey Stengel

1967 Red Ruffing, Branch Rickey,* Lloyd Waner

1968 Joe Medwick, Kiki Cuyler, Goose Goslin

1969 Stan Musial, Roy Campanella, Stan Coveleski, Waite Hoyt

1970 Lou Boudreau, Earle Combs, Ford Frick,* Jesse Haines

1971 Jake Beckley, Dave Bancroft, Chick Hafey, Harry Hooper, Joe Kelley, Rube Marquard, George Weiss,* Satchel Paige

1972 Sandy Koufax, Yogi Berra, Early Wynn, Lefty Gomez, Will Harridge,* Ross Youngs, Josh Gibson (NL), Buck Leonard (NL)

1973 Warren Spahn, Billy Evans,* George Kelly, Mickey Welch, Monte Irvin, Roberto Clemente

1974 Mickey Mantle, Whitey Ford, Jim Bottomley, Jocko Conlan,* Sam Thompson, Cool Papa Bell (NL)

1975 Ralph Kiner, Earl Averill, Bucky Harris,* Billy Herman, Judy Johnson (NL)

1976 Robin Roberts, Bob Lemon, Roger Connor, Fred Lindstrom, Cal Hubbard,* Oscar Charleston (NL)

1977 Ernie Banks, Amos Rusie, Joe Sewell, Al Lopez,* Martin Dihugo (NL), John Henry Lloyd (NL)

1978 Eddie Mathews, Addie Joss, Larry MacPhail*

1979 Willie Mays, Warren Giles,* Hack Wilson

1980 Al Kaline, Duke Snider, Chuck Klein, Tom Yawkey*

1981 Bob Gibson, Johnny Mize, Rube Foster (NL)

1982 Hank Aaron, Frank Robinson, Travis Jackson, Happy Chandler*

1983 Brooks Robinson, Juan Marichal, George Kell, Walter Alston*

1984 Luis Aparicio, Harmon Killebrew, Don Drysdale, Rick Ferrell, Pee Wee Reese

1985 Hoyt Wilhelm, Lou Brock, Enos Slaughter, Arky Vaughan

1986 Willie McCovey, Bobby Doerr, Ernie Lombardi

Individual Batting and Pitching Streaks

A significant majority of the great batting and pitching streaks occurred between 1920 and 1941. Foremost among them is probably Joe DiMaggio's hitting streak in 1941, which began inauspiciously on May 15 when DiMaggio collected a meager single off Eddie Smith of the White Sox. Two months later the streak reached 56 games after DiMaggio rapped a double and two singles against Al Milnar and Joe Krakauskas of the Indians. The following night, on July 17, at Cleveland Stadium, DiMaggio was stopped by Al Smith and Jim Bagby but more by third baseman Ken Keltner and shortstop Lou Boudreau. Keltner converted two hard shots down the third-base line into outs, and in DiMaggio's last at bat, in the eighth inning, Boudreau fashioned a double play out of a smash that DiMaggio later said was among the hardest balls he ever hit. During his 56-game streak DiMaggio hit .408 with 91 hits in 223 at bats. That same year Ted Williams of the Boston Red Sox lost the MVP Award to DiMaggio although he hit .406 for the entire season.

Longest National League Hitting Streak
44 games—Pete Rose, Cincinnati, 1978; stopped on August 1 by Larry McWilliams and Gene Garber of the Atlanta Braves.

Willie Keeler, Baltimore, 1897. Prior to Keeler's 44-game streak, the record was held by Bill Dahlen of the Chicago White Stockings, who hit safely in 42 straight games in 1894, breaking George Davis's year-old mark of 33 games. Dahlen's streak ended on August 7 against Cincinnati in a game in which the White Stockings made 20 hits, five each by Bill Lange and Cap Anson, who preceded and followed Dahlen in the Chicago batting order. According to some record books, Dahlen began a 28-game streak the next day, meaning that he narrowly missed putting together a 71-game skein, but the second streak is still the subject of dispute.

Most Consecutive Base Hits, No Bases on Balls Intervening
AL—12—Walt Dropo, Detroit, July 14 and 15, 1952
NL—10—Jake Gettman, Washington, September 10 and 11, 1897; Ed Konetchy, Brooklyn, June 28, June 29 and July 1, 1919

Most Consecutive Games Hitting at Least One Home Run
NL—8—Dale Long, Pittsburgh, May 19 through May 28, 1956
AL—6—Frank Howard, Washington, May 12 through May 18, 1968

Most Consecutive Games Collecting at Least One RBI
NL—17—Ray Grimes, Chicago, 1922. For many years Grimes's mark went unrecognized because a back injury sidelined him for a nine-day stretch during the streak.
AL—13—Taft Wright, Chicago, 1941. Wright's RBI skein ended five days after DiMaggio's hitting streak began.

Most Consecutive Games Played
2130—Lou Gehrig, New York Yankees, 1925–39. Unquestionably the most remarkable streak of this or any other era, Gehrig's skein began on June 1, 1925, when he pinch-hit for shortstop Pee Wee Wanninger; continued because regular first baseman Wally Pipp was beaned in batting practice by Charlie Caldwell (who later earned fame for a streak of his own when he coached Princeton to two straight undefeated football seasons); seemed destined for an early end on July 5, 1925, until Fred Merkle fainted from the heat in the ninth inning after playing the whole game at first base for the Yankees; took a small detour on September 28, 1930, when Gehrig played left field while Babe Ruth pitched and Harry Rice played first base; aroused only mild attention until 1933 when Gehrig surpassed the previous record of 1,307 games set by former Yankees shortstop Everett Scott (whose own streak ended when he was replaced by Pee Wee Wanninger, the man Gehrig pinch-hit for to start his skein); came within a hair of being terminated in 1934 when Gehrig was beaned in a midseason exhibition game; and seemed definitely over a month later when he had to be carried off the field after suffering a back injury, only to see

him penciled in the lineup the following day at shortstop and then replaced by a pinch runner after leading off the game with a single. The streak finally ended on May 2, 1939, when Gehrig, already showing the debilitating effects of the neuromuscular disease that just two years later would claim his life, removed himself from the lineup, allowing Babe Dahlgren to play the entire game at first base. Prior to Scott, the consecutive game record was held by third baseman George Pinckney, who played 577 straight games for the old Brooklyn Bridegrooms. Steve Garvey holds the National League record, playing in 1207 consecutive games before a thumb injury ended his string on July 30, 1983.

Most Consecutive Wins by a Pitcher, League
NL—24—Carl Hubbell, New York Giants, 1936–37
AL—17—Johnny Allen, Cleveland, 1936–37
           Dave McNally, Baltimore, 1968–69

Most Consecutive Wins by a Pitcher, Season, League
NL—19—Tim Keefe, New York Giants, 1888
Rube Marquard, New York Giants, 1912. On July 3, 1912, after beating Brooklyn 2–1, Marquard had an incredible 19–0 record, which should actually **have** been 20–0. Earlier in the season Jeff Tesreau had been credited with a victory that ought to have gone to Marquard, who relieved Tesreau in the top of the ninth inning of a game in which the Giants were trailing and then saw them come back and win in their final turn at bat.

AL—16—Walter Johnson, Washington, 1912
Joe Wood, Boston, 1912; beating Johnson on September 1 to tie Johnson's brand-new record

Lefty Grove, Philadelphia, 1931; missing his chance for an AL season-record 17th straight win when he lost 1–0 to the Browns on August 23, after left-fielder Jimmy Moore, spelling Al Simmons, who took the day off, misplayed a fly ball, leading to the game's only run.

Schoolboy Rowe, Detroit, 1934

Most Consecutive Wins by a Pitcher in His Home Park
20—Lefty Grove, Boston Red Sox, May 3, 1938, through May 12, 1941. In the process Grove forever buried the notion that a southpaw could not win in Fenway Park.

Most Consecutive Wins by a Relief Pitcher

22—Roy Face, Pittsburgh Pirates, 1958–59. Face was only two short of Hubbell's alltime-record 24 straight wins when he lost his next-to-last decision in 1959 after getting off to a 17–0 start.

Most Consecutive Wins by a Pitcher with a Last-Place Team

15—Steve Carlton, Philadelphia Phillies, 1972. Carlton's record streak helped make him a 27-game winner with a team that won only 59 games.

World Series Play: 1920–41

FRANCHISE SUMMARY

Team	League	WS Record through 1941	Last year in WS
Boston	American	5–0	1918
Cleveland	American	1–0	1920
Boston	National	1–0	1914
New York	American	9–3	1941
Cincinnati	National	2–1	1940
Chicago	American	2–1	1919
Philadelphia	American	5–3	1931
St. Louis	National	3–2	1934
Pittsburgh	Natonal	2–2	1927
New York	National	4–8	1937
Washington	American	1–2	1933
Chicago	National	2–7	1938
Detroit	American	1–5	1940
Philadelphia	National	0–1	1915
Brooklyn	National	0–3	1941

Yearly Highlights
1920—Cleveland (AL) defeated Brooklyn (NL) 5 games to 2

Indians player-manager Tris Speaker platooned at three positions—first base, left field and right field—and got a trio of wins from Stan Coveleski, the last pitcher until 1946 to win three in a Series. The Indians also received the first Series grand-slam homer from Elmer Smith, the first Series homer by a pitcher from Jim Bagby, and Bill Wamby's unassisted triple play, the only one in Series history. Cleveland won the pennant despite losing the AL's premier shortstop, Ray Chapman, who was killed by a Carl Mays pitch in August.

1921—New York (NL) defeated New York (AL) 5 games to 3

The first Subway Series and also the last Series played on a best-five-of-nine format. Waite Hoyt of the Yankees pitched three complete games without allowing an earned run but lost one of them, the Series finale, on an error by shortstop Roger Peckinpaugh. In Game Three, the Giants pounded a Series-record 20 hits while winning 13–5.

1922—New York (NL) defeated New York (AL) 4 games to 0

When the best the Yankees could do was a tie in Game Two, manager Miller Huggins was nearly fired, and John McGraw and his Giants seemed to have permanently cemented the Yankees into place as the city's second-best team. Of Babe Ruth, who hit only .118 in the Series, sportswriter Joe Vila wrote: "The exploded phenomenon didn't surprise the smart fans who long ago realized that he couldn't hit brainy pitching. Ruth, therefore, is no longer a wonder. The baseball public is onto his real worth as a batsman and in the future, let us hope, he will attract just ordinary attention."

1923—New York (AL) defeated New York (NL) 4 games to 2

Casey Stengel hit two game-winning homers for the Giants, the first one inside the park, but Ruth, just a year after Vila's put-down, broke out of his Series slump with a vengeance, hitting .368 and hammering three homers.

1924—Washington (AL) defeated New York (NL) 4 games to 3

The most exciting Series to date. Washington won the deciding game in 12 innings, Walter Johnson getting the victory in relief. The winning run came home when Early McNeely's ground ball hit a pebble and bounced over Giants third baseman Fred Lingstrom's head. In McGraw's last Series game he was outfoxed by Senators manager Bucky Harris, who started right-hander Curly Ogden, allowed him to pitch to the required one batter and then brought in lefty George Mogridge, saddling the Giants with a lineup of left-handed hitters.

1925—Pittsburgh (NL) defeated Washington (AL) 4 games to 3

In the eighth inning of Game Three, with the Senators leading 4–3 and two out, Earl Smith of the Pirates hit a drive headed into the temporary right-centerfield seats in Griffith Stadium, but Sam Rice dove over the wall and came out of the crowd clutching the ball. Second base umpire Rigler signaled the catch, but many observers felt that Rice had wrestled the ball out of a fan's hand. On his way to becoming the Series hero when he also led both teams with 12 hits, Rice saw his dream fade when the Pirates, down three games to one, pulled out the next two contests and then rallied to win the seventh game, getting 15 hits and nine runs off Walter Johnson, who was making his last Series appearance. Roger Peckinpaugh, the AL's MVP in 1925, once again became the Series goat when he made eight errors.

1926—St. Louis (NL) defeated New York (AL) 4 games to 3

For the third year in a row the Series went the full seven games. The deciding clash was played in a steady drizzle at Yankee Stadium. Pitching in relief, Pete Alexander struck out the Yankees' Tony Lazzeri with the bases loaded and two out in the seventh inning, preserving a 3-2 Cardinals lead. The Series ended when Babe Ruth was caught trying to steal second base with two out in the ninth inning.

1927—New York (AL) defeated Pittsburgh (NL) 4 games to 0

Herb Pennock of the Yankees had a perfect game going in Game Three until Pie Traynor ended it with one out in the eighth. Ruth and Lou Gehrig between them knocked in 12 runs while the Pirates scored only 10.

1928—New York (AL) defeated St. Louis (NL) 4 games to 0

Ruth set several Series records as he hit three homers and batted .625 while Gehrig knocked home nine runs against a Cardinals pitching staff that had a 6.09 Series ERA.

1929—Philadelphia (AL) defeated Chicago (NL) 4 games to 1

Howard Ehmke broke Ed Walsh's Series record when he fanned 13 Cubs in the opener. The Cubs led 8–0 in the seventh inning of Game Four but lost 10–8 as the A's put on the most amazing one-inning rally in Series history.

1930—Philadelphia (AL) defeated St. Louis (NL) 4 games to 2

Al Simmons and Jimmie Foxx both had a good Series, but it was the pitching of Lefty Grove and George Earnshaw, each of whom won two games, that beat the Cards.

1931—St. Louis (NL) defeated Philadelphia (AL) 4 games to 3

The Cards were led by Pepper Martin, who hit .500 and stole five bases, and Bill Hallahan, who recorded two wins and saved the seventh game.

1932—New York (AL) defeated Chicago (NL) 4 games to 0

Ruth may or may not have "called" his shot in Game Three, but in any event it was his second homer of the game and last in Series play. It came in the fifth inning of a 4–4 game, against Charlie Root, on an 0–2 pitch, a high inside change-up. The homer overrode Gehrig's overall Series effort of three homers and eight RBIs.

1933—New York (NL) defeated Washington (AL) 4 games to 1

In their first Series, Carl Hubbell and Mel Ott of the Giants were the pitching and hitting stars. Hubbell won two games without giving up an earned run, and Ott slugged two homers, the second bringing home the deciding run in the 10th inning of the final game.

1934—St. Louis (NL) defeated Detroit (AL) 4 games to 3

In the sixth inning of the final game, Joe Medwick of the Cardinals slid hard into Tigers third baseman Marv Owen, nearly triggering a riot in Briggs Stadium. When Detroit fans pelted Medwick with fruit and vegetables as he tried to take his left-field post in the bottom of the inning, Commissioner Landis ordered him removed from the game for his own protection. The Cardinals were ahead at the time 9–0 and didn't protest Landis's decision, but if the score had been closer, one wonders whether Landis would not have been forced to declare the first forfeit in Series history.

1935—Detroit (AL) defeated Chicago (NL) 4 games to 2

Lon Warneke's two fine pitching efforts were all the Cubs could point to, as the Tigers made do without Hank Greenberg, who was injured early in the Series.

1936—New York (AL) defeated New York (NL) 4 games to 2

After losing the opener 6–1 to Carl Hubbell, the Yankees scored 42 runs in the next five games, including a record 18 in Game Two.

1937—New York (AL) defeated New York (NL) 4 games to 1

Hubbell's win in Game Four was all that prevented the Yankees from sweeping.

1938—New York (AL) defeated Chicago (NL) 4 games to 0

Stan Hack of the Cubs hit .471 to lead all Series batters. The rest of the accolades once again belonged to the Yankees.

1939—New York (AL) defeated Cincinnati (NL) 4 games to 0

The Reds hung tough before losing the opener 2–1 in the ninth inning and took the Yankees to 10 innings before dropping Game Four but managed only 12 singles in the other two contests.

1940—Cincinnati (NL) defeated Detroit (AL) 4 games to 3

Two complete-game victories by both Bucky Walters and Paul Derringer sparked the Reds to their first untainted World Championship.

1941—New York (AL) defeated Brooklyn (NL) 4 games to 1

In Game Three, Fred Fitzsimmons of the Dodgers blanked the Yankees for seven innings before a line drive off the bat of Yankees pitcher Marius Russo broke his kneecap and forced him to leave the game. The Dodgers ultimately lost 2–1 and then dropped Game Four in the ninth inning when Tommy Henrich fanned for what should have been the final out of a 4–3 Dodgers victory, only to have the third strike elude catcher Mickey Owen and Henrich reach first base. Before the Yankees were retired they scored four runs and broke open the most competitive Series they had been in since 1926.

SECTION 4

SECTION 4

Famous Firsts:
1942–60

1942—Ted Lyons sets a post deadball era record when he makes 20 starts and completes all 20 games.

1943—To save on rubber, which is in short supply during the war, a new balata baseball is manufactured and used. It results in no home runs being hit in the first 11 games of the season and shutouts in 11 of the first 29 games. Finally, the balls left over from 1942 are brought out of the closet while balls with a better quality of rubber cement are rushed into production.

1944—On July 20, in a game against the Yankees, Nels Potter of the Browns becomes the first pitcher ever to be ejected expressly for violating the spitball rule.

1945—The Washington Senators miss becoming the only team in modern history to vault from last place to a pennant the following year when they lose their final game of the season to the A's in extra innings on a fly ball that outfielder Bingo Binks, who's neglected to don sunglasses after the sun breaks through late in the day, loses in the brightness.

1945—The National League's leader in pitching wins, leader in pitching losses, runner-up in stolen bases and the Red Sox leader in saves all have the same last name—Barrett—and no two of them are related.

1947—Pitcher Bill Voiselle of the Braves, who resides in Ninety-Six, North Carolina, becomes the first player to wear the name of his hometown on the back of his uniform when he appears on the field bearing number 96.

1947—Bonus baby Joe Tepsic stings the Dodgers and quits rather than be sent to the minors after spending the 1946 season with the club.

1947—"Howling Hilda" Chester, now at her peak, lets other Dodgers fans know how she feels about Tepsic's betrayal. With her ringing cow bells and shouts to Dodgers players until they wave to her in their seat in the Ebbets Field bleachers, Chester prefers the sobriquet "Queen of the Bleachers" to "Howling Hilda." Before each game she can be seen carrying a banner with her name on it and earning the price of admission by selling songsheets at the corner of Dekalb Avenue and Flatbush Extension. When the Dodgers are out of town, she bides her time by selling newspapers in downtown Brooklyn. Chester has her counterparts in Mary Ott, the "Horse Lady of St. Louis," who for 25 years has been the scourge of umpires and visiting players to Sportsman's Park, and "Megaphone Lolly" Hopkins in Boston. Hopkins, however, is considerably more genteel than Ott and much less partisan than Chester; she bestows her cheers not only on Braves and Red Sox players but also on players from visiting teams should they happen to do something that pleases her.

1948—There are no Hildas or Lollys or Marys in Cleveland, but there is Joe Early, a night watchman, who writes to Indians owner Bill Veeck, asking how come players are always honored—why not a fan every now and then? Why not indeed, responds Veeck, and he has a special night for Early at which Early receives an outhouse, a backfiring Model T and some weird animals, plus a Ford convertible, luggage, a refrigerator, a washing machine, a watch, a stereo, clothes and lots more. Between Veeck's promotions and the first Cleveland pennant-winner in 28 years, the Indians draw 2,620,627 and shatter every all-time attendance record.

1949—Mel Allen is first heard to utter the line that made him famous, "How about that?" when Joe DiMaggio returns to the New York lineup after being disabled by a bone spur and cracks a hit his first time up. Another colorful bit of work from that same era, though never heard nationally, comes from Pittsburgh's Rosie Rosewell, who says, each time Ralph Kiner cranks one out of Forbes Field, "Open the window, Aunt Minnie, here it comes!" pauses a moment, and then shatters a light bulb over the air.

1951—Bill Veeck, now the owner of the Browns, hires Eddie Gaedel, a three-foot-seven-inch midget, and uses him as a pinch hitter for leadoff man Frank Saucier in the bottom of the first inning of a game on August 19 against Detroit. Pitcher Bob Cain of the Tigers, after he realizes it isn't a gag and stops laughing, walks Gaedel on four pitches. American League president Will Harridge is appalled when he learns of Veeck's latest innovation and orders Gaedel's at-bat stricken from the record book until it's pointed out to him by Veek that the game's stats will thereupon make it seem that Cain pitched to no one.

1951—Russ Hodges utters the most famous single line ever mouthed by a play-by-play announcer when he ecstatically shouts, shrieks and sobs, "The Giants win the pennant!" over and over again after Bobby Thomson's three-run homer abruptly ends the National League pennant playoff series between the Giants and the Dodgers.

1953—Paul Pettit, the Pirates' $100,000 bonus baby, posts a 7.11 ERA but manages to win a game, for which the Pirates are grateful. Cleveland's $100,000 bonus baby, Billy Joe Davidson, in contrast, never even throws a single pitch in a major-league game.

1954—The sacrifice fly rule, tinkered with for years, sometimes in effect and other times not, is once again adopted and this time remains on the books; a batter who hits a run-scoring fly ball is henceforth not charged with time at bat.

1954—Players for the first time are no longer allowed to leave their gloves on the playing field while their team is at bat.

1950s—Warning tracks are at last required in the outfields of all major-league parks. Padded fences, however, will not be mandatory until the 1970s.

1956—Robin Roberts of the Phillies is tagged for a National League record 46 home runs on his way to surrendering an all-time career record 502 homers.

1957—The American League makes batting helmets mandatory. Prior to this many players have already begun wearing them.

1957—Pedro Ramos of the Senators surrenders 43 home runs, a new American League season record.

1960—Jerry Holtzman of the *Chicago Sun Times* helps initiate the crediting of "saves" to relief pitchers.

1960—White Sox owner Bill Veeck is the first to put names on the backs of his team's uniforms. Veeck also unveils an exploding scoreboard in Comiskey Park. On the other hand, Veeck's crosstown rival, the Chicago Cubs, calmly ally themselves with the Red Sox and remain the last clubs to have a manually operated scoreboard until 1986, when the Oakland A's turn back the clock and convert their scoreboard to a human-run operation.

Batting Title
Record Holders

Ted Williams and Stan Musial were unquestionably the elite hitters in their respective leagues during the period between 1942 and 1960. The last two players to retire with career averages above .330, they each set numerous offensive records, not the least of which are their league marks for the longest span of time between their first and last batting titles. Williams took his initial American League crown in 1941 and his final crown an all-time record 17 years later; Musial holds the National League record with a 14-year spread between his first triumph in 1943 and his last in 1957.

Most Batting Titles Won
  AL—12—Ty Cobb, last in 1919
  NL—8—Honus Wagner, last in 1911

Other Players Who Won Four or More Batting Titles
  7—Rod Carew (AL), last in 1978
     Stan Musial (NL), last in 1957
     Rogers Hornsby (NL), last in 1928
  6—Ted Williams (AL), last in 1958
  4—Bill Madlock (NL), last in 1983
     Roberto Clemente (NL), last in 1967
     Harry Heilmann (Al), last in 1927

Most Batting Titles Won Prior to 1901
  5—Dan Brouthers led the National League in 1882, 1883, 1889 and 1892 and the American Association in 1891. The only other players ever to lead two different major leagues batting were Pete Browning, who won the American Association batting crown in 1882 and 1885 and the Players League batting crown in 1890, and Ed Delahanty, National League in 1899 and American League in 1902.

Most Consecutive Batting Titles Won
AL—9—Ty Cobb, 1907–15
NL—6—Rogers Hornsby, 1920–25

Youngest Batting Title Winner
AL—Al Kaline, Detroit, 1955; 20 years old
NL—Pete Reiser, Brooklyn, 1941; 22 years old

Oldest Batting Title Winner
AL—Ted Williams, Boston, 1958; 40 years old
NL—Honus Wagner, Pittsburgh, 1911; 37 years old

Oldest Player to Win His First Batting Title
NL—Al Oliver, Montreal, 1982; 35 years old
AL—Charlie Gehringer, Detroit, 1937; 34 years old

Most Batting Title Winners, Team
NL—22—Pittsburgh; won by 10 different players; last winner was Bill Madlock in 1983.
AL—18—Detroit; 12 won by Ty Cobb, four by Harry Heilmann, and one each by Charlie Gehringer and Al Kaline, the last winner in 1955

Fewest Batting Title Winners, Team
NL—0—New York Mets; Houston Astros; Giants while in San Francisco
AL—0—Milwaukee Brewers; Toronto Blue Jays; Seattle Mariners; Washington–Texas Rangers; A's while in Oakland

Most Seasons Since Last Batting Title Winner, Team
AL—43—Chicago; last winner was Luke Appling in 1943. Appling, who also won in 1938, is the only White Sox player ever to lead the AL in batting.
NL—32—New York–San Francisco Giants; last winner was Willie Mays in 1954

Only Third Basemen to Win More Than One Batting Title
NL—4—Bill Madlock, 1975, 1976, 1981 and 1983
AL—3—Wade Boggs, 1983, 1985, and 1986
—2—George Brett, 1976 and 1980

Last Shortstop to Win a Batting Title
AL—Lou Boudreau, Cleveland, 1944
NL—Dick Groat, Pittsburgh, 1960. Only three shortstops

have won NL batting titles since 1901—Honus Wagner, Arky Vaughan and Groat—and all three played for the Pirates.

Only Catchers to Win a Batting Title
NL—Bubbles Hargrave, Cincinnati, 1926
  Ernie Lombardi, Cincinnati, 1938, and Boston, 1942
AL—None

Only Pitcher Ever to Win a Batting Title
Guy Hecker, Louisville (AA), 1886. Hecker was one of a kind. Nicknamed "The Big Blond," he didn't begin his professional career until he was in his mid-twenties and played only nine seasons in the majors after his belated start. But he packed so many extraordinary feats into his brief career that he could occupy a full page in the all-time record book by himself. As a rookie with Louisville in 1882, Hecker authored a no-hitter, only the second in American Association history, which was further distinguished by the fact that his teammates made six errors behind him. Two years later he won 52 games for Louisville, an Association record. In 1886 Hecker slipped to only 27 wins but hit .342, edging out teammate Pete Browning for the AA batting crown by two points. That same season, in a game against Baltimore on August 15, Hecker hit three home runs, the only AA player ever to do so, and in addition crossed the plate seven times, an all-time one-game record. Now the possessor of batting, slugging and pitching marks that can never be surpassed, Hecker was still not done. Versatile enough to play elsewhere when he wasn't pitching, he set an unsurpassable *fielding* record on October 9, 1887, when he became the first player in major-league history to play an entire game at first base without handling a single chance.

Most Recent Batting Title Winner to Repeat the Following Season
NL—Dave Parker, Pittsburgh, 1977–78
AL—Wade Boggs, Boston, 1985–86

Most Recent Player to Win a Batting Title without Hitting a Home Run
AL—Rod Carew, Minnesota, 1972
NL—Zack Wheat, Brooklyn, 1918

Fewest Base Hits by a Batting Title Winner
NL—102—Ernie Lombardi, Boston, 1942
AL—127—Ty Cobb, Detroit, 1914

Biggest Leap in Average from Previous Season by Batting Title Winner
NL—97 points—Carl Furillo, Brooklyn, 1953; hit .247 in 1952, .344 in 1953
AL—85 points—Mickey Vernon, Washington, 1946; hit .268 in 1943, .353 in 1946 after losing two years to military service

Biggest Drop in Average Season after Winning Batting Title
AL—118 points—Norm Cash, Detroit, 1962; hit .361 in 1961, .243 in 1962
NL—99 points—Willie McGee, St. Louis, 1986; hit .353 in 1985, .254 in 1986

Most Discouraging Season after Winning Batting Title
NL—Rico Carty, Atlanta, 1971. Carty hit .366 to win the NL batting title in 1970, then missed all of 1971 while being treated for tuberculosis. He never again had a season as a full-time regular, and only the DH rule in the American League saved his career.
AL—George Sisler, St. Louis, 1923. After Sisler won the AL batting crown in 1922, surgery for sinus blockages that affected his eyesight idled him for the entire 1923 season; he was never again the same player.

Only Players to Win Two Batting Titles with Averages Below Their Career Averages
Ty Cobb, Detroit, 1906 (.350), 1907 (.324); .367 career average
Ted Williams, Boston Red Sox, 1947 (.343), 1958 (.328); .344 career average

Multiple Batting Title Winners Who Retired with Career Averages Below .300
AL—Carl Yastrzemski, Boston, 1963, 1967 and 1968; .285 career average
Pete Runnels, Boston, 1960 and 1962; .291 career average
Ferris Fain, Philadelphia, 1950 and 1951; .290 career average
NL—None

Highest Batting Average to Win Batting Title, since 1901
NL—.424—Rogers Hornsby, St. Louis, 1924
AL—.422—Nap Lajoie, Philadelphia, 1901

Highest Batting Average Failing to Win Batting Title, since 1901
AL—.408—Joe Jackson, Cleveland, 1911; runner-up to Ty Cobb's .420. Cobb's .401 average in 1922, second to George Sisler's .420, is the only other .400 season in this century that failed to win a batting crown.

NL—.393—Babe Herman, Brooklyn, 1930; runner-up to Bill Terry's .401

Lowest Average to Win Batting Title
AL—.301—Carl Yastrzemski, Boston, 1968
NL—.320—Larry Doyle, New York Giants, 1915

Closest Batting Title Races
First place—Snuffy Stirnweiss of the Yankees won the AL batting crown in 1945 by less than a thousandth of a point, hitting .30854 to Tony Cuccinello's .30845. After missing the batting title by the narrowest margin in history, Cuccinello was released by the White Sox and never again played in the majors.

Second Place—George Kell, Detroit, won the AL batting crown in 1949 by .00016 of a point over Ted Williams, Boston Red Sox.

Third Place—Chick Hafey, St. Louis Cardinals, won the NL batting crown in 1931 by .00028 of a point over Bill Terry, New York Giants. Both hit .349 when their averages were rounded off. In third place with a .348 average was Jim Bottomley of the Cardinals.

Fourth Place—Alex Johnson, California Angels, won the AL batting crown in 1970 by .00037 of a point over Carl Yastrzemski, Boston Red Sox.

Most Disputed Batting Title
First Place—For 70 years Ty Cobb was credited with winning the 1910 AL batting title by a single point—.385 to .384—over Nap Lajoie of Cleveland despite efforts on Lajoie's behalf by St. Louis Browns manager Jack O'Connor and coach Harry Howell, who instructed rookie third baseman Red Corriden to play deep each time Lajoie batted in a doubleheader on the last day of the season. Corriden's

positioning allowed Lajoie to beat out eight bunts and resulted in both O'Connor and Howell being barred from future major-league jobs. In 1981 the *Sporting News* discovered that Lajoie had won after all—.384 to .383—because Cobb received double credit for a 2-for-3 game, and two hitless at bats were omitted from his statistics. The *Sporting News* is right, yet it's also true that Lajoie's season-ending flurry of hits was tainted. Your choice who the real winner was.

Second Place—In 1976 George Brett of the Kansas City Royals won the AL batting title over teammate Hal McRae when outfielder Steve Brye of the Minnesota Twins allowed a fly ball Brett hit on his last at bat of the season to fall safely. Brye made only a token attempt to deny he'd deliberately engineered Brett's batting title win and justified his machinations by claiming that Brett, a third baseman, was more deserving of the crown than McRae, a designated hitter. Again, your choice who really won.

Handicapped Players

In 1945 the St. Louis Browns purchased Pete Gray, the MVP the previous year in the Southern Association. The Browns claimed they were seeking outfield help, but cynics felt Gray's acquisition was only an attempt to bolster sagging attendance, as he had only one arm. Gray played 77 games for the 1945 Browns. It was a remarkable achievement for a man missing a limb, but Gray was not the only severely handicapped player to make it all the way to the major leagues.

Most Successful One-Armed Player
Hugh "One Arm" Daily. Daily pitched in the National League, Union Association and American Association from 1882 to 1887. In 1883, pitching for Cleveland, he led the National League in bases on balls and threw a no-hitter against Philadelphia; the following year he led all Union Association hurlers in strikeouts. No known photographs of Daily have survived, unfortunately, but we know it was his left arm that was lacking and that, since he was a pitcher, he couldn't have worn a glove while in the field. Reportedly, Daily fielded hard-hit balls by first blocking them with a pad attached to his truncated left forearm.

Major-League Pitcher Overcoming the Greatest Handicap
Bert Shepard, a former minor-league pitcher, lost a leg after being shot down over Germany in World War II while serving as an Army Air Corps pilot. Outfitted with an artificial leg, he was signed as a coach by the Washington Senators in 1945. After pitching in several exhibition games, he made a relief appearance on August 14 in the regular-season game against the Red Sox and gave up only one run in five innings. Shepard, who came to bat three times during

his relief stint, also classifies as the hitter overcoming the greatest handicap. In 1948, while managing the Class B Waterbury, Connecticut, club, he played several games at first base.

Most Successful Handicapped Pitcher, since 1901

Luther "Dummy" Taylor, a deaf-mute, won 21 games for the New York Giants in 1904 and 112 games over a nine-year career. One of only two deaf-mutes to play in the majors, after leaving baseball Taylor worked as a housefather at the Illinois School for the Deaf in Jacksonville, where he helped Dick Sipek, who was partly deaf, to become a good enough outfielder to play with the Cincinnati Reds in the middle 1940s.

Most Successful Handicapped Pitcher, since Taylor

Many players have had lengthy major-league careers despite missing toes and fingers, two Hall of Famers, Three Finger Brown and Red Ruffing, among them; Gray, Shepard and Daily were the only three who managed to play without a limb. But another Daley—Buddy Daley—pitched in the American League for 10 years with nearly as great a handicap. Daley had a withered right arm, the result of an injury incurred at birth, but was still able to win 60 games, plus one in the 1961 World Series.

Smallest Player

Eddie Gaedel, the midget Bill Veeck hired in 1951, stood three feet seven inches and weighed 67 pounds. Apart from Gaedel, the smallest player was five-foot-two-inch Nin Alexander, who played a handful of games in 1884, but the smallest player to play a full season in the majors was probably Dicky Pearce, listed as having been only five feet, three-and-a-half inches. The smallest player to become a star was Dummy Hoy, who was five foot four inches and weighed 148 pounds. Hoy was easily the most successful handicapped player of all time; not only was he diminutive but he was a deaf-mute. His dual handicap kept him from making the major leagues until he was given a chance in 1888 by Washington at age 26. He went on to play 14 seasons and compile over 2000 hits. Among the many other successful small players were Harry Chappas, five feet, three inches; Hugh Nicol, five feet, four inches; Davy Force, five feet, four inches; Willie Keeler, five feet, four-and-a-half inches; Sparky Adams, five feet, four-and-a-half inches; Freddy Patek, five feet, five inches; Albie Pearson, five feet, five inches; and Bobby Shantz, five feet, six inches but only 139 pounds. Special mention: Ernie Oravetz, an outfielder with the Washington Senators for two years in the 1950s, was not only five feet, four inches but also wore glasses.

Tallest Player

Johnny Gee, who won seven games in the National League between 1939 and 1946, was six feet, nine inches—an inch taller than Gene Conley, the most successful tall player. Conley won 91 games for the Braves, Phillies and Red Sox in the 1950s and early 1960s. At one point in his career Conley also played with the NBA Boston Celtics during the winter months.

First Player to Wear Glasses

Will White, pitcher, 1877–86, and a 229-game winner

First Player in the 20th Century to Wear Glasses

Lee Meadows, St. Louis Cardinals, 1915

First Player Other Than a Pitcher to Wear Glasses

George Toporcer, St. Louis Cardinals, 1921

First Catcher to Wear Glasses

Clint Courtney, New York Yankees, 1951

First Winner of Most Valuable Player Award to Wear Glasses

NL—Jim Konstanty, Philadelphia, 1950
AL—Dick Allen, Chicago, 1972

First League Leader in a Major Hitting Department to Wear Glasses

NL—Chick Hafey, St. Louis, 1931, won the batting title.
AL—Bob Dillinger, St. Louis, 1948, had the most base hits.

First 20-Game Winner to Wear Glasses, since 1901

NL—Lee Meadows, Pittsburgh, 1926 (20–9)
AL—Mel Harder, Cleveland, 1934 (20–12)

First Player With One Eye

AA—Billl Irwin, Cincinnati pitcher, 1886

AL—Hi Jasper, pitcher for Chicago, Cleveland and St. Louis from 1914 to 1919.

NL—Tom Sunkel, pitcher for St. Louis, New York and Brooklyn from 1937 to 1944

Firsts by Black Players

The first black professional baseball player, according to most sources, was John Jackson, who played under the name of Bud Fowler with the Newcastle, Pennsylvania, club in 1872. During the next two decades a number of other black players made their marks in the minor leagues. The two best probably were second baseman Frank Grant, who broke in with Buffalo in the International League in 1886 and was called the "Black Fred Dunlap," and George Stovey, the leading pitcher in the International League in the mid-1880's. Grant and Stovey would have both undoubtedly played in either the American Association or the National League, along with many other black players who were their contemporaries, had they not encountered a latent prejudice that emerged and soon permeated all of organized baseball when the Toledo American Association club hired the Walker brothers in 1884.

First Black Major-League Player
   Probably catcher Fleet Walker with Toledo in 1884, followed shortly thereafter by his younger brother Welday, an outfielder. Fleet actually made his professional debut with Toledo a year earlier when the team was in the Northwest League. In 50 games he batted .251, and the following season, facing stronger AA pitching, raised his average to .263, a highly respectable showing for a catcher in an era when many backstoppers hit below .200. The Walkers first attracted the attention of Toledo manager Charlie Morton while they were playing for Oberlin College. Welday did little in the few major-league games he played, but Fleet was good enough to keep another rookie catcher, Deacon McGuire, on the bench for much of the 1884 season. McGuire would go on to become the first player to catch in over 1500

major-league games, while Walker's big-league experience would last only a few months. Not all historians agree, however, that the Walkers were the first black major leaguers. In 1882 the Providence Grays signed catcher Sandy Nava and used him for the next three seasons to spell their regular backstopper Barney Gilligan. Nava, the first native San Franciscan to play in the majors, explained his dark complexion by saying he was Cuban. Whether or not Nava was actually black is impossible to determine now, but it may be significant that when prejudice began mushrooming later in the decade he was phased out of the major leagues.

First Professional Black Player in the 20th Century

Technically, it was Jimmy Claxton, who pitched briefly in 1916 for the Oakland Oaks in the Pacific Coast League, but once again there is lots of room for debate. In 1901 John McGraw tried to sign Charlie Grant, a black second baseman, to a contract with the Baltimore Orioles, who were about to begin their fledgling season in the American League. To circumvent the issue of Grant's color, McGraw presented him as Tokohama, a full-blooded Cherokee Indian, after he saw a creek with that name on a wall map in the Hot Springs, Arkansas, hotel where the Orioles were staying during spring training. But White Sox owner Charlie Comiskey, among others, saw through the hoax and blocked Grant's signing. A few years later, as manager of the New York Giants, McGraw attempted to hire a Cuban pitcher named Jose Mendez, but Mendez's nickname alone—"the Black Matty"—unified rival National League clubs against McGraw's integration effort. In 1911, however, the Cincinnati Reds successfully managed to sign two light-skinned Cubans named Rafael Almeida and Armando Marsans. Almeida failed to stick, but Marsans proved to be a pretty good outfielder and paved the way for other clubs, the Washington Senators in particular, to import more Cuban players. All of course were light-skinned, but there have been numerous light-skinned Latin players who, since the color line was finally broken, have acknowledged their ancestry was at least partially black. So it's safe to say, I think, that one or two black players besides the Walkers—and one hopes a lot more than that—found ways before 1946 to get past the color barrier.

First Black American Player Officially Accepted by Organized Baseball in the 20th Century
Jackie Robinson in 1946 with the Montreal Royals, Brooklyn's International League farm club. In his first game in organized baseball, on April 18, 1946, at Roosevelt Stadium in Jersey City, Robinson collected three singles and a home run off Jersey City's Phil Oates.

First Black American to Play in the National League
Jackie Robinson. He made his major-league debut with Brooklyn on April 15, 1947, against the Boston Braves, went hitless, and was 0-for-20 after his first five games. Robinson ended the 1947 season with a .297 batting average, led the National League in stolen bases, and was named Rookie of the Year.

First Black American to Play in the American League
Larry Doby, Cleveland, 1947. Used mainly at second base and as a pinchhitter, Doby hit only .156 in 29 games. Moved to center field the following spring, he hit .301 and sparked the Indians to their first pennant since 1920.

First Black American to Pitch in the National League
Dan Bankhead, Brooklyn, 1947. Used as a reliever in four games, he had an 0–0 record but homered in his first major-league at bat. In the fall he became the first black pitcher to play in a World Series—though not the first to pitch in one—when he got into a game as a pinch runner.

First Black American to Pitch in the American League
Satchel Paige, Cleveland, 1948. Paige was also the first black to win a game and the first to pitch a shutout, both occurring in his first major-league start. On October 10, 1948, he became, in addition, the first black to pitch in a World Series game when he worked two-thirds of an inning in relief.

First Black Pitcher to Win a World Series Game
Joe Black, Brooklyn, started and won the first game of the 1952 Series.

First Black Pitcher to Throw a No-Hitter
Sam Jones, Chicago Cubs, May 12, 1955, against Pittsburgh

First Black Pitcher to Win 20 Games in a Season
   NL—Don Newcombe, Brooklyn, 1955 (20–5)
   AL—Mudcat Grant, Minnesota, 1965 (21–7)

First Black Manager
   AL—Frank Robinson, Cleveland, 1975
   NL—Frank Robinson, San Francisco, 1981

First Black to Be a League Leader in Fielding Average
   NL—Jackie Robinson, Brooklyn, 1948, led all second basemen with a .980 FA.
   AL—Vic Power, Kansas City A's, 1957, led first basemen with a .998 FA.

First Black Umpire
   Emmett Ashford, American League, 1965. Ashford retired in 1970 and died of a heart attack in 1980.

YOUR FAVORITE TEAM'S FIRST BLACK PLAYERS

(Teams in Existence Prior to 1961)

Team	First Black Player	Second Black Player	First Black Regular
Brooklyn Dodgers	Jackie Robinson, 1947	Dan Bankhead, 1947	Jackie Robinson, 1947
Cleveland Indians	Larry Doby, 1947	Satchel Paige, 1948	Larry Doby, 1948
St. Louis Browns	Hank Thompson, 1947	Willard Brown, 1947	Satchel Paige, 1952
New York Giants	Hank Thompson, 1949	Monte Irvin, 1949	Hank Thompson, 1950
Boston Braves	Sam Jethroe, 1950	Luis Marquez, 1951	Sam Jethroe, 1950
Chicago White Sox	Minnie Minoso, 1951	Sam Hairston, 1951	Minnie Minoso, 1951
Philadelphia A's	Bob Trice, 1953	Vic Power, 1954	Vic Power, 1954
Chicago Cubs	Ernie Banks, 1953	Gene Baker, 1953	Banks and Baker, 1954
Pittsburgh Pirates	Curt Roberts, 1954	Sam Jethroe, 1954	Curt Roberts, 1954
St. Louis Cards	Tom Alston, 1954	Brooks Lawrence, 1954	Curt Flood, 1958
Cincinnati Reds	Nino Escalera, 1954	Chuck Harmon, 1954	Frank Robinson, 1956
Washington Senators	Carlos Paula, 1954	Joe Black, 1957	Carlos Paula, 1954

Team	First Black Player	Second Black Player	First Black Regular
New York Yankees	Elston Howard, 1955	Harry Simpson, 1957	Elston Howard, 1959
Philadelphia Phillies	John Kennedy, 1957	Chuck Harmon, 1957	Pancho Herrera and Tony Taylor, 1960
Detroit Tigers	Ozzie Virgil, 1958	Larry Doby, 1958	Jake Wood, 1961
Boston Red Sox	Pumpsie Green, 1959	Earl Wilson, 1959	Willie Tasby, 1960

Note: The St. Louis Browns, the third team to integrate, never had a black regular until after the franchise moved to Baltimore (Bob Boyd, 1956). Paige, who had a 12–10 record in 138 innings in 1952, was the first black to see more than token action with the team.

Thompson and Irvin debuted in the same game with the Giants in 1949; ditto Banks and Barker with the Cubs in 1953 and Escalera and Harmon with the Reds in 1954.

Some sources credit Hairston with being the White Sox first black player in July 1951; by then, however, Minoso had already been with the team for several weeks.

FIRST BLACK LEAGUE LEADERS

Batting

Department	National League	American League
Batting Average	Jackie Robinson, Brooklyn, 1949	Tony Oliva, Minnesota, 1964
Slugging Average	Willie Mays, N.Y. Giants, 1954	Larry Doby, Cleveland, 1952
Home runs	Willie Mays, N.Y. Giants, 1955	Larry Doby, Cleveland, 1952
RBIs	Monte Irvin, N.Y. Giants, 1951	Larry Doby, Cleveland, 1954
Stolen Bases	Jackie Robinson, Brooklyn, 1947	Minnie Minoso, Chicago, 1951
Hits	Willie Mays, S.F. Giants, 1960	Minnie Minoso, Cleveland, 1960
Runs	Frank Robinson, Cincinnati, 1956	Larry Doby, Cleveland, 1952
Doubles	Hank Aaron, Milwaukee, 1955	Minnie Minoso, Chicago, 1957
Triples	Hank Thompson, N.Y. Giants, 1952	Minnie Minoso, Chicago, 1951

Department	National League	American League
Bases on Balls	Jim Gilliam, Los Angeles, 1959	Dick Allen, Chicago, 1972 Roy White, New York, 1972
Strikeouts	Pancho Herrera, Philadelphia, 1960	Larry Doby, Cleveland, 1952
Total Bases	Willie Mays, N.Y. Giants, 1955	Tony Oliva, Minnesota, 1964

Pitching

Wins	Don Newcombe, Brooklyn, 1957	Mudcat Grant, Minnesota, 1965
Losses	Sam Jones, Chicago, 1955	Orlando Pena, Kansas City A's, 1963
Winning Pct.	Don Newcombe, Brooklyn, 1955	Mudcat Grant, Minnesota, 1965
Shutouts	Bob Gibson, St. Louis, 1962	Mudcat Grant, Minnesota, 1965
Strikeouts	Don Newcombe, Brooklyn, 1951	Al Downing, New York, 1964
ERA	Sam Jones, San Francisco, 1959	Luis Tiant, Cleveland, 1968
Bases on Balls	Sam Jones, Chicago, 1955	Earl Wilson, Boston, 1963
Complete Games	Juan Marichal, San Francisco, 1964	Fergie Jenkins, Texas, 1974

Awards

Rookie of the Year	Jackie Robinson, Brooklyn, 1947	Tony Oliva, Minnesota, 1964
Most Valuable Player	Jackie Robinson, Brooklyn, 1949	Elston Howard, New York, 1963
Cy Young	Don Newcombe, Brooklyn, 1956	Vida Blue, Oakland, 1971

Eagle-eyed Hitters

Ted Williams owned many records when he retired in 1960. Most have since been broken, but one that still stands is his career mark for the highest bases on balls average. Williams walked .208 percent of the times he stepped to the plate: Max Bishop, with a career bases on balls average of .204, is the only other player above .200. Williams also still holds the record for the most consecutive seasons as a league leader in bases on balls—six, from 1941 through 1949, excepting the 1943, 1944 and 1945 seasons when he was in the military service.

Most Seasons League Leader in Bases on Balls
    AL—11—Babe Ruth, last in 1933
    NL—6—Mel Ott, last in 1942

Most Seasons 100 or More Bases on Balls
    AL—13—Babe Ruth, last in 1934
    NL—10—Mel Ott, last in 1942. Ott also set an all-time major-league record in 1942 when he received 100 or more walks for he seventh consecutive season.

Most Bases on Balls, Season
    AL—170—Babe Ruth, New York, 1923
    NL—148—Eddie Stanky, Brooklyn, 1945
            Jimmy Wynn, Houston, 1969

Fewest Bases on Balls, Season, Minimum 500 at Bats
    AL—6—George Stovall, Cleveland, 1909; 565 at bats
    NL—9—Virgil Stallcup, Cincinnati, 1949; 575 at bats

Fewest Bases on Balls, 154-Game Season, League Leader in Bases on Balls
    NL—69—Hack Wilson, Chicago, 1926
    AL—90—Willie Kamm and Johnny Mostil, Chicago, 1925

Most Intentional Bases on Balls, Season
45—Willie McCovey, San Francisco, 1969

Most Bases on Balls, Season, Pinch Hitter
AL—18—Elmer Valo, Washington, 1960
NL—16—Harry McCurdy, Philadelphia, 1933
    Merv Rettenmund, San Diego, 1977

Most Consecutive Games Receiving at Least One Base on Balls
AL—22—Roy Cullenbine, Detroit, July 2 through July 24, 1947
NL—15—Darrell Evans, Atlanta, April 9 through April 27, 1976

Most Bases on Balls, Game, Since 1893
AL—6—Jimmie Foxx, Boston, June 16, 1938
NL—5—held by many players, but Mel Ott of the New York Giants, who walked five times in a game on four separate occasions, is the only player ever to do it more than twice.

MOST BASES ON BALLS, CAREER, TOP 10

	Years Active	*Bases on Balls*
1. Babe Ruth	1914–35	2056[1]
2. Ted Williams	1939–60	2019
3. Joe Morgan	1963–84	1865
4. Carl Yastrzemski	1961–83	1844
5. Mickey Mantle	1951–68	1734
6. Mel Ott	1926–47	1708
7. Eddie Yost	1944–62	1614[2]
8. Stan Musial	1941–63	1599
9. Pete Rose	1963–	1566[3]
10. Harmon Killebrew	1954–75	1559

[1]The only player on the top 10 list who was active before 1920.

[2]The only leadoff hitter on the list and also the only player with fewer than 2000 career hits.

[3]With so many modern players on the list, you should rightfully wonder where the eagle-eyed hitters of the game's early days rank. Ty Cobb, for one, is only 17th in career bases on balls. Willie Keeler, five feet, four-and-a-half inches and reputedly the most deft bat handler ever, is nowhere to be found—he had just 524 walks in 8594 at bats.

Most Intentional Bases on Balls, Game
5—Mel Ott, New York Giants, on October 5, 1929, in the second game of a doubleheader against the Phillies and the last game of the season. Ott began the game one home run behind the Phillies Chuck Klein in the NL home run derby; to ensure Klein of the crown, Phillies pitchers purposely passed Ott every time he came to bat.

First Player to be Given an Intentional Pass with the Bases Loaded
Nap Lajoie, Philadelphia Athletics, May 23, 1901, while he was en route to the Triple Crown.

Most Bases on Balls, Season, Team
AL—835—Boston, 1949
NL—732—Brooklyn, 1947

Fewest Bases on Balls, Career, Minimum 5000 at Bats
174—George Stovall, 1904–15; 5218 at bats

Fewest Bases on Balls, Career, Minimum 4000 at Bats
138—Jesus Alou, 1963–79; 4345 at bats. Alou also seldom struck out, so fielders, knowing that contact was imminent, were unusually alert when he came to bat.

Fewest Bases on Balls, Career, Minimum 1500 at Bats
25—Rob Picciolo, 1977–85; 1628 at bats. In 1979 Picciolo, probably the most impatient hitter in history, walked only three times in 348 at bats.

HIGHEST ON-BASE PERCENTAGE, CAREER, TOP TEN
(Minimum 1000 games)

		Years Active	On Base Pct.
1.	Ted Williams	1939–1960	.483
2.	Babe Ruth	1914–35	.474
3.	John McGraw	1891–1906	.464[1]
4.	Billy Hamilton	1888–1901	.455
5.	Lou Gehrig	1923–39	.447
6.	Rogers Hornsby	1915–37	.434
7.	Ty Cobb	1905–28	.433

		Years Active	On base Pct.
8.	Jimmie Foxx	1925–45	.430
9.	Tris Speaker	1907–28	.427
10.	Ferris Fain	1947–55	.424[2]

[1]McGraw and Hamilton were two of the best players in the 1890s at coaxing walks. Even so, the generally inflated batting averages of the period resulted in their being higher on the list than they probably belong.

[2]The one real surprise on the list. Eddie Yost, Ted Williams, Eddie Joost and Eddie Stanky were the recognized masters at drawing walks in the late 1940s and early 1950s, but Fain was just as good. One illustration of how difficult it is to achieve a career on-bases percentage of .400 or better: In 1980 Mike Hargrove's career percentage was .405; it subsequently slipped below .400, but before it did he was the only active player above that figure, and there have been none since who retired with a .400 percentage.

The Four Most Interesting Teams between 1942 and 1960

1946 BROOKLYN DODGERS
W-96 L-60
Manager: Leo Durocher

Regular Lineup—1B, Ed Stevens; 2B, Eddie Stanky; 3B, Cookie Lavagetto; SS, Pee Wee Reese; RF, Dixie Walker; CF, Carl Furillo; LF, Pete Reiser; C, Bruce Edwards; P, Joe Hatten; P, Kirby Higbe; P, Vic Lombardi; P, Hank Behrman; P, Hugh Casey.

With only one regular, Walker, hitting .300 and Higbe's 17 wins leading the pitching staff, the Dodgers nevertheless succeeded in ending the regular season tied with the heavily favored Cardinals. They were swept in the two-of-three pennant playoff series yet seemed on the verge of replacing the Cards as the NL's next great dynasty, especially when they won the flag in 1947. And while it's true that the Dodgers did win five more pennants in the next decade, many observers felt they perennially seemed to fall short of expectations—one game short each season, to be exact. The 1946 club set a painful pattern; it was the first of three Dodgers teams in a six-year period to lose the pennant by dint of dropping its last game of the season. Moreover, of the six World Series the Dodgers participated in between 1947 and 1956, they lost five of them, all to the Yankees. Had the Dodgers defeated the Cards in 1946 and thereupon started off their reign as the NL's top team by proving to themselves that they could win the big game, it is conceivable that they would have won 9 pennants in the next 11 years rather than 6, and that they, and not the Yankees, would have been the era's dominant club.

1950 BOSTON RED SOX
W-94 L-60
Manager: Joe McCarthy

Regular Lineup—1B, Walt Dropo; 2B; Bobby Doerr; 3B Johnny Pesky; SS, Vern Stephens; RF, Al Zarilla; CF, Dom DiMaggio; LF, Ted Williams; C, Birdie Tebbetts; P. Mel Parnell; P, Ellis Kinder; P, Joe Dobson; P, Chuck Stobbs.

This team ought to have won its third consecutive pennant but instead ended up with three hairline misses, losing in 1948 to the Indians in a pennant playoff game, to the Yankees in 1949 by dropping the last two games after leading by one game with two to go, and to the Yankees again in 1950 despite hitting .302 as a unit and scoring 1027 runs, both figures records for the era. Analysts pointed to the season-ending broken elbow Ted Williams sustained in the All-Star Game as the reason the Sox came up short in 1950, yet it's hard to see how they could have needed more hitting. What did them in was a dreadful 4.88 staff ERA—a full run worse than in 1949—and an AL-high 748 bat on balls. Mel Parnell, with an 18–10 record, was the only pitcher whose ERA was under 4.00, but even Parnell failed to match his 1949 performance, when he won 25 games. The most exciting post-World War II offensive show, the Sox featured a utilityman, Billy Goodman, who wasn't good enough to crack the regular lineup even though he won the AL batting crown with a .354 average. It was sad to see them fade. The 1950 season was both their last gasp and McCarthy's; he quit after it was over, the team slipped to a distant third in 1951 and then started tumbling swiftly toward mediocrity. Those who loved hitting in those years still talk wistfully about the classic Series matchup they never got to see—the Rex Sox versus the Dodgers.

1956 CINCINNATI REDS
W-91 L-63
Manager: Birdie Tebbetts

Regular Lineup—1B, Ted Kluszewski; 2B, Johnny Temple; 3B, Ray Jablonski; SS, Roy McMillan; RF, Wally Post; CF, Gus Bell; LF, Frank Robinson; C, Ed Bailey; P, Brooks

Lawrence; P, Johnny Klippstein; P, Joe Nuxhall; P, Art Fowler; P, Hal Jeffcoat; P, Hersh Freeman.

McMillan hit three home runs and Temple hit just two, but the rest of the team clubbed 216, spurring Reds fans to vote the entire starting lineup to the All-Star team the following year, and who can argue that their chauvinism was all that wrongheaded? Had Bell hit one more four-bagger, the Reds would have been the first team in history to have four 30-homer men; as it was, they tied the 1947 Giants' record for the most home runs in a 154-game season. Weak pitching did them in—what else?—but the Big Red Machine in the 1970s was pallid in comparison to this team. The only comparable club in recent history was the 1963 Twins.

1959 MILWAUKEE BRAVES
W-86 L-70
Manager: Fred Haney

Regular Lineup—1B, Joe Adcock; 2B, Felix Mantilla; 3B, Eddie Mathews; SS, Johnny Logan; RF, Hank Aaron; CF, Billy Bruton; LF, Wes Covington; C, Del Crandall; P. Warren Spahn; P, Lew Burdette; P, Bob Buhl; P, Joey Jay; P, Don McMahon.

Not a great team in any sense but good enough to have easily won its third consecutive pennant if Red Schoendienst hadn't been idled for the entire season by tuberculosis. Minus Schoendienst, the Braves tried seven players at second base before going with 35-year-old Bobby Avila in the stretch drive. Avila had been on the downside of the hill for about five years by then and played his last innings in the two-game pennant playoff loss to the Dodgers. Equally responsible for the Braves' also-ran status, though not as well publicized, was Haney's stubborn insistence on platooning lefty Frank Torre at first base with righty Joe Adcock. Torre hit .228 and had one homer; Adcock batted .292 and clubbed 25 homers. No one could fault Haney for the loss of Schoendienst, but his Adcock-Torre experiment played a large hand in his being replaced at the close of the season by Chuck Dressen.

Minor League Feats and Firsts

The first minor league was the International Association, formed in 1877. A second minor-league circuit, the League Alliance, also tried to get off the ground that same year but failed to complete its schedule. In 1879 the Western League, the first minor league to endure for a substantial length of time, was founded by Ted Sullivan. Five years later the International League, the oldest minor league still in existence, began as the Eastern League. By 1903 there were 13 minor-league teams, and ten years later the total had climbed to 40. In 1949, the peak of what is now seen to have been the golden age of organized baseball, there were 59 minor leagues in operation. Many were forced to close their doors, however, when major-league teams began televising games into their areas. Even the relatively stable Triple A leagues underwent severe upheavals once the two major leagues began transferring franchises in the 1950s and placed teams in Milwaukee, Kansas City, Baltimore, San Francisco and Los Angeles, all former AAA bastions. Major-league expansion in the 1960s and 1970s removed several more Triple A strongholds from minor-league circuits. In 1986 there were 16 minor leagues, about the same number there have been for the past decade, with three of them organized exclusively for first-year professional players.

First Minor-League Pennant Winner
The Tecumseh club of London, Ontario, which won the 1877 International Association flag with a team batting average of .191; St. Paul was leading the League Alliance that same year when it disbanded.

Biggest Crowd to See a Minor-League Game
In 1982, 65,666 fans turned out for an American Associa-

tion game between Denver and Omaha. The previous record had been held by the Miami Marlins, who drew 57,000 to the Orange Bowl on August 7, 1956, to watch Satchel Paige beat Columbus in an International League game. In 1941 the Jersey City Giants of the IL set a record when they sold 65,391 tickets for their home opener at Roosevelt Stadium, but since the park held only 40,000 all ticket buyers could not, and obviously did not, attend the game.

First Minor-League Team to Draw 1 Million Fans in a Season
The Louisville Redbirds in 1983 had a total attendance of 1,052,438, the current all-time minor-league record.

Best Minor-League Team Ever
By almost unanimous consensus the 1919–25 Baltimore Orioles, who won an organized-baseball record seven pennants in a row after losing their star southpaw Ralph Worrell, who won 25 games in 1918 at age 19 and then perished in the flu epidemic. In 1919 the Orioles featured Max Bishop at second base; 23-year-old coal miner Joe Boley at shortstop; Fritz Maisel, down from the majors, at third base; Merwin Jacobson in center field; and Otis Lawry, the International League's top hitter with a .364 average. A year later Jacobson led the IL with a .404 mark, the league's highest average since 1897, and 20-year-old Lefty Grove was purchased from Martinsburg in the Blue Ridge League to augment an already solid mound staff that was led by Harry Frank, Jack Ogden and Jack Bentley. The 1920 Orioles won the IL flag by a record 26½ games and demolished St. Paul in the Little World Series.

In 1921 the Orioles won 119 games in a 168-game season and a record 27 games in a row. The team easily triumphed again in 1922 as owner-manager Jack Dunn continued to resist offers from major-league teams for his stars like Grove and Bishop, although he did auction off Jack Bentley to the Giants for $65,000 at the end of the season.

Good as Grove was, however, the club's best pitcher in 1923 was Rube Parnham with a 33–7 record and a season-ending string of 20 wins in a row. Parnham had earlier pitched briefly with the Philadelphia A's, but several other Orioles stars like outfielder Clarence Pitt, the IL's top hitter in 1923, and first baseman Clayton Sheedy, never got a major-league opportunity at all, in part because of Dunn's refusal to let go of his players until his price was met. At the conclusion of the 1923 season, with rival IL clubs tiring of the Orioles' dominance and pressing league officials to end the circuit's holdout against the major-league draft system that embraced the rest of organized baseball, Dunn finally agreed to sell Max Bishop to the A's for $25,000 but held on to Joe Boley until 1927 when the A's forked over $65,000. By then Boley was 31 years old and on the downside of his career.

Lefty Grove was more fortunate; he went to the A's for $100,600 after a 26–6 season in 1924. In his five years with the Orioles, Grove won 108 games and lost only 36, giving him a combined major- and minor-league record of 411 wins and 190 losses, easily the highest winning percentage in organized baseball history. Preparing for Grove's departure, the Orioles signed 24-year-old amateur pitching star George Earnshaw late in the 1924 season and kept him until the spring of 1928 when he too was sold to the A's—for $70,000. In 1925 Earnshaw, Jack Ogden and Tommy Thomas still gave the Orioles the most formidable pitching staff in the minors and spurred the club to its seventh straight pennant with help from outfielders Maurice Archdeacon and Twitchy Dick Porter, the IL's batting champ in 1924 and again in 1927. Earnshaw, Ogden and Thomas were all in the majors by the 1928 season, but Dunn clung to Porter until a few weeks before his death in October of 1928 when Porter was finally sold to Cleveland for $40,000. By the time Porter left the Orioles he was 28 years old.

A few last comments. Great as the Orioles were, they had one glaring weakness. At no time during their seven-year rein could Dunn manage to land a top-flight catcher. On that count, and that count alone, the team was below major-league caliber. Many observers believed that in all other respects the Orioles were better than most of the teams in the majors. The best evidence of that was that the A's, who wound up with the majority of Dunn's stars, emerged as the game's strongest team by the end of the decade.

Now, to answer your two questions. How did Connie Mack corral so many of those great Orioles? Well, it didn't hurt that he and Dunn were both Irish. The more interesting question is how did the A's come up with all that dough in the mid-1920s after suffering a long series of last-place clubs that drew hardly any fans at all and then, despite winning three pennants in a row, fall on such hard times by the early 1930s that Mack had to sell almost all of his purchased Orioles? There was a depression on, sure, but was that the whole story? It would take space that I don't have to spare in this book and a grasp of Mack's rather strange psychological makeup that no one may ever have to tell you why I don't think it was.

Second-Best Minor-League Team Ever
Ironically, while the Orioles were dashing to seven straight International League pennants, the Fort Worth Panthers of the Texas League won seven consecutive percentage championships between 1919 and 1925, losing the pennant only in 1919 in a split-season playoff to the Shreveport Gassers, the first-half winner, and then sweeping both halves of the league race for the next six years. Managed by Jake Atz, the "Cats" featured first baseman Clarence "Big Boy" Kraft, who collected 55 homers in 1924 (at the time a minor-league record) and 196 RBIs, still a Texas League record, then retired and was replaced in 1925 by Ed Konetchy, a former longtime major-league star. Atz's top moundsmen were Paul Wachtel, who won a Texas League-record 232 games, and Joe Pate. Many of the Cats stars saw big-league duty at some point in their careers, but apart from Konetchy only pitcher Wilcy Moore and shortstop Topper Rigney were more than marginal performers in the majors.

Worst Minor League Team Ever
In 1926 Reading of the International League posted a 31–129 record and .194 winning percentage while finishing an organized baseball-record 75 games behind pennant-winning Toronto.

Most Recent Minor-League Team that Staked a Legitimate Claim to Being Major League
In 1945 Paul Fagan bought a one-third interest in the San Francisco Seals from owner Charlie Graham and immediately vowed to bring major-league baseball to San Francisco and soon—as soon, the fact was, as he succeeded in having the Pacific Coast League certified as a third major league. Fagan, the scion of a San Francisco banking family, was at first viewed as a crackpot by members of the major-league establishment, but his vision suddenly took on a frightening tinge of reality when he began implementing it. Fagan believed that the path to big-league recognition lay in getting

all PCL teams to stop selling their star players to major-league clubs and start paying them big-league salaries. Accordingly, he saw to it that the 1946 Seals were better paid than many of their major-league counterparts and arranged for them to travel first class and stay in the best hotels. His reward in 1946 was a new minor-league attendance record, and San Francisco's reward was a Seals pennant behind pitcher Larry Jansen's 30–6 season and the stellar work of second baseman Hugh Luby, the PCL's Most Valuable Player that year, and first baseman Ferris Fain. Fagan's plan collapsed when other PCL club owners refused to match his largesse and undermined him by arranging working agreements with major-league teams that cemented the PCL's minor-league status, but for that one year the Seals looked, traveled, played and were paid like major leaguers. Ferris Fain, for one, balked when he was sold to the Philadelphia A's because he would have to take a cut in salary.

Number of Home Runs Babe Ruth Hit in the Minor Leagues
Just one. It came on September 5, 1914, while Ruth, pitching for the Baltimore Orioles, was shutting out Toronto 9–0. Ruth was the first great Baltimore player that Jack Dunn auctioned to a major-league club. Dunn had hoped to hang onto Ruth awhile longer but encountered money problems when the Federal League put a team in Baltimore to compete with the Orioles. Why did Ruth go to the Boston Red Sox instead of Philadelphia like so many of Dunn's latter-day stars? Actually Ruth came very close to winding up with the A's. Connie Mack was given first crack at him but declined, and Dunn then contacted Boston owner Joe Lannin, who also happened to be Irish, as was the Red Sox player-manager, Bill Carrigan. John McGraw, of the same persuasion, felt betrayed when Dunn sold Ruth without first offering the Babe to the Giants.

All-time Organized-Baseball Record for Most Home Runs in an Inning
3—Gene Rye, Waco, Texas League, May 6, 1930, against Beaumont; Waco scored 18 runs in the inning and won 22–4. Rye, whose real name was Mercantelli, appeared briefly with the Boston Red Sox the following year and went 7-for-39, all singles.

Organized Baseball Record for Best Season by a Pitcher
Bob Riesener had a perfect 20–0 record in 1957 for Alexandria in the Evangeline League; in 1949, 40-year-old right-hander Orie Arntzen of Albany in the Eastern League posted a 25–2 record and was voted the Minor League Player of the Year by the *Sporting News*; but many consider Bill Kennedy's 1946 season with Rocky Mount in the Coastal Plains League to be the most awesome year ever by a minor-league hurler. Kennedy, who later had an eight-year major-league career, mainly as a reliever, had a 28–3 record, with 456 strikeouts and a 1.03 ERA in 280 innings.

Longest Hitting Streak in Organized Baseball History
Joe DiMaggio went on a 61-game tear for the San Francisco Seals in 1933 as a prelude to his major-league 56-game record, but the all-time record belongs to outfielder Joe Wilhoit of Wichita in the Western League, who in 1919 hit in 69 straight games. Wilhoit had earlier played four seasons in the majors and hoped his skein would earn him a return ticket, but it didn't happen.

Organized Baseball Record for Highest Season Batting Average
.477—Walter Malmquist, York, Nebraska State League, 1913

Organized Baseball Record for Most Home Runs in a Season
72—Joe Bauman, Roswell Rockets, Longhorn League, 1954. Bauman, a 32-year-old first baseman, also had 224 RBIs, hit an even .400 and had a .916 slugging average.

Organized Baseball Record for Most RBIs in a Season
254—Bob Crues, Amarillo, West Texas–New Mexico League, 1948. In addition, Crues hit .404 and had 69 home runs.

Organized Baseball Record for Most Home Runs in a Game
8—Nig Clarke, Corsicana, Texas League, June 15, 1902. That day Corsicana and Texarkana moved their game to Ennis and played in the morning to circumvent the Sunday blue laws then in force. In the tiny Ennis park, Corsicana eked out a 51–3 win as Clarke went 8-for-8, all four-baggers. The class of the Texas League at the time, Corsicana posted a record 27 straight wins in 1902, led by Clarke, who later made the major leagues as a catcher with Cleveland.

Organized Baseball Record for Best Single-Game Performance by a Pitcher

On June 13, 1952, Ron Necciai, pitching for Bristol, a Pittsburgh farm club in the Class D Appalachian League, threw a no-hitter and struck out 27 batters in a nine-inning game. That same summer a teammate of his, Bill Bell, threw three no-hitters, two of them back-to-back. By the end of the 1952 season Pittsburgh owner Branch Rickey, groping for ways to bolster the last-place Pirates, had rushed both Necciai and Bell up to the majors, where they were hit hard, lost confidence and never recovered it.

Best Minor-League Player Prior to World War II

Plenty of grist for argument here, but I recommend Ike Boone, who won five minor league batting titles in four different circuits—the Southern Association in 1921, the Texas League in 1923, the Pacific Coast League in 1929 and the International League in 1931 and 1934. With the San Francisco Mission Reds in 1929, Boone hit .407 and had 55 homers and 323 hits, leading the Pacific Coast League in all these departments; in addition, he collected 553 total bases, an all-time organized-baseball season record. A year later Boone was hitting .448 for the Mission Reds after 83 games when he was acquired by Brooklyn. Boone was among the rare minor-league *wunderkinds* who hit nearly as well in the majors—.319 in 356 games and .330-plus in his only two seasons as a regular. The rap against him was that he was slow afoot and a lackadaisical outfielder, the same rap borne by Smead Jolley and, to a lesser extent, Buzz Arlett, two PCL contemporaries of Boone's who many contend were his superiors. Another PCL star of the same vintage, Ox Eckhardt, was lightly regarded by major-league scouts because he fashioned his astronomical minor-league batting averages by hitting to the opposite field rather than with power.

Best Minor League Player since World War II

Rocky Nelson gets my vote. Unlike Boone, Arlett and Jolley, who hit well when given opportunities in the majors, and Eckhardt, who never got a real opportunity, Nelson was given chance after chance in the late 1940s and early 1950s but flopped so many times that it seemed inevitable he would finish out his career in the International League, where he won two Triple Crowns. But then Pittsburgh gave him one last shot in 1959 at age 34, and he responded with two good seasons while sharing first base with Dick Stuart, another minor-league sensation no one really believed would ever produce in the majors.

Career Home Run Leader, American Association

Bunny Brief, 256. Brief also led the PCL in 1916 with 33 homers. In 569 major-league at bats, he hit .223 and had only five homers.

Career Home Run Leader, International League

Ollie Carnegie, 258. Frozen for years in the high minors, Carnegie never played a single game in the majors.

Career Home Run Leader, Pacific Coast League

Buzz Arlett, 251. Arlett began as a pitcher with the Oakland Oaks and still holds the PCL record for the most putouts in a season by a pitcher, one of the many paradoxes in a career that was restricted to the minors for all but one year supposedly because of weak glovework. Like Brief, Arlett cut a swath in more than one Triple A league. In 1932 he twice hit four home runs in a game for Baltimore and led the International League with 54 homers and 144 RBIs. For how he did in his lone year in the majors, see both "Rookie Records" and "Final Season Records."

MINOR LEAGUE CAREER PITCHING LEADERS

Wins

	Minor-League Wins	Major-League Wins
1. Bill Thomas	383	—[1]
2. Joe Martina	349	6[2]
3. George Payne	348	1
4. Tony Freitas	342	25
5. Alex McColl	332	4[3]

[1]Thomas collected 383 wins despite losing three full seasons, from 1947 through 1949, when he was declared ineligible after being implicated in an Evangeline League betting scandal.

[2]All six wins came as a 35-year-old rookie with the 1924 Washington Senators. His last major-league appearance was a perfect relief inning in the World Series that fall.

[3]Another longtime minor leaguer who got his sole major-league chance with a pennant-bound Washington team. McColl came to the Senators when he was 39—in time to pitch two perfect relief innings in the 1933 World Series.

Most Wins in One League
295—Frank Shellenback, Pacific Coast League. Won 10 games as a 19-year-old rookie with the 1918 White Sox, then was cut when he started poorly in 1919 and never again made it out of the high minors.

Most Losses in One League
235—Herman Pillette and Spider Baum, Pacific Coast League

Most Games Pitched
1015—Bill Thomas

MINOR LEAGUE CAREER BATTING LEADERS

Highest Average

	Minor League	Major League
1. Ike Boone	.370	.319
2. Ox Eckhardt	.367	.192[1]
3. Smead Jolley	.366	.305
4. Carl East	.365	.286

Most Home Runs

1. Hector Espino	462	—
2. Buzz Arlett	432	18
3. Nick Cullop	420	11[2]
4. Merv Connors	400	8
5. Joe Hauser	399	79[3]

Most RBIs

1. Nick Cullop	1856	67
2. Buzz Arlett	1786	72
3. Jim Poole	1784	140[4]
4. Larry Barton	1751	—
5. Spencer Harris	1745	46

Most Hits

1. Spencer Harris	3617	94
2. Harry Strom	3486	—
3. Eddie Hock	3474	1
4. George Whiteman	3388	70
5. Snake Henry	3384	14[5]
6. Jigger Statz	3356	737[6]

Most Stolen Bases

	Minor League	Major League
1. George Hogriever	947[1]	48[7]

[1]Holds the all-time organized-baseball record for highest career batting average, even ahead of Ty Cobb's, which is lowered by his minor-league stats.

[2]One of the last American Indian players, he also showed good power in the majors but struck out too much to stick.

[3]Both preceded and followed Jim Poole as the Philadelphia A's regular first baseman. A knee injury gave the job to Poole, but Hauser later reclaimed it for a time while Jimmie Foxx was still learning the position. Small for a first sacker, only five-feet, ten-and-a-half inches—but a bomber in the high minors. In 1930 Hauser hit 63 home runs for Baltimore and had 443 total bases, an International League record. With Minneapolis in the American Association three years later, he set an all-time Triple A record when he clubbed 69 homers.

[4]Became expendable when the A's acquired Jimmie Foxx and Hauser recovered from his knee injury. His 29 seasons in organized baseball are the most by any player who wasn't a pitcher. Among pitchers, George Brunet leads with 33 seasons, followed by Herman Pillette who, like Poole, put 29 years into the game. Brunet is an original. Apart from being the only minor-league pitching great to have a significant major-league career—324 games and 15 seasons—he's one of the small number of post-1950 players to forge a second life for himself in the minors after his major-league days ended. Still active in 1985 at age 50, Brunet had a 244–242 minor-league record in 668 games.

[5]Did poorly when the Braves gave him a crack at their first-base job in the early 1920s—but at least he got a chance in the majors, however brief. Larry Barton, who came along a few years later when the game was overstocked with good-hitting first basemen, never did.

[6]His 3356 hits all came with the Los Angeles Angels in the PCL. When his major-league total is added to them, he stands fourth on the all-time organized-baseball career hit list, behind only Pete Rose, Ty Cobb and Hank Aaron.

[7]Many of his minor-league seasons were in the 1890s before the modern rule for determining a stolen base was evolved. As a result, his true stolen base total is probably quite a bit less.

Switch Hitters' Records

In 1950 Jim Russell of the Brooklyn Dodgers became the first switch hitter in major-league history to homer from both sides of the plate for the second time in the same game. Russell's record lasted less than six years. On May 18, 1956, Mickey Mantle of the New York Yankees had his third switch-hit homer game. By the time he was done Mantle would have 10 of them and hold most of the other all-time switch-hit slugging records as well.

First Switch Hitter to Homer from Both Sides of the Plate in the Same Game
  AL—Wally Schang, Philadelphia, September 8, 1916, at Shibe Park off Allan Russell and Slim Love of the Yankees
  NL—Augie Galan, Chicago, June 15, 1937

First Switch Hitter of Note
  Bob "Death to Flying Things" Ferguson, New York Mutuals, 1871. Active in the major leagues until 1884, Ferguson was the first switch hitter to collect 1000 career hits.

First Switch Hitter to Collect 2000 Career Hits
  George Davis, Chicago White Sox, 1902. Davis collected 2688 hits altogether, the switch-hit career record until Pete Rose broke it in 1976.

First Switch Hitter to Collect 3000 Career Hits
  Pete Rose, Cincinnati Reds, 1978. In 1984 Rose also of course became the first switch hitter to make 4000 hits.

First Switch Hitter to Collect 100 Hits from Each Side of the Plate in a Season
  NL—Garry Templeton, St. Louis, 1979
  AL—Willie Wilson, Kansas City Royals, 1980

First Switch Hitter to Win a Batting Title
AA—Tommy Tucker, Baltimore Orioles, 1889
AL—Mickey Mantle, New York, 1956
NL—Pete Rose, Cincinnati, 1968

SEASON BATTING RECORDS

Department	National League	American League
Batting Average	.362, George Davis, New York, 1893 .348, Frankie Frisch, New York, 1923* .348 Pete Rose, Cincinnati, 1969*	.365, MICKEY MANTLE, New York, 1956
Slugging Average	.615, Ripper Collins, St. Louis, 1934	.705, MICKEY MANTLE, New York, 1956
Home Runs	35, Ripper Collins, St. Louis, 1934	54, MICKEY MANTLE, New York, 1961
RBIs	134, GEORGE DAVIS, New York, 1897 128, Ripper Collins, St. Louis, 1934*	130, Mickey Mantle, New York, 1956*
Hits	230, PETE ROSE, Cincinnati, 1973	230, WILLIE WILSON, K.C. Royals, 1980
Doubles	51, PETE ROSE, Cincinnati, 1978	46, John Anderson, Milwaukee, 1901
Triples	27, GEORGE DAVIS, New York, 1893 19, Max Carey, Pittsburgh, 1923* 19, Garry Templeton, St. Louis, 1979*	21, Willie Wilson, K.C. Royals, 1985
Total Bases	369, Ripper Collins, St. Louis, 1934	376, MICKEY MANTLE, New York, 1956
Bases on Balls	116, Miller Huggins, St. Louis, 1910	146, MICKEY MANTLE, New York, 1957
Runs	140, MAX CAREY, Pittsburgh, 1922	133, Willie Wilson, K.C. Royals, 1980
Pinch Hits	22, Red Schoendienst, St. Louis, 1962	24, DAVE PHILLEY, Baltimore, 1961
Stolen Bases	110, VINCE COLEMAN, St. Louis, 1985	83, Willie Wilson, K.C. Royals, 1979

Department	National League	American League
At Bats	695, Maury Wills, Los Angeles, 1962	705, WILLIE WILSON, K.C. Royals, 1980
Strikeouts	115, Vince Coleman, St. Louis, 1985	126, MICKEY MANTLE, New York, 1961
Fewest Strikeouts (Minimum 500 ABs)	10, FRANKIE FRISCH, St. Louis, 1927	21, Buck Weaver, Chicago, 1919

*Record since 1901
Note: Tommy Tucker of the Baltimore Orioles (AA) hit .372 in 1889, the all-time highest season average by a switch hitter.

Only Switch Hitter to Win a Triple Crown
Mickey Mantle, New York Yankees, 1956

First Switch Hitter to Hit for the Cycle
NL—Max Carey, Pittsburgh, June 20, 1925
AL—Mickey Mantle, New York, May 23, 1957

CAREER BATTING RECORDS

Department	Name	Years Active	Record No.
Batting Average	Frankie Frisch	1919–37	.316
Slugging Average	Mickey Mantle	1951–68	.557
Home Runs	Mickey Mantle	1951–68	536
RBIs	Mickey Mantle	1951–68	1509
Hits	Pete Rose	1963–	4256
Doubles	Pete Rose	1963–	746
Triples	George Davis	1890–1909	167
Total Bases	Pete Rose	1963–	5752
Bases on Balls	Mickey Mantle	1951–1968	1734
Runs	Pete Rose	1963–	2165
Pinch Hits	Dave Philley	1941–62	93
Stolen Bases	Max Carey	1910–1929	738
At Bats	Pete Rose	1963–	14,053
Strikeouts	Mickey Mantle	1951–68	1710

Most Unsung Career Record Held by a Switch Hitter
Don Buford (1963–72) grounded into only 33 double plays in 4553 at bats—a ratio of one to every 138 at bats, the best in history.

Great Batting Debuts

Late in the 1951 season the St. Louis Browns brought out-fielder Bob Nieman up from Oklahoma City in the Texas League. On September 14 Brownie fans watched him face pitcher Mickey McDermott of the Red Sox and become the first—and to date only—player to homer in his first two at bats in the majors. Bert Campaneris of the Kansas City A's is otherwise the one player in this century to hit two homers in his initial major-league game—in his first and fourth at bats on July 23, 1964. The first player to homer twice in his inaugural game .was Princeton Charlie Reilly, who did it with Columbus in the American Association on October 9, 1889. Reilly, a switch hitter, played in five more games and batted .478 before the curtain descended on the 1889 season. It was mostly downhill for him after his great debut—he hit only .250 in an eight-year career—although in 1892 he became one of the first three players in history to get a pinch hit.

First Player to Homer in His Initial at Bat
   Bill Duggleby, Philadelphia Phillies, April 21, 1898. Duggleby, a pitcher, did it up big, bringing home four runs with his circuit clout. Nearly 90 years have passed since that spring afternoon, but Duggleby remains the only player to hit a grand slam in his first at bat.

Second Player to Homer in His First at Bat
   Johnny Bates, Boston Braves, April 12, 1906

First American League Player to Homer in His First at Bat
   Earl Averill, Cleveland Indians, April 16, 1929. Averill was also the first future Hall of Famer to break in with a homer. The only other Hall of Famer to debut similarly was

pitcher Hoyt Wilhelm of the New York Giants on April 25, 1952. In his second at bat Wilhelm tripled. He then played 20 years in the majors without ever hitting another home run or triple.

Second Pitcher to Homer in His First at Bat
Clise Dudley, Brooklyn Dodgers, April 29, 1929

First American League Pitcher to Homer in His First at Bat
Bill Lefebvre, Boston Red Sox, June 10, 1938

First Black Player to Homer in His First at Bat
Dan Bankhead, Brooklyn Dodgers, August 20, 1947. It was his only hit that year and the only homer in his career.

First American League Black Player to Homer in His First at Bat
Gates Brown, Detroit Tigers, June 19, 1963

Only Expansion Team Player to Homer in His First at Bat in Team's Inaugural Game
Al Woods, Toronto Blue Jays, April 7, 1977, as a pinch hitter in the fifth inning

Only Players on Opposing Teams to Homer in Their First at Bats in the Same Game
Emmett Mueller, Philadelphia Phillies, and Ernie Koy, Brooklyn Dodgers, April 19, 1938

Winners of the "Three Musketeers" Award
On September 20, 1981, Gary Gaetti, Tim Laudner and Kent Hrbek of the Minnesota Twins all homered in their first-major league games, Gaetti's coming in his first at bat.

Most Unlikely Player to Homer in His First at Bat (Pitchers Excluded)
Shortstop Buddy Kerr of the New York Giants hit one out the first time he stepped to the plate on September 8, 1943. Five years later Kerr became the last Giants regular to play a full season in the Polo Grounds without hitting a single home run.

Most Recent Player to Homer in His First at Bat
Jay Bell, Cleveland Indians, September 29, 1986, off Bert Blyleven of the Twins. Bell's clout—on the first pitch he saw

in the major leagues—was the record-breaking 47th gopher ball Blyleven served up in 1986.

Winner of the "Not Easily Intimidated" Award
Facing Warren Spahn in his initial major-league game, on May 24, 1957, Cubs outfielder Frank Ernaga homered in his first at bat and then tripled his next time up against Spahn.

Greatest Debut by a Hall of Famer
On June 30, 1894, Louisville outfielder Fred Clarke introduced himself to the National League by clubbing five hits in his first game. The only other player to debut with a five-hit game was Cecil Travis of the Senators on May 16, 1933, in a 12-inning contest.

Players Who Got Four Hits in Their First Games
Casey Stengel, Brooklyn Dodgers, July 27, 1912
Art Shires, Chicago White Sox, August 20, 1928
Spook Jacobs, Philadelphia A's, April 13, 1954
Willie McCovey, San Francisco Giants, July 30, 1959, including two triples
Mack Jones, Milwaukee Braves, July 13, 1961
Ted Cox, Boston Red Sox, September 17, 1977
Kirby Puckett, Minnesota Twins, May 8, 1984
Special Mention—Pitcher Russ Van Atta debuted with the Yankees on April 25, 1933, by collecting four hits in the process of shutting out the Senators 16–0.

The Five Greatest One-Game Wonders
First Place—The Houston Colt 45s started an all-rookie lineup on September 29, 1963, including outfielder Johnny Paciorek, who was a perfect 3-for-3, walked twice, scored four runs and drove in three. A back injury felled Paciorek in 1964, and he never worked his way back to the majors.

Second Place—Third baseman Ray Jansen of the St. Louis Browns went 4-for-5 on September 30, 1910, in his only look at major-league pitching. Jansen's four hits are the all-time one-game record.

Third Place—In 1933 catcher Aubrey Epps of the Pirates went 3-for-4 in his only big-league game and knocked in three runs.

Fourth Place—White Sox catcher Chuck Lindstrom, son of Hall of Famer Fred Lindstrom, tripled and walked in his lone game in 1958, then quit with a perfect 1.000 career batting average and a record 3.000 slugging average, breaking the old mark of 2.000 set in 1912 by Ed Irvin, another one-game wonder.

Fifth Place—In 1944 Steve Biras of the Indians went 2-for-2 in his only game, singling as a pinch hitter and then staying in the game at second base and singling again, giving him a 1.000 career batting average and two RBIs.

Catchers' Records

The period between 1942 and 1960 was a prime time for receivers. In 1942 Ernie Lombardi won a batting title, the last catcher ever to do so, and four years later Buddy Rosar became the first backstopper to post a perfect 1.000 fielding average. Furthermore, the 1951 season was the first in which catchers were chosen as the Most Valuable players in both leagues, something that has happened only one other time in history—at the close of the 1955 season.

SEASON BATTING RECORDS

Department	National League	American League
Batting Average	.394, JACK CLEMENTS, Philadelphia, 1895 .367, Babe Phelps, Brooklyn, 1936*	.362, Bill Dickey, New York, 1936
Slugging Average	.630, GABBY HARTNETT, Chicago, 1930	.617, Bill Dickey, New York, 1936
Home Runs	41, ROY CAMPANELLA, Brooklyn, 1953	37, Carlton Fisk, Chicago, 1985
RBIs	142, ROY CAMPANELLA, Brooklyn, 1953	133, Bill Dickey, New York, 1937
Runs	103, Roy Campanella, Brooklyn, 1953	118, MICKEY COCHRANE, Philadelphia, 1932
Hits	193, TED SIMMONS, St. Louis, 1975	192, Yogi Berra, New York, 1950
Doubles	42, Terry Kennedy, San Diego, 1982	42, MICKEY COCHRANE, Philadelphia, 1930
Triples	13, TIM McCARVER, St. Louis, 1966 JOHNNY KLING, Chicago, 1903	12, Mickey Cochrane, Philadelphia, 1928

Department	National League	American League
Total Bases	317, Roy Campanella, Brooklyn, 1953	318, YOGI BERRA, New York, 1950
Bases on Balls	125, GENE TENACE, San Diego, 1977	121, Darrell Porter, K.C. Royals, 1979
Stolen Bases	24, Johnny Kling, Chicago, 1902	36, JOHN WATHAN, K.C. Royals, 1982
Strikeouts	113, Randy Hundley, Chicago, 1966	120, LANCE PARRISH, Detroit, 1984
Fewest Strikeouts (Minimum 400 ABs)	14, Ernie Lombardi, Cincinnati, 1938	8, MICKEY COCHRANE, Philadelphia, 1929

*Record since 1901
Note: All catchers' seasons that contained 15 or more games at other positions are excluded, and where ties exist—i.e., between Kennedy and Cochrane for most doubles—the all-time record holder is considered to be the catcher who played the fewest games elsewhere. The lone exceptions are Fisk, Tenace and Porter, all of whom played more than 15 games at other positions but collected so many more home runs and bases on balls respectively than the runners-up to their league records that excluding them would result in recognizing a much lesser achievement.

Most Games, Career, at Catcher
1918—Al Lopez, 1928–47. But Bob Boone, who has caught in 1808 games, seems likely to break Lopez's mark sometime late in the 1987 season.

Most Consecutive Games at Catcher
312—Frankie Hayes, Philadelphia A's and Cleveland Indians, October 3, 1943, through April 21, 1946

EVOLUTION OF SEASON RECORD FOR BEST FIELDING AVERAGE

	Team	League	Year	Average
Doug Allison	Hartford	National	1876	.881[1]
Pop Snyder	Louisville	National	1877	.910[2]
Pop Snyder	Boston	National	1878	.912
Pop Snyder	Boston	National	1879	.925
Silver Flint	Chicago	National	1880	.932
Charlie Bennett	Detroit	National	1881	.962[3]

Team	League	Year	Average
Chief Zimmer	Cleveland	National	1896	.972
Malachi Kittredge	Boston	National	1901	.984
Ossee Schrecken-gost	Philadelphia	American	1905	.984
Johnny Kling	Chicago	National	1907	.987
Bill Bergen	Brooklyn	National	1908	.989
George Gibson	Pittsburgh	National	1912	.990[4]
Hank Severeid	St. Louis	American	1923	.993
Mickey Cochrane	Philadelphia	American	1930	.993
Shanty Hogan	New York	National	1931	.996
Bill Dickey	New York	American	1931	.996
Earl Grace	Pittsburgh	National	1932	.998
Buddy Rosar	Philadelphia	American	1946	1.000[5]

[1]The catcher for the 1869–70 Cincinnati Red Stockings, Allison was 30 years old by the time the National League was formed, and 1876 was his last season as a regular.

[2]May have been the best catcher of his era, but he jumped to the American Association in 1882, thereby sacrificing the disproportionate recognition that National League players have received from historians.

[3]Bennett had a .966 fielding average in 1888 but in only 74 games, fewer than the 60 percent of his team's games required to qualify as a fielding leader. Another catcher, Farmer Vaughn, fielded .969 in 1893, but included in his average were some 40 games he played at other positions.

[4]In only 94 games, just barely qualifying as the new record holder.

[5]Yogi Berra fielded 1.000 in 1958 but caught only 85 games. The National League record was set by Wes Westrum of the New York Giants when he fielded .999 in 1950.

Best Career Fielding Average
    .993—Bill Freehan, 1961–76

Most Seasons League Leader in Fielding Average
    AL—8—Ray Schalk, last in 1922
    NL—7—Gabby Hartnett, last in 1937

Most Consecutive Errorless Games
    148—Yogi Berra, New York Yankees, July 28, 1957 through May 10, 1959. During his streak Berra also set the record for most consecutive errorless chances—950.

Most Chances Accepted, Career
    10,734—Bill Freehan, 1961–76

Most Chances Accepted, Season

1221—Johnny Edwards, Houston Astros, 1969. That year the Astros' pitchers set the all-time season record for most strikeouts. All the one-game records for most chances accepted are similarly held by the battery-mates of strikeout record-setters.

Most Assists, Season

NL—214—Pat Moran, Boston 1903; he did it while catching only 107 games.

AL—212—Oscar Stanage, Detroit, 1911

Most Seasons League Leader in Assists

AL—6—Jim Sundberg, last in 1981

NL—6—Gabby Hartnett, last in 1935

Del Crandall, last in 1960

Most No-hitters Caught, Career

4—Ray Schalk; the last one was Charlie Robertson's perfect game on April 30, 1922

Only Catcher since Ernie Lombardi to Hit .300 or More Five Times

Thurman Munson, last in 1977

Most Recent Left-hander to Catch in a Major-League Game

Mike Squires, Chicago White Sox, last in 1980

Most Games Caught by Left-hander, Since 1901

46—Tom Doran, Boston Red Sox, 1904–06 (13); Detroit Tigers, 1905 (33).

Greatest Left-handed Catcher

Jack Clements, 1884–1900; .286 career batting average in 1157 games

Most Gold Glove Awards

10—Johnny Bench, 1967–83

Men for All Seasons

Heisman Trophy Winners to Play Major-League Baseball

On June 20, 1986, Auburn running back Bo Jackson, the number one pick in the NFL draft, spurned a reported $7 million deal with the Tampa Bay Buccaneers to sign a baseball contract with the Kansas City Royals. When Jackson was added to the Royals' roster in September, he became only the second former Heisman Trophy winner to play in a major-league game. Those of you who are up on your general sports history can not only name the first but also remember him as one of the last great single-wing tailbacks: Vic Janowicz, Ohio State, 1950. Janowicz won as a junior, then floundered through his final college season after the new Buckeye coach, Woody Hayes, installed a T-formation, which diluted his triple-threat talents. But the Pirates still thought enough of Janowicz's overall athletic ability to make him a bonus baby. After two undistinguished seasons with the Pirates in the mid-1950s, Janowicz opted to pursue a pro football career with the Washington Redskins instead, but that too ended when he was in a near-fatal auto accident.

Members of the Pro Football Hall of Fame Who Played Major League Baseball

There are seven: Jim Thorpe, Paddy Driscoll, Red Badgro, Ernie Nevers, George Halas, Greasy Neale and Ace Parker. None of them even remotely threatened to become a Hall of Famer in both sports, but all except Driscoll and Badgro had their moments. Parker homered in his first major-league at bat; Nevers surrendered two of Babe Ruth's 60 home runs in 1927; Thorpe drove in the winning run in the famous double no-hit game in 1917; Neale starred for the Reds in the 1919 World Series; and Halas played a few games for the 1919 Yankees in right field, a position that would be occupied the following year by Babe Ruth.

Only Member of Both the Pro Football and Pro Baseball Hall of Fame

Cal Hubbard, a star tackle in the NFL, was enshrined in Cooperstown as well as in Canton, Ohio, after a long career as a National League umpire. Hank Soar, Charlie Moran and George Magerkurth were other umpires who played in the NFL. Soar also coached the Providence Steamrollers in the Basketball Association of America, a forerunner of the NBA.

Only Major-League Manager Who also Served as Head Coach in the NFL

Hugo Bezdek managed the Pirates from 1917 through 1919 and later coached the Pittsburgh Steelers.

First Athlete to Play in Both a Rose Bowl Game and a World Series

Jackie Jensen, an All-American running back at Cal, played in the 1949 Rose Bowl game against Northwestern and later played for the Yankees in the 1950 World Series. Chuck Essegian, who teamed with Gary Kerkorian and Harry Hugasian to give Stanford the nation's best-ever Armenian backfield, in 1959 became the second athlete to play in both a Rose Bowl game and a World Series.

Other College Football Stars Who Played in the Major Leagues

The list is too long to mention everyone. Among those who had successful major-league careers were Jackie Robinson, Glenn Wright, Lou Gehrig, George Stirnweiss, Spud Chandler, Blondie Ryan, Billy Werber, Del Pratt, Luke Sewell, Ted Kluszewski, Sam Chapman, Eldon Auker, Lloyd Merriman, Frank Grube, Harvey Hendrick, Wes Schulmerich, Eddie Morgan, Rick Leach, Bill Carrigan, Red Wilson, Joe Sparma, Tom Haller, Galen Cisco, Harry Agganis, Carl Reynolds, Riggs Stephenson, Gee Walker, Kirk Gibson, Al Dark, Jake Gibbs, Bernie Allen, Ron Darling, Norm Cash and Frankie Frisch. Bud Metheny, Eric Tipton and Bob Finley were three outstanding running backs who played in the majors during World War II when rosters were thinned by the draft; Finley, the catalyst on the top-ranked SMU

Mustangs in 1935, was never more than a reserve catcher even with draft-depleted Philadelphia Phillies and might have done better to consider a pro football career. Among the others who achieved stardom on college gridirons but were only marginal major leaguers were Jesse Hill, Johnny Herrnstein, Tom Gastall, Dean Look, Bill Renna, Harley Boss, Chick Outen, Larry Bettencourt, Don Lund, Steve Korcheck, Carroll Hardy, Jerry Schoonmaker, Paul Giel, David Morey, Tom Yewcic, Haywood Sullivan, George Spencer and Mike Miley.

Athletes who Played Both Pro Football and Major-League Baseball Prior to World War II

In the 1920s and 1930s it was not at all uncommon for major-league baseball players to give pro football a whirl during the off-season. Among the many not previously mentioned who did were Chuck Dressen, Evar Swanson, Tom Whelan, Mike Wilson, Russ Young, Ab Wright, Ernie Vick, Pid Purdy, Jim Levey, Hoge Workman, Joe Vance, Al Pierotti, Ossie Orwoll, Garland Buckeye, Walt Masters, Bert Kuczynski, Red Smith, Wallie French, Bob Fothergill, Charlie Berry and Walt Gilbert.

Athletes Who Played Both Pro Football and Major-League Baseball after World War II

Beginning in the early 1940s it became increasingly difficult to combine both sports. Now that both baseball and football have lengthened their seasons, it's altogether impossible. The last athlete to play both pro sports on a major-league level was Tom Brown, an outfielder with the 1963 Senators who later played on the first Super Bowl winner, the 1966 Green Bay Packers. Among the other two-sport pro athletes since 1941 are Jim Castiglia, Steve Filipowicz, Pete Layden, Norm Bass, Rex Johnston and Cliff Aberson.

Only College Basketball All-American to Win a Major-League MVP Award

Dick Groat, winner of the National League MVP award in 1960, had been an All-American at Duke before he signed a bonus contract with the Pirates. Groat also played for a short time in the National Basketball Association.

Athletes Who Played Both Pro Basketball and Major-League Baseball Prior to World War II

Before World War II a number of major leaguers regularly switched their sliding pads for short pants during the winter months. Pro basketball was a loose operation then at best with a short season and lots of franchise transfers, but the biggest reason it was relatively simple for major leaguers to play both sports was that pro basketball teams hadn't yet become repositories for seven-footers. The game still had plenty of room for a good small man, and there were many of them, including several of the following two-sporters: Harry Riconda, Ralph Miller, Ed Wineapple, Bert Lewis and Rusty Saunders. No famous baseball names here, but Saunders, a four-game outfielder with the 1927 Philadelphia A's, was well-known among court followers. He played some 20 years on the pro circuit and was deep into his forties before he finally put away his sneakers.

Athletes Who Played Both Pro Basketball and Major-League Baseball after World War II

The most recent athlete to play both is Boston Celtics star Danny Ainge, who dropped baseball after being stymied by major-league pitching—he hit .187 in 88 games for Toronto in 1981. Others who have had dual careers since World War II are Frankie Baumholtz, Howie Schultz, Chuck Connors, Del Rice, Bill McCahan, Hank Biasetti, George Crowe, Irv Noren, Steve Hamilton, Cotton Nash, Dave Debusschere, Ron Reed, Johnny Gee, Dick Ricketts and Gene Conley. Conley was the best in both worlds; DeBusschere, the best pro basketball player also to play major-league baseball; and Reed, a teammate of DeBusschere's on the 1966–67 Detroit Pistons, the best baseball player also to play pro basketball.

Other Athletes for All Seasons

The best major-league baseball player who later became a pro golfer was Ken Harrelson, but Sammy Byrd, known in his days with the Yankees as "Babe Ruth's Caddy" because he often served as a late-inning defensive replacement for Ruth, was the best pro golfer who had been a former major-league baseball player. The greatest track-and-field athlete who also played major-league baseball was of course Jim Thorpe. Not far behind Thorpe, who was probably the greatest all-around athlete in major-league history, was Vern Kennedy, a 21-game winner for the White Sox in 1936 and winner of the decathlon at the Penn Relays in 1927.

Pinch-hitting Feats

Pinch hitters really began to come into their own in the 1950s, and no player did more to elevate their status than Peanuts Lowrey when he tagged 22 pinch bingles for the Cardinals in 1953. Close on Lowrey's heels followed Ron Northey, Dave Philley, Elmer Valo, Smokey Burgess and Jerry Lynch, and by the end of the decade most teams had at least one player whose sole job was to sit patiently in the dugout and await pivotal situations, usually late in a game, when his bat was needed.

First Pinch Hitter
Most sources agree that it was pitcher Mickey Welch of the New York Giants, on September 10, 1889, and that he fanned.

First Player to Be Used as a Pinch Hitter Twice in a Season
In 1891 the rules were changed, allowing teams to substitute for any player during a game at any time. Previously substitutes could be used only in the event of an injury or with the opposing team's permission, which was not always granted. The St. Louis Browns of the American Association used pitcher Jack Stivetts as a pinch hitter twice in 1891, but he failed to deliver on both occasions. Yet the choice was a sound one, for Stivetts went on to post a .297 career batting average, the all-time highest among pitchers who worked at least 2000 innings.

First Successful Pinch Hitter
Jack Doyle of the Cleveland Spiders. In a game at Brooklyn on June 7, 1892, he batted for pitcher George Davies and singled. Doyle was also successful in two of his next three tries in the role, but strangely was used as a pinch

hitter only five times in his long career and not at all in the six seasons he played in the 1900s. He retired in 1905 with a .301 career batting average and a .600 (3-for-5) batting average as a pinch hitter.

EVOLUTION OF THE SEASON PINCH-HIT RECORD

Player	Team	League	Year	Pinch Hits
Jack Doyle	Cleveland	National	1892	1[1]
John Sharrott	Philadelphia	National	1893	2[2]
Doggie Miller	Louisville	National	1896	6
Duke Farrell	Washington	National	1897	8[3]
Sammy Strang	New York	National	1905	8
John Hoey	Boston	American	1907	8
Dode Criss	St. Louis	American	1908	12[4]
Ted Easterly	Cleveland-Chicago	American	1912	13
Doc Miller	Boston	National	1913	20[5]
Sam Leslie	New York	National	1932	22[6]
Peanuts Lowrey	St. Louis	National	1953	22[7]
Dave Philley	Baltimore	American	1961	24
Vic Davalillo	St. Louis	National	1970	24
Jose Morales	Montreal	National	1975	25

[1]Two members of the Pittsburgh Pirates, Princeton Charlie Reilly and none other than Connie Mack, also had pinch hits in 1892.

[2]Tied by several players between 1893 and 1896.

[3]The first great pinch hitter. Until he went 1-for-11 in 1904, Farrell was averaging close to .500 in pinch-hit roles.

[4]The only player to be a league leader in pinch hits four consecutive seasons (1908–11), Criss was also the first pitcher in the American League to serve as a pinch-hitting specialist.

[5]Pinch hitters have generally followed great seasons with poor ones. Miller was one of the rare exceptions. After setting a new season pinch-hit record in 1913, he averaged .343 as a pinch hitter the following year—yet was released by the Reds.

[6]Leslie's feat was so unpublicized that when Lowrey collected 22 pinch hits in 1953 many sportswriters thought he'd set a new record and that the old one belonged to Ed Coleman of the Browns, who made 20 pinch hits in 1936.

[7]Lowrey's season is viewed as something of a fluke because he went 9-for-69 as a pinch hitter in 1954-55, but check what he did in 1952—13-for-27—one of the best years ever among pinch hitters with more than 25 at bats.

.400 SEASONS BY PINCH HITTERS
(Minimum 35 at bats)

Player	Team	Year	Hits/AB's	Average
Ed Kranepool	New York Mets	1974	17–35	.486
Gates Brown	Detroit Tigers	1968	18–39	.472
Frenchy Bordagaray	St. Louis Cards	1938	20–43	.465
Rick Miller	Boston Red Sox	1983	16–35	.457
Jose Pagan	Pittsburgh Pirates	1969	19–42	.452
Joe Cronin	Boston Red Sox	1942	18–42	.429
Don Dillard	Cleveland Indians	1961	15–35	.429
Candy Maldonado	San Francisco Giants	1986	17–40	.425
Merritt Ranew	Chicago Cubs	1963	17–41	.415
Carl Taylor	Pittsburgh Pirates	1969	17–41	.415
Dave Philley	Philadelphia Phils	1958	18–44	.409
Frankie Baumholtz	Chicago Cubs	1955	15–37	.405
Jerry Lynch	Cincinnati Reds	1961	19–47	.404
Jerry Turner	San Diego Padres	1978	20–50	.400
Chet Laabs	St. Louis Browns	1940	14–35	.400

Best World Series Performance by a Pinch Hitter
Dusty Rhodes of the New York Giants hit a home run and two singles and netted six RBIs as a pinch hitter in the first three games of the 1954 World Series.

First Player to Hit a Pinch Home Run in a World Series
Yogi Berra, New York Yankees, October 2, 1947, at Ebbets Field. The first player to hit two pinch homers in a World Series was Chuck Essegian of the Los Angeles Dodgers in the second and sixth games of the 1959 Series, both coming at Comiskey Park.

First Player to Hit Pinch Home Runs in Successive Games
Ray Caldwell, New York Yankees, June 10 and June 11, 1915. Caldwell was a pitcher.

First Player to Hit Pinch Home Runs in Both Games of a Doubleheader
AL—Joe Cronin, Boston, June 17, 1943
NL—Hal Breeden, Montreal, July 13, 1973

Most Pinch Home Runs, Season
NL—6—Johnny Frederick, Brooklyn, 1932
AL—5—Joe Cronin, Boston, 1943

First Player to Homer as a Pinch Hitter in Three Consecutive Plate Appearances
Del Unser, Philadelphia Phillies, 1979. A year earlier Lee Lacy of the Dodgers homered in three consecutive official at bats but received a base on balls during his streak.

First Player to Homer As a Pinch Hitter in His First Major League at Bat
NL—Eddie Morgan, St. Louis, April 14, 1936
AL—Ace Parker, Philadelphia, April 30, 1937

Most Plate Appearances, Season, by a Pinch Hitter
NL—86—Merv Rettenmund, San Diego, 1977
AL—81—Elmer Valo, Washington and New York, 1960; including a pinch-hit record 18 bases on balls.

Lowest Season Batting Average by a Pinch Hitter, Minimum One Hit
.030—Chick Outen, Brooklyn, 1933; one hit in 33 at bats. An outstanding hitter in the minors—he rapped .341 for Jersey City in 1932—Outen batted .248 overall for Brooklyn in 1933, his lone test against big-league pitching.

TOP 10 IN CAREER PINCH HITS

		Years Active	Pinch Hits
1.	Manny Mota	1962–80	150
2.	Smokey Burgess	1949–67	145[1]
3.	Jose Morales	1973–85	123
4.	Jerry Lynch	1954–66	116
5.	Red Lucas	1923–38	114[2]
6.	Steve Braun	1971–85	113
7.	Gates Brown	1963–75	108
	Terry Crowley	1969–83	108
9.	Mike Lum	1967–81	103
10.	Rusty Staub	1963–85	100

[1]Gets my vote as the best ever. Even as a rookie he was a rugged pinch hitter—he had 12—and if it hadn't been for a terrible final season, he would have had a career pinch-hit average of well over .300.

[2]Lucas, a pitcher, in 1935 became the first player to make 100 pinch hits, and he held the career record for most pinch hits until 1965 when Burgess broke it. Ham Hyatt, in 1917, was the first player to collect 50 career pinch hits. In 1913 Hyatt also became the first player to hit three pinch home runs in a season.

First Player to Hit 10 Pinch Home Runs
   Cy Williams. He retired in 1930 with only 41 career pinch hits, but 11 of them were homers.

Most Career Pinch Home Runs
   20—Cliff Johnson. Playing for Toronto, he broke Jerry Lynch's old mark of 18 when he hit his 19th on August 5, 1984, against Oakland.

First Player to Hit Three Pinch Grand Slam Home Runs
   Ron Northey, Chicago Cubs, September 18, 1950. Willie McCovey and Rich Reese have since tied Northey's record for the most pinch grand slams. In 1956 Northey hit .376 as a pinch hitter for the White Sox (15-for-39), remarkable in itself, but even more extraordinary is that 13 of his 15 hits came with two strikes on him.

THE TOP 10 CAREER PINCH HITTERS
(Minimum 100 Pinch-hit at Bats)

	Years Active	At Bats	Hits	Average
1. Gordy Coleman	1959–67	120	40	.333
2. Ward Miller	1909–17	110	36	.327
3. Doc Miller	1910–14	120	39	.325
4. Rod Carew	1967–85	124	40	.323
5. Al Kaline	1953–74	115	37	.322[1]
6. Tommy Davis	1959–76	197	63	.320
7. Elmer Smith	1914–25	123	39	.319
8. Estel Crabtree	1929–44	116	37	.319
9. Earl Smith	1919–30	129	41	.318
10. Bibb Falk	1920–31	114	36	.316[2]

[1]Hall of Famers, for the most part, have been undistinguished pinch hitters. Aside from Kaline, only Bill Terry among those with 100 or more pinch-hit at bats has a career average (.301) of over .300.
[2]The difference of only 17 points between the 1st and 10th players on the list indicates how difficult it is to be consistently successful as a pinch hitter. Among players with 200 or more pinch-hit at bats, only Bob Fothergill, who hit exactly .300, was able to post a .300 career batting average.

Lowest Career Batting Average as Pinch Hitter, Minimum 300 at Bats
   .204—Mike Jorgensen, 1968–85; 72 hits in 353 bats

Lowest Career Batting Average as Pinch Hitter, Minimum 200 at Bats
.176—Russ Synder, 1959–70; 49 hits in 278 at bats

THE 10 WORST PINCH HITTERS OF ALL TIME
(Minimum 100 Pinch-hit at Bats)

		Years Active	At Bats	Hits	Average
1.	Ivan Murrell	1963–74	180	21	.117
2.	Ted Kubiak	1967–76	123	15	.122
3.	Al Zarilla	1943–53	120	15	.125
4.	Woody Held	1954–69	147	19	.129
5.	Lou Klimchock	1958–70	161	21	.130
6.	J. C. Martin	1959–72	109	16	.148
7.	Dick Nen	1963–70	102	15	.147
8.	Hector Cruz	1973–82	128	19	.148
9.	Billy Klaus	1952–63	120	18	.150
10.	Roger Repoz	1964–72	133	20	.150

Cy Young Award Winners

The Cy Young Award was originated in 1956. It was initially intended to honor only the top major-league pitcher each season, but by 1967 the feeling that the best pitcher in each league should be honored yearly had gained sway, and a second award was added.

First Cy Young Winner
Don Newcombe, Brooklyn Dodgers, 1956

First left-hander to Win a Cy Young
Warren Spahn, Milwaukee Braves, 1957

First American League Pitcher to Win a Cy Young
Bob Turley, New York Yankees, 1958

First Cy Young Winner for a Team Other Than a Pennant Winner
NL—Don Drysdale, Los Angeles, 1962
AL—Dean Chance, Los Angeles, 1964

First to Win Two Cy Youngs
Sandy Koufax, Los Angeles Dodgers, 1965. When he won again in 1966, Koufax also became the first pitcher to win three times.

Other Three-Time Winners
NL—Tom Seaver, New York Mets, 1969, 1973 and 1975
AL—Jim Palmer, Baltimore, 1973, 1975 and 1976

Only Four-Time Winner
Steve Carlton, Philadelphia Phillies, 1972, 1977, 1980 and 1982. When he won in 1972, Carlton also became the only pitcher to cop the award while playing for a last-place team.

First Relief Pitcher to Win a Cy Young
   NL—Mike Marshall, Los Angeles, 1974
   AL—Sparky Lyle, New York, 1977

Only Rookie to Win a Cy Young
   Fernando Valenzuela, Los Angeles Dodgers, 1981

Youngest Cy Young Winner
   NL—Dwight Gooden, New York Mets, 1985, age 20; 15
days younger than Valenzuela the year he won
   AL—Bret Saberhagen, Kansas City Royals, 1985, age 21

Oldest Cy Young Winner
   AL—Early Wynn, Chicago, 1959, age 39
   NL—Steve Carlton, Philadelphia, 1982, age 37

Most Wins by Starting Pitcher Who Won a Cy Young
   AL—31—Denny McLain, Detroit, 1968
   NL—27—Steve Carlton, Philadelphia, 1972

Fewest Wins by Starting Pitcher Who Won a Cy Young, 1981 Excepted
   AL—18—Pete Vuckovich, Milwaukee, 1982
   NL—18—Mike Scott, Houston, 1986

Lowest ERA by Cy Young Winner
   AL—1.04—Rollie Fingers, Milwaukee, 1981
   NL—1.12—Bob Gibson, St. Louis, 1968

Highest ERA by Cy Young Winner
   AL—3.66—LaMarr Hoyt, Chicago, 1983
   NL—3.12—Bob Gibson, St. Louis, 1970

Only Pitcher to Win a Cy Young after Being Traded in Midseason
   Rick Sutcliffe, Chicago Cubs, 1984. Sutcliffe, who started
the year with Cleveland, is also the only winner to play in
both leagues in the same season.

25-Game Winners Who Failed to Win a Cy Young
   NL—Juan Marichal, San Francisco, and on three different occasions, no less—1963, 1966 and 1968, when he won
26 games

AL—Jim Katt, Minnesota, 1966; Mickey Lolich, Detroit, 1971

Only Pitcher to Win a Cy Young in Both Leagues
Gaylord Perry, Cleveland (AL), 1972; San Diego (NL), 1978

Batters' Strikeout Records

In 1956 outfielder Jim Lemon of the Washington Senators fanned 138 times, setting a new all-time record. Four years later Mickey Mantle of the Yankees collected his 1000th strikeout in only his 10th season, and another Senator, Harmon Killebrew, completed his second of a record six straight seasons in which he fanned over 100 times. Twenty years later Lemon, Mantle and Killebrew would no longer hold any major season or career strikeout records, yet they still loom today as probably the three leading harbingers of the home-run-or-bust syndrome that had already begun to permeate the game by the late 1950s.

The National League began keeping accurate batters' strikeout stats in 1910, and the American League followed suit three years later. From 1876 to 1896 the National League had counted batters' strikeouts and then, for no overwhelming reason, ceased doing it for the next 14 years. The American Association kept track of the batters' strikeouts in only 2 of its 10 seasons as a major league—1889 and again in 1891. Records of batters' strikeouts are also available for the lone Players League season in 1890.

Since foul balls were not universally counted as strikes until 1903, and batters received four strikes as late as 1887, the natural assumption is that strikeouts in the game's early years were relatively infrequent. But the stats that are available to us indicate otherwise. In 1886, with the mound still only 50 feet from the plate and pitchers now allowed to throw overhand, Matty Kilroy, a rookie left-hander with the Baltimore Orioles in the American Association, fanned 513 hitters. An individual breakdown of Kilroy's victims is impossible to reconstruct a century later, but Tom Brown, rightfielder for the Pittsburgh Alleghenies, was quite likely his main one. Brown led the Players League in fanning the air in 1890, the American Association in 1891 and the National League in three of the next four seasons. Even without the strikeout totals from 6 of the 16 years he played, Brown finished in 1898 with 708 whiffs. Including his six lost years, he probably struck out around 1,100 times, making him the only player to top 1,000 until Babe Ruth came along.

Chronology of Significant Strikeout Milestones

1884—Sam Wise, shortstop for the Boston Red Stockings, struck out 104 times, a record that stood until 1914.

1887—John Morrill of the Boston Red Stockings became the first player to strike out 500 times in his career.

1892—Tom Brown, playing with Louisville in the National League, became the first player to strike out 90 or more times two years in a row.

1892—Pud Galvin concluded his career with 630 strikeouts in only 2702 at bats; a pitcher, Galvin sometimes played the outfield between mound assignments and had a .202 batting average despite the frequency with which he fanned.

1930—Babe Ruth became the first player to strike out 1000 times in his career

1932—Bruce Campbell of the St. Louis Browns struck out 104 times, the first to top 100 since 1914.

1934—Harlond Clift of the Browns became the first third baseman to strike out 100 or more times in a season.

1935—First baseman Dolf Camilli of the Phillies became the first National Leaguer since 1884 to strike out 100 times in a season.

1937—Frank Crosetti of the Yankees became the first shortstop to strike out 100 or more times in a season.

1940—Chet Ross of the Boston Braves set a new rookie strikeout record when he fanned 127 times.

1949—The last season in which neither league had a player who struck out 100 times.

1958—Harry Anderson of the Phillies topped the National League with 95 strikeouts, the last league leader to fan less than 100 times.

1963—John Bateman of the Houston Colt 45s became the first catcher to fan 100 or more times in a season.

1966—Mickey Mantle of the Yankees became the first player to fan 1500 times.

1966—George Scott of the Boston Red Sox set an American League rookie strikeout record by fanning 152 times.

1978—In his 11th season Bobby Bonds of the Texas Rangers struck out for the 1500th time, the quickest any player has ever reached 1500 K's.

1978—Pirates leadoff hitter Omar Moreno had only two home runs yet struck out 104 times.

1979—Lou Brock retired with 1730 strikeouts and only 149 home runs, further proof that it isn't only sluggers who have fallen prey to the whiff syndrome.

1983—Reggie Jackson of the Angels became the first player to strike out 2000 times.

1984—Juan Samuel of the Phillies fanned 168 times, setting an all-time rookie record.

1986—Reggie Jackson of the Angels became the first player to fan 2500 times.

1986—Pete Incaviglia of the Rangers fanned 185 times to set both a new all-time rookie and American League record, José Canseco of the A's (175) and Danny Tartabull of the Mariners (157) also topped George Scott's old AL rookie mark.

EVOLUTION OF BATTERS' SEASON STRIKEOUT RECORD
(Since 1913)

	Team	League	Year	K's
Danny Moeller	Washington	American	1913	103[1]
Gus Williams	St. Louis	American	1914	120
Vince DiMaggio	Boston	National	1938	134
Jim Lemon	Washington	American	1956	138
Jake Wood	Detroit	American	1961	141[2]
Harmon Killebrew	Minnesota	American	1962	142
Dave Nicholson	Chicago	American	1963	175[3]
Bobby Bonds	San Francisco	National	1969	187
Bobby Bonds	San Francisco	National	1970	189

[1]The 1913 season was the first in which both leagues began keeping complete and official strikeout records. Moeller was the first documented player to fan 100 times in a season since Sam Wise in 1884.

[2]Also broke Chet Ross's rookie record in 1961; the new mark lasted only until 1966.

[3]Nicholson fanned 573 times in 1419 career at bats—a strikeout average of .404. Counting only those times his bat made contact, he hit .356, making him an even more exciting player than Dave Kingman or Reggie Jackson, if they happen to be your brand of excitement. Kingman's strikeout average through

the 1986 season was .272; Jackson's was a mere .262. They rank one and two as the easiest strikeout victims among active players, but in comparison to Nicholson they both seem like Joe Sewell. But before we get to Sewell and the other players at the opposite end of the spectrum from Nicholson, Kingman and Jackson, consider this: Through the 1986 season some 100 players had either topped or were within swinging range of 1000 career strikeouts, but only two of them—Babe Ruth and Jimmie Foxx—finished their careers prior to 1959.

TOP 10 IN CAREER STRIKEOUTS

		Years Active	K's
1.	Reggie Jackson	1967–	2500
2.	Willie Stargell	1961–82	1935
3.	Tony Perez	1964–86	1869[1]
4.	Dave Kingman	1971–	1816
5.	Bobby Bonds	1968–81	1757
6.	Mike Schmidt	1972–	1744
7.	Lou Brock	1961–79	1730[1]
8.	Mickey Mantle	1951–68	1710
9.	Harmon Killebrew	1954–75	1699
10.	Lee May	1965–82	1570

[1]Never a league leader in K's.

THE 10 HARDEST BATTERS TO STRIKE OUT
(Minimum 10 Seasons since 1901)

		Years Active	AB's	K's	AB/K Ratio
1.	Joe Sewell	1920–33	7132	113	63 to 1
2.	Lloyd Waner	1927–45	7732	173	45 to 1[1]
3.	Nellie Fox	1947–65	9232	216	43 to 1
4.	Tommy Holmes	1942–52	4992	122	41 to 1[2]
5.	Tris Speaker	1907–28	7899	220	36 to 1[3]
6.	Stuffy McInnis	1909–27	6667	189	35 to 1
7.	Andy High	1922–34	4440	130	34 to 1
8.	Sam Rice	1915–34	9269	275	34 to 1
9.	Frankie Frisch	1919–37	9112	272	34 to 1
10.	Edd Roush	1913–31	7363	215	34 to 1[4]

[1]As a part-time outfielder and pinch hitter with the Pirates, Braves and Reds in 1941, Waner made over 230 plate appearances without striking out a single time.

[2]In 1945 Holmes led the National League in home runs with 28 and in fewest strikeouts with nine, the only such double winner in history.

[3]Speaker's and McInnis's stats prior to 1913 are excluded because their strikeout totals for their earlier seasons are unavailable.

[4]Roush's 1914–15 Federal League K totals are unavailable.

The Five Most Remarkable Batters' Strikeout Feats in This Century

First Place—Tommy Holmes's all-time record double win in 1945

Second Place—Ted Williams hit 521 career home runs and fanned only 709 times.

Third Place—Joe DiMaggio hit 361 career home runs and fanned only 369 times.

Fourth Place—Joe Sewell's last strikeout in the 1930 season came on May 26 when White Sox lefty Pat Caraway zapped him twice in the same game. The only other pitcher ever to fan Sewell twice in a game was the equally obscure Cy Warmoth, who did it in 1923. Warmoth had a mere 54 strikeouts in his career. In 1931 Caraway totaled only 55 strikeouts in 220 innings.

Fifth Place—Nellie Fox played 98 consecutive games in 1958 without striking out, breaking the old record of 89 games, set in 1932 by third baseman Carey Selph of the White Sox shortly before he was released.

Special Mention—In 1935 catcher Lee Head of Knoxville in the Southern Association fanned only one time in 122 games and 402 at bats.

World Series Play: 1942–60

FRANCHISE SUMMARY

Team	League	WS Record Through 1960	Last Year in WS
Los Angeles	National	1–0	1959
Boston	American	5–1	1946
New York	American	18–7	1960
St. Louis	National	6–3	1946
Cleveland	American	2–1	1954
Cincinnati	National	2–1	1940
Pittsburgh	National	3–2	1960
Chicago	American	2–2	1959
Milwaukee	National	1–1	1958
Washington	American	1–2	1933
Detroit	American	2–5	1945
Chicago	National	2–8	1945
Philadelphia	National	0–2	1950

Became Defunct between 1942 and 1960

Philadelphia	American	5–3	1931
Boston	National	1–1	1948
New York	National	5–9	1954
Brooklyn	National	1–8	1956
St. Louis	American	0–1	1944

Yearly Highlights
1942—St Louis (NL) defeated New York (AL) 4 games to 1

After dropping the Series opener, the Cards got two
complete-game wins from rookie Johnny Beazley, plus a

shutout from Ernie White, and took the next four games to hand the Yankees their first Series loss since 1926.

1943—New York (AL) defeated St. Louis (NL) 4 games to 1

The Yankees' retaliation for the 1942 wipeout featured two superbly pitched games by Spud Chandler, the AL's MVP in 1943.

1944—St. Louis (NL) defeated St. Louis (AL) 4 games to 2

The last series to be played entirely in one stadium—antiquated Sportsman's Park—was also the Browns' one and only fall appearance. Their pitchers allowed only 16 runs in the six games, but Cardinals pitchers gave up just 12.

1945—Detroit (AL) defeated Chicago (NL) 4 games to 3

Hal Newhouser of the Tigers had a Series ERA of 6.10 but won two games, including the clincher. Hank Borowy of the Cubs became the first pitcher since Jack Coombs in 1916 to win a Series game in both leagues.

1946—St. Louis (NL) defeated Boston (AL) 4 games to 3

Considered one of the great Series, but only the first and last games were tight. Moreover, the two stars, Ted Williams and Stan Musial, hit .200 and .222 respectively. But Harry Brecheen of the Cardinals won three games, and Enos Slaughter tallied the run that won the Series in the eighth inning of Game Seven by scoring all the way from first base on Harry Walker's single when Red Sox shortstop Johnny Pesky hesitated a fraction of a second before relaying Leon Culberson's throw to the plate.

1947—New York (AL) defeated Brooklyn (NL) 4 games to 3

The first Series to be televised. The opener drew a record 73,365 to Yankee Stadium as Guy Lombardo and his orchestra entertained and Met Opera soprano Helen Jepson sang the national anthem. Although sloppily played for the most part, this Series ranks among the most exciting because of two events: Bill Bevens's near no-hitter in Game Five and Al Gionfriddo's catch of Joe DiMaggio's 415-foot drive the following day with two Yankees aboard.

1848—Cleveland (AL) defeated Boston (NL) 4 games to 2

The last Series until 1967 that did not include either a New York team or a former New York team. The Braves won the opener 1–0 on a single by Tommy Holmes, which drove home Phil Masi from second base after Masi had seemingly been picked off in a carefully timed play between Indians pitcher Bob Feller and shortstop Lou Boudreau. It was the closest Feller would ever come to a Series victory. The fifth game, in Cleveland, drew an all-time Series record crowd of 86,288.

1949—New York (AL) defeated Brooklyn (NL) 4 games to 1

The 1949 Series also began with a 1–0 game, won by the Yankees on Tommy Henrich's homer leading off the bottom of the ninth inning. It was the closest Don Newcombe of the Dodgers would ever come to a Series victory. Brooklyn's lone bright spot came in Game Two when Preacher Roe turned the tables on the Yankees and blanked them 1–0.

1950—New York (AL) defeated Philadelphia (NL) 4 games to 0

Phillies manager Eddie Sawyer pulled the biggest Series surprise since Connie Mack started Howard Ehmke in the 1929 opener when he named reliever Jim Konstanty to start the lid-lifter. But for the third straight year the Series began with a 1–0 game, won once again by the Yankees behind Vic Raschi. Although swept, the Phils were in every game except the last one until the final out.

1951—New York (AL) defeated New York (NL) 4 games to 2

The Giants, sparked by Eddie Stanky, won two of the first three games but then fell prey to Joe DiMaggio, playing in his last Series, and a 13-run assault in Game Five.

1952—New York (AL) defeated Brooklyn (NL) 4 games to 3

The Dodgers went up three games to two, but superlative relief pitching by Allie Reynolds helped the Yankees snatch the last two contests. Reynolds also pitched a 2–0 shutout in Game Four.

1953—New York (AL) defeated Brooklyn (NL) 4 games to 2

Billy Martin became the only player to make 12 hits in a 6-game Series and drove in the winning run in the ninth inning of the last game. The Dodgers became the first team to hit .300 in a Series and lose.

1954—New York (NL) defeated Cleveland (AL) 4 games to 0

Dusty Rhodes of the Giants delivered three game-winning hits, two of them as a pinch hitter, and Willie Mays broke hearts all over Cleveland when he robbed Vic Wertz of a probable game-winning two-run triple with a back-to-the-plate catch in the eighth inning of the opener.

1955—Brooklyn (NL) defeated New York (AL) 4 games to 3

In their eighth try the Dodgers finally managed to win their first and only Series while in Brooklyn. The hero was Johnny Podres with two complete-game victories, including a 2–0 shutout in the finale.

1956—New York (AL) defeated Brooklyn (NL) 4 games to 3

Don Larsen's perfect game gave the Yankees a 3–2 lead in the Series, but Clem Labine pitched a brilliant 10-inning 1–0 win for the Dodgers the following day, setting up what promised to be a highly dramatic final game. It disappointed— the Yankees won 9–0 behind Johnny Kucks—which is why this Series, aside from Larsen's perfect game, is seldom mentioned among the great ones even though it was Brooklyn's last fall appearance.

1957—Milwaukee (NL) defeated New York (AL) 4 games to 3

Lew Burdette of the Braves pitched three complete-game victories, the last two of them shutouts, and Hank Aaron had 11 hits and seven RBIs.

1958—New York (AL) defeated Milwaukee (NL) 4 games to 3

Down three games to one, the Yankees beat Burdette twice and Warren Spahn once to become the first team since the Pirates in 1925 to come back from so large a Series deficit. Bob Turley pitched a 7–0 shutout in Game Five, saved Game Six and then won the final game with a six-and-two-thirds-inning relief stint.

1959—Los Angeles (NL) defeated Chicago (AL) 4 games to 2

The first Series involving a West Coast team and the last one involving a Chicago team. Ted Kluszewski provided most of the White Sox offense with three homers and 10 RBIs but could do little with Dodgers relief ace Larry Sherry, who won two games and saved the other two L.A. victories. Charlie Neal of the Dodgers knocked in six runs and led all batters with 10 hits.

1960—Pittsburgh (NL) defeated New York (AL) 4 games to 3

For the first time a seven-game Series ended with a home run when Bill Mazeroski of the Pirates led off the bottom of the 10th inning by depositing a Ralph Terry pitch over the Forbes Field left-field wall. In his last World Series as a manager, Casey Stengel saw his Yankees hit .338, set a Series record for runs and total bases, and still contrive to lose. Pittsburgh pitchers had a collective 7.11 ERA, the poorest ever by a Series participant, let alone a winner.

SECTION 5

Famous Firsts:
1961–76

1961—For the first time in 60 years two cities are given new major-league franchises. One of them, the Washington Senators, replacing the old Washington Senators, who have moved to Minnesota, plays the first game involving an expansion team on April 10 at Griffith Stadium, a 4–3 loss to the Chicago White Sox, the team that, perhaps fittingly, played the very first American League game back in 1901.

1962—The National League reluctantly follows the American League's lead and swells to 10 teams by granting franchises to groups representing Houston and New York. Houston plays the first game involving an NL expansion team on April 10 and, perhaps fittingly, triumphs over the Chicago Cubs, the lone participant in the very first major-league season back in 1876 that has survived until 1962 without any interruptions or franchise transfers.

1962—Borrowing a page from the old Baltimore Orioles' scrapbook, the San Francisco Giants win the NL pennant after groundskeeper Marty Schwab drenches the infield at Candlestick Park, supposedly to keep the dust from billowing in the stiff winds there—but the Dodgers scream that it was done to slow down their leading base thief, Maury Wills, the first player in modern history to swipe more than 100 sacks in a season. Significantly, perhaps, Schwab is voted a full World Series share by Giants players.

1965—An amateur rookie draft is at long last instituted, major-league teams selecting free-agent players in the reverse order of their finish. The Yankees, the leading opponents of the draft, immediately topple to sixth place, their first second-division finish in 40 years.

1965—As a signal that the complete game is soon to become an endangered species, the Dodgers use three pitchers to shut out the Astros on September 3 and then need four pitchers to shut them out again the following day.

1966—Red Barber, possibly the finest baseball broadcaster ever, is fired after 34 years in the booth when he appalls the Yankees brass by asking his TV cameraman to pan the stands in Yankee Stadium on an afternoon when only 413 fans turn out to watch the Yankees first cellar finisher since 1912.

1968—Dick McAuliffe of the Tigers sets a record when he becomes the first American League player to play more than 150 games in a season without grounding into a double play.

1969—Both major leagues expand to twelve teams and divide into two divisions, the champs in each division meeting in a best-three-of-five League Championship Series at the end of the regular season to determine the pennant winner and World Series representative.

1969—The "Bleacher Bums" make their official debut at Wrigley field and root the Cubs to their highest finish since 1945. They are too far from the action, however, to follow the movements of the Cubs catcher Randy Hundley's flip-over mitt, the first of its kind, or to see the hands of Expos outfielder Rusty Staub, the first to popularize batting gloves.

1969—John Hollison dies in Chicago. His obituary neglects to mention that he was the last surviving major-league pitcher who worked on a mound only 50 feet from home plate.

1970—Chick Cargo dies in Rochester, New York. His obituary neglects to mention that he was the last surviving major-league player to have batted against a pitcher throwing from a mound only 50 feet from home plate.

1970—Traded by the Cardinals to the Phillies, outfielder Curt Flood refuses to report to his new team and elects to test the reserve clause instead. Flood sets off a chain of events that within six years will merit him a few moments of silent thanks each evening around the dinner table of every major-league player.

1970—Major-league umpires refuse to work the League Championship Series games and force a settlement that increases their salaries and benefits. During the coming decade the umpires will repeatedly display their willingness to strike until their demands are met.

1971—The Pirates begin wearing form-fitting double-knit uniforms. Later in the decade the White Sox will experiment with short pants. By 1987 the Pirates' uniforms will be a mix of V-neck jerseys, pants with waistbands and Cap Anson-style caps.

1971—Ron Hunt of the Expos sets a modern record when he's hit by 50 pitches. In 1974 Hunt will retire with a 20th-century record of 243 HBP's.

1972—The players stage a 13-day strike, the first general strike in major-league history, and delay the opening of the season for 10 days. Commissioner Bowie Kuhn rules that games lost due to the strike will not be made up. As a result, the Tigers win the AL Eastern Division by dint of playing and winning one more game than the Red Sox. The Tigers half-game margin of victory is the smallest in either major league since 1908 when a similar ruling against playing makeup games gave the Tigers the flag by half a game over Cleveland.

1972—Milt Pappas of the Cubs becomes the first pitcher in history to post 200 career wins without ever winning 20 games in a season.

1973—The American League, after voting unanimously in favor of the designated hitter rule, uses designated hitters for pitchers for the first time in major-league history. The National League disdains the notion of a designated hitter and refuses to go along with the rule. Research into the history of the designated hitter idea reveals that it was first suggested in 1928 by National League president John Heydler, and that NL owners were all for it but couldn't get the support of the AL, which roundly vetoed it.

1974—Fergie Jenkins of the Texas Rangers becomes the last AL pitcher to appear in the lineup as a batter. In the game against the Twins, he singles in the sixth inning to break up a no-hitter and then goes on to triumph 2–1 for his 25th win.

1975—Catfish Hunter, the first star player to get himself declared a free agent, starts his first season with the Yankees, the team that won the bidding war for his services.

1975—Pitchers Andy Messersmith and Dave McNally, having played all season without signing contracts, demand free agency and are granted it by arbitrator Peter Seitz, the same man who declared Hunter a free agent. Seitz's decision results in a modification of the reserve clause and a shift in the balance of power from the owners to the players.

1976—Don Driessen of the Reds becomes the first player to serve as a dh in a World Series game.

Expansion Team Firsts

On April 11, 1961, the Los Angeles Angels became the first major-league expansion team to register a victory when they bested Baltimore 7–2 in their very first game. The following year the Houston Colt 45s became the first National League expansion team to win a game when they blasted the Cubs 11–2 in their inaugural contest. In contrast, the New York Mets debuted by losing their first nine games and went on to set a new 20th-century record for the most losses in a season. But in 1969 the Mets rewarded their followers and flabbergasted their critics by becoming the first expansion team to win a division title, a pennant and a World championship.

First American League Expansion Team to Win a Division Title
Kansas City Royals, 1976

First American League Expansion Team to Win a Pennant
Kansas City Royals, 1980

First American League Expansion Team to Win a World Championship
Kansas City Royals, 1985

First Expansion Team to Occupy Sole Possession of First Place
AL—The Los Angeles Angels swept a twin bill from the Senators on July 4, 1962, and moved briefly into first place. They ultimately finished third, making them the first expansion club to achieve a first-division finish.

NL—The Mets surged past the Cubs into the NL Eastern Division lead for the first time on September 10, 1969, after taking a doubleheader from the Expos.

First Second-Wave Expansion Team to Win a Division Title
    AL—Kansas City Royals, 1976
    NL—Montreal, 1981

First Second-Wave Expansion Team to Win a Pennant
    AL—Kansas City Royals, 1980
    NL—San Diego, 1984

First Second-Wave Team to Win a World Championship
    AL—Kansas City Royals, 1985
    NL—None

First Third-Wave Expansion Team to Win a Division Title
    AL—Toronto, 1985

First Season Two Expansion Teams Opposed Each Other in a League Championship Series
    AL—1982—California versus Milwaukee
    NL—1986—New York Mets versus Houston

FIRST EXPANSION TEAM PLAYERS TO BE LEAGUE LEADERS

Batting

Department	National League	American League
Batting Average	Al Oliver, Montreal, 1982	ALEX JOHNSON, California, 1970
Slugging Average	None	FRANK HOWARD, Washington, 1968
Home Runs	Dave Kingman, New York, 1982	FRANK HOWARD, Washington, 1968
RBIs	Dave Winfield, San Diego, 1979	FRANK HOWARD, Washington, 1970
Hits	Al Oliver, Montreal, 1982	GEORGE BRETT, Kansas City, 1975
Runs	Tim Raines, Montreal, 1983	ALBIE PEARSON, Los Angeles, 1962*
Doubles	RUSTY STAUB, Houston, 1967	Amos Otis, Kansas City, 1970
Triples	Roger Metzger, Houston, 1971 Joe Morgan, Houston, 1971	BOBBY KNOOP, California, 1966

Department	National League	American League
Total Bases	Dave Winfield, San Diego, 1979	FRANK HOWARD, Washington, 1968
Stolen Bases	Ron Le Flore, Montreal, 1980	TOMMY HARPER, Seattle Pilots, 1969
Bases on Balls	JOE MORGAN, Houston, 1965**	FRANK HOWARD, Washington, 1970
Strikeouts	JIM WYNN, Houston, 1967	FRANK HOWARD, Washington, 1967

*First AL major offensive department leader from an expansion team.
**First NL major offensive department leader from an expansion team.

Pitching

Wins	Tom Seaver, New York, 1969	DEAN CHANCE, Los Angeles, 1964
Losses	ROGER CRAIG, New York, 1962	George Brunet, California, 1967
Winning Pct.	TOM SEAVER, New York, 1969	Paul Splittorff, Kansas City, 1979
Starts	JERRY REUSS, Houston, 1973	Dennis Leonard, Kansas City, 1978
Complete Games	Tom Seaver, New York, 1973	DEAN CHANCE, Los Angeles, 1964
Innings	Randy Jones, San Diego, 1976	DEAN CHANCE, Los Angeles, 1964
Shutouts	John Matlack, New York, 1974	DEAN CHANCE, Los Angeles, 1964
ERA	Tom Seaver, New York, 1970	DICK DONOVAN, Washington, 1961*
Strikeouts	TOM SEAVER, New York, 1970	Nolan Ryan, California, 1972
Bases on Balls	Bill Stoneman, Montreal, 1969	BO BELINSKY, Los Angeles, 1962
Games Pitched	RON HERBEL, N.Y.-S.D., 1970	Ken Sanders, Milwaukee, 1971
Saves	HAL WOODESHICK, Houston, 1964**	Minnie Rojas, California, 1967

Awards

Cy Young	Tom Seaver, New York, 1969	DEAN CHANCE, Los Angeles, 1964

Department	National League	American League
MVP	None	JEFF BURROUGHS, Texas, 1974
Rookie of the Year	TOM SEAVER, New York, 1967	Lou Piniella, Kansas City, 1969

*First AL leader from an expansion team.
**First NL leader from an expansion team in a department other than losses.

Home Run Feats

In 1961, to the dismay of many who regarded Babe Ruth's slugging records as inviolate, Roger Maris of the Yankees clubbed 61 home runs, breaking Ruth's season record of 60, set in 1927. Thirteen years later Hank Aaron of the Braves shattered Ruth's career record of 714 circuit clouts. Many of Ruth's home run marks still stand, however, and among them are two that will surely never be broken. In 1927 Ruth hit more home runs all by himself than every team in the American League except his own Yankees. Eight years later, upon joining the Boston Braves for what would be his final major-league season, he became the first player to hit three home runs in a game in both leagues when he thrice found the seats on May 25, 1935, at Forbes Field. Another of Ruth's records that seems likely to endure is his season mark for most homers on the road—32—also set in 1927, although George Foster of the Reds came remarkably close to equaling it in 1977 before finishing with 31.

Most Home Runs at Home, Season
   AL—39—Hank Greenberg, Detroit, 1938; he had 58 altogether
   NL—34—Ted Kluszewski, Cincinnati, 1954; but only 15 on the road

Most Seasons League Leader in Home Runs
   AL—12—Babe Ruth, last in 1931
   NL—7—Ralph Kiner, 1946 through 1952 consecutive

Most Home Runs, Season, 1901 through 1919
   NL—24—Gavvy Cravath, Philadelphia, 1915
   AL—29—Babe Ruth, Boston, 1919; breaking Socks Seybold's league record of 16, set in 1902 with Philadelphia

Most Home Runs, Season, 1920 through 1941
   AL—60—Babe Ruth, New York, 1927
   NL—56—Hack Wilson, Chicago, 1930, the all-time NL record

Most Home Runs, Season, 1942 through 1960
   NL—54—Ralph Kiner, Pittsburgh, 1949
   AL—52—Mickey Mantle, New York, 1956

Most Home Runs, Seasons, 1961 through 1976
   AL—61—Roger Maris, New York, 1961
   NL—52—Willie Mays, San Francisco, 1965

Most Home Runs, Season, Since 1977
   NL—52—George Foster, Cincinnati, 1977
   AL—46—Jim Rice, Boston, 1978

First Player to Homer in Every Park in Use During His Career
   Harry Heilmann. He homered in Braves Field, Forbes Field, Ebbets Field, Wrigley Field, Crosley Field and the Baker Bowl for the first time in 1930, the season he came to Cincinnati from the Tigers. Previously he had homered in all nine American League stadiums in which he'd played—Shibe Park, Comiskey Park, Sportsman's Park (used also by the Cardinals), Cleveland's League Park, Navin Field, Fenway Park, Yankee Stadium, the Polo Grounds (used by both the Yankees and the Giants until 1923) and Griffith Stadium.

First Player to Hit 30 or More Home Runs in a Season in Both Leagues
   Dick Stuart, Pittsburgh (NL) 1961, Boston (AL) 1963

First Player to Hit 40 or More Home Runs in a Season in Both Leagues
   Darrell Evans, Atlanta (NL) 1973, Detroit (AL) 1985

Most Times Hitting Three or More Home Runs in a Game
   6—Johnny Mize. First done while with the Cardinals on July 13, 1938; last done on September 15, 1950, while with the Yankees

Most Times Hitting Two or More Home Runs in a Game
   72—Babe Ruth. He hit three homers in a game twice, once in each league, and never hit four in a game.

Players Who Hit Four Home Runs in a Game

AL—Lou Gehrig, New York, June 3, 1932. The first player to hit four in a game in the 20th century, he picked the day John McGraw quit as manager of the Giants to do it and so got second billing in the sports pages.

Pat Seerey, Chicago, July 18, 1948, in an 11-inning game. He hit only .231 that season with 19 homers and was cut early the following year.

Rocky Colavito, Cleveland, June 10, 1959. He did it in Baltimore's Memorial Stadium, at the time a very tough park to homer in.

NL—Bobby Lowe, Boston, May 30, 1894. In Boston's 20–11 win over Cincinnati, Lowe also singled, giving him 17 total bases, after he'd gone 0-for-6 in a morning game that day.

Ed Delahanty, Philadelphia, July 13, 1896. At Chicago, in a 9–8 loss to the Colts.

Chuck Klein, Philadelphia, July 10, 1936. In a 10-inning game at Forbes Field, a rugged place for sluggers prior to 1947.

Gil Hodges, Brooklyn, August 31, 1950. He did it at Ebbets Field, making him the lone player in this century prior to Bob Horner—Lowe is the only other one—to hit four homers in a game in his home park.

Joe Adcock, Milwaukee, July 31, 1954. Also at Ebbets Field. Adcock had a double in addition, giving him 18 total bases, the one-game record.

Willie Mays, San Francisco, April 30, 1961.

Mike Schmidt, Philadelphia, April 17, 1976. At Wrigley Field in a 10-inning game won 18–16 by the Phillies after they trailed 13–2 at one point.

Bob Horner, Atlanta, July 6, 1986. At Atlanta, in an 11–8 loss to Montreal, making him the first player since Delahanty to hit four homers in a losing cause.

The "Lucky Spectator" Award

Pitcher Billy Loes was either a teammate or an opponent of four players who hit four homers in a nine-inning game—Hodges, Adcock, Colavito and Mays—and so was on hand when each of them did it.

Only Pitchers to Hit Three Home Runs in a Game

Guy Hecker, Louisville (AA), August 16, 1886
Jim Tobin, Boston (NL), May 13, 1942. A good hitter,

Tobin hammered six homers in 1942, more than anyone else on the club except Max West and Ernie Lombardi.

Last Player to Hit Two Grand Slam Homers in a Game
Frank Robinson, Baltimore Orioles, June 26, 1970; in a 12–2 win over Washington.

First Player to Hit Three Grand Slam Homers in a One-Week Span
Lou Gehrig, New York Yankees, August 29, August 31 and September 1, 1931. Jim Northrup of the Tigers and Larry Parrish of the Rangers have also hit three four-run homers in a week's time.

First Team to Hit Two Grand Slam Homers in the Same Inning
Minnesota, July 18, 1962, Harmon Killebrew and Bob Allison doing the damage

Most Grand Slam Home Runs in a Season
5—Ernie Banks, Chicago Cubs, 1955; breaking Babe Ruth's record of four, set in 1919

Only Pitcher to Hit Two Grand Slam Home Runs in a Game
Tony Cloninger, Atlanta Braves, July 3, 1966. Moreover, Cloninger is the only National League player ever to do it.

Most Consecutive Games Hitting at Least One Home Run, Pitcher
4—Ken Brett, Philadelphia Phillies, June 9, 13, 18 and 23, 1973. His only home runs that season.

Last American League Pitcher to Homer in a Regular-Season Game, Batting as Pitcher
Roric Harrison, Baltimore, October 3, 1972

Most Home Runs, Season, as Team's Leadoff Batter in Game
11—Bobby Bonds, San Francisco Giants, 1973. Bonds also holds the career record with 35 leadoff homers.

Most Home Runs, Season, Against One Team
14—Lou Gehrig, New York Yankees, 1936; against Cleveland

Most Home Runs, Season, by Runner-up to League Leader
AL—54—Mickey Mantle, New York, 1961
NL—47—Ted Kluszewski, Cincinnati, 1955

Most Home Runs, Season, through April 30
11—Willie Stargell, Pittsburgh Pirates, 1971
    Graig Nettles, New York Yankees, 1974
    Mike Schmidt, Philadelphia Phillies, 1976

Most Home Runs, Season, through May 31
20—Mickey Mantle, New York Yankees, 1956

Most Home Runs, Season, through June 30
30—Babe Ruth, New York Yankees, 1928

Most Home Runs, Season, through July 31
41—Babe Ruth, New York Yankees, 1928
    Jimmie Foxx, Philadelphia A's, 1932

Most Home Runs, Season, through August 31
51—Roger Maris, New York Yankees, 1961

Most Home Runs, Season, through September 30
60—Babe Ruth, New York Yankees, 1927
    Roger Maris, New York Yankees, 1961

Only Team with Two Players Who Hit 50 or More Home Runs
The 1961 New York Yankees. Roger Maris, 61, and Mickey Mantle, 54.

Only Team with Three Players Who Hit 40 or More Home Runs
The 1973 Atlanta Braves. Dave Johnson, 43, Darrell Evans, 41, and Hank Aaron, 40.

Only Team with Four Players Who Hit 30 or More Home Runs
The 1977 Los Angeles Dodgers. Steve Garvey, 33, Reggie Smith, 32, Ron Cey, 30, and Dusty Baker, 30.

PLAYERS WITH 50 OR MORE HOMERS
IN A SEASON

	Team	League	Year	Home Runs
Roger Maris	New York	American	1961	61[1]
Babe Ruth	New York	American	1927	60
Babe Ruth	New York	American	1921	59
Hank Greenberg	Detroit	American	1938	58
Jimmie Foxx	Philadelphia	American	1932	58
Hack Wilson	Chicago	National	1930	56
Babe Ruth	New York	American	1920	54
Babe Ruth	New York	American	1928	54
Ralph Kiner	Pittsburgh	National	1949	54
Mickey Mantle	New York	American	1961	54
Mickey Mantle	New York	American	1956	52
Willie Mays	San Francisco	National	1962	52
George Foster	Cincinnati	National	1977	52
Ralph Kiner	Pittsburgh	National	1947	51
Johnny Mize	New York	National	1947	51
Willie Mays	New York	National	1955	51
Jimmie Foxx	Boston	American	1938	50[2]

[1] Had only one homer before May 3, 1961, the Yankees' 17th game, but then hit 11 in the rest of May.

[2] The only player to hit 50 in a season with two different franchises and also the only player besides Mantle to hit 50 in a season and fail to win his league's home run crown.

Most Controversial Home Run Ever

AL—George Brett's two-run "pine tar" blast for the Royals on July 24, 1983, which beat the Yankees 5–4 and had the odd effect, after all the disputes were settled, of causing *both* clubs to go into a tailspin and fall out of contention.

NL—The famous homer that should have been but wasn't. Dave Augustine's seeming game-winning blast for the Pirates in the 13th inning on September 30, 1973, against the Mets was ruled to have bounced off the top of the wall, allowing Cleon Jones to retrieve the ball and the Mets to throw the winning run out at the plate. The Mets ultimately won the game and the NL Eastern Division title. The Pirates will always feel they were robbed, and Augustine never hit another home run in the majors.

Last Team to Go a Full Season without Finding the Seats in Its Home Park
The 1945 Washington Senators. Their only homer at Griffith Stadium was an inside-the-park four-bagger by first baseman Joe Kuhel. Griffith Stadium was so cavernous that Sam Rice played a record 19 seasons with the Senators without ever hitting a fair ball into the seats in his home park.

Last Player to Hit Two Inside-the-Park Home Runs in a Game
Greg Gagne, Minnesota, October 4, 1986; against the White Sox. Gagne was the first player to accomplish this feat since Dick Allen of the White Sox on July 31, 1972, who did it, oddly enough, against Minnesota.

First Player to Hit One over the Green Monster
Hugh Bradley of the Red Sox tagged the first homer over the left-field wall in Fenway shortly after the park first opened its doors in 1912. It was his only homer all season. In 1914, playing for the Pittsburgh Rebels in the Federal League, Bradley had no homers in 427 at bats.

First Player to Clear the Left-Field Wall in Braves Field
Frank Snyder, New York Giants, 1926, more than 11 years after Braves Field hosted its first game. The place was so mammoth that between 1915 and 1928, when the fences were moved in, only seven balls were hit out of the park.

Fewest Home Runs, Season, Since 1901, by League Leader in Home Runs
NL—6—Tommy Leach, Pittsburgh, 1902. Leach hiked his total to seven in 1903, but all of them were inside-the-park—as were most of his four-baggers in 1902.
AL—7—Sam Crawford, Detroit, 1908
          Braggo Ruth, Cleveland, 1915

Home Run Leaders Who Never Hit Another Four-Bagger in the Majors
Fred Odwell, Cincinnati Reds, 1905; Dave Brain, Boston Braves, 1907

Most At Bats, Season, without Hitting a Home Run
NL—672—Rabbit Maranville, Pittsburgh, 1922
AL—658—Doc Cramer, Boston, 1938

PLAYERS WITH 500 OR MORE CAREER HOME RUNS

	Years Active	Home Runs
Hank Aaron	1954–76	755
Babe Ruth	1914–35	714[1]
Willie Mays	1951–73	660
Frank Robinson	1956–76	586
Harmon Killebrew	1954–75	573
Reggie Jackson	1967–	542
Mickey Mantle	1951–68	536
Jimmie Foxx	1925–45	534
Ted Williams	1939–60	521
Willie McCovey	1959–80	521
Eddie Mathews	1952–68	512
Ernie Banks	1953–71	512
Mel Ott	1926–47	511[2]

[1]Total would be 715 if Ruth were credited with a game-winning homer he hit in 1918 that rules of that time rated only a triple because the winning run scored from first base.
[2]Was third on the all-time career list as recently as the spring of 1960.

Most Home Runs, Career, by a Pitcher
38—Wes Ferrell, 1927–41. Right behind Ferrell are Bob Lemon with 37, Red Ruffing with 36 and Warren Spahn and Earl Wilson with 35.

Most Grand Slam Home Runs, Career
23—Lou Gehrig, 1923–39

Most Inside-the-Park Home Runs, Career
51—Sam Crawford, 1899–1917

Most Home Runs, Career, All of Them Inside-the-Park
9—Miller Huggins, 1904–16

Most Home Runs, Career, without Ever Being a League Leader in Home Runs
475—Stan Musial, 1941–63

Most Seasons Homering in All Parks Played In
11—Babe Ruth, last in 1931. Even granting that in Ruth's day there were only 8 parks, as opposed to 14 now in the American League, it's still an extraordinary record. Hank Aaron, the NL record holder, did it nine times, last in 1966 when there were 10 different parks to conquer.

Not with a Whimper

In 1966 an arthritic condition in his left elbow forced Sandy Koufax to retire after he'd enjoyed one of the finest seasons ever by a pitcher. Koufax easily broke Henry Schmidt's 63-year-old record for most wins by a pitcher in his final major-league season and went out with the biggest bang of any pitcher in history.

RECORD HIGHS BY PLAYERS IN THEIR FINAL SEASON*

Pitching

Department	Name	Team	League	Year	Record No.
Wins	Sandy Koufax	Los Angeles	National	1966	27
ERA	Ned Garvin	Brooklyn-N.Y.	Nat.-Am.	1904	1.72
Winning Pct.	Larry French	Brooklyn	National	1942	.789
Losses	Pete Dowling	Mil.-Cleve.	American	1901	26
Innings	Sandy Koufax	Los Angeles	National	1966	323
Starts	Sandy Koufax	Los Angeles	National	1966	41
Complete Games	Jack Cronin	Brooklyn	National	1904	33[1]
Shutouts	Henry Schmidt	Brooklyn	National	1903	5[2]
	Buttons Briggs	Chicago	National	1905	5
	Joe McGinnity	New York	National	1908	5
	George Kaiserling	Newark	Federal	1915	5
	Sandy Koufax	Los Angeles	National	1966	5
Strikeouts	Sandy Koufax	Los Angeles	National	1966	317
Bases on Balls	Henry Schmidt	Brooklyn	National	1903	120
Games	Bill Wakefield	N. Y. Mets	National	1964	62

Depart-ment	Name	Team	League	Year	Record No.
Saves	Russ Christopher	Cleveland	American	1948	17
	Rollie Fingers	Milwaukee	American	1985	17

*Excluding players who retired before 1901 or were declared ineligible.

[1]Quit at age 30 rather than suffer through another season with Brooklyn like 1904 when he had a 2.70 ERA but lost 23 games.

[2]Even though Schmidt won 21 games in 1903, Brooklyn didn't retain him. Another of the many outstanding pitchers the club let slip through its fingers in the early part of the century, he played only that one season in the majors.

Batting

Depart-ment	Name	Team	League	Year	Record No.
Batting Ave.	Sam Dungan	Washington	American	1901	.320[1]
	Bill Keister	Philadelphia	National	1903	.320[2]
Slugging Ave.	Buzz Arlett	Philadelphia	National	1931	.538[3]
Home Runs	Ted Williams	Boston	American	1960	29[4]
RBIs	Joe Wood	Cleveland	American	1922	92
Hits	Irv Waldron	Mil.-Wash.	American	1901	186[5]
Runs	Ike Davis	Chicago	American	1925	105
Doubles	Jack Burns	St. L.-Detroit	American	1936	37
Triples	Ernie Gilmore	Kansas City	Federal	1915	15[6]
Total Bases	Steve Evans	Brklyn.-Balt.	Federal	1915	234[7]
Games	Chick Stahl	Boston	American	1906	155
Stolen Bases	Dave Fultz	New York	American	1905	44
Bases on Balls	Roy Cullenbine	Detroit	American	1947	137[8]
Strikeouts	Howie Goss	Houston	National	1963	128
Fewest Strikeouts (Minimum 500 ABs)	Joe Sewell	New York	American	1933	64
At Bats	Tony Lupien	Chicago	American	1948	617[9]

[1]Played in the National League in the early 1890s and did fairly well, then slipped down to the minors. In 1900, the American League's last year as a minor league, Dungan was its leading hitter.

[2]Probably the most enigmatic figure of all time, Keister hit at least .300 in every one of his five seasons as a regular and showed good power, yet never

found a team or a position he could call home. The Phillies dropped him after 1903 even though he led the club in RBIs and was second in batting.

[3]In 1931, his only major-league season, Arlett hit .313, had 18 homers, knocked in 72 runs and had the fifth-highest slugging average in the National League.

[4]Had a .645 slugging average in his final season but batted only 310 times. Similarly, Chicken Hawkes of the Phillies hit .322 in his 1925 finale but had only 320 at bats. The all-time record for the highest batting average by a player in his final season belongs to Dave Orr, who hit .373 for the Brooklyn Players League entry in 1890 before he suffered a stroke and had to quit. Orr also holds the all-time record for most triples, RBIs and total bases.

[5]Almost as mysterious as Keister, Waldron hit .311 in 141 games and led the American League in at bats in its inaugural season. Like Arlett, he got only that one taste of major-league life; and also like Arlett, he played most of his career in the Pacific Coast League.

[6]For those of you who are unwilling to acknowledge the Federal League was a major circuit, the alternate record holders are: Tommy Long, 14 triples with the 1917 Cardinals; Sam Dungan, 233 total bases with the 1901 Senators.

[7]Among the top outfielders in the National League before he jumped to the Federal League in 1914, Evans was one of several FL stars who were persona non grata after the Feds folded.

[8]Granted, Cullenbine hit only .224 in 1947. But he led the American League in walks, ranked fourth in home runs and was second on the Tigers in RBIs. Like Lupien, he was cut; and like Lupien's replacement, George Vico, his replacement in 1948, was gone by the end of the following year.

[9]Another first baseman who got short-changed in the late 1940s. An excellent fielder and a deft base thief, Lupien wasn't considered a strong enough hitter for a first sacker—he had just six homers in 1948—and lost his job to Charlie Kress, who had all of one homer in 1949.

Outfielders' Records

Outstanding outfielders were probably more plentiful during the 1960s and 1970s than at any other time in history. Six of the top 10 in career games played in the outfield—Willie Mays, Hank Aaron, Lou Brock, Al Kaline, Roberto Clemente and Vada Pinson—were active throughout most of the period; Curt Flood set the all-time record for the best season fielding average and several other glove marks; Aaron broke Babe Ruth's career record for home runs; Roger Maris broke Ruth's season home run record; and Brock established many new season and career stolen base standards.

SEASON BATTING RECORDS

Batting Average	National League	American League
Batting Average	.438, HUGH DUFFY, 1894 .398, Lefty O'Doul, Philadelphia, 1929*	.420, Ty Cobb, Detroit, 1911
Slugging Average	.723, Hack Wilson, Chicago, 1930	.847, BABE RUTH, New York, 1920
Home Runs	56, Hack Wilson, Chicago, 1930	61, ROGER MARIS, New York, 1961
RBIs	190, HACK WILSON, Chicago, 1930	171, Babe Ruth, New York, 1921
Hits	254, LEFTY O'DOUL, Philadelphia, 1929	253, Al Simmons, Philadelphia, 1925
Runs	196, BILLY HAMILTON, Philadelphia, 1894 158, Chuck Klein, Philadelphia, 1930*	177, Babe Ruth, New York, 1921

Batting Average	National League	American League
Doubles	64, Joe Medwick, St. Louis, 1936	67, EARL WEBB, Boston, 1931
Triples	36, OWEN WILSON, Pittsburgh, 1912	26, Joe Jackson, Cleveland, 1912 26, Sam Crawford, Detroit, 1914
Total Bases	445, Chuck Klein, Philadelphia, 1930	457, BABE RUTH, New York, 1921
Bases on Balls	148, Jim Wynn, Houston, 1969	170, BABE RUTH, New York, 1923
Stolen Bases	118, Lou Brock, St. Louis, 1974	130, RICKEY HENDERSON, Oakland, 1982
Strikeouts	189, BOBBY BONDS, San Francisco, 1970	185, Pete Incaviglia, Texas, 1986
Fewest Strikeouts (Minimum 500 ABs)	8, LLOYD WANER, Pittsburgh, 1933	9, Dale Mitchell, Cleveland, 1952

*Record since 1901

Most Games, Career, in the Outfield
2943—Ty Cobb, 1905–1928

Most Consecutive Games in the Outfield
897—Billy Williams, Chicago Cubs, September 11, 1963, through June 13, 1969

Best Career Fielding Average
.993—Terry Puhl, 1977–86

Most Seasons League Leader in Fielding Average
AL—6—Amos Strunk, last in 1920
NL—5—Mike Griffin, last in 1898

Most Consecutive Errorless Games
226—Don Demeter, Philadelphia Phillies and Detroit Tigers, September 3, 1962, through July 6, 1965. During that span Demeter played a number of games at other positions where he did make errors.

Most Consecutive Errorless Chances
568—Curt Flood, St. Louis Cardinals, September 3, 1965, through June 4, 1967

EVOLUTION OF SEASON RECORD FOR
BEST FIELDING AVERAGE

	Team	League	Year	Average
Paul Hines	Chicago	National	1876	.923
John Glenn	Chicago	National	1877	.948
Joe Hornung	Boston	National	1881	.948
Tom Dolan	St. Louis	Association	1883	.957[1]
Jim O'Rourke	New York	National	1888	.960
Jim Fogarty	Philadelphia	National	1889	.961[2]
Jim Fogarty	Philadelphia	Players	1890	.963
Mike Griffin	Brooklyn	National	1892	.986[3]
Harry Bay	Cleveland	American	1904	.987
Sam Crawford	Detroit	American	1905	.988
Fielder Jones	Chicago	American	1906	.988
Ed Hahn	Chicago	American	1907	.990
Wildfire Schulte	Chicago	National	1908	.994
Sammy West	Washington	American	1928	.996[4]
Dick Porter	Cleveland	American	1933	.996
Harry Craft	Cincinnati	National	1940	.997
Danny Litwhiler	Philadelphia	National	1942	1.000
Rocky Colavito	Cleveland	American	1965	1.000
Curt Flood	St. Louis	National	1966	1.000[5]

[1]May have been one of the greatest outfielders ever but was so poor a hitter that no team could afford to carry him for his fielding alone. Set an all-time record in 1883 when he threw out 62 base runners trying to advance.

[2]Among the very best outfielders in his day but took ill late in the 1890 season and died early in 1891 at 27.

[3]Not a fluke season by any means. Griffin owned the surest outfield glove in the game for nearly a decade.

[4]The best fielder in his time. His arm went dead in 1930 but came back as strong as ever—he led the AL in double plays in 1932.

[5]Several outfielders have had perfect fielding averages since 1966, but none had as many chances as Flood with 396.

Most Chances Accepted, Career
7461—Tris Speaker, 1907–28

Most Chances Accepted, Season
566—Taylor Douthit, St. Louis Cardinals, 1928. It was the only year Douthit handled anywhere near that number of chances. Second to Douthit is Richie Ashburn, who had 560 chances in 1951. Ashburn is the only outfielder to han-

dle over 520 chances in a season more than once—he did it four times, last in 1957.

Most Chances Accepted, Game, Nine Innings

13—Earl Clark, Boston Braves, May 10, 1929. Clark was only 21 at the time and seemed ready to take over the Braves' regular centerfield slot, but he never made it.

Most Assists, Season, Since 1901

44—Chuck Klein, Philadelphia Phillies, 1930. Klein played shallow in his home park, the Baker Bowl, which had a short right field, and threw out several batters at first base on what ought to have been singles.

Most Runners Thrown Out at Plate, Game

3—Jack McCarthy, Chicago Cubs, April 26, 1905. The Pirates provided the opposition that day and repeatedly challenged McCarthy's 36-year-old arm on short fly balls. Notwithstanding his having risen to the test, McCarthy lost his job to Wildfire Schulte.

Most Gold Glove Awards

12—Roberto Clemente, 1955–72
    Willie Mays, 1951–73

Triple Crown Winners

In 1967 Carl Yastrzemski won the Triple Crown when he led the American League in batting and RBIs and tied Harmon Killebrew of the Twins for the top spot in home runs. Only a year earlier Frank Robinson had won the Triple Crown after the Orioles acquired him from the Reds. After a ten-year hiatus since Mickey Mantle's Triple Crown season in 1956, Robinson's and Yastrzemski's triumphs seemed to signal that hitters like Chuck Klein, Jimmie Foxx, Lou Gehrig and Ted Williams, who were capable of winning a Triple Crown and who had been relatively abundant in the 1930s and 40s, were once again going to emerge. Instead however, 19 seasons have passed since 1967, and Yastrzemski still remains the last Triple Crown winner.

Closest Since 1967 to Winning a Triple Crown

AL—Dick Allen, Chicago, led in homers and RBIs and was third in batting in 1972. Jim Rice, Boston, also led in homers and RBIs and was third in batting in 1978.

NL—Mike Schmidt, Philadelphia, led in homers and RBIs and was fourth in batting in 1981

TRIPLE CROWN WINNERS

	Team	League	Year	HRs	RBIs	BA
Paul Hines	Providence	National	1878	4	58	.358[1]
Tip O'Neill	St. Louis	Association	1887	14	123	.435[2]
Hugh Duffy	Boston	National	1894	18	145	.438
Nap Lajoie	Philadelphia	American	1901	14	125	.422
Ty Cobb	Detroit	American	1909	9	115	.377[3]
Heinie Zimmerman	Chicago	National	1912	14	98	.372
Rogers Hornsby	St. Louis	National	1922	42	152	.401[4]

	Team	League	Year	HRs	RBIs	BA
Rogers Hornsby	St. Louis	National	1925	39	143	.403
Chuck Klein	Philadelphia	National	1933	28	120	.368[5]
Jimmie Foxx	Philadelphia	American	1933	48	163	.356
Lou Gehrig	New York	American	1934	49	165	.363
Joe Medwick	St. Louis	National	1937	31	154	.374[6]
Ted Williams	Boston	American	1942	36	137	.356[7]
Ted Williams	Boston	American	1947	32	114	.343
Mickey Mantle	New York	American	1956	52	130	.353[8]
Frank Robinson	Baltimore	American	1966	49	122	.316
Carl Yastrzemski	Boston	American	1967	44	121	.326

[1]Disputed. Some sources give the batting title in 1878 to Abner Dalrymple.
[2]Led the American Association in every major hitting department in 1887—runs, hits, total bases, slugging average, doubles and triples as well as the three TC departments.
[3]The only TC winner also to lead his league in stolen bases.
[4]The case against Hornsby being the all-time greatest second baseman always starts with the fact that everybody hit a ton during his peak years. Really? Who else between 1920 and 1940 won two Triple Crowns, let alone hit .400 three times?
[5]Despite winning the Triple Crown, he wasn't selected the MVP.
[6]Last National League player to win a Triple Crown.
[7]Lost out in the MVP voting to Joe Gordon of the Yankees.
[8]The only TC winner who also hit 50 homers in the same season.

NUMBER OF TIMES LED THE THREE TC DEPARTMENTS*

	BA	HRs	RBIs	Total Wins
Babe Ruth	1	12	6	19
Ty Cobb	12	1	4	17
Ted Williams	6	6	4	16
Rogers Hornsby	7	2	4	13
Honus Wagner	8	0	4	12
Hank Aaron	2	4	4	10
Stan Musial	7	0	2	9
Lou Gehrig	1	3	5	9
Jimmie Foxx	2	4	3	9
Johnny Mize	1	4	3	8
Dan Brouthers	5	2	1	8[1]
Cap Anson	3	0	4	7
Nap Lajoie	3	1	3	7
Chuck Klein	1	4	2	7
Ed Delahanty	2	1	3	6

	BA	HRs	RBIs	Total Wins
Mickey Mantle	1	4	1	6
Joe DiMaggio	2	2	2	6
Sam Thompson	1	2	2	5
Carl Yastrzemski	3	1	1	5
Willie Mays	1	4	0	5
Joe Medwick	1	1	3	5

Active Players

	BA	HRs	RBIs	Total Wins
Dave Parker	2	0	1	3^2
Don Mattingly	1	0	1	2

[*]Includes only players who won at least one batting title and one of the other two TC departments.

[1]RBI totals for Brouthers and Anson are incomplete. It is possible, even likely, that each won at least one more RBI crown.

[2]Parker and Mattingly are the only two active players who have won a batting title and a second TC department. Of the pair, Mattingly would seem to have the better chance of someday winning the Triple Crown, and there are probably no other active players at the moment who, realistically, have more than an outside shot.

Close, But No Cigar, Awards

First Prize—Cy Seymour of the Reds led the National League in every major hitting department except home runs in 1905. He lost the TC by the margin of one home run; the NL leader in homers that year was a teammate of Seymour's, Fred Odwell, who never hit another home run in the majors.

Second Prize—Ted Williams led the AL in homers and RBIs in 1949 but missed taking his third Triple Crown when he lost the batting title to George Kell by .00016 of a point.

Third Prize—Stan Musial missed a Triple Crown in 1948 by a single home run; that season he led the National League in every other major hitting department.

Fourth Prize—Al Rosen of the Indians led the American League in homers and RBIs in 1953 but lost the batting title to Mickey Vernon by a single point when he failed by an eyelash to beat out an infield hit in his last at bat of the season.

Fifth Prize—By today's rules Jimmie Foxx would have won a Triple Crown in 1932 as well as in 1933. He led in homers and RBIs but lost the AL batting title by three points to Dale Alexander, who had only 392 at bats. Foxx came close again in 1938 when he led in batting and RBIs and clubbed 50 homers but lost the home run crown to Hank Greenberg, who had 58.

Sixth Prize—Ty Cobb led the AL in batting and RBIs in 1911 but fell one home run short of winning his second TC. In 1907 Cobb also missed a TC when he finished tied for second in homers.

Seventh prize—Rogers Hornsby came nearly as close as Ted Williams to winning three TCs. In 1921 he led the NL in batting and RBIs but trailed home run leader George Kelly by two circuit clouts.

Eighth Prize—Gavvy Cravath of the Phillies led the NL in homers and RBIs in 1913 but lost the batting crown to Jake Daubert of the Dodgers by nine points.

Closest Babe Ruth Came to Winning a Triple Crown

In 1924 Ruth led the AL in homers and batting average but finished second in RBIs, eight behind Goose Goslin of the Senators. Two years later Ruth won the homer and RBI crowns but trailed batting leader Heinie Manush of the Tigers by six points.

Closest Hank Aaron Came to Winning a Triple Crown

In 1963 Aaron led the NL in homers and RBIs but finished third in batting seven points behind the winner, Tommy Davis.

Great Shutout Feats

More shutouts were pitched in 1968 than in any other season since the end of the deadball era as pitchers savored their last months before mound heights were shaved and the strike zone was reduced to edge the balance of power once again toward the batters' side of the scale. That year Don Drysdale established a new all-time record for consecutive shutout innings, Bob Gibson fashioned the most shutouts by any pitcher since the end of the deadball era, and the Mets' Jim McAndrew also set a shutout record, albeit one he would rather not own.

Most Shutout Games, Season, since 1901
    NL—16—Pete Alexander, Philadelphia, 1916
    AL—13—Jack Coombs, Philadelphia, 1910

Most Shutout Games, Season, since 1920
    NL—13—Bob Gibson, St. Louis, 1968
    AL—11—Dean Chance, Los Angeles, 1964

Most Shutout Games, Season, 1920 through 1941
    NL—10—Carl Hubbell, New York Giants, 1933
    AL—6—Done by nine pitchers, last by Bob Feller, Cleveland, 1941

Most Shutout Games, Season, 1942 through 1960
    NL—10—Mort Cooper, St. Louis, 1942
    AL—9—Bob Feller, Cleveland, 1946
            Bob Lemon, Cleveland, 1948

Most Shutout Games by Left-hander, Season, since 1901
    NL—11—Sandy Koufax, Los Angeles, 1963. Second only to Ed Morris of the Pittsburgh Alleghenies in the American Association, who had 12 in 1886.

AL—9—Ron Guidry, New York, 1978
Babe Ruth, Boston, 1916

Most Seasons League Leader in Shutouts
NL—7—Pete Alexander, last in 1921
AL—7—Walter Johnson, last in 1924

Most Consecutive Shutouts Pitched
NL—6—Don Drysdale, Los Angeles, 1968
AL—5—Don White, Chicago, 1904

Most Consecutive Shutout Innings Pitched
NL—58—Don Drysdale, Los Angeles, 1968. Drysdale began his streak with a shutout on May 14; after pitching three more complete-game shutouts in succession, he led the Giants 3–0 in the ninth inning on May 31 at Dodger Stadium and then filled the bases with none out. With a 2–2 count, Drysdale's next pitch hit Giants catcher Dick Dietz, apparently forcing home a run and ending the shutout skein. But plate umpire Harry Wendelstadt ruled that Dietz hadn't tried to dodge the pitch. With the count now 3–2, Dietz popped out to short left field, and Drysdale then got the next two batters, preserving his streak. The Dodgers claimed that Wendelstadt's call was both correct and courageous; Giants vice president Chub Feeney said it would have been courageous if he'd made it in San Francisco. The skein was finally broken on June 8, 1968, in the fourth inning of Drysdale's try for a seventh straight shutout when Phillies outfielder Howie Bedell hit a sacrifice fly.

AL—55⅔—Walter Johnson, Washington, 1913; including two relief appearances

Most Consecutive Shutout Innings Pitched by Left-hander
45⅓—Carl Hubbell, New York Giants, 1933

Most Consecutive Shutout Innings Pitched, Beginning of Career
NL—25—George McQuillan, Philadelphia, 1908
AL—22—Boo Ferriss, Boston, 1945. Ferriss is one of nine pitchers who threw shutouts in their first two major-league games. McQuillan, whose shutout string included relief appearances, is not among them.

Most Spectacular Pitching Job, First Two Major-League Games

Jim Hughes of the Baltimore Orioles threw a two-hit shutout in his major-league debut on April 18, 1898, then no-hit the Boston Beaneaters four days later in his second start. Hughes won 23 games as a rookie and 28 in his sophomore year, then got married and spent the 1900 season pitching in a California outlaw league after his new bride refused to go East.

Most Innings Needed to Win Shutout in First Start

11—Jesse Stovall, Cleveland September 3, 1903. Stovall, brother of Cleveland first baseman George Stovall, beat Detroit 1–0. The Tigers were so impressed by his overtime masterpiece that they acquired him after the season, then cut him loose when he had a 3–13 record in 1904.

Only Player to Pitch a Complete-Game Shutout in the Lone Game He Pitched

Catcher John Ryan was sent to the mound by the St. Louis Cardinals in the second game of a doubleheader in 1902. Despite throwing a three-hit shutout, he was never again tried as a pitcher.

Most Hits Surrendered While Pitching a Shutout

NL—14—Larry Cheney, Chicago, versus the New York Giants on September 14, 1913

AL—14—Milt Gaston, Washington, versus Cleveland on July 10, 1928

The Team That Never Learned How to Pick Them II

The only time a St. Louis Browns pitcher led the American League in whitewashes was in 1929 when three Brownies —Sam Gray, George Blaeholder and Al Crowder—all tied for the top spot with four shutouts.

Most Shutout Games Lost, Season

NL—11—Bugs Raymond, St.Louis, 1908.

AL—10—Walter Johnson, Washington, 1909; five of them to the White Sox

Most Consecutive Shutout Games Lost, Season

4—Jim McAndrew, New York Mets, 1968; he gave up only six runs in his four losses. No other pitcher has ever lost more than two shutouts in a row.

Pitcher with Whom McAndrew Could Most Sympathize
Erv Kantlehner, Pittsburgh, had a 2.26 ERA in 1915 but only a 6–12 record as the Pirates were blanked 8 times in his 18 starts.

Most Consecutive Shutout Wins, Team
NL—6—Pittsburgh, June 2 through June 6, 1903, amid an all-time record 56 straight shutout innings from June 1 to June 9
AL—5—Baltimore, September 2 through September 6, 1974

Most Shutout Games Won in a Season, Team
NL—32—Chicago, 1907 and 1909
AL—30—Chicago, 1906

Most Shutout Games Lost in a Season, Team
NL—33—St. Louis, 1908; 11 of them behind Bugs Raymond
AL—29—Washington, 1909; 10 of them behind Walter Johnson

Most Consecutive Games Without Being Shut Out, Team
AL—308—New York, August 3, 1931, through August 2, 1933. The streak was ended by Lefty Grove of the A's, who blanked the Yankees 7–0.
NL—182—Philadelphia, August 17, 1893, through May 10, 1895

TOP 10 IN CAREER SHUTOUTS

		Years Active	Shutouts
1.	Walter Johnson	1907–27	110
2.	Pete Alexander	1911–30	88
3.	Christy Mathewson	1900–1916	83
4.	Cy Young	1890–1911	77
5.	Eddie Plank	1901–17	70[1]
6.	Three Finger Brown	1903–16	63
7.	Warren Spahn	1942–65	63
8.	Tom Seaver	1967–	61
9.	Ed Walsh	1904–17	58[2]
	Don Sutton	1966–	58

[1]Southpaw record.
[2]Only non-200-game winner in top 10.

Most Consecutive Innings Without Scoring, Team
AL—48—Philadelphia, September 22 to September 26, 1906
NL—48—Chicago, June 15 to June 21, 1968. During their scoreless skeins both the A's and the Cubs lost four consecutive shutout games, tying a record held by several teams but most notably the Astros, who had it happen to them in 1963 and again only three years later.

Most 1–0 Games Won, Career
38—Walter Johnson, Johnson also lost an all-time record 26 1–0 games and 65 shutout games altogether, also an all-time record.

Only Pitcher to Complete 100 or More Games without Ever Pitching a Shutout
Jim Hughey, 1891–1900, registered exactly 100 complete games but no shutouts. His career record was 28–80, giving him a .266 winning percentage, the all-time poorest among pitchers in over 100 decisions. In Hughey's defense he pitched for the 1898 St. Louis Browns and the 1899 Cleveland Spiders, two of the worst teams in the last century.

Most Complete Games since 1901 without Pitching a Shutout
45—Roy Mahaffey, 1927–36

Only Pitcher since 1901 to Throw a No-hitter But Never a Shutout
Ed Lafitte of the Brooklyn Tip Tops in the Federal League held the Kansas City Packers hitless on September 19, 1914, while beating them 6–2. Lafitte, whose family tree included the pirate Jean Lafitte, won 35 games in the majors between 1909 and 1915, but none was a shutout. Bumpus Jones, who no-hit Pittsburgh 7–1 on October 15, 1892, in his first major-league game, also never pitched a shutout. The following year the mound was moved 10½ feet farther from the plate, and Jones, unable to adjust to the added distance, was cut by Cincinnati after being battered to the tune of a 10.32 ERA in his first seven games.

The Three Most Interesting Teams Between 1961 and 1976

1967 CHICAGO WHITE SOX
W-89 L-73
Manager: Eddie Stanky

Regular Lineup—1B, Tom McCraw; 2B, Wayne Causey; 3B, Don Buford; SS, Ron Hansen; RF, Ken Berry; CF, Tommy Agee; LF, Pete Ward; C, J. C. Martin; P, Gary Peters; P, Joel Horlen; P, Tommy John; P, Bob Locker; P, Hoyt Wilhelm; P, Wilbur Wood.

Nobody ever thought much of Stanky as a manager, but he kept this club in the tight 1967 American League race until the last week of the season when a doubleheader loss to Kansas City left the battle to the Red Sox, Twins and Tigers. The White Sox best hitters in 1967, Buford and Berry, batted .241; Ward led in RBIs with 62; Agee in runs with 73 and total bases with 196; and the club scored almost 200 runs less than pennant-winning Boston. But Stanky's pitching tandem of Peters and Horlen, coupled with a superlative bullpen crew of Wilhelm, Locker and Wood, made for a lot of close low-scoring games. The Sox team batting average of .225 and slugging average of .320 are both record lows for a first-division team since the end of deadball era. Peters, Horlen and John ranked first, second and fourth in the AL in ERA, but John's 2.47 figure was a shade too high for a team that averaged just over three runs a game, and he finished with a 10–13 record.

1972 CINCINNATI REDS
W-95 L-59
Manager: Sparky Anderson

Regular Lineup—1B, Tony Perez; 2B, Joe Morgan; 3B, Dennis Menke; SS, Dave Concepcion; RF, Cesar Geronimo; CF, Bobby Tolan; LF, Pete Rose; C, Johnny Bench; P, Jack Billingham; P, Ross Grimsley; P, Gary Nolan; P, Clay Carroll, P, Tom Hall; P, Pedro Borbon; P, Don Gullett; P, Wayne Simpson; P, Jim McGlothlin.

The Reds easily won the NL Western Division by 10½ games over the Astros, beat the favored Pirates in the LCS when Bob Moose wild-pitched home the pennant-winning run in the bottom of the ninth inning of Game Five, then took the A's to seven games in the World Series before losing the finale 3–2. Unlike Cincy teams later in the decade, this club had only one .300 hitter, Rose at .307, and only Bench with 100 RBIs. The Reds trailed the Astros uncharacteristically in batting, runs and even home runs and got a league-low 25 complete games from their starters. But what Anderson lacked in mound quality he made up for in depth. Much like the 1939 Yankees, who lacked a real staff leader but had nine heavy contributors, the Reds had eight pitchers who worked in more than 120 innings and a ninth, Carroll, who saved 37 games. The staff workhorse was Billingham with only 218 innings, and fragile Nolan, the top winner, had just 15 victories. The team won the division with timely hitting and a strong bullpen, but in the postseason the hitters did little, and it was the starting pitchers who, unexpectedly, came through. In the Series the Reds got only one poor starting effort—from McGlothlin in Game Five. Likewise, only Gullett in the first game of the LCS put on a bad show. The 1972 season was Joe Morgan's first as a Red—and the first time the public really became aware of his tremendous versatility, as he led the NL in runs, bases on balls, steals and fielding while hitting .292.

1974 OAKLAND ATHLETICS
W-90 L-72
Manager: Al Dark

Regular Lineup—1B, Gene Tenace; 2B, Dick Green; 3B, Sal Bando; SS, Bert Campaneris; RF, Reggie Jackson; CF, Bill North; LF, Joe Rudi; C, Ray Fose; P, Catfish Hunter; P, Vida Blue; P, Ken Holtzman; P, Rollie Fingers.

The A's won their division with the second-lowest team batting average in the AL, no reliable dh's, no .300 hitters and only Catfish Hunter of the starters having a good season— Holtzman was 19–17, Blue was 17–15—but the staff had the league's top ERA, and Fingers posted 17 saves. In the LCS the A's beat Baltimore in four games, losing only the first one, and then almost swept the Dodgers in the Series before dropping the fifth game. Dark got solid years from Rudi and Jackson and 103 RBIs from Bando on a .243 average, but the A's hit only .183 as a team in the LCS and .211 in the Series, creating the impression, in retrospect, that they won their third straight world title on habit as much as anything else.

Relievers' Records

In 1970 Hoyt Wilhelm became the first pitcher to appear in 1000 games, Mike Marshall gave up trying to be a starter and moved permanently to the bullpen, and Rollie Fingers, after registering only one complete game in 19 starts, began thinking that he might be wise to do the same. Fifteen years later the three of them held almost every major season and career relief record and were all strong candidates for the title of best relief pitcher ever.

Asked to name the first great reliever, most historians cite Firpo Marberry, but I'd split the honor between Three Finger Brown and Ed Walsh, with Christy Mathewson and Chief Bender only a notch beyond. When those four pitched, a "save" was still some 50 years away from being added to the game's vocabulary, but managers were already well aware that certain pitchers were especially adept at protecting a late-inning lead and were not at all hesitant to yank their starters when the game was on the line and to bring on the staff ace. Brown, for example, averaged over 10 relief appearances a season, and after it was decided what constituted a save and today's standards were applied to yesterday's box scores, he was credited with leading the National League in saves four consecutive years and being the first pitcher to chalk up more than 10 saves in a season. Walsh was only slightly less prized for his relief work. Four of his 40 wins in 1908 came as a reliever, and in addition he collected seven saves.

Just as effective as Brown and Walsh, a generation later, was Lefty Grove. During his peak years he was probably the best southpaw bullpen stopper in the game. After he was traded to the Red Sox, Grove was used almost exclusively as a starter, but between 1925 and 1933 he won 28 games in relief and saved 51 others.

Greatest Season by a Relief Pitcher Prior to 1893
First Prize—Jack Manning, Boston Red Caps, 1876. Manning, a rightfielder, doubled as a change pitcher and won four games and saved five others in relief of starters.
Second Prize—Bill Hutchinson, Chicago White Stockings, 1891. The last pitcher to win 40 games two years in a row, Hutchinson numbered 7 relief victories and a save among his 43 wins in 1891.

Greatest Season by a Relief Pitcher Between 1893 and 1920
First Prize—Tom Hughes, Boston Braves, 1915. He had a 20–14 record overall but was a perfect 10–0 as a reliever with five saves.
Second Prize—Nig Cuppy, Cleveland Spiders, 1894. He was 8–0 in relief, the first great season by a bullpenner after the mound was moved to its present location.

First Relief Pitcher to Collect 100 Saves
Firpo Marberry, in 1934, pitching for the Tigers. He retired with 101 saves and also won 94 games as a starter.

First Relief Pitcher to Collect 200 Saves
Hoyt Wilhelm, in 1969, pitching for the Angels. He finished with 227 saves.

First Relief Pitcher to Collect 300 Saves
Rollie Fingers, in 1982, pitching for the Brewers. He retired at the end of the 1985 season with 347 saves, the all-time career record.

First Relief Pitcher Selected for an All-Star Game
Jack Russell, Washington Senators, 1934. The first reliever to pitch in an All-Star Game was Mace Brown of the Pirates, in 1938.

First Relief Pitcher to Appear in 60 or More Games Two Consecutive Seasons
Ace Adams, New York Giants, 1942–43. He went on to appear in 60-plus games four straight seasons during World War II.

First Relief Pitcher to Appear in Half His Team's Games
John Wyatt, Kansas City A's, 1964. He had a 9–8 record in 81 games.

First Relief Pitcher to Appear in 90 Games in a Season
Wayne Granger, Cincinnati Reds, 1969. Posted 27 saves in 90 games.

First Relief Pitcher to Appear in 100 Games in a Season
Mike Marshall, Los Angeles Dodgers, 1974. He made 106 appearances, the all-time record, and also set the current American League record in 1979 when he appeared in 90 games for the Twins.

Most Relief Appearances, Season, by a Left-hander
AL—88—Wilbur Wood, Chicago, 1968
NL—86—Craig Lefferts, San Diego, 1986

Most Relief Innings, Season
NL—208—Mike Marshall, Los Angeles, 1974, shattering the old all-time record of 167 innings, set in 1945 by Andy Karl of the Phillies
AL—168⅓—Bob Stanley, Boston, 1982

Season Tandem Record for Relief Appearances
NL—178—Kent Tekulve (94) and Enrique Romo (84), Pittsburgh, 1979
AL—160—Wilbur Wood (88) and Hoyt Wilhelm (72), Chicago, 1968

Relief Pitcher with the Most Underappreciated Career
Lindy McDaniel. He pitched in 987 games and 2140 innings between 1955 and 1975. Never on a pennant winner, let alone a division winner, he had 172 saves and also won 22 games as a starter.

Best Career by a Reliever Who Began as a Starter
Phil Regan. Dropped in 1965 by the Tigers after successive seasons in which he went 4–10 and 1–5 as a starter, Regan was used exclusively in relief by the Dodgers in 1966 and responded with a 14–1 record and 21 saves, the best all-around season ever by a National League reliever. He finished in 1972 with 92 career saves and 58 relief wins.

Best Career by a Starter Who Began as a Reliever
Phil Niekro, hands down. The runner-up is just as clearcut. Wilbur Wood, after eight years in the bullpen, was made a starter by the White Sox in 1971 and won 20 games the next four years in a row.

Best Final Season by a Reliever
Jim Willoughby departed in 1978 after registering 13 saves in 59 games for the White Sox, and Rollie Fingers collected 17 saves in 1985, his final season, but neither had a particularly overwhelming ERA. Hence the award must go to Russ Christopher, who had 17 saves and a 2.90 ERA as the Indians bullpen ace in 1948 before a weak heart forced him to retire prematurely.

Greatest One-Game Relief Performance
Ernie Shore. On June 23, 1917, in the first game of a doubleheader at Fenway Park, Shore relieved Babe Ruth after Ruth was booted by homeplate umpire Brick Owens for arguing a ball-four call to Washington leadoff hitter Ray Morgan. Red Sox catcher Pinch Thomas was also ejected for joining Ruth's protest. The new catcher, Sam Agnew, cut down Morgan trying to steal second base, and Shore then retired the next 26 batters in a row and is credited with having pitched a perfect game despite not pitching a complete game.

Relief Pitcher Who Did the Most to Aid His Own Cause
NL—Emil Yde, Pittsburgh, June 15, 1924. Trailing the Cubs in the ninth inning, Yde doubled home the tying run and then tripled home the winning run in the 14th inning.
AL—Babe Birrer, Detroit, July 19, 1955. After entering the game in relief, he hit two three-run homers.

Relief Pitcher Who Did the Least to Aid His Own Cause
Ed Rommel, Philadelphia A's, July 10, 1932. In the process of working an American League-record 17 innings in relief, he gave up 29 hits and 14 runs to Cleveland batters, yet emerged the winning pitcher when the A's pushed across their 18th run in the top of the 18th inning. It was Rommel's 171st and last major-league victory, and he had the additional distinction of helping Johnny Burnett of the Indians make nine hits, an all-time one-game record. The A's stuck with Rommel because they brought only two able-bodied pitchers to Cleveland that day and had no one left after Connie Mack lifted starter Lew Krausse.

Least Productive Season by a Reliever
In 1986 Ed Vande Berg of the Dodgers pitched in 60 games without recording a single save and collected just one

win. Only one other reliever, Arnie Earley of the Red Sox in 1965, has had a less productive season. In 57 games Earley posted an 0–1 record and no saves.

Most Career Mound Appearances by a Reliever Who Never Started a Game

899—Sparky Lyle, 1967–82. Second at the moment is Kent Tekulve with 853 appearances.

Winners of the "You-Had-to-Be-Paying-Attention-to-See-Them-in-Action" Award

First Prize—Joe Hoerner (1963–77) appeared in 493 games but logged only 563 innings of work.

Second Prize—Fred Gladding (1961–73), 450 games and 601 innings

Third Prize—Ron Willis (1966–70), 188 games and 238 innings

Fourth Prize—Randy Moffitt (1972–83), 534 games and 782 innings

Fifth Prize—Steve Hamilton (1961–72), 421 games and 664 innings. Included in his career stats are 17 starts and three complete games.

Special Award—Bill Henry (1952–69) appeared in 527 games and made 44 starts in his 16-year career but only once, in 1965, worked 100 innings.

Proof That It Doesn't Pay for a Reliever to Start Off Too Meteorically

Butch Metzger began his career in the mid-1970s with 12 straight wins in relief, breaking the rookie record of 10 straight relief wins set in 1952 by Eddie Yuhas of the Cardinals. Before Yuhas, the record belonged to Joe Pate, who was 9–0, all in relief, for the 1926 Athletics. Now you probably know that Metzger won only 18 games before his arm went, but Yuhas and Pate fared even worse. Neither ever won another game after his rookie season.

Best Season Ever by a Reliever

True, Roy Face was 18–1 in 1959, Phil Regan went 14–1 in 1966, Jim Konstanty and Willie Hernandez both were selected MVPs, and Hernandez, Rollie Fingers and Sparky Lyle all won Cy Young Awards, but John Hiller still gets my vote. In 1973 he had a 10–5 record in relief, a 1.44 ERA, 124 strikeouts in 125 innings—but the clincher was his 38 saves, a southpaw record until 1966 when Dave Righetti of the Yankees netted 46 saves.

EVOLUTION OF THE SEASON SAVE RECORD SINCE 1901

	Team	League	Year	Saves
Joe McGinnity	New York	National	1904	5[1]
Claude Elliott	New York	National	1905	6[2]
George Ferguson	New York	National	1906	7
Ed Walsh	Chicago	American	1908	7
Frank Arellanes	Boston	American	1909	8[3]
Three Finger Brown	Chicago	National	1911	13
Firpo Marberry	Washington	American	1924	15
Firpo Marberry	Washington	American	1925	15
Firpo Marberry	Washington	American	1926	26[4]
Joe Page	New York	American	1949	27
Ellis Kinder	Boston	American	1953	27
Luis Arroyo	New York	American	1961	29
Ted Abernathy	Chicago	National	1965	31[5]
Jack Aker	Kansas City	American	1966	32
Wayne Granger	Cincinnati	National	1970	35
Clay Carroll	Cincinnati	National	1972	37
John Hiller	Detroit	American	1973	38
Dan Quisenberry	Kansas City	American	1983	45
Bruce Sutter	St. Louis	National	1984	45
Dave Righetti	New York	American	1986	46

[1]Before 1904 the 20th-century record was three, held by many. McGinnity tied Jack Manning's all-time record, set in 1876.

[2]Never pitched again in the majors after 1905.

[3]The only saves of his career.

[4]By 1926 Marberry, you'd think, would have spawned an onslaught of bullpen records, but over the next 30 years Johnny Murphy was the only other relief pitcher to collect 100 saves, and as late as 1946 Ken Raffensberger, mainly a starter, led the National League in saves with just six.

[5]Had 148 career saves, all of them after he passed his 30th birthday.

EVOLUTION OF SEASON RECORD FOR
RELIEF WINS, SINCE 1893

	Team	League	Year	Relief Wins
Frank Killen	Pittsburgh	National	1893	5
Nig Cuppy	Cleveland	National	1894	8
Tom Hughes	Boston	National	1915	10
Elam Vangilder	St. Louis	American	1925	11
George Dauss	Detroit	American	1926	11[1]
Wilcy Moore	New York	American	1927	13[2]
Mace Brown	Pittsburgh	National	1938	15[3]
Jim Konstanty	Philadelphia	National	1950	16[4]
Roy Face	Pittsburgh	National	1958	18[5]

[1]The final 11 wins of a career in which he won 221, all for the Tigers.
[2]Won 19 games altogether in this, his rookie season, and also had 13 saves.
[3]Lost the most important game played that season when he surrendered the famous "homer in the gloamin' " to Gabby Harnett of the Cubs.
[4]Probably the finest season by a reliever prior to Hiller's 1973 season—he also had 22 saves and appeared in 74 games, the most ever by a pitcher in a 154-game season.
[5]The American League record belongs to John Hiller, who won 17 for the Tigers in 1974; Hiller also lost 14 games that year and holds the all-time season record for most relief decisions—31.

TOP 10 IN CAREER SAVES

	Years Active	Saves
1. Rollie Fingers	1968–85	341
2. Bruce Sutter	1976–	286
3. Goose Gossage	1972–	278
4. Sparky Lyle	1967–82	238
5. Dan Quisenberry	1979–	229
6. Hoyt Wilhelm	1952–72	227
7. Roy Face	1953–69	197
8. Gene Garber	1969–	194
9. Mike Marshall	1965–81	187
10. Tug McGraw	1965–84	180

TOP 10 IN CAREER RELIEF WINS

		Years Active	Relief Wins
1.	Hoyt Wilhelm	1952–72	123
2.	Lindy McDaniel	1955–75	119
3.	Rollie Fingers	1968–75	107
4.	Sparky Lyle	1967–85	99
5.	Roy Face	1953–69	96
6.	Mike Marshall	1965–81	92
	Goose Gossage	1972–	92
8.	Don McMahon	1957–74	90
9.	Tug McGraw	1965–84	89
10.	Clay Carroll	1964–78	88

The 20 Most Lopsided
Trades since 1901

At the conclusion of the 1965 season the Reds felt they needed more quality pitchers to become a contender and sent Frank Robinson to Baltimore for starting pitcher Milt Pappas, reliever Jack Baldschun and a promising young outfielder named Dick Simpson. Simpson never panned out, Baldschun proved to be almost through, and the trade began to seem just about the worst one ever made when Robinson won the American League Triple Crown in 1966 and led Baltimore to its first World Championship while the Reds faded from fourth place to seventh. No question the swap worked out badly for the Reds, but it was far from being the all-time worst deal. While Robinson went on to hit 586 career home runs and make the Hall of Fame, Pappas didn't do all that shabbily either. He won 99 games in the National League before retiring and 207 altogether, not exactly the figures of a washout. Here are 20 swaps that, I think, make the Robinson-Pappas transaction look rather good. Excluded are all deals in which a sizable chunk of cash—more than $25,000—sweetened the package and made it too tempting for impoverished club owners to resist. Also excluded is the infamous trade in which the Giants got Christy Mathewson from the Reds for a washed-up Amos Rusie. Not only did it occur near the end of 1900, but the prime mover in the deal, John Brush, knew that he'd soon be leaving the Reds to join the Giants and hence was acting clandestinely in his own best interest.

1905—The Red Sox sent rookie George Stone to the Browns for aging Jesse Burkett. Stone leads the American League in total bases in 1905; Burkett hits .257. The following year Stone wins the AL batting title, Burkett is playing out the string in the minors, and the Red Sox plummet to the cellar two years after winning the pennant.

1907—Cleveland deals rebellious holdout pitcher Earl Moore to the Yankees for Walter Clarkson, brother of 328-game winner John Clarkson. Moore doesn't get along in New York either and drops to the minors but resurfaces with the Phillies late in the 1908 season and becomes the ace of their staff. Walter Clarkson wins four games for Cleveland and is cut in 1908 as the Indians, short of pitching, lose the pennant by half a game.

1910—The Cardinals swindle the Reds out of Miller Huggins, Rebel Oakes and Frank Corridon for the price of Fred Beebe and Al Storke. Storke dies before spring training begins, and Beebe plays only one year for the Reds.

1919—Cleveland gets Larry Gardner, Charlie Jamieson and Elmer Myers from the A's for Braggo Roth. Gardner and Jamieson became vital cogs in the Indians' 1920 World Championship team; the A's ship Roth to the Red Sox in midseason. For the Indians, the deal makes up, partially, for the 1915 transaction with the White Sox in which they got Roth for Shoeless Joe Jackson.

1934—Convinced that Wes Ferrell's lame arm won't recover, the Indians send him to the Red Sox along with Twitchy Dick Porter in return for Bob Weiland and Bob Seeds. Ferrell wins 59 games for the Red Sox over the next three seasons, Weiland wins one game for Cleveland, and Seeds is cut after being unable to crack the Indians lineup.

1938—The Phillies send Dolf Camilli to Brooklyn for Eddie Morgan. Morgan never plays a single game for the Phils; Camilli has four 100-plus RBI seasons for the Dodgers and in 1941 leads the NL in both homers and RBIs. (In the Phillies' defense, some sources claim that owner Gerry Nugent got a fair-sized wad of cash too.)

1947—The Phils get Al Lakeman from the Reds for Ken Raffensberger and Hugh Poland. Lakeman hits .159 as the Phils' backup catcher; for the next six years Raffensberger is one of the NL's top pitchers. With Raffensberger, the Phils conceivably could have won two more pennants in that period; without him they are lucky to win one.

1950—The A's send Nellie Fox to the White Sox for catcher Joe Tipton. Tipton never becomes more than a sub; Fox should one day become a Hall of Famer.

1954—The Orioles give up on Roy Sievers and send him to Washington for Gil Coan. Coan turns out to be about finished; in 1957 Sievers becomes the Senators' first home run king.

1959—The Pirates package Frank Thomas, Jim Pendleton, Whammy Douglas and Johnny Powers and ship them to the Reds for Harvey Haddix, Smokey Burgess and Don Hoak. Thomas is a bust in 1959 for the Reds; the others are even bigger disappointments. In 1960 Haddix, Burgess and Hoak lead the Pirates to their first flag since 1927.

1960—The Indians get Norm Cash in a deal with the White Sox and swiftly present him to the Tigers in return for Steve Demeter, whom they expect will fill their third base hole. Which Demeter does—for all of three games. Cash leads the AL in batting in 1961 and goes on to a long and productive career.

1969—The Seattle Pilots snare Lou Piniella from Cleveland in the expansion draft, grow disenchanted with him in spring training and swap him to their sister expansion club, the Kansas City Royals, for John Gelnar and Steve Whitaker. Piniella wins the Rookie of the Year award in 1969; Seattle wins a move to Milwaukee.

1969—Not content with aging third baseman Ed Charles, the Mets deal Amos Otis and Bob Johnson to the Royals for Joe Foy. Foy hits .236 in 1970 and is out of the majors the following year; Otis plays until 1985 and posts higher career totals in every major batting department than any of the Mets' career leaders.

1971—The greatest year ever for trades if you're not a fan of the Mets, Giants or Astros. The Giants start off the season by passing future home-run king George Foster along to the Reds for Frank Duffy and Vern Geishert.

1971—Still in quest of a third baseman, the Mets grab Jim Fregosi from the Angels for Leroy Stanton, Don Rose and Francisco Estrada . . . and throw in pitcher Nolan Ryan.

1971—At the end of the season the Astros deliver John Mayberry to the Royals for Jim York and Lance Clemons. In a three-year period the Royals have now acquired Mayberry, Lou Piniella and Amos Otis just about for free.

1971—Duffy's not what they're looking for, so when the season's over the Giants send him to Cleveland for sore-armed Sam McDowell and manage in the same deal to unload aging Gaylord Perry, who has only 179 wins left in his right arm.

1972—To get Danny Carter the Red Sox divest themselves of Sparky Lyle. Lyle posts 35 saves for the Yankees in 1972 and later wins the Cy Young award; Carter never again plays regularly.

1975—In December, the Yankees obtain Willie Randolph, Dock Ellis and Ken Brett from the Pirates for Doc Medich. Medich wins eight games for Pittsburgh in 1976; Ellis wins 17 for the Yankees, and Randolph becomes one of the top second baseman in the American League for the next decade.

1978—The Indians test switch-hitting shortstop Alfredo Griffin in a few games, find him wanting and ship him to Toronto for reliever Victor Cruz. Cruz wins three games for Cleveland in 1979; Griffin wins the Rookie of the Year award and becomes one of the AL's best glove men at shortstop for the next decade.

Workhorse Records

In 1971 Mickey Lolich of the Tigers pitched 376 innings, the most by any hurler since 1917. The following year Wilbur Wood topped Lolich's post-deadball record when he logged 377 innings for the White Sox. Wood's total was the most by a left-hander since Irv Young pitched 378 innings for the Boston Braves in 1905.

Before 1893, when the mound distance was increased by 10½ feet, pitchers routinely worked 500 or more innings in a season, led by Will White of Cincinnati, who pitched 683 innings in 1879 while the mound was still only 45 feet from the plate. Until the early 1920s pitchers were still expected to finish almost every game they started and paced themselves accordingly. After that, inning totals dipped so sharply that in 1925, for the first time in major-league history, a league leader in innings pitched worked fewer than 300 innings.

Most Innings Pitched, Season, since 1901
    AL—464—Ed Walsh, Chicago, 1908
    NL—434—Joe McGinnity, New York Giants, 1904

Most Innings Pitched, Season, 1920 through 1941
    NL—363—Pete Alexander, Chicago, 1920
    AL—358—George Uhle, Cleveland, 1923

Most Innings Pitched, Season, 1942 through 1960
    AL—371—Bob Feller, Cleveland, 1946; the post-deadball record for a 154-game season
    NL—347—Robin Roberts, Philadelphia, 1953

Most Innings Pitched, Season, 1961 through 1976
    AL—377—Wilbur Wood, Chicago, 1972
    NL—346—Steve Carlton, Chicago, 1972

Most Innings Pitched, Season, since 1977
 NL—342—Phil Niekro, Atlanta, 1979
 AL—319—Jim Palmer, Baltimore, 1977

Most Seasons League Leader in Innings Pitched
 NL—7—Pete Alexander, last in 1920
 AL—5—Bob Feller, last in 1947
     Walter Johnson, last in 1916

Fewest Innings Pitched by League Leader in Innings Pitched, 1981 Excluded
 AL—256—Early Wynn, Chicago, 1959
 NL—261—Fernando Valenzuela, Los Angeles, and Joaquin Andujar, St. Louis, 1984

First Season League Leader in Innings Pitched Had Fewer than 300 Innings
 AL—1925—Herb Pennock, New York, led with 277 IPs
 NL—1926—Pete Donohue, Cincinnati, led with 286 IPs

Most Seasons 400 or More Innings Pitched, since 1901
 2—Ed Walsh, Chicago White Sox, 1907 and 1908; Joe McGinnity, New York Giants, 1903 and 1904

Most Seasons 300 or More Innings Pitched, since 1901
 11—Christy Mathewson, last in 1914

Most Consecutive Seasons 300 or More Innings Pitched, since 1901
 9—Walter Johnson, 1910–18

Most Consecutive Seasons 300 or More Innings Pitched, since 1920
 NL—6—Robin Roberts, Philadelphia, 1950–55
 AL—4—Wilbur Wood, Chicago, 1971–74

Most Innings Pitched, Game
 NL—26—Leon Cadore, Brooklyn, and Joe Oeschger, Boston, May 1, 1920
 AL—24—Jack Coombs, Philadelphia, and Joe Harris, Boston, September 1, 1906

Second-Most Innings Pitched, Game
NL—22—Bob Smith, Boston, May 17, 1927. Smith lost 4–3 to the Cubs in 22 innings, the longest complete-game decision in National League history.
AL—21—Ted Lyons, Chicago, May 24, 1929, lost 6–5 to Detroit in 21 innings.

Most Relief Innings Pitched, Game
NL—18⅓—Zip Zabel, Chicago, June 17, 1915, winning 4–3 in 19 innings over Jeff Pfeffer of the Dodgers, who went all the way
AL—17—Ed Rommell, Philadelphia, July 10, 1932, winning 18–17 in 18 innings over Cleveland.

Most Relief Innings Pitched, Career
1870—Hoyt Wilhelm, 1952–72

TOP 10 IN CAREER INNINGS PITCHED

		Years Active	*Innings*
1.	Cy Young	1890–1911	7357
2.	Pud Galvin	1879–92	5941
3.	Walter Johnson	1907–27	5926
4.	Gaylord Perry	1962–83	5352
5.	Phil Niekro	1964–	5273
6.	Warren Spahn	1942–65	5246
7.	Pete Alexander	1911–30	5189
8.	Kid Nichols	1890–1906	5061
9.	Steve Carlton	1965–	5055
10.	Tim Keefe	1880–93	5052

Great Feats of Precocity

Robin Yount became the youngest regular in American League history when he won the Brewers shortstop job in 1974 shortly after celebrating his 18th birthday. The youngest National League regular, also only 18 at the time, was Johnny Lush, who alternated between first base and the outfield for the 1904 Phillies. Unlike Yount who went on to become a long-time star, Lush was gone from the majors by the age of 24 after leading a hapless Cardinals team in wins and ERA. Trapped on weak clubs, embroiled in frequent holdouts and disputes with managers, he took his talented arm to the Pacific Coast League where he pitched with equal distinction—and bad luck—for several more seasons. With Portland in 1914 for example, he tossed a no-hitter against Venice that he lost 1–0 on a teammate's two-base error followed by a passed ball. Lush was the first player in this century to leave his mark on the game before the age of twenty, but he and Yount were far from being the only players who carved their first niches in the record book while they were still teenagers.

Youngest Player to Hit a Home Run since 1901
Tommy Brown, who in 1944 played 46 games at shortstop for the Dodgers as a 16-year-old high school student, banged a circuit clout off Preacher Roe of the Pirates on August 20, 1945, when he was just 17 years, 4 months and 14 days old.

Youngest Player to Get a Pinch Hit since 1901
AL—Mel Acosta, Washington, 1913, at age 17
NL—Mel Ott, New York Giants, 1926, at age 17; he was 9-for-24 that season as a pinch hitter.

Youngest to Pitch in a Game since 1901

NL—Joe Nuxhall, still a month and a half shy of his 16th birthday, pitched two-thirds of an inning for Cincinnati on June 10, 1944, in the Reds' 18–0 loss to the Cardinals.

AL—Carl Scheib, Philadelphia, September 6, 1943, when he was 16 years, 8 months and 5 days old

Youngest Pitcher to Start a Game since 1901

Bonus baby Jim Derrington was still a couple of months shy of his 17th birthday when the White Sox gave him a starting assignment in 1956. He lost it, was 0–1 in 20 games in 1957 and was gone from the majors before he turned eighteen.

Youngest 20-Game winner

No pitcher has been a 20-game winner before his 20th birthday since the mound was moved to its present distance from the plate. But before that happened there were several teenage 20-game winners. The youngest was Willie McGill, who won 20 in the American Association in 1891 at age 17; as a 16-year-old McGill had become the youngest ever to pitch a complete-game victory when he beat Buffalo on May 20, 1890, while toiling for Cleveland in the Players League. By 1896 McGill, one of the more prodigious imbibers of his day, was finished.

Youngest 25-Game Winner

Jumbo McGinnis, St. Louis Browns (AA), 1882, at age 18 won 25 games; the following year he won 28, giving him 53 wins before his 20th birthday.

First Teenage 20-Game Winner

Among those who consider the National Association a major league, Tommy Bond is regarded as the first teenage 20-game winner—he had a 22–32 record at age 18 with the 1874 Brooklyn Atlantics. In any case, Bond became the youngest 30-game winner in 1876 when he racked up 31 victories for Hartford while still just 20 years old, as well as being the youngest 40-game winner the following season with Boston.

Most Luckless Teenage Pitcher

Larry McKeon set an American Association record for most losses in a season when he was beaten 41 times in 1884 as an 18-year-old rookie with Indianapolis.

Best Debut by a Teenager Pitcher
Von McDaniel of the Cardinals threw a two-hit 2–0 shutout against the Dodgers at age 18 on June 15, 1958.

Youngest Catcher since 1901
Bob Williams, New York Yankees, had just turned 17 when he caught his first major-league game in 1911.

BEST SEASONS BY TEENAGERS*

Batting

Department	National League	American League
Batting Average	.322, MEL OTT, New York, 1928	.290, Tony Conigliaro, Boston, 1964
Slugging Average	.524, Mel Ott, New York, 1928	.530, TONY CONIGLIARO, Boston, 1964
Home Runs	18, MEL OTT, New York, 1928	24, TONY CONIGLIARO, Boston, 1964
RBIs	82, PHIL CAVARRETTA, Chicago, 1935	52, Tony Conigliaro, Boston, 1964
Hits	162, PHIL CAVARRETTA, Chicago, 1935	139, Al Kaline, Detroit, 1954
Runs	85, PHIL CAVARRETTA, Chicago, 1935	45, Ty Cobb, Detroit, 1906
Doubles	28, PHIL CAVARRETTA, Chicago, 1935	21, Tony Conigliaro, Boston, 1964
Triples	12, PHIL CAVARRETTA, Chicago, 1935 12, FRED LINDSTROM, New York, 1925	7, Ty Cobb, Detroit, 1906
Total Bases	238, PHIL CAVARRETTA, Chicago, 1935	214, Tony Conigliaro, Boston, 1964
Stolen Bases	17, Cesar Cedeno, Houston, 1970	23, TY COBB, Detroit, 1906
Bases on Balls	59, RUSTY STAUB, Houston, 1963	35, Tony Conigliaro, Boston, 1964
Strikeouts	61, Phil Cavarretta, Chicago, 1935	78, TONY CONIGLIARO, Boston, 1964

Pitching

Department	National League	American League
Wins	17, Dwight Gooden, New York, 1984	19, WALLY BUNKER, Baltimore, 1964
Losses	10, Cal McLish, Brooklyn, 1944	12, FRANK SHELLENBACK, Chicago, 1918

Department	National League	American League
Starts	32, Gary Nolan, Cincinnati, 1967	36, BOB FELLER, Cleveland, 1938
Complete Games	8, Gary Nolan, Cincinnati, 1967	20, BOB FELLER, Cleveland, 1938
Innings	227, Gary Nolan, Cincinnati, 1967	278, BOB FELLER, Cleveland, 1938
Games	40, BILLY McCOOL, Cincinnati, 1964	39, Bob Feller, Cleveland, 1938
Shutouts	5, GARY NOLAN, Cincinnati, 1967	4, Joe Wood, Boston, 1909
Bases on Balls	73, Dwight Gooden, New York, 1984	208, BOB FELLER, Cleveland, 1938
Strikeouts	276, DWIGHT GOODEN, New York, 1984	240, Bob Feller, 1938
ERA	2.58, Gary Nolan, Cincinnati, 1967	2.21, JOE WOOD, Boston, 1909

*Includes players since 1901 who ended the season still short of their 20th birthday—batters in at least 100 games, pitchers in at least 154 innings.

Great Milestone Achievements

On April 8, 1974, Hank Aaron of the Braves surpassed what had once seemed an unattainable milestone when he hit his 715th home run off Al Downing of the Dodgers. The only comparable achievement occurred on September 11, 1985, at Riverfront Stadium when Pete Rose singled off Eric Show of San Diego to collect his 4192d career hit 57 years to the day after Ty Cobb played his last game and retired with a record that for the next half-century was believed to be even more unassailable than Ruth's. Here is a partial chronology of other great milestone achievements.

1897—On July 18 Cap Anson became the first player in history to make 3000 hits.

1910—Pitching for Cleveland, Cy Young won his 500th game on July 19, beating Washington 5–4 in 11 innings.

1914—On June 9 Honus Wagner of the Pirates became the first player in this century and only the second in history to make 3000 career hits.

1915—Eddie Plank of the Federal League St. Louis Terriers became the first southpaw to win 300 games.

1916—Sam Crawford of Detroit collected his 312th and final triple.

1921—Still in the early stages of his career, Babe Ruth of the Yankees hit his 137th home run, breaking Roger Conner's career record of 136.

1923—On May 25 Ty Cobb scored his 1741st run, moving him ahead of Wagner. Cobb retired with 2244 runs, another all-time record that now seems within Rose's reach if he plays in 1987.

1923—Cobb went 4-for-4 on September 20 against the Red Sox at Fenway Park, breaking Wagner's record for career hits.

1927—On July 19, now with the Athletics, Cobb wreaked revenge on Detroit for letting him go by garnering his 4000th career hit, a double, off Sam Gibson of the Tigers. Remarkably, Cobb himself didn't realize what he'd achieved in that less record-concerned time until he read about it in the paper that evening.

1927—On September 30 Babe Ruth shattered his own record of 59 when he hammered his 60th homer of the season off Tom Zachary of Washington.

1928—Tris Speaker of the A's collected his 793d and last career double.

1929—Pete Alexander of the Cardinals netted his 373d career victory, staggering to a 19–16 decision over the Phillies. Released shortly thereafter by the Cards, Alexander left convinced that his last victory had put him one ahead of Christy Mathewson and given him the National League record for career wins, but 15 years later a review of Mathewson's stats revealed he'd been deprived of a win in 1902 that ought to have been credited to him, bringing his total also up to 373.

1935—Babe Ruth, wearing a Boston Braves uniform, collected his 2056th and last walk.

1936—Outfielder Woody Jensen of the Pirates totaled 396 at bats, the all-time record for a 154-game season. The quintessential contact hitter, Jensen struck out only 19 times that year and picked up just 16 walks.

1937—Rogers Hornsby hit .321 in 20 games for the St. Louis Browns and then retired at 41 with a .358 career average, the all-time highest by a right-handed hitter.

1939—On May 2 the Yankees beat Detroit 22–2 at Briggs Stadium without Lou Gehrig's name appearing in the box score for the first time in 2131 games played by the Yankees.

1941—Lefty Grove of the Red Sox, after a long struggle, became the second left-hander to win 300 games.

1942—Paul Waner of the Braves made his 3000th career hit, the last player to do so until 1957.

1960—On July 19 Juan Marichal of the Giants experienced the best mound debut ever by a future Hall of Famer when he pitched a 2–0 one-hitter against the Phillies.

1961—Roger Maris of the Yankees broke Ruth's season home run record when he hit his 61st round-tripper on October 1 off Tracy Stallard of the Red Sox.

1963—Warren Spahn's first win of the season gave him 328 career victories, breaking Eddie Plank's southpaw record.

1963—Early Wynn became the First American League hurler since 1941 to win 300 games when he beat Kansas City.

1970—Willie Mays became the first black player to make 3000 hits.

1972—Roberto Clemente made his 3000th and final career hit, a double off John Matlack of the Mets in the Pirates' last night home game of the season.

1974—Al Kaline of the Tigers became the first American Leaguer since Tris Speaker in 1925 to collect 3000 hits when he doubled on September 24 against Dave McNally of Baltimore.

1975—Bob Watson of Houston scored the 1,000,000th major-league run on May 4 in a game against the Giants.

1979—On September 23, against the Mets, Lou Brock of the Cardinals stole his 938th and final base.

1981—On June 10, just before the players went out on strike, Pete Rose of the Phillies made his 3630th hit to tie Stan Musial's National League record.

1981—Steve Carlton of the Phillies broke Bob Gibson's National League record when he recorded his 3118th career strikeout on September 21 in a 17-inning 1–0 loss to Montreal.

1983—Cal Ripken of the Orioles set a new all-time record when he played every inning of every regular-season, League Championship Series and World Series game played by his team.

1984—Pete Rose played in his 3309th game, breaking Carl Yastrzemski's all-time record for the most games played.

1984—Pete Rose collected his 4000th hit, a double off Jerry Koosman of the Phils, exactly 21 years after making his first hit.

1985—On July 11 Nolan Ryan of the Astros became the first pitcher in history to notch 4000 strikeouts when he fanned Danny Heep of the Mets.

1985—Rod Carew of the Angels collected his 3000th hit on August 4 off Frank Viola of the Twins, making him the first infielder since Eddie Collins to attain the 3000-hit circle. That same day Tom Seaver of the White Sox beat the Yankees 4–1 at Yankee Stadium for his 300th win. It was the first time in history that two players had achieved such important milestone figures on the same date.

1985—Cal Ripken of the Orioles played his 5342d consecutive inning, breaking the all-time record of 5341 consecutive innings, set by Buck Freeman of the Red Sox on June 5, 1905. Ripken ended the 1986 season with a streak of 6864 innings without respite.

1985—Phil Niekro of the Yankees nailed his 300th win on October 6, the last day of the season, by beating Toronto 8–0. It was the first time since 1890 that two pitchers picked up their 300th wins in the same year.

1986—Steve Carlton of the Giants on August 5 became the first southpaw to collect 4000 strikeouts.

World Series Play: 1961–76

FRANCHISE SUMMARY

Team	League	WS Record Thru 1976	Last WS	LCS Record Thru 1976	Last LCS
Oakland	American	3–0	1974	3–2	1975
New York	American	20–10	1976	1–0	1976
St. Louis	National	8–4	1968	—	—
Pittsburgh	National	4–2	1971	1–4	1975
Cleveland	American	2–1	1954	—	—
Boston	American	5–3	1975	1–0	1975
Los Angeles	National	3–2	1974	1–0	1974
Cincinnati	National	4–4	1976	4–1	1976
Chicago	American	2–2	1959	—	—
Baltimore	American	2–2	1971	3–2	1974
New York	National	1–1	1973	2–0	1973
Detroit	American	3–5	1968	0–1	1972
Chicago	National	2–8	1945	—	—
Minnesota	American	0–1	1965	0–2	1970
San Francisco	National	0–1	1962	0–1	1971
Philadelphia	National	0–2	1950	0–1	1976
Atlanta	National	—	—	0–1	1969

Became Defunct between 1961 and 1976

Milwaukee	National	1–1	1958	—	—

Yearly Highlights

1961—New York (AL) defeated Cincinnati (NL) 4 games to 1

Whitey Ford broke Babe Ruth's World Series record for consecutive scoreless innings as the Yankees won easily under their new manager, Ralph Houk.

1962—New York (AL) defeated San Francisco (NL) 4 games to 3

Ralph Terry nearly became the first pitcher to lose the seventh game in two World Series on the final pitch of the game. Instead he became the first pitcher to win a seventh game 1–0 as Yankees second baseman Bobby Richardson speared Willie McCovey's line drive in the bottom of the ninth inning with two out and runners on second and third.

1963—Los Angeles (NL) defeated New York (AL) 4 games to 0

The first renewal of the Yankees-Dodgers rivalry since the Brooklyn franchise had fled to the West coast, and the first time the Yankees had been swept in a Series since the Giants did it to them in 1922.

1964—St. Louis (NL) defeated New York (AL) 4 games to 3

Also for the first time since 1922, the Yankees lost back-to-back Series—despite Bobby Richardson's all-time record 13 hits—when a weary Bob Gibson of the Cardinals staggered to a 7–5 win in the deciding game.

1965—Los Angeles (NL) defeated Minnesota (AL) 4 games to 3

The Dodgers dropped the first two games in Minnesota but then got three shutouts, two of them by Sandy Koufax, to win a Series that had only one close game, the finale.

1966—Baltimore (AL) defeated Los Angeles (NL) 4 games to 0

The Dodgers were held scoreless the last $33\frac{2}{3}$ innings of the Series by Orioles reliever Moe Drabowsky, who fanned a record-tying six in a row in the opener, followed by three Orioles starting pitchers—Jim Palmer, Wally Bunker and Dave McNally—who had notched only one shutout among them during the regular season.

1967—St. Louis (NL) defeated Boston (AL) 4 games to 3

The seventh game found both Bob Gibson of the Cardinals and Jim Lonborg of the Red Sox shooting for their third wins, the first time that so dramatic a matchup had ever occurred in a Series. Gibson emerged with the victory but shared laurels with teammate Lou Brock, who hit .414 and stole a record seven bases.

1968—Detroit (AL) defeated St. Louis (NL) 4 games to 3

Once again Brock hit over .400 and swiped seven bases, and Gibson and his mound rival both started the seventh game in search of their third Series victories. But this time Gibson's opponent, Mickey Lolich, prevailed as Curt Flood of the Cardinals misplayed a long fly ball into a two-run triple. An inning earlier Lolich had extinguished a St. Louis rally by picking both Flood and Brock off first base. The Series MVP, Lolich brought the Tigers back after they trailed three games to one and aided his own cause in his first Series win by hitting the only home run of his long major-league career. Gibson achieved a measure of solace when he set an all-time Series record by fanning 17 Tigers in the opener.

1969—New York (NL) defeated Baltimore (AL) 4 games to 1

The most improbable world champs ever, the Mets fulfilled their fans' wildest fantasy by capturing four straight after dropping the opener. Prior to the 1969 season each league had expanded to 12 teams and split into two divisions, necessitating a best-three-of-five league Championships Series to determine the pennant winner. The Mets won the first National League LCS, besting the Atlanta Braves three games to none. The Orioles likewise won the first American League LCS three games to none over Minnesota.

1970—Baltimore (AL) defeated Cincinnati (NL) 4 games to 1

The Reds won the fourth game to avert a sweep. Both LCS runners-up, Minnesota and Pittsburgh, once again fell in three straight.

1971—Pittsburgh (NL) defeated Baltimore (AL) 4 games to 3

Led by Roberto Clemente's bat, Nelson Briles's shutout in Game Four and Steve Blass's two complete-game wins, including the series finale, the Pirates rallied after being down two games to none. Game Three, in Pittsburgh, was the first Series contest to be played at night. In LCS play, the Orioles swept Oakland and Pittsburgh bested San Francisco three games to one.

1972—Oakland (AL) defeated Cincinnati (NL) 4 games to 3

The A's Series hero, Gene Tenace, hit .348 and collected four homers and nine RBIs after hitting .225 in the regular season. For the first time in Series history no pitcher on either team registered a complete game. Also for the first time, both LCSes were competitive, the A's needing five games to dispose of Detroit and Pittsburgh taking the Reds to the full five games before losing on a ninth-inning wild pitch.

1973—Oakland (AL) defeated New York (NL) 4 games to 3

Well-pitched games from starters Jerry Koosman and John Matlack, abetted by Tug McGraw's superb relief work, nearly brought the Mets their second World Championship in five years, but the A's got even better relief pitching from Rollie Fingers, who had two saves, and Darold Knowles, who also had two saves and became the first pitcher to appear in every game of a seven-game Series. Again, both LCSes went down to the wire, the Mets beating the Reds in five behind Tom Seaver while Catfish Hunter shut down the Orioles in the fifth game without a single Baltimore runner getting as far as third base.

1974—Oakland (AL) defeated Los Angeles (NL) 4 games to 1

The A's got complete games from Vida Blue and Ken Holtzman to beat the Orioles 3–1 in the LCS, and Don Sutton blanked the Pirates in the opener of the National League LCS, which the Dodgers also won three games to one. But in the World Series, for the third year in a row, no pitcher tossed a complete game. Reliever Rollie Fingers, with a win and two saves, was the Series MVP. The A's, in becoming the first team other than the Yankees to win three straight World Championships, also may have become, in the opinion of many observers, the last team ever to do it.

1975—Cincinnati (NL) defeated Boston (AL) 4 games to 3

In LCS play, the Reds took out the Pirates in three straight, and the Red Sox did the same to Oakland, setting up what promised to be one of the better Series of the decade. It turned out to be possibly the best Series ever. Boston's Luis Tiant broke what was becoming a disturbing pattern by pitching two complete-game victories, and the

Red Sox came from three runs back in the eighth inning of Game Six to tie the Reds in regulation length and then even the Series on a 12th-inning homer by Carlton Fisk. But in Game Seven, the Red rallied from a 3–0 deficit to win their first World Championship in 35 years on Joe Morgan's two-out single in the ninth inning. The Reds scored 29 runs in the Series, the Red Sox scored 30, and both pitching staffs had an identical 3.88 ERA. The most even matchup in history, both statistically and on the field, was probably resolved by the Reds having a deeper bullpen. At the wire, Red Sox manager Darrell Johnson found himself with no one to bring in but rookie lefty Jim Burton. Burton's loss in the seventh game was the last decision he recorded in the majors.

1976—Cincinnati (NL) defeated New York (AL) 4 games to 0

The most one-sided Series since 1963—the Yankees were competitive only in the second game—followed the Reds' three-zip blowout of the Phillies in the National League LCS. The Yankees, on the other hand, needed five games in the LCS to shake the Kansas City Royals, the first American League expansion team to qualify for postseason play. The fifth game seemed headed for extra innings until Chris Chambliss of the Yankees snapped a 6–6 deadlock by leading off the bottom of the ninth inning with a homer off Royals reliever Mark Littell. Mobbed by Yankees fans, Chambliss was unable to complete his home run trot around the bases. Hours later he crept out of the clubhouse, accompanied by two policemen, and touched home plate to make his pennant-winning run official.

SECTION 6

Famous Firsts:
1977–86

1977—The American League bloats to 14 teams after granting new franchises to Toronto and Seattle. There are now 26 clubs in the major leagues, the most since the frantically unstable 1884 season when the uninvited Union Association joined the American Association in its war with the National League.

1977—Paddy Livingston dies in Cleveland. His obituary notes that he played for the Indians but neglects to mention that he was the last surviving member of the American League's class of 1901, its first year as a major circuit.

1978—The Yankees beat the Red Sox 5–4 at Fenway Park to cop the first division playoff game in history.

1979—Willie Stargell of the Pirates and Keith Hernandez of the Cardinals become the first players to be selected co-MVPs.

1980—A new stat—game-winning RBIs—is introduced to give analysts additional fodder to trot out when they're debating who the greatest clutch hitter is. Jack Clark of the second-division San Francisco Giants leads the majors in GWRs in 1980 and ties for the top spot the next two seasons.

1981—On June 12 the players go on strike for the second time in history and shut down the season for 50 days.

1982—Joel Youngblood becomes the first player to get hits for two different teams in two different cities on the same day when he's traded by the Mets to the Expos following an afternoon game on August 4 and scurries to Philadelphia in time to play in the game that night for Montreal.

1982—Relief pitcher Greg Minton of the Giants sets a new major-league record when he twirls 269⅓ innings over four seasons without surrendering a home run.

1982—In the wake of dire forecasts that the 1981 strike will disenchant fans with the game, the Dodgers demolish the season attendance record by drawing 3,608,881 fans.

1983—First baseman Pete Rose of the Phillies becomes the first player since the end of the deadball era to play a full season at the position for a pennant winner without hitting a home run.

1984—Jim Rice of the Red Sox sets a new major-league record when he grounds into 36 double plays.

1985—Don Baylor of the Yankees is hit by 24 pitches, tying the American League record, set first by Kid Elberfeld in 1911.

1985—Wade Boggs of the Red Sox becomes the first player in 55 years to make 240 hits in a season.

1985—Don Sutton, never a strikeout leader, becomes the first pitcher ever to fan 100 or more hitters in 20 consecutive seasons. By September he is on the same team with Reggie Jackson, the first hitter to fan 100 or more times in 17 consecutive seasons (1981 excepted).

1985—The two League Championship Series are expanded to a best 4-of-7 format, and the Kansas City Royals promptly establish the record for being the first team to rally from a 3–1 deficit to win an LCS.

1986—On April 30, pitching against the Seattle Mariners at Fenway Park, Roger Clemens of the Red Sox becomes the first hurler in history to fan 20 hitters in a nine-inning game.

1986—Don Sutton of the Angels beats the Texas Rangers 5–1 on June 18 for his 300th career victory, making him the first 300-game winner in history who needed more than 20 full seasons to do it and only once was a 20-game winner.

1986—Don Baylor of the Red Sox breaks the American League record that he previously shared with Kid Elberfeld when he is hit by 35 pitches. His career total of 227 leaves him only 16 short of Ron Hunt's modern record.

1986—Indians knuckleballer Phil Niekro extends his own all-time major-league record when he throws his 217th wild pitch.

1986—Bert Blyleven of the Twins surrenders 50 home runs, shattering Robin Roberts's former all-time record of 46 by a comfortable margin.

1986—On September 29, for the first time in history, two brothers face each other as rookie starting pitchers when Greg Maddux of the Cubs beats older brother Mike of the Phillies 8–3.

The Most Difficult
Pitchers to Beat

His 24–4 record and .857 winning percentage in 1986 not only brought Boston's Roger Clemens the Cy Young and MVP awards but narrowly missed equalizing Ron Guidry's incredible performance eight years earlier for the Yankees. In 1978 Guidry had the greatest season ever by a left-hander, a 25-game winner and, for that matter, a 20-game winner when he posted a 25–3 record and an .893 winning percentage. Guidry's mark shattered the old record for the highest winning percentage by a 20-game winner—.880—set by Preacher Roe of the Brooklyn Dodgers in 1951 when he won 22 games and lost only 3. But Roe still holds the National League record.

Highest Winning Percentage, Season, Minimum 15 Wins
   NL—.947—Roy Face, Pittsburgh, 1959 (18–1). At one point in the season Face had a 17–0 record.
   AL—.938—Johnny Allen, Cleveland, 1937 (15–1). Allen was 15–0 until he lost his last start of the season.

Most Wins in a Season without a Loss
   Al—12—Tom Zachary, New York, 1928. The runner-up is Dennis Lamp, who had a perfect 11–0 record for Toronto in 1985.
   NL—10—Howie Krist, St. Louis, 1942. The runner-up, Ken Holtzman of the Cubs, began the 1967 season by winning his first nine games, then was called away to do military service.

Highest Winning Percentage by a Rookie 20-Game Winner
   NL—.833—King Cole, Chicago, 1910 (20–4)
   AL—.813—Russ Ford, New York, 1910 (26–6)

Highest Winning Percentage by a Rookie since 1893, Minimum 10 Decisions
NL—.900—Al Orth, Philadelphia, 1895 (9–1)
AL—.900—Whitey Ford, New York, 1950 (9–1). In 1926 Joe Pate of the Philadelphia A's was a perfect 9–0 as a reliever.

Most Wins without a Loss, Only Season in Majors
3—Luke Nelson, New York Yankees, 1919.
   Danny Osborn, Chicago White Sox, 1975

Most Seasons League Leader in Winning Percentage
AL—5—Lefty Grove, last in 1939
NL—3—Ed Reulbach, 1906–08 consecutive

Only Pitcher to Lead Both the NL and the AL in Winning Percentage
Jack Chesbro, Pittsburgh (NL), 1901 and 1902; New York (AL), 1904

Most Seasons League Leader in Winning Percentage before 1901
3—Bob Caruthers, St. Louis (AA), 1885 and 1887; Brooklyn (AA), 1889

Only Two-Time League Leader in Winning Percentage with a Career WP below .500
Larry Benton of the New York Giants led the National League in winning percentage in 1927 and again in 1928 but finished with a 127–128 record.

Highest Career Winning Percentage, Minimum 150 Decisions
.717—Spud Chandler, 1937–47 (109–43). Chandler didn't win his first game until he was nearly 30. He lost almost two full seasons to military service during World War II and parts of several other seasons to arm ailments. Against that he played for the Yankees, who won seven pennants while he was with them. Prior to joining the Yankees, Chandler posted a mediocre 47–41 record in six minor-league seasons.

Highest Career Winning Percentage, Pitcher Never on a Pennant Winner, Minimum 150 Wins
.626—Addie Joss, Cleveland, 1902–10 (159–95)

TOP 10 IN CAREER WINNING PERCENTAGE*
(Minimum 200 Decisions)

	Years Active	Wins	Losses	Pct.
1. Whitey Ford	1950–67	236	106	.690[1]
2. Dave Foutz	1884–94	147	66	.690
3. Bob Caruthers	1884–92	218	99	.688[2]
4. Lefty Grove	1925–41	300	141	.680[3]
5. Ron Guidry	1975–	163	80	.671
6. Christy Mathewson	1900–16	373	187	.665
7. Larry Corcoran	1880–87	177	90	.663
8. Sam Leever	1898–1910	194	100	.660[4]
9. Sandy Koufax	1955–66	165	81	.665
10. Johnny Allen	1932–44	142	75	.654

[1]Had a .720 winning percentage through 1964, then lost 22 games and won only 20 in his last three seasons.

[2]Had a .708 winning percentage before posting a 2–10 record for the 1892 St. Louis Browns in his final season as a pitcher.

[3]The top winning percentage among 300-game winners.

[4]Had a 36–38 career record after his first three seasons but then fashioned an incredible .718 winning percentage from 1901 through 1910.

Highest Career Winning Percentage since 1961 (Retired Pitchers Only)
.686—Don Gullett, 1970–78 (109–50). In his last four seasons he won 44 games, lost only 13 and had a .772 winning percentage.

Highest Career Winning Percentage, Minimum 40 Decisions
.771—Howie Krist, 1937–46 (37–11). After his first four seasons he had an unbelievable 26–4 career record.

Highest Career Winning Percentage, Minimum 20 Decisions
.871—Luis Aloma, 1950–53 (18–3). In between bouts of arm trouble he also netted 15 saves and pitched a shutout in his only starting assignment.

Most Career Wins without a Loss
4—Ben Shields, 1924–31. Although pounded in almost every game he pitched—he had an 8.27 career ERA—he was somehow never beaten.

Highest Career Winning Percentage as a Relief Pitcher, Minimum 50 Decisions
   .718—Hugh Casey, 1935–49 (51–20).

Only Pitcher with a .600 Career Slugging Average and Winning Percentage
   Babe Ruth, 1914–25; had a .671 winning percentage (94–96) and a .690 slugging average.

The All-time Worst Fielders

When third baseman Butch Hobson of the Red Sox fielded .899 in 133 games in 1978, he became the first regular player in 62 years to post a fielding average that was below .900.

Last Regular Prior to Hobson to Field below .900
Charlie Pick, Philadelphia A's, 1916. Primarily a third baseman, Pick fielded .899 in 116 games.

Last National Leaguer to Field Below .900 in More Than 100 Games
Heinie Zimmerman, Chicago Cubs, 1914, had an .897 fielding average in 146 games, most of them at third base. Playing shortstop right beside Zimmerman was Red Corriden, who fielded .894 in 107 games. Somehow the Cubs still managed to finish in the first division.

Lowest Fielding Average by a National League Regular since 1914
Dick Allen, Philadelphia, 1967, fielded .908 at third base. The following season he was put in the outfield.

Last Regular Outfielder to Field Below .900
Guy Zinn, New York Yankees, 1912; fielded .899 in 106 games.

Lowest Fielding Average by a Regular Player since 1901
If we drop back a year to 1900, we find Piano Legs Hickman at third base for the New York Giants fielding a grand .842 and making 86 errors. But the record since 1901, when the majors became a two-league operation, belongs to Bill Keister, who fielded .851 and made 97 errors while playing shortstop for the 1901 Baltimore Orioles.

Most Errors, Season, by a Player since 1901
Johnny Gochnauer, Cleveland shortstop, 1903; made 98 errors and fielded .869.

Most Errors, Season, by First Baseman since 1901
Once again, by dropping back a year to 1900, we find Jack Doyle, who made 43 errors with the Giants, most of them, we might imagine, while trying to handle Piano Legs Hickman's throws. The record since 1901 is held by Jerry Freeman, who racked up 41 miscues with Washington in 1908.

Most Errors, Season, by a Catcher since 1901
41—Oscar Stanage, Detroit Tigers, 1911. Rather bizarrely, Stanage also holds the American League record for most assists in a season.

First Player to Make 100 Errors in a Season
Frank Fennelly, shortstop for Cincinnati in the American Association in 1886, collected 117 boots, a figure that was tied by shortstop Herman Long of the Kansas City AA team in 1889. Some authorities say Fennelly and Long share the all-time record for most errors in a season; the Macmillan *Baseball Encyclopedia* claims that Billy Shindle of the Philadelphia Players League entry netted 119 errors in 1890.

Last Player to Make 100 Errors in a Season
Rookie shortstop Joe Sullivan was charged with 102 errors and had an .860 fielding average for Washington in 1893.

Last Player to Make 90 or More Errors in a Season
Johnny Gochnauer, Cleveland, 1903; along with his 98 errors he batted .185.

Last Player to Make 80 or More Errors in a Season
Neal Ball, shortstop New York Yankees, 1908; a year before he became the first player to perform an unassisted triple play.

Last Player to Make 70 or More Errors in a Season
Buck Weaver, shortstop Chicago White Sox, made exactly 70 errors in 1913. The year before he had 71 boots. Despite his high number of miscues, Weaver had relatively

decent fielding averages for that time, and one suspects that he accumulated so many errors mostly because he got to more balls than the average shortstop. Switched to third base in 1916, he became one of the outstanding hot corner glove men of his era.

Last Player to Make 60 or More Errors in a Season
Al Brancato, shortstop Philadelphia A's, 1941; 61 errors and a .915 fielding average.

Last Player to Make 50 or More Errors in a Season
Roy Smalley, shortstop Chicago Cubs, 1951; 51 errors and a .945 fielding average. No apologies here. Cubs fans in the early fifties, harkening back to Tinker to Evers to Chance, cynically coined the chant "Miksis to Smalley to Addison Street." When Cubs managers Frankie Frisch and Phil Cavarretta wanted to rest Smalley's scatter-arm, they were stuck with Tommy "Buckshot" Brown at shortstop. In 1951 Brown fielded .911 and was second on the team in errors to Smalley, although he played in just 61 games.

Base-stealing Feats

What player was the most proficient base thief ever? The most prolific? We're watching both of them perform right now. Indeed the majority of season and career base-stealing records have been set in the past 15 years.

Most Stolen Bases, Season
AL—130—Rickey Henderson, Oakland, 1982; also swiped 108 bases in 1983 and 100 in 1980.
NL—118—Lou Brock, St. Louis, 1974. The only other players who stole 100 or more bases in a season were Maury Wills, who grabbed 104 with the 1962 Dodgers, and Vince Coleman, 110, as a rookie with the 1985 Cardinals and 107 in 1986, his sophomore season.

Most Stolen Bases, Season, 1901 through 1919
AL—96—Ty Cobb, Detroit, 1915
NL—81—Bob Bescher, Cincinnati, 1911

Most Stolen Bases, Season, 1920 through 1941
AL—63—Sam Rice, Washington, 1920
NL—52—Max Carey, Pittsburgh, 1920

Most Stolen Bases, Season, 1942 through 1960
AL—61—George Case, Washington, 1943
NL—50—Maury Wills, Los Angeles, 1960

Most Stolen Bases without Being Caught, Season
AL—16—Jimmy Sexton, Oakland, 1982
NL—12—Miguel Dilone, Pittsburgh, 1977

Most Consecutive Stolen Bases without Being Caught
NL—38—Davey Lopes, Los Angeles; broke Max Carey's

old record of 31, set in 1922, on August 9, 1975; streak ended when he was nailed on August 24.

AL—32—Willie Wilson, Kansas City Royals, 1980; Tod Cruz, Chicago, 1980–81. Prior to Wilson and Cruz, the AL record was 26, set in 1977 by Mitchell Page of Oakland.

Most Successful Thefts of Home, Season
　　AL—7—Rod Carew, Minnesota, 1969
　　NL—7—Pete Reiser, Brooklyn, 1946

First Player to Steal Home Twice in a Game
　　Joe Tinker, Chicago Cubs, June 28, 1910

Last Pitcher to Steal Home
　　Curt Simmons, St. Louis Cardinals, September 1, 1963, in a 7–3 win over the Phils

Most Stolen Bases, Game
　　6—Eddie Collins, Philadelphia A's, September 11 and September 22, 1912. Collins's dual feats, occurring only 11 days apart, were the only times in modern history that a player stole more than five bases in a game.

Most Seasons League Leader in Stolen Bases
　　NL—10—Max Carey, last in 1925
　　AL—9—Luis Aparicio, 1956–64 consecutive

Most Seasons 50 or More Stolen Bases
　　NL—12—Lou Brock, last in 1976
　　AL—8—Ty Cobb, last in 1917

Most Players with 50 or More Stolen Bases in a Season, Team
　　AL—3—Oakland, 1976: Bill North (75), Bert Campaneris (54), Don Baylor (52)
　　NL—3—San Diego, 1980: Gene Richards (61), Ozzie Smith (57), Jerry Mumphrey (52).

Most Stolen Bases, Season, Team
　　NL—347—New York Giants, 1911
　　AL—341—Oakland, 1976

Best Stolen Base Percentage, Season, Minimum 35 Attempts
NL—.962—Max Carey, Pittsburgh, 1922; 51 steals in 53 tries
AL—.943—Amos Otis, Kansas City Royals, 1970; 33 steals in 35 tries

Lowest Stolen Base Percentage, Season, Minimum 20 Attempts
.133—Larry Gardner, Cleveland Indians, 1920; three steals in 23 tries

Most Times Caught Stealing, Season
AL—42—Rickey Henderson, Oakland, 1982; 130 steals in 172 tries.
NL—36—Miller Huggins, St. Louis, 1914; 32 steals in 68 tries. Huggins's stolen base percentage that season—well below .500— was not atypical of the deadball era.

Most times Caught Stealing, Season, Team
NL—149—Chicago, 1924; 137 steals in 286 tries
AL—123—Oakland, 1976; 341 steals in 464 tries

Fewest Stolen Bases, Season, by League Leader in Stolen Bases
AL—15—Dom DiMaggio, Boston, 1950
NL—18—Stan Hack, Chicago, 1938

Fewest Stolen Bases, Season, by Team
AL—13—Washington, 1957; club leader was Julio Becquer with 3
NL—17—St. Louis, 1949; club leader was Red Schoendienst with 8

Highest Batting Average, Season, since 1901, by League Leader in Steals
AL—.420—Ty Cobb, Detroit, 1911
NL—.354—Honus Wagner, Pittsburgh, 1908

Lowest Batting Average, Season, since 1901, by League Leader in Steals
NL—.219—Danny Murtaugh, Philadelphia, 1941
AL—.225—George Case, Cleveland, 1946

Winner of the "Making Them Count" Award
In 1958 first baseman Vic Power, playing for Cleveland and the Kansas City A's, stole only three bases all year, but two of them were thefts of home—and in the same game, no less.

Winner of the "Right Man for the Job" Award
Inserted as a pinch runner on September 1, 1909, rookie Bill O'Hara of the New York Giants promptly stole both second and third base; called on again to pinch run the following day, he did the same thing. Not only is O'Hara the only pinch runner to swipe two bases on consecutive days, he's the lone pinch runner to swipe two sacks on more than one occasion.

Winner of the "Stemming the Tide" Award
On May 11, 1897, catcher Duke Farrell of Washington threw out a record eight would-be base thieves. Farrell's opposite, and the winner of the "In Over His Head" Award, is Branch Rickey, who helplessly watched 13 Washington Senators base runners steal on him while he was catching for the Yankees on June 28, 1907.

Most Combined Home Runs and Stolen Bases, Season, Minimum 30 Home Runs
86—Ken Williams, St. Louis Browns, 1922. Williams, who was also the first player to collect 30 or more homers and 30 or more stolen bases in the first season, seems likely to have his record broken very soon—perhaps even in 1987—by Eric Davis, Kirk Gibson or Joe Carter.

MEMBERS OF THE 30/30 CLUB

	Team	Year	Thefts	Homers	Total
Ken Williams	St. Louis Browns	1922	47	39	86
Willie Mays	New York Giants	1956	40	36	76
Willie Mays	New York Giants	1957	38	35	73
Hank Aaron	Milwaukee Braves	1963	31	44	75
Bobby Bonds	San Francisco Giants	1969	45	32	77
Tommy Harpes	Milwaukee Brewers	1970	38	31	69
Bobby Bonds	San Francisco Giants	1973	43	39	82
Bobby Bonds	New York Yankees	1975	30	32	62
Bobby Bonds	California Angels	1977	41	37	78
Bobby Bonds	Chicago-Texas	1978	43	31	74

Most Consecutive Games without Being Caught Stealing
1,206—Gus Triandos, 1953–65. Triandos played his entire career without ever being caught stealing. He tried only once to swipe a base, and that was while playing for Baltimore in 1958 in a game the Orioles were losing so badly to the Yankees that the Yankees didn't bother to make a play on him.

Fewest Stolen Bases, Career, 2,400 or More Games Played
19—Harmon Killebrew, 1954–75 (2,435 games). Nearly half of Killebrew's thefts—8—came in 1969. Killebrew also has the fewest triples (24) of any player in over 2000 games.

TOP 10 IN CAREER STOLEN BASES

	Years Active	*Stolen Bases*
1. Lou Brock	1961–79	938
2. Ty Cobb	1905–28	892
3. Eddie Collins	1906–30	743
4. Max Carey	1910–29	738
5. Honus Wagner	1897–1917	703[1]
6. Joe Morgan	1963–84	689
7. Rickey Henderson	1979–	660[2]
8. Bert Campaneris	1964–83	631[3]
9. Maury Wills	1959–72	586
10. Davey Lopes	1972–	555

[1]In 1897, Wagner's rookie year, a stolen base was still customarily awarded whenever a runner advanced an extra base on a hit or an out. As a result, all stolen base records set before 1898, when the modern scoring rule was established, are impossible to compare to records set afterward and have been omitted from this section.

[2]The most prolific base thief in history, he has averaged 82.5 stolen bases a season.

[3]In 1969 he stole 62 bases in 70 tries, the highest success rate of any American League player with more than 60 attempts in a season. Tim Raines of the Expos, who swiped 70 sacks in 79 attempts for an .886 percentage in 1985, holds the all-time record; in 1986 Raines posted identical stolen base stats to tie his own mark.

Most Career Thefts of Home
35—Ty Cobb, 1905–28. George Burns, 1911–25, is second with 27.

Most Times Caught Stealing, Career
    307—Lou Brock, 1961–79. No other player is even close.

Highest Stolen Base Percentage, Career, Minimum 400 Attempts
    .870—Tim Raines. At the conclusion of the 1986 season, Raines had 461 stolen bases in 530 attempts, easily the best average in history. Willie Wilson with an .841 success rate and Davey Lopes (.831) also rank among the all-time leaders in theft efficiency.

Loyalty Records

In 1982 Carl Yastrzemski completed his 23d season in a Boston Red Sox uniform, tying Brooks Robinson's all-time record for playing the most seasons with the same team. Yastrzemski's retirement left Bill Russell heir to the loyalty record among active players. In 1986 Russell played his 18th consecutive season with the Dodgers. Since free agency was made part of the game in 1975, only nine other players who began their careers before then—Mike Schmidt, Robin Yount, Dave Concepcion, Dennis Leonard, Dwight Evans, Bob Forsch, Jim Rice, Charlie Moore and George Brett—were still playing with their original teams during the 1986 season.

Record for Most Seasons with One Team Before Brooks Robinson Broke It
22—Al Kaline, Detroit Tigers, 1953–74
    Mel Ott, New York Giants, 1926–47
    Stan Musial, St. Louis Cardinals, 1941–63
    Cap Anson, Chicago White Stockings, 1876–97. Anson's share of the record is open to dispute since he played with the Rockford Forest Citys and Philadelphia Athletics in the National Association for five seasons prior to 1876.

Team That for Some Perverse Reason Inspired the Most Loyalty
The Chicago White Sox from 1914 through 1950. Beginning in 1914, Red Faber pitched 20 years for them without ever playing with another team. Ted Lyons pitched 21 years for the Pale Hose from 1923 through 1946. And shortstop Luke Appling gave the Sox his entire 20-year career from 1930 through 1950. Faber came to the club in time to play on two pennant winners, but Lyons and Appling were not so fortunate. Lyons holds the record for playing the most

pennantless seasons with the same team, and Appling is second to him.

ENTIRE CAREER WITH ONE TEAM RECORD HOLDERS

Batting

Department	Name	Years Active	Team	Record
Games	Carl Yastrzemski	1961–83	Boston Red Sox	3308
At Bats	Carl Yastrzemski	1961–83	Boston Red Sox	11,988
Hits	Stan Musial	1941–63	St. Louis Cardinals	3630
Home Runs	Mickey Mantle	1951–68	New York Yankees	536
RBIs	Lou Gehrig	1923–29	New York Yankees	1991
Runs	Stan Musial	1941–63	St. Louis Cardinals	1949
Doubles	Stan Musial	1941–63	St. Louis Cardinals	725
Triples	Bid McPhee	1882–99	Cincinnati Reds	189
Total Bases	Stan Musial	1941–63	St. Louis Cardinals	6134
Stolen Bases	Clyde Milan	1907–22	Washington Senators	495
Bases on Balls	Ted Williams	1939–60	Boston Red Sox	2019
Strikeouts	Mickey Mantle	1951–68	New York Yankees	1710
Batting Average	Ted Williams	1939–60	Boston Red Sox	.344
Slugging Average	Ted Williams	1939–60	Boston Red Sox	.634

Pitching

Wins	Walter Johnson	1907–27	Washington Senators	416
Losses	Walter Johnson	1907–27	Washington Senators	279
Winning Pct.	Whitey Ford	1950–67	New York Yankees	.690
Games	Walter Johnson	1907–27	Washington Senators	802

Department	Name	Years Active	Team	Record
Innings Pitched	Walter Johnson	1907–27	Washington Senators	5924
Starts	Walter Johnson	1907–27	Washington Senators	666
Complete Games	Walter Johnson	1907–27	Washington Senators	532
ERA	Addie Joss	1902–10	Cleveland Indians	1.88
Strikeouts	Walter Johnson	1907–27	Washington Senators	3508
Bases on Balls	Bob Feller	1936–56	Cleveland Indians	1764

The All-time Loyalty All-Star Team*

Position	Name	Team	Years Played	Total
First Base	Cap Anson	Chicago White Stockings	1879–97	19
Second Base	Bid McPhee	Cincinnati Reds	1882–99	18
Third Base	Brooks Robinson	Baltimore Orioles	1958–75	18
Shortstop	Dave Concepcion	Cincinnati Reds	1970–86	17
Outfield	Al Kaline	Detroit Tigers	1954–72	19
Outfield	Roberto Clemente	Pittsburgh Pirates	1955–72	18
Outfield	Clyde Milan	Washington Senators	1908–21	14
Catcher	Bill Dickey	New York Yankees	1929–43	15
Pitcher	Walter Johnson	Washington Senators	1907–27	21
Pitcher	Ted Lyons	Chicago White Sox	1923–46	21
Pitcher	Red Faber	Chicago White Sox	1914–33	20
Pitcher	Mel Harder	Cleveland Indians	1928–47	20

*Limited to players who became institutions both because they spent their entire careers with the same team and because they were regulars at the same positions without any interruptions during the years cited. The lone exceptions are Lyons, who lost years to the military service, Kaline, who was a utility outfielder during the regular season in 1968 but played every game in the World Series, and Concepcion, the Reds regular shortstop in 1986 until injured in mid-season.

Mobility Records

Carl Yastrzemski and Alex Johnson dovetailed in 1970 when they fought it out all season for the American League batting crown, which Johnson won by a fraction of a point, but from then on their careers diverged probably as much as those of any two players in modern history. By the time Johnson left in 1976 he had played at least one full season with eight different teams, a 20th-century record.

Most Teams Played for between 1901 and 1960

Since 1961, when expansion increased the number of teams in the major leagues, Ken Brett, Bob Miller and Tommy Davis have all worn a record 10 different uniforms, but prior to expansion the record was held by Dick Littlefield, who pitched for nine different teams between 1950 and 1958. He appeared with the Red Sox, the White Sox, the Tigers, the Browns, the Pirates, the Cardinals, the Giants, the Cubs and the Milwaukee Braves—and, in addition, pitched three games in a Baltimore uniform after the Browns franchise was transferred there in 1954.

One of a Kind

Mike Torrez. Between 1974 and 1978 he pitched for the Expos, the Orioles, the A's, the Yankees and the Red Sox, winning at least 14 games with each club. No other player in history has done so much for so many teams in such a short space of time.

Proof That the More Things Change the More They Stay the Same

Due to the expansion and free agency, player mobility seems to be at an all-time apex in the 1980s, but that isn't really the case. Exactly a century ago things were equally in a state of flux, as can be seen by the career of Jersey Bakely. In 1884 Bakely embarked on an odyssey that took him not only to four different teams in his next four seasons in the majors but also to four different leagues. Bakely actually pitched for six different clubs during that span. He spent the 1884 season with Philadelphia, Wilmington and Kansas City in the Union Association, then was out of the majors until 1888, when he pitched for Cleveland in the American Association. The following year he found himself still with Cleveland but in the National League, and in 1890 he jumped to the Cleveland entry in the Players League. In each of the four seasons he pitched at least 300 innings, giving him an additional record for being the only pitcher ever to figure in a minimum of 30 decisions in four different major leagues.

Proof That the More Things Change the More They Stay the Same, II

Don Mincher broke in with the Washington Senators in 1960, then went to Minnesota when the franchise transferred there the following year. In 1971 he found himself with the expansion Washington Senators and must have felt that he'd come full circle upon learning that the franchise would be transferring to Texas in 1972 and he'd be going with it.

Players in 1000 or More Games at Two Different Positions

Ernie Banks (1953–71); 1259 games at first base, 1125 games at shortstop

Stan Musial (1941–1963); 1896 games in the outfield, 1016 games at first base

Ron Fairly (1958–1978); 1218 games at first base; 1037 games in the outfield.

Rod Carew (1967–75); 1128 games at second base, 1065 games at first base

Ironically, both Banks and Musial would have made the Loyalty All-Star Team if they'd remained at their original positions.

Only Player in 500 or More games at Four Different Positions

Pete Rose (1963–); 1327 games in the outfield, 948 games at first base, 634 games at third base, 628 games at second base. Rose is the only player ever to have played regularly at four different positions.

Players Who Were Regulars at Three Different Positions (since 1893)

Wid Conroy, 1901–11; shortstop, third base, outfield
Frankie Gustine, 1939–50; second base, third base, shortstop
Nixey Callahan, 1894–1913; pitcher, outfield, third base
Eric McNair, 1929–42; shortstop, second base, third base
Billy Goodman, 1947–62; second base, first base, third base
Ray Boone, 1948–60; shortstop, third base, first base
Gill McDougald, 1951–60; third base, shortstop, second base

Harmon Killebrew, 1954–75; third base, first base, outfield
Joe Torre, 1960–77; catcher, third base, first base
Pete Runnels, 1951–64; shortstop, second base, first base
Dick Allen, 1963–77; third base, outfield, first base
Jimmy Brown, 1937–46; second base, shortstop, third base
Don Buford, 1963–72; second base, third base, outfield
Buddy Myer, 1925–41; second base, shortstop, third base
Dan Meyer, 1974–85; outfield, first base, third base
Don Money, 1968–83; third base, second base, shortstop
Deron Johnson, 1960–76; first base, third base, outfield
Bill Keister, 1896–1903; second base, shortstop, outfield
Barry McCormick, 1895–1904; second base, shortstop, third base

Players since 1893 Who Pitched in 100 games and Had 1000 hits
Babe Ruth (1914–1935); 163 games pitched, 2873 hits.
Cy Seymour (1896–1913); 140 games pitched, 1723 hits.

Players since 1893 to qualify for the Batting Title and ERA Crown in Same Season
Nixey Callahan, Chicago Colts, 1897; 190 innings pitched, 94 games played
Harry Howell, Baltimore Orioles, 1902; 199 innings pitched, 96 games played

Only Player since 1901 to Play 15 or More Games at Every Position
Art Hoelskoetter, 1905–08. The all-time jack-of-all-trades, in his four seasons with the St. Louis Cardinals, he was tried at every job, including that of pinch hitter, in at least 15 games.

The Hitless Wonders

Duane Kuiper and Johnnie LeMaster both finished their careers in 1985 with performances that cemented their rankings among the leading Hitless Wonders of all time. Kuiper, by failing to hit a home run, kept intact his record for the fewest home runs of any player in history with 3000 or more career at bats, and LeMaster's .119 season vaulted his career batting average into 10th place on the list of the all-time weakest hitters.

THE 20 WORST HITTERS*

		Years Active	At Bats	Batting Ave.	Slugging Ave.
1.	Davy Force	1876–88	2950	.211	.249
2.	Jerry Kindall	1956–65	2057	.213	.327
3.	Bobby Wine	1960–72	3172	.215	.286
4.	Dal Maxvill	1962–75	3443	.217	.259[1]
5.	Joe Quest	1878–88	2282	.217	.267
6.	Darrell Chaney	1969–79	2113	.217	.288
7.	George McBride	1901–20	5526	.218	.264[2]
8.	Skeeter Webb	1932–48	2274	.219	.268
9.	Lee Tannehill	1903–12	3778	.220	.273
10.	Johnnie LeMaster	1978–85	3167	.223	.290
11.	Jimmy Canavan	1891–97	2064	.223	.344
12.	Ed Brinkman	1961–75	6045	.224	.300
13.	Pop Smith	1880–91	4176	.224	.317
14.	George Strickland	1950–60	2824	.224	.311
15.	Enzo Hernandez	1971–78	2327	.224	.266[3]
16.	Roger Repoz	1964–72	2145	.224	.390[4]
17.	John Kennedy	1962–74	2110	.225	.323[5]
18.	Gorman Thomas	1973–86	4677	.225	.448[6]

	Years Active	At Bats	Batting Ave.	Slugging Ave.
19. Charlie O'Leary	1904–13	3230	.226	.273[7]
20. Bill Greenwood	1882–90	2170	.226	.287

*Minimum 2000 career at bats. Pitchers and catchers excluded.

[1]Has the lowest slugging average of any player in this century who batted over 3000 times.

[2]A model of consistency. As Washington's regular shortstop from 1908 through 1916, he never hit more than .235 or less than .203.

[3]No fewer than six of the top 15 on this list were shortstops active in the last 15 years. Hernandez was the prototype—low average, low on base percentage, little run production.

[4]If you remember Repoz at all, you remember him as one of a host of slugging outfielders in the 1960s who connected now and then but mostly just struck out a lot. More than that, he has the lowest career average ever among outfielders with 2000 or more at bats.

[5]The list, as you've already spotted, is constituted almost entirely of players active before 1920 and after 1960. The weakest hitter between 1920 and World War II, and also the only member of the top 25, was Rabbit Warstler, a shortstop and second baseman, who hit .229 between 1930 and 1940.

[6]Despite his low average, Thomas has been a steady, and sometimes spectacular, run producer. In contrast, Rick Miller, also an outfielder from the same period, had a .269 career average on 3887 at bats but only 369 RBIs and 552 runs.

[7]Coaching for the Browns in 1934, O'Leary was called on once to pinch hit and singled—at age 52.

LOWEST SEASON BATTING AVERAGE BY POSITION
(Minimum 300 at Bats)

Position	Name	Team	Year	At Bats	BA	SA
First Base	George Scott	Boston Red Sox	1968	350	.171	.237
Second Base	Mickey Doolan	Brooklyn Dodgers	1918	308	.179	.218
Third Base	Dave Roberts	San Diego Padres	1974	318	.167	.252
Shortstop	George McBride	St. Louis Cards	1906	313	.169	.208
Outfield	George Wright	Texas Rangers	1985	363	.190	.242
Catcher	Bill Bergen	Brooklyn Dodgers	1909	346	.139	.156

(Minimum 400 at Bats)

Position	Name	Team	Year	At Bats	BA	SA
First Base	Dave Kingman	New York Mets	1982	535	.204	.432
Second Base	Billy Hallman	Cleveland-Phillies	1902	464	.185	.235[1]
Third Base	Eddie Zimmerman	Brooklyn Dodgers	1911	417	.185	.264
Shortstop	Ed Brinkman	Washington Senators	1965	444	.185	.257[2]
Outfield	Curt Blefary	Baltimore Orioles	1968	451	.200	.322[3]
Catcher	Billy Sullivan	Chicago White Sox	1908	430	.191	.228

(Minimum 500 at Bats)

Position	Name	Team	Year	At Bats	BA	SA
First Base	Dave Kingman	New York Mets	1982	535	.204	.432
Second Base	Bobby Lowe	Detroit Tigers	1904	507	.207	.258
Third Base	Don Wert	Detroit Tigers	1968	536	.200	.299
Shortstop	Monte Cross	Philadelphia A's	1904	503	.189	.256
Outfield	Gorman Thomas	Milwaukee-Cleveland	1983	535	.209	.379
Catcher	Randy Hundley	Chicago Cubs	1968	553	.226	.311[4]

(Prior to 1901*)

Position	Name	Team	Year	At Bats	BA	SA
First Base	Milt Scott	Baltimore (AA)	1886	482	.190	.242
Second Base	Joe Gerhardt	New York (NL)	1885	399	.155	.195[5]
Third Base	Art Whitney	Kansas City (AA)	1891	358	.193	.240
Shortstop	Charlie Bastian	Philadelphia (NL)	1885	389	.167	.252[6]
Outfield	Jim Lillie	Kansas City (NL)	1886	416	.175	.197
Catcher	Henry Sage	Toledo (AA)	1890	275	.149	.229

*Minimum 350 at bats; for catchers, participation in at least half of team's games.

[1] In 1902 the Phillies replaced Hallman with Pete Childs, who hit .194 and had a .206 slugging average, the lowest in this century among players with over 400 at bats.

[2] Cleveland shortstop Johnny Gochnauer hit .185 both in 1902 and 1903, but each year his average was a few thousandths of a point higher than Brinkman's.

[3] Willie Kirkland hit a fraction above .200 for Cleveland in 1962, as did Clyde Milan for Washington in 1909; Blefary's 1968 average was actually a shade below .200. Still, a case can be made that technically Milan had the

poorest season since Blefary played a number of games behind the plate in 1968.

[4]Hundley's not-all-that-terrible batting average in 1968 ranks as the worst mostly because catchers who aren't hitting much seldom got 500 at bats in a season.

[5]Called "Move Up Joe," Gerhardt did anything but that with men on base. A decent hitter early in his career, he tailed off dramatically after pitchers began throwing overhand.

[6]Bastian, Tom McLaughlin and Henry Esterday were the three most inept of the many weak-hitting shortstops in the 1880s, suggesting that the philosophy then with regard to shortstops may have been very like that in our own time.

Most Consecutive at Bats without Hitting a Home Run

3278—Eddie Foster, 1910–23. Foster collected six career home runs in 5652 at bats, but all came early in his career. He connected for the last time near the beginning of the 1916 season.

Most Career at Bats without Hitting a Home Run, since 1901

1931—Tom Oliver, 1930–33. Second to Oliver is Irv Hall, an infielder with the Philadelphia A's during World War II who went homerless in 1904 at bats.

THE 12 LOWEST CAREER HOME RUN PERCENTAGES[*]

		Years Active	At Bats	Home runs	HR Pct.
1.	Bill Holbert	1876–88	2335	0	.00000[1]
2.	Duane Kuiper	1975–85	3379	1	.00029
3.	Davy Force	1876–86	2950	1	.00034
4.	Emil Verban	1944–50	2911	1	.00034[2]
5.	Jimmy Slagle	1899–1908	4994	2	.00040
6.	Johnny Bassler	1913–27	2319	1	.00044[3]
7.	Floyd Baker	1938–49	2280	1	.00044
8.	Woody Woodward	1963–71	2187	1	.00047
9.	Freddie Maguire	1922–31	2120	1	.00047
10.	Al Bridwell	1905–15	4167	2	.00048
11.	Tommy Thevenow	1924–38	4164	2	.00048[4]
12.	Ed Hahn	1905–10	2045	1	.00049

[*]Players who had home run percentages below .00050 in 2000 or more career at bats.

[1]Holds the all-time record for the most career at bats without hitting a home run.

[2]Got his chance during the war when he was 29. Did little his rookie year, but then hit .412 in the 1944 World Series and went on to a productive career. In 1949 he struck out only twice in 343 at bats.

[3]Shared the Detroit catching job during the 1920s with Larry Woodall, who hit only one home run in 1317 career at bats. The only .300 career hitter on the "Powerless" list, Bassler was still catching in the Pacific Coast League when he was in his middle forties.

[4]Hit his only two home runs in 1926 and also homered in the 1926 World Series. All three were inside-the-park circuit clouts. Thevenow's bizarrely condensed power display is second only to Johnny Cooney's. In 3372 at bats between 1921 and 1944, Cooney hit just two home runs—and they came on successive days in 1939.

Lowest Career Batting Average, Minimum 1,000 at Bats

.175—Ray Oyler, 1965–70. Detroit won the pennnat in 1968 with Oyler playing shortstop and hitting .135 in 111 games. The only other player in this century who posted a sub-.200 career batting average in 1000 or more at bats—catchers again excepted—was Rich Morales, 1967–74, who finished at .195.

Lowest Career Batting Average, Minimum 500 at Bats

.161—John Vukovich, 1970–81. In 1971, while sharing the Phillies' third-base job with Don Money, Vukovich hit .166 in 74 games and had a .189 slugging average.

Most Career at Bats without Ever Getting a Hit, Pitchers Included

41—Randy Tate, New York Mets, 1975; went 0-for-41 in his only season. Excluding pitchers, the lowest career average among players who got at least one hit belongs to Skeeter Shelton, an outfielder who was give a 10-game trial by the Yankees in 1915 and went 1-for-40, giving him an .025 career mark.

Most Career at Bats without Ever Getting a Hit, Pitchers Excluded

23—Mike Potter, St. Louis Cardinals, 1976–77
Larry Littleton, Cleveland Indians, 1981

Most Career at Bats Exclusively as a Pinch Hitter, .000 Career Batting Average

13—Paul Dicken, Cleveland Indians, 1964, 1966

LOWEST CAREER BATTING AVERAGE
BY POSITION
(Minimum 3,000 at Bats)

Position	Name	Years Active	At Bats	BA
First Base	Dave Kingman	1971–	6677	.236[1]
Second Base	Bobby Knoop	1964–72	3622	.236
Shortstop	Bobby Wine	1960–72	3172	.215
Third Base	Lee Tannehill	1903–12	3778	.220[2]
Outfield	Gorman Thomas	1973–86	4677	.225
Catcher	Bill Bergen	1901–11	3028	.170[3]
Pitcher (Minimum 200 ABs)	Ron Herbel	1963–71	206	.029[4]

[1] Also played the outfield and as a designated hitter.

[2] Also played some at shortstop and second base; the only Hitless Wonder who was actually a member of the original Hitless Wonders—the 1906 Chicago White Sox.

[3] Had only a .201 career slugging average. Reportedly a great defensive catcher, but I'm more inclined to believe he stuck around so long because he spent his last eight seasons with Brooklyn. The Dodgers in those years seemed to have entered into some sort of Faustian compact to make their pitchers survive on as little hitting support as possible.

[4] Went 0-for-47 in 1964, his worst season, but the record belongs to Bob Buhl, who went 0-for-70 in 1962 for the Braves and Cubs. The AL Season record for futility is held by Bill Wight of the White Sox, who went 0-for-61 in 1950.

The Three Most Interesting
Teams since 1977

1977 KANSAS CITY ROYALS
W-102 L-60
Manager: Whitey Herzog

Regular Lineup—1B, John Mayberry; 2B, Frank White; 3B, George Brett; SS, Freddie Patek; RF, Al Cowens; CF, Amos Otis; LF, Tom Poquette; C, Darrell Porter; P, Dennis Leonard; P, Jim Colborn; P, Paul Splittorff; P, Andy Hassler; P, Marty Pattin; P, Doug Bird; P, Larry Gura.

After posting the best regular-season record ever by an AL expansion club, the Royals were only three outs away from winning the American League pennant. Before they got them the Yankees scored three runs and beat them in the ninth inning of the fifth and final LCS game for the second year in a row. Probably the finest Royals team ever, much stronger than either the 1980 or 1985 clubs, they not only had a solid lineup but a good bench and the deepest pitching staff in the league. With just a very slight reordering of events, Herzog could have taken them to four pennants in five years—and they didn't miss by all that much in 1979, either. The Yankees, Reds and A's are remembered as the dominant teams of the 1970s, but the Royals were on a par with them and may even have been the best of them all.

1980 HOUSTON ASTROS
W-93 L-70
Manager: Bill Virdon

Regular Lineup—1B, Art Howe; 2B, Joe Morgan; 3B, Enos Cabell; SS, Craig Reynolds; RF, Terry Puhl; CF, Cesar Cedeno; LF, Jose Cruz; C, Alan Ashby; P, Joe Niekro; P, Nolan Ryan; P, Ken Forsch; P, Vern Ruhle; P, J. R. Richard; P, Joe Sambito; P, Dave Smith; P, Frank LaCorte.

The Astros came to Dodger Stadium on the last weekend of the season needing to win only one game of a three-game set to clinch their first division title. They lost all three but won the one-game playoff for the right to meet the Phillies in the LCS. After splitting the first two games in Philadelphia, Virdon got a super 11-inning 1–0 shutout from Niekro in Game Three. Playing at home and only one step away from taking the pennant, the Astros then dropped two straight 10-inning games. In Game Five, they led 5–2 in the top of the eighth with Ryan pitching, but Ryan couldn't hold off the Phillies, nor could relief ace Sambito. For the first time in their history the Astros, in 1980, had two .300 hitters, Cedeno and Cruz, plus a pitching staff that could have been unstoppable if Richard hadn't suffered a midseason stroke. An ill-fated club, tenacious to the end, but one break short of winning it all. The same could be said for the 1981 team, which lost the division playoff by a hair to the Dodgers, who went on to win the World Series, and, of course, the 1986 team.

1983 PHILADELPHIA PHILLIES
W-90 L-72
Manager: Pat Corrales and Paul Owens

Regular Lineup—1B, Pete Rose; 2B, Joe Morgan; 3B, Mike Schmidt; SS, Ivan DeJesus; RF, Von Hayes; CF, Gary Maddox; LF, Gary Matthews; C, Bo Diaz; P, Steve Carlton; P, John Denny; P, Ron Reed; P, Charlie Hudson; P, Al Holland, P, Marty Bystrom.

Maddox, their top-hitting regular, hit only .275; they had only one regular younger than 30, no 20-game winners, got only a 15–16 season from staff ace Carlton, eight wins from their number three starter Hudson, and a 6–9 record from Bystrom, their fourth starter. Yet they won their division by six games, romped over the Dodgers in the LCS and won the World Series opener before the Orioles burst their bubble and took four straight. The three big reasons for their unexpected win were Denny's 19 victories, Holland's 25 saves and Schmidt's 40 homers and 109 RBIs. But other contenders got equally good seasons from their top players, and none had a first baseman who hit .245 and had just 45 RBIs. The real catalyst on this club was 39-year-old Morgan, who hit only .230 but scored 72 runs and collected 89 walks in just 404 at bats. Many believe this team, and not the 1973 Mets, was the weakest pennant winner since the 1944 St. Louis Browns—but it may also have been the most savvy team ever. Whether they would have come together if Corrales had remained at the helm may be the only real grist for argument here.

Third Baseman's Records

The proliferation of great third basemen in the past 20 years has yet to be studied and understood. As a point of comparison, only one third baseman active before 1908—Jimmy Collins—is in the Hall of Fame. No one can predict for sure how many third basemen active at the moment will make it, but three seems an extremely conservative guess, and it may be as many as six or seven. From whence did they suddenly all appear?

SEASON BATTING RECORDS

Department	National League	American League
Batting Averages	.391, JOHN MCGRAW, Baltimore, 1899 .379, Fred Lindstrom, New York, 1930*	.390, George Brett, K.C. Royals, 1980
Slugging Average	.644, Mike Schmidt, Philadelphia, 1981	.664, GEORGE BRETT, K.C. Royals, 1980
Home Runs	48, MIKE SCHMIDT, Philadelphia, 1980	43, Al Rosen, Cleveland, 1953
RBIs	135, Eddie Mathews, Boston, 1953	145, AL ROSEN, Cleveland, 1953
Runs	143, John McGraw, Baltimore, 1898 130, Pete Rose, Cincinnati, 1976*	145, HARLOND CLIFT, St. Louis, 1936
Hits	231, Fred Lindstrom, New York, 1928, 1930	240, WADE BOGGS, Boston, 1985
Doubles	51, Pete Rose, Cincinnati, 1978	56, GEORGE KELL, Detroit, 1950

Department	National League	American League
Triples	27, GEORGE DAVIS, New York, 1893 27, JIMMY WILLIAMS, Pittsburgh, 1899 22, Tommy Leach, Pittsburgh, 1902*	22, Bill Bradley, Cleveland, 1903
Total Bases	363, Eddie Mathews, Boston, 1953	367, AL ROSEN, Cleveland, 1953
Bases on Balls	131, Bob Elliott, Boston, 1948	151, EDDIE YOST, Washington, 1956
Stolen Bases	59, Art Devlin, New York, 1905	74, FRITZ MAISEL, New York, 1914
Strikeouts	180, MIKE SCHMIDT, Philadelphia, 1975	172, Jim Presley, Seattle, 1986
Fewest Strikeouts (Minimum 500 ABs)	7, Pie Traynor, Pittsburgh, 1929	3, JOE SEWELL, New York, 1932

*Record since 1901.
Note: Harmon Killebrew of the Twins hit 49 homers in 1969 but played almost half the season at first base. Woody English of the Cubs scored 152 runs in 1930 while playing 83 games at third base and 78 games at shortstop; since his total is higher than the record at both positions, he can conceivably be regarded as the all-time record holder at either.

Most Games, Career, at Third Base
  2,870—Brooks Robinson, 1955–77

Most Consecutive Games at Third Base
  576—Eddie Yost, Washington, July 3, 1951, through May 11, 1955

Best Career Fielding Average
  .971—Brooks Robinson, 1955–77

Most Seasons League Leader in Fielding Average
  AL—11—Brooks Robinson, last in 1975
  NL—6—Heinie Groh, last in 1924
       Ken Reitz, last in 1981

EVOLUTION OF SEASON RECORD FOR BEST FIELDING AVERAGE

	Team	League	Year	Average
Joe Battin	St. Louis	National	1876	.867[1]
Bill Hague	Providence	National	1879	.925[2]
Chappy McGarr	Boston	National	1890	.933
Billy Nash	Boston	National	1894	.933[3]
Lave Cross	Philadelphia	National	1895	.940
Bill Clingman	Louisville	National	1897	.947
Lave Cross	Cleveland-St. Louis	National	1899	.959[4]
Harry Steinfeldt	Chicago	National	1907	.967
Terry Turner	Cleveland	American	1911	.970[5]
Hans Lobert	Philadelphia	National	1913	.974
Larry Gardner	Cleveland	American	1920	.976
Heinie Groh	New York	National	1924	.983[6]
Willie Kamm	Cleveland	American	1933	.984[7]
Hank Majeski	Philadelphia	American	1947	.988
Don Money	Milwaukee	American	1974	.989

[1] A victim of the fair-foul rule change. Slumped to .199 in 1877 after hitting .300 the previous year.

[2] A fluke season—Hague never again came within 80 points of his record. Art Whitney's .924 FA with Pittsburgh in 1887 is probably a truer peak figure for the period.

[3] Rated by many the best fielding third baseman prior to 1900.

[4] Never received anywhere near the press that Hall of Famer Jimmy Collins did, but had better career stats in almost every major department.

[5] Also played shortstop and second base in 1910 but was in enough games at third base to be the recognized fielding leader. Led AL third basemen in FA again in 1912.

[6] Still the NL season record; broke his own former record of .975, set in 1923.

[7] Those who saw both Kamm and Brooks Robinson play rank them about equal and, in any case, the two best glovemen ever at third base.

Most Consecutive Errorless Games

97—Jim Davenport, San Francisco, July 29, 1966, through April 28, 1968. Davenport was a utility infielder by the late 1960s and during the skein also played other positions where he did make errors.

Most Consecutive Errorless Chances

261—Don Money, Milwaukee Brewers, September 28, 1973, through July 16, 1974. Money's season FA record was largely the result of his long errorless streak.

Most Chances Accepted, Career
  8,902—Brooks Robinson, 1955–77

Most Chances Accepted, Season
  603—Harlond Clift, St. Louis Browns, 1937

Most Chances Accepted, Game, Nine Innings
  13—Done by several third basemen; last by Roy Hughes, Chicago Cubs, August 29, 1944

Most Assists, Season
  412—Graig Nettles, Cleveland Indians, 1971

Most Seasons League Leader in Assists
  AL—8—Brooks Robinson, last in 1974
  NL—7—Ron Santo, 1962–68 consecutive

Greatest Left-handed Third Baseman
  Hick Carpenter, 1879–92, played 1,059 games at third base and a scattering of games at shortstop and second base. Carpenter was probably not only the best southpaw third baseman but the best southpaw infielder, period. The last lefty infielder of note was Kid Mohler, a second baseman with the San Francisco Seals in the Pacific Coast League as late as the early teens. Mohler played three games in the majors at age 19 in 1894 before commencing his long minor-league career. The last southpaw infielder to play regularly in the majors was Bill Huhlen, a shortstop with the 1896 Phillies. Don Mattingly of the Yankees, who played several games at third base in 1986, is the most recent southpaw infielder.

Most Gold Glove Awards
  16—Brooks Robinson, 1955–77. Only pitcher Jim Kaat has won as many Gold Gloves.

Red-hot Rookies

Fernando Valenzuela and Dwight Gooden, the most exciting rookie pitchers since Herb Score, exploded onto the scene in the 1980s only four years apart, and in 1986 Todd Worrell of the Cardinals shattered the yearling record for saves by a wide margin in the process of copping the NL Rookie of the Year Award. None of the three managed to win 20 games, something only one first-year pitcher—Tom Browning of the Reds—has done in this decade, but Valenzuela and Gooden also each set an all-time rookie record. Gooden's is well known, but you may need to check the list below before you remember Valenzuela's.

ROOKIE RECORD HOLDERS*

Batting

Department	National League	American League
Batting Average	.373, George Watkins, St. Louis, 1930	.408, JOE JACKSON, Cleveland, 1911
Slugging Average	.621, GEORGE WATKINS, St. Louis, 1930	.609, Ted Williams, Boston, 1939
Home Runs	38, WALLY BERGER, Boston, 1930 38, FRANK ROBINSON, Cincinnati, 1956	37, Al Rosen, Cleveland, 1950
RBIs	119, Wally Berger, Boston, 1930	145, TED WILLIAMS, Boston, 1939
Hits	223, LLOYD WANER, Pittsburgh, 1927	217, Tony Oliva, Minnesota, 1964

*Qualifications for rookie status are the same as those employed by the Official Major League Scoring Committee as of 1971.

Department	National League	American League
Runs	135, ROY THOMAS, Philadelphia, 1899 133, Lloyd Waner, Pittsburgh, 1927**	132, Joe DiMaggio, New York, 1936
Doubles	52, JOHNNY FREDERICK, Brooklyn, 1929	47, Fred Lynn, Boston, 1975
Triples	27, JIMMY WILLIAMS, Pittsburgh, 1899 25, Tommy Long, St. Louis, 1915**	19, Home Run Baker, Philadelphia, 1909
Total Bases	352, Dick Allen, Philadelphia, 1964	374, HAL TROSKY, Cleveland, 1934 374, TONY OLIVA, Minnesota, 1964
Stolen Bases	110, VINCE COLEMAN, St. Louis, 1985	50, John Cangelosi, Chicago, 1986
Bases on Balls	115, ROY THOMAS, Philadelphia, 1899 100, Jim Gilliam, Brooklyn, 1953**	107, Ted Williams, Boston, 1939
Pinch Hits	20, JOE FRAZIER, St. Louis, 1954	17, Sammy Hale, Detroit, 1920
Strikeouts	168, Juan Samuel, Philadelphia, 1984	185, PETE INCAVIGLIA, Texas, 1986
Fewest Strikeouts (Minimum 500 ABs)	17, BUDDY HASSETT, Brooklyn, 1936	25, Tom Oliver, Boston, 1930

Pitching

Department	National League	American League
Wins	30, BILL HOFFER, Baltimore, 1895 28, Pete Alexander, Philadelphia, 1911**	26, Russ Ford, New York, 1910
Losses	28, STILL BILL HILL, Louisville, 1896 25, Harry McIntyre, Brooklyn, 1905**	26, Bob Groom, Washington, 1901
Games	78, Tim Burke, Montreal, 1985	80, MITCH WILLIAMS, Texas, 1986
Starts	41, IRV YOUNG, Boston, 1905	36, Roscoe Miller, Detroit, 1901

Department	National League	American League
Complete Games	41, IRV YOUNG, Boston, 1905	35, Roscoe Miller, Detroit, 1901
Innings Pitched	378, IRV YOUNG, Boston, 1905	332, Roscoe Miller, Detroit, 1901 332, Scott Perry, Philadelphia, 1918
Winning Pct.	.833, KING COLE, Chicago, 1910	.813, Russ Ford, New York, 1910
Strikeouts	276, DWIGHT GOODEN New York, 1984	245, Herb Score, Cleveland, 1955
Bases on Balls	185, SAM JONES, Chicago, 1955	168, Elmer Myers, Philadelphia, 1916
Shutouts	8, FERNANDO VALEN-ZUELA, L.A., 1980	8, RUSS FORD, New York, 1910 8, REB RUSSELL, Chicago, 1913
Saves	36, TODD WORRELL, St. Louis, 1986	23, Doug Corbett, Minnesota, 1980
ERA	1.11, BABE ADAMS, Pittsburgh, 1909	1.39, Harry Krause, Philadelphia, 1909

**Record since 1901.

Only Rookie to Win a Batting Title
Tony Oliva, Minnesota Twins, 1964 (.323)

Only Rookie to Be a League Leader in Home Runs
Al Rosen, Cleveland Indians, 1950 (37)

Oldest Rookie 20-Game Winner
Jim Turner, Boston Braves, 1937, 34 years old (20–11). Lou Fette, a rookie 30-year-old teammate of Turner's, also won 20. Henry Schmidt is the only other rookie pitcher since 1901 to win 20 games at age 30.

Only Rookie Pitcher to Win 20 Games While Pitching Less Than 200 Innings
Bob Grim, New York Yankees, 1954 (20–6; 199 innings pitched). Grim is not only the only rookie to accomplish this, but the only pitcher in history.

Most Recent Rookie 20-Game Winners
NL—Tom Browning, Cincinnati, 1985 (21–9)
AL—Bob Grim, New York, 1954 (20–6)

Best Season by Rookie Batter Who Failed to Win Rookie of the Year Award

Minnie Minoso, Chicago White Sox, 1951, hit .326, led the AL in triples and stolen bases and was fifth in slugging, but lost out to the Yankees Gil McDougald.

Best Season by Rookie Pitcher Who Failed to Win Rookie of the Year Award

Gene Bearden, Cleveland Indians, 1948, had a 20–7 record and led the AL with a 2.43 ERA, but lost the award to Al Dark of the Boston Braves in the last season only one rookie honor was given.

Only Team in Existence since 1947 That Has Never Had a Rookie of the Year Winner

Pittsburgh. Ironically, in 1946, the last season no official rookie award was given, Ralph Kiner of the Pirates was generally regarded to be the top rookie in the majors, although Del Ennis of the Phillies copped the *Sporting News* yearling award.

Life-Begins-At-40 Records

When 46-year-old Phil Niekro garnered his 300th win by blanking Toronto 8–0 on the last day of the 1985 season, he also became the oldest major-league pitcher ever to toss a shutout, replacing Satchel Paige, who was a few months younger when he whitewashed the Tigers 1–0 in 12 innings on August 6, 1952. Between them Niekro and Paige hold a number of the "Life-Begins-at-40" records.

Oldest Player to Hit a Home Run
AL—46—Jack Quinn, Philadelphia, 1930. Quinn, a pitcher, is also the oldest player to make more than one hit in a season—he collected four in 1932 when he was 48.
NL—46—Cap Anson, Chicago, 1897

Oldest Player to Hit a Grand Slam Home Run since 1901
43—Tony Perez, Cincinnati, in 1985

Oldest Player to Participate in a Major-League Game
Satchel Paige pitched three shutout innings for the Kansas City A's at age 59 (or maybe older) on September 25, 1965, against the Boston Red Sox. The only hit off Satch was a single by Carl Yastrzemski.

Oldest Player to Hit Safely in a Major-League Game
Minnie Minoso went 1-for-8 at age 53 as a dh for the Chicago White Sox in 1976; his lone hit, a single, came on September 12. Nick Altrock was a slightly younger 53-year-old when he played right field for the White Sox on October 6, 1929, and got a hit in his only trip to the plate.

First 40-Year-Old to Play in a Major-League Game
Dickey Pearce, a standout shortstop in the 1850s, hung on long enough to play 25 games with St. Louis in 1876, the National League's inaugural year. But if you're among those who credit the National Association with being a major league, the honor goes to Harry Wright, who played a single game in the outfield for the 1875 Boston Red Caps after he turned 40. Wright also played one game for Boston in 1876.

First Player Who Was Still a Regular at Age 40
Joe Start, Providence Grays, 1883. Start, a first baseman, remained a regular player until he was nearly 44 years old.

Oldest Rookie
NL—43—Diomedes Olivo, Pittsburgh, 1962, had a 5–1 record and seven saves in 62 games.
AL—42—Satchel Paige, Cleveland, 1948, had a 6–1 record in 27 games.

Oldest Rookie to Play in Over Half His Team's Games
Chuck Hostetler hit .298 in 90 games as a 41-year-old rookie outfielder with the 1944 Detroit Tigers.

Oldest Rookie to Play Enough to Qualify for a Batting Title
Earle Brucker played 102 games for the 1937 Philadelphia A's at age 36—the rules then required a player to participate in two-thirds of his team's games to qualify for a batting title. In 1938 Brucker actually did lead all American League batters when he hit .374—but in only 53 games.

Oldest Rookie to Go on to a 20-Year Career
Hoyt Wilhelm, 29 when he came to the New York Giants in 1952, retired in 1972 after playing 21 years in the majors.

Oldest Games Caught after Age 40
220—Deacon McGuire, 1884–1912. Some historians, myself among them, consider this to be the most impressive of all the "Life-Begins-at-40" accomplishments.

Oldest 20-Game Winner
NL—42—Warren Spahn, Milwaukee, 1963 (23–7)
AL—41—Cy Young, Boston, 1908 (21–11)

Oldest League Leader in a Major Pitching Department
NL—48—Jack Quinn, Brooklyn, 1932; led in saves with 8. Also the NL save leader in 1931 with 15.
AL—42—Jim Turner, New York, 1945, led in saves with 10.

Oldest League Leader in a Major Batting Department
AL—40—Ted Williams, Boston, 1958, hit .328 to win the batting title.
NL—40—Cap Anson, Chicago, 1891, led in RBIs with 120.

LIFE-BEGINS-AT-40 SEASON BATTING RECORDS

Department	National League	American League
Batting Average	.335, Cap Anson, Chicago, 1895 .325, Pete Rose, Philadelphia, 1981*	.357, TY COBB, Philadelphia, 1927
Slugging Average	.508, STAN MUSIAL, St. Louis, 1962	.482, Ty Cobb, Philadelphia, 1927
Home Runs	20, Hank Aaron, Atlanta, 1974	29, TED WILLIAMS, Boston, 1960
RBIs	120, CAP ANSON, Chicago, 1891 82, Stan Musial, St. Louis, 1962*	94, Ty Cobb, Philadelphia, 1927
Hits	172, Pete Rose, Philadelphia, 1982	207, SAM RICE, Washington, 1930
Runs	87, Cap Anson, Chicago, 1895 82, Willie Mays, San Francisco, 1971*	121, SAM RICE, Washington, 1930
Doubles	32, Honus Wagner, Pittsburgh, 1915	35, SAM RICE, Washington, 1930
Triples	17, HONUS WAGNER, Pittsburgh, 1915	13, Sam Rice, Washington, 1930
Total Bases	243, Honus Wagner, Pittsburgh, 1915	271, SAM RICE, Washington, 1930
Stolen Bases	25, DAVEY LOPES, Chicago-Houston, 1986	22, Ty Cobb, Philadelphia, 1927

Department	National League	American League
Bases on Balls	112, Willie Mays, San Francisco, 1971	121, LUKE APPLING, Chicago, 1949
Strikeouts	123, WILLIE MAYS, San Francisco, 1971	115, Reggie Jackson, California, 1986
Fewest Strikeouts (Minimum 500 ABs)	32, Pete Rose, Philadelphia, 1982	14, SAM RICE, Washington, 1930

*Record since 1901.

Note: Record holders are players who were at least 40 years old before the end of the season in which they set the mark. Batting and slugging average record holders must have had enough plate appearances to qualify for the batting title.

The Leading Losers

Hugh Mulcahy is the only major leaguer who has ever been saddled with the unwelcome nickname of "Losing Pitcher," but rather surprisingly he owns none of the major records for pitching losses. Three of them have been set since 1981—by Jose DeLeon, Terry Felton and George Frazier. Do you know what they are?

Lowest Winning Percentage, Season, Minimum 20 Decisions
    AL—.050—Jack Nabors, Philadelphia, 1916 (1–19)
    NL—.095—Jose DeLeon, Pittsburgh, 1985 (2–19)

Most Losses, Season, without a Win
    AL—12—Steve Gerkin, Philadelphia, 1945
    NL—12—Russ Miller, Philadelphia, 1929

Most Consecutive Losses, Season
    AL—19—Bob Groom, Washington, 1909
               Jack Nabors, Philadelphia, 1916
    NL—18—Roger Craig, New York Mets, 1963
               Cliff Curtis, Boston, 1910. Curtis also lost his first five decisions in 1911, giving him 23 consecutive losses, an all-time record. Before going into a tailspin in 1910, he had a 6–5 record and two shutouts.

Most Seasons League Leader in Losses
    NL—4—Phil Niekro, Atlanta, 1977–80 consecutive
    AL—4—Bobo Newsom, last in 1945; done with four different teams
           Pedro Ramos, 1958-61, consecutive

Most Consecutive Losses, Start of Career
16—Terry Felton, Minnesota, April 18, 1980, through September 12, 1982; breaking Guy Morton's record of 13, set with Cleveland in 1914.

Last 25-Game Loser
Ben Cantwell, Boston Braves, 1935. His 4–25 record is the worst since 1901 by a 25-game loser. Just two years earlier, in 1933, Cantwell had rung up a 20–10 record with the Braves to lead all National League pitchers in *winning* percentage.

Most Losses, Season, 162-Game Schedule
24—Roger Craig, New York Mets, 1962
   Jack Fisher, New York Mets, 1964

Most Losses, Season, by Relief Pitcher
NL—16—Gene Garber, Atlanta, 1979 (6–16)
AL—14—Darold Knowles, Washington, 19780 (2–14 but had 27 saves)
   John Hiller, Detroit, 1974 (17–14)
   Mike Marshall, Minnesota, 1979 (10–14)

Most Losses, Season
48—John Coleman, Philadelphia Phillies, 1883 (12-48). Despite his monstrous number of losses, Coleman was the Phillies' ace—the rest of their mound staff had an aggregate 5–33 record.

Most Losses, Season, since 1893
33—Red Donahue, St. Louis Browns, 1897. But Donahue was not the last 30-game loser. That distinction belongs to Jim Hughey of Cleveland, who had a 4–30 record in 1899.

Most Losses, Season, since 1901
29—Vic Willis, Boston Braves, 1905. He also dropped 25 decisions in 1904, making him the last pitcher to lose 24 or more games two years in a row.

Most Losses, Season, since 1920
27—Paul Derringer, St. Louis Cardinals–Cincinnati Reds, 1933

Most Losses, Only Major-League Season

37—George Cobb, Baltimore Orioles, 1892 (10–37). In 1876, his one and only season, Dory Dean had a 4–26 record with Cincinnati, which played just 65 games. Cobb's record, in contrast, came in the first season that the National League experimented with a 154-game schedule. Another one-year hurler, Florence Sullivan of the AA Pittsburgh Alleghenies, lost 35 of his team's 108 decisions in 1884.

Most Losses, Only Major-League Season, since 1901

NL—18—Ham Iburg, Philadelphia, 1902
AL—13—Orie Arntzen, Philadelphia, 1945
        Troy Herriage, Kansas City A's, 1956
        Jeff Byrd, Toronto, 1977
FL—20—Hank Keupper, St. Louis, 1914

Only 30-Game Winner Who Later Lost 20 Games in a Season

Denny McLain, Washington, 1971 (10–22); Detroit, 1968 (31–6)

Only Pitcher since 1901 to Lose 20 Games for a Pennant-winning Team

George Mullin, Detroit, 1907 (20–20)

Lowest Winning Percentage by Pitcher on a Pennant-Winner, Minimum 20 Decisions

NL—.345—Larry French, Chicago, 1938 (10–19)
AL—.350—Bill Bevens, New York, 1947 (7–13). In 1986 Tom Seaver of the pennant winning Red Sox also had a 7–13 record, but six of his losses came with the second-division White Sox.

Most Losses, Season, in a World Series

3—George Frazier, New York Yankees, 1981; all of them in relief

Most Fantastic Turnaround from One Season to the Next

Earl Hamilton was cut by the St. Louis Browns after he had a 0–9 record in 1917. Brought back to the majors by Pittsburgh in 1918, Hamilton posted a perfect 6-0 record and an 0.83 ERA in six starts.

TOP 10 IN CAREER LOSSES

	Years Active	Losses
1. Cy Young	1890–1911	313
2. Pud Galvin	1879–92	309
3. Walter Johnson	1907–27	279
4. Gaylord Perry	1962–83	265
5. Phil Niekro	1964–	261
6. Jack Powell	1897–1912	255[1]
7. Eppa Rixey	1912–33	251
8. Robin Roberts	1946–66	245
Warren Spahn	1942–65	245
10. Early Wynn	1939-63	244

[1]Has a .493 career winning percentage, one of only two 200-game winners who finished below .500. The other is Bobo Newsom with a .487 winning percentage.

MOST LOSSES, CAREER, WITH .000 WINNING PERCENTAGE

	Years Active	Career Record
Terry Felton	1979–82	0–16
Steve Gerkin	1945	0–12
Charlie Stecher	1890	0–10
Archie Reynolds	1968–72	0–8
Paul Brown	1961–63, 1968	0–8
Walter Craddock	1955–58	0–7
Tommy McCarthy	1884–94	0–7[1]
Roy Bruner	1939–41	0–7
Ed O'Neil	1890	0–7[2]
Charlie Barnabe	1927–28	0–7

[1]Made the Hall of Fame as an outfielder, but his first season, as a 19-year-old pitcher-outfielder with the 1884 Boston Union Association team, is best forgotten. He was 0–7 on the mound and hit only .215; throughout his career he was used occasionally as a relief pitcher, but never to any greater effect than he exhibited in 1884.

[2]O'Neil and Charlie Stecher were teammates in 1890 on the AA Philadelphia A's, who ended the season with probably the worst pitching staff in history.

Lowest Career Winning Percentage since 1901, Minimum 200 Decisions
.372—Milt Gaston, 1924–34 (97–164). Gaston, who never pitched in the minor leagues, had a 5–3 record as a 28-year-old rookie with the 1924 Yankees and was 15–14 with the Browns in 1925 after being traded to them but finished below .500 every other season.

Lowest Career Winning Percentage since 1901, Minimum 150 Decisions
.314—Buster Brown, 1905–13 (48–105); died before the 1914 season began.

Lowest Career Winning Percentage since 1901, Minimum 100 Decisions
.304—Bill Bailey, 1907–1922 (34–78). Bailey had a 4-1 record as a rookie, but it was his lone bright spot. His nadir came in 1910 with the Browns when he was 2–18 overall and 0–17 as a starting pitcher.

Lowest Career Winning Percentage since 1901, Minimum 50 Decisions
.206—Ike Pearson, 1939–48 (13–50); including a 7–40 record as a starter. Signed by the pitcher-hungry Phillies after graduating from the University of Mississippi, Pearson was thrown into the breech without a minor-league apprenticeship and suffered for it his whole career.

Lowest Career Winning Percentage, Cy Young Award Winner
.448—Randy Jones, 1973–82 (100–123)

Lowest Career Winning Percentage, Pitcher with ERA below 3.00 in over 100 Decisions
.350—George Bell, 1907–11 (43–80). Seventeen of Bell's 43 wins were shutouts, and he had a fine 2.85 ERA. One of the most luckless pitchers ever, his misfortune was twofold: He was bound by the reserve clause to Brooklyn, at the time a rotten team, and he didn't get to the majors until he was 32 years old.

All-time Winner of the Hugh Mulcahy Award
Ike Butler had a 1–10 record with the 1902 Baltimore

Orioles in his only year in the majors. Discouraged, he signed with Portland, where he set a Pacific Coast League record in 1903 when he lost 31 games and then tied his own mark the following year when he dropped 31 more.

Father-and-Son Firsts

In 1986 Hal McRae's son Brian went to spring training with the Royals and stands a chance of making the club soon. In the event he does, and his father is still active, it will be the first time a father and son have played in the major leagues in the same season, let alone for the same team.

First Son to Play for a Team Managed by His Father
Earl Mack, Philadelphia A's, 1910; son of Connie Mack. When Dale Berra played with the Yankees for a short while under his father's tutelage in 1985, it was only the second time in major-league history a son had been managed by his father. In 1987 Cal Ripken is slated to become the first son to play as a regular for his father.

First Father and Son to Play in the Majors
Herman and Jack Doscher. A third baseman with Troy, beginning in 1879, Herman wasn't much of a player, nor was his son, who pitched briefly for the Cubs and Dodgers in the early 1900s. The second father-and-son combo to make the majors, the Meinkes—Frank and son Bob—had even less impact.

First Father and Son Who Both Had Lengthy Careers
The Sullivans, Billy, Sr., and Billy, Jr. The elder Sullivan played for the White Sox in the first part of the century and was a fine catcher but a weak hitter. His son, also a catcher, was the antithesis. Billy, Jr., hit .351 for Cleveland in 1935, but his defensive skills were such that he caught more than half his team's games only once and was moved behind the plate after failing to cut it as both a third baseman and a first baseman. The Sullivans were also the first father and

son to play in a World Series—Billy I in 1906 with the White Sox, and Billy II in 1940 with the Tigers.

Other Fathers and Sons Who Both Had Lengthy Careers
Earl Averill, Sr., and Jr. George and Dick Sisler. Ray and Bob Boone. Marty and Matt Keough. Ernie and Don Johnson. Mike and Tommy Tresh. Pinky and Milt May. Joe Schultz, Sr., and Jr. Mel Queen and son Mel. Dick Schofield and son Dick. Yogi and Dale Berra. Bob and Terry Kennedy. Maury and Bump Wills. Joe Coleman and son Joe. Dizzy and Steve Trout. Jim Bagby, Sr., and Jr. Vern and Vance Law. Jim and Mike Hegan. Max and Hal Lanier. Dolf and Doug Camilli. Gus and Buddy Bell. Roy Smalley, II and III. Oscar Ray Grimes, Sr., and Jr. Thornton and Don Lee.

Only Father and Son to Play for the Same Team in the Same Decade
Earle Brucker, Sr., and Jr., both caught for the A's in the 1940s. Unlike the Sullivans, Brucker *père* could hit, whereas his son couldn't. Brian McRae promises to be the second son to play for the same team as his father in the same decade. Should Barry Bonds be traded to the Cubs or Cardinals before the 1980s are out, he would be the third.

First Father and Son Both to Pitch in the Majors
Willie Mills, New York Giants, 1901; Art Mills, Boston Braves, 1927. Neither ever won a game.

Only Father and Son Each to Win a Game before His 20th Birthday
Lew Krausse, Sr., Philadelphia A's, 1931; Lew Krausse, Jr., Kansas City A's, 1961.

Only Father and Son Each to Be a League Leader in Innings Pitched
Jim Bagby, Sr., Cleveland, 1920, led the AL with 340 innings pitched; Jim Bagby, Jr., Cleveland, 1943, equaled his father's feat by pitching in 273 innings.

Only Father and Son Each to Be a League Leader in Losses
Herman Pillette, Detroit, 1923, led the AL with 19 losses; Duane Pillette, St. Louis, 1951, tied for the AL lead with 14 losses.

Only Father and Son Each to Be a League Leader in Pinch Hits
Joe Schultz, Sr., St. Louis Cardinals, 1919, led the NL with eight pinch hits; Joe Schultz, Jr., St. Loius Browns, led the AL in pinch hits in both 1945 and 1946.

First Black Father and Son to Play in the Majors
Sam Hairston, Chicago White Sox, 1951, saw two of his sons make the majors—John in 1969 with the Cubs, and later Jerry, who broke in with the 1973 White Sox. Maury Wills became the second black father to have a son make it when Bump won the Rangers' second base job in 1977.

Longest Span between First Games Played in Majors by a Father and Son, Since 1901
36 years—Jack Lively, Detroit Tigers, 1911; Bud Lively, Cincinnati Reds, 1947. Both were pitchers; Jack was 62 years old when his son reached the majors.

All-time Longest Span between First Games Played in Majors by a Father and Son
43 years—Charlie Ganzel, St. Paul (UA), 1884; Babe Ganzel, Washington Senators, 1927. The elder Ganzel, among the game's leading catchers in the 1890s, had been dead 13 years by the time Babe made the majors, but his younger brother John, a first baseman with several teams in the early part of the century, was still alive to see it.

Only Father to Have Two Sons Who Won Batting Titles
Ewart Walker, who pitched for Washington between 1909 and 1912, fathered both Dixie and Harry Walker. Dixie won the NL batting title in 1944; Harry won it in 1947. Moreover, Ewart's brother Ernie played in the majors for the Browns in the mid-teens, giving the Walkers a second record for being the only family who had two generations of brothers make it to the top.

LEADERS IN COMBINED CAREER HITS*

1. Gus and Buddy Bell — 4096
2. George, Dick and Dave Sisler — 3557
3. Eddie Collins, Sr. and Jr. — 3377
4. Maury and Bump Wills — 2941
5. Ewart, Dixie and Harry Walker — 2883
6. Ray and Bob Boone — 2761
7. Yogi and Dale Berra — 2645

LEADERS IN COMBINED CAREER WINS*

1. Dizzy and Steve Trout — 244
2. Jim Bagby, Sr. and Jr. — 224
3. Ed Walsh and son Ed — 206
4. Joe Coleman and son Joe — 194

*Batters contributing at least one hit and pitchers at least one win to the family total.

The Most Prolific Hitters

In 1985 Pete Rose established a new all-time record for career base hits and Wade Boggs became the first American League player since 1928 to make 240 hits in a season.

PLAYERS WHO MADE 240 OR MORE HITS IN A SEASON

	Team	League	Year	Hits
George Sisler	St. Louis.	American	1920	257
Lefty O'Doul	Philadelphia	National	1929	254
Bill Terry	New York	National	1930	254
Al Simmons	Philadelphia	American	1925	253
Rogers Hornsby	St. Louis	National	1922	250
Chuck Klein	Philadelphia	National	1930	250
Ty Cobb	Detroit	American	1911	248
George Sisler	St. Louis	American	1922	246
Willie Keeler	Baltimore	National	1897	243
Babe Herman	Brooklyn	National	1930	241
Heinie Manush	Detroit	American	1928	241
Jesse Burkett	Cleveland	National	1896	240
Wade Boggs	Boston	American	1985	240

Most Seasons League Leader in Hits
  AL—8—Ty Cobb, last in 1919
  NL—7—Pete Rose, last in 1981

Most Seasons 200 or More Hits
  NL—10—Pete Rose, last in 1979
  AL—9—Ty Cobb, last in 1924

Most Consecutive Seasons 200 or More Hits
NL—8—Willie Keeler, 1894 through 1901
NL since 1901—5—Chuck Klein, 1929 through 1933
AL—5—Al Simmons, 1929 through 1933
      Charlie Gehringer, 1933 through 1937

Most Consecutive Seasons 200 or More Hits, Start of Career
3—Johnny Pesky, Boston Red Sox, 1942, 1946 and 1947; he missed the 1943 through 1945 seasons while in military service.

First Players to Make 200 or More Hits in a Season
NL—Sam Thompson, Detroit, 1887 (203 hits)
AA—Tip O'Neill, St. Louis, 1887 (225 hits)
      Pete Browning, Louisville, 1887 (220 hits)
      Denny Lyons, Philadelphia, 1887 (209 hits)
AL—Nap Lajoie, Philadelphia, 1901 (229 hits)

All-Time Organized-Baseball Record for Most Hits in a Season
325—Paul Strand, Salt Lake City, Pacific Coast League, 1923. Strand, who had earlier flopped as a teenage pitcher with the Boston Braves, returned to the majors at age 30 in 1924, but finished his career in the minors after hitting .228 in 47 games for the Philadelphia A's.

Fewest Hits, Season, Minimum 150 Games
NL—80—Dal Maxvill, St. Louis, 1970; batted 399 times in 152 games.
AL—82—Ed Brinkman, Washington, 1965; batted 444 times in 154 games.

Most Hits in a Nine-Inning Game
NL—7—Wilbert Robinson, Baltimore, June 10, 1892; went 7-for-7. Rennie Stennett, Pittsburgh, September 16, 1975; went 7-for-7 and twice had two hits in an inning as the Pirates blasted the Cubs 22–0, the worst shutout shellacking in this century.
AL—6—Held by many players. Only one AL player, Cesar Gutierrez of Detroit, has ever gone 7-for-7, and that was in a 12-inning game on June 21, 1970. For the season Gutierrez netted only 101 hits and hit .243; after 1970 he made just seven more hits in the majors.

All-Time Major-League Record for Most Hits in a Game
9—Johnny Burnett, Cleveland, July 10, 1932; went 9-for-11 in an 18-inning game against Philadelphia.

First Player to Go 6-For-6 in a Nine-Inning Game
Davy Force, Philadelphia, June 27, 1876. He hit .230 that season and was arguably the weakest hitter of all time.

First Teammates Each to Get Six Hits in the Same Nine-Inning Game
Hick Carpenter and Long John Reilly of the American Association Cincinnati Red Stockings on September 12, 1883. Both went 6-for-7.

PLAYERS WHO MADE 3,000 OR MORE CAREER HITS

	Years Active	Hits
Pete Rose	1963–	4256[1]
Ty Cobb	1905–28	4191[2]
Hank Aaron	1954–76	3771
Stan Musial	1941–63	3630
Tris Speaker	1907–28	3515
Honus Wagner	1897–1917	3430
Carl Yastrzemski	1961–83	3419[3]
Eddie Collins	1906–30	3311
Willie Mays	1951–73	3251
Paul Waner	1926–45	3152
Nap Lajoie	1896–1916	3251
Rod Carew	1967–85	3053
Cap Anson	1876–97	3041
Lou Brock	1961–79	3023
Al Kaline	1953–74	3007
Roberto Clemente	1955–72	3000

[1] Holds the record for the most hits in the National League, having played his entire career there. Cobb is of course the American League record holder.

[2] Disputed figure. Many historians believe that Cobb was credited with an extra hit in 1910 and his correct total should be 4190.

[3] The first player to make 3000 hits on less than a .290 career batting average, Yaz was down to .285 by the time he retired. Kaline and Brock are the only other members of the 300-hit club who finished with career batting averages below .300.

The Strikeout Kings

On April 30, 1986, in the course of beating Seattle, Roger Clemens of the Red Sox became the first pitcher in history to fan 20 batters in a nine-inning game. Less than a month later, on May 28, Joe Cowley of the White Sox set a modern record when he started off his game against the Rangers by striking out the first seven hitters who faced him. Cowley's record lasted only until September 23, 1986, when Jim Deshaies of the Astros fanned the first eight Dodgers he faced in the course of pitching his first Major League complete game. Clemens, Cowley and Deshaies are just three of the multitude of pitchers in recent years who have toppled almost all the existing season and career strikeout records.

Most Consecutive Strikeouts, Game
10—Tom Seaver, New York Mets, April 22, 1970. Seaver fanned 19 San Diego Padres in the game, tying the former nine-inning record, and broke Mickey Welch's old mark of nine consecutive strikeouts, set against Philadelphia on August 28, 1884, when Welch, pitching for the New York Gothams (soon to become the Giants), opened the game by fanning the first nine Phillies he faced—the all-time record Deshaies was shooting for until he faltered after striking out Jose Gonzalez.

Most Consecutive Strikeouts by a Rookie in His First Game
7—Sammy Stewart, Baltimore Orioles, September 1, 1978, against Cleveland. A starting pitcher at the time, Stewart failed to finish the game despite his strikeout skein and was also knocked out early in his next start. The following season Earl Weaver made him a reliever.

Most Strikeouts by a Rookie in His First Start
NL—15—Karl Spooner, Brooklyn, September 22, 1954
J. R. Richard, Houston, September 5, 1971
AL—12—Elmer Myers, Philadelphia, October 6, 1915. Moreover, Myers threw a two-hit shutout. The following season he led the AL in losses with 23 and set the AL rookie record for most bases on balls.

First Pitcher to Strike out 19 Batters in a Game
Charlie Sweeney, Providence Grays, June 7, 1884. Exactly one month later Hugh Daily of Chicago fanned 19 hitters in a Union Association game. Daily, as you no doubt know, had only one arm, but Sweeney apparently had a less overt but ultimately more insidious handicap. He jumped to the Union Association in the midst of the 1884 season, paving the way for Hoss Radbourn to set all sorts of iron-man records while bringing Providence the pennant. By 1887 Sweeney, possibly the most gifted pitcher of his time, had drifted from the majors altogether although just 24 years old, and shortly thereafter he wound up in San Quentin, convicted of manslaughter.

First Pitcher to Strike out 18 Batters in a game, Mound 60 Feet 6 Inches From The Plate
AL—Bob Feller, Cleveland, October 2, 1938, against Detroit
NL—Sandy Koufax, Los Angeles, August 31, 1959, against San Francisco. Koufax also fanned 18 Cubs on April 24, 1965, making him the only NL pitcher who twice struck out 18 or more batters in a game.

First Pitcher to Strike Out 19 Batters in a Game, Mound 60 Feet 6 Inches From The Plate
NL—Steve Carlton, St. Louis, September 15, 1969, against the pennant-winning Mets. The following year Tom Seaver of the Mets, while breaking Welch's consecutive strikeout mark, became the second pitcher to do it.
AL—Nolan Ryan, California, August 12, 1974. In 1976 Ryan also had an 18-K effort and became the first AL hurler who twice fanned 18 or more batters in a game.

Most Strikeouts, Game, by a Rookie
18—Bill Gullickson, Montreal, September 10, 1980

Most Strikeouts, Game, Extra Innings Included
21—Tom Cheney, Washington Senators, September 12, 1962, against Baltimore, in 16 innings

Most Strikeouts, Season
AL—383—Nolan Ryan, California, 1973. His record-breaking strikeout was Rich Reese of the Twins—on his last pitch of the season.

NL—382—Sandy Koufax, Los Angeles, 1965

Most Strikeouts, Season, 1901 Through 1919
AL—349—Rube Waddell, Philadelphia, 1904. Waddell's total is now universally accepted, but after Bob Feller notched 348 K's in 1946 it was hotly contested for some while by many authorities, who felt that Waddell had been credited with more strikeouts in 1904 than he'd earned and Feller was now the true modern record holder.

NL—267—Christy Mathewson, New York Giants, 1903

Most strikeouts, Season, 1920 through 1941
NL—262—Dazzy Vance, Brooklyn 1924
AL—261—Bob Feller, Cleveland, 1940

Most Strikeouts, Season, 1942–60
AL—348—Bob Feller, Cleveland, 1946
NL—246—Sandy Koufax, Los Angeles, 1960

Most Strikeouts, Season, since 1977
AL—341—Nolan Ryan, California, 1977
NL—313—J. R. Richard, Houston, 1979

Most Seasons League Leader in Strikeouts
AL—12—Walter Johnson, last in 1924
NL—7—Dazzy Vance, 1922–28 consecutive

Most Seasons 300 or More Strikeouts
5—Nolan Ryan, last in 1977. Ryan tied the record too for the most seasons with 200 or more strikeouts when he did it for the 10th time in 1985 equaling Tom Seaver, who last accomplished it in 1978.

Most Consecutive Seasons 200 or More Strikeouts
9—Tom Seaver, 1968–76

Most Seasons 100 or More Strikeouts
21—Don Sutton, 1966–86 consecutive

Most Significant Milestone Strikeout
Now that it seems clear that Nolan Ryan will retire with more career strikeouts than Steve Carlton, my vote goes to Ryan's whiff of the Expos' Brad Mills on April 27, 1983, giving him his 3509th career strikeout and tying him with Walter Johnson.

Most Strikeouts, Season, Team
NL—1221—Houston, 1969; led by Don Wilson with 235
AL—1189—Cleveland, 1967; led by Sam McDowell with 236

First Team to Top 1000 Strikeouts in a Season
Los Angeles Dodgers, 1959, notched 1077; led by Don Drysdale with 242

Fewest Strikeouts, Season, Since 1901, by League Leader in Strikeouts
AL—113—Bob Newsom, Washington, and Tex Hughson, Boston, 1942
NL—134—Dazzy Vance, Brooklyn, 1922

Most Recent League Leader to Have Fewer Than 200 Strikeouts (1981 Excluded)
AL—187—Len Barker, Cleveland, 1980
NL—188—Jack Sanford, Philadelphia, 1957

Most Consecutive Years, League, without a Pitcher Who Had 200 or More Strikeouts
NL—16—1942 through 1957, from Johnny Vander Meer, who had 202 K;s in 1941, to Sam Jones with 205 K's in 1958
AL—13—1917 through 1929, from Walter Johnson with 228 K's in 1916 to Lefty Grove, 209 K's in 1930

Most Consecutive Years, Individual, without Registering 100 Strikeouts in a Season
21—Ted Lyons, 1923–46. Lyons, a 260-game winner, never once in his long career came even close to notching 100 strikeouts in a season; his high was 74 in 1933.

TOP 10 IN CAREER STRIKEOUTS

	Years Active	Strikeouts
1. Nolan Ryan	1966–	4277
2. Steve Carlton	1965–	4040[1]
3. Tom Seaver	1967–	3640
4. Gaylord Perry	1962–83	3534[2]
5. Walter Johnson	1907–27	3509[3]
6. Don Sutton	1966–	3431
7. Phil Niekro	1964–	3277[4]
8. Fergie Jenkins	1965–83	3192
9. Bob Gibson	1959–75	3117
10. Bert Blyleven	1970–	3090[5]

[1]Southpaw record. Mickey Lolich, the runner-up, is 12th on the all-time list. Jerry Koosman, if you can believe it, is the fourth-most prolific lefty strikeout king in history and 16th on the all-time list.

[2]Never a league leader in strikeouts; nor, for that matter, was Sutton.

[3]The only top 10 member who was active before 1959.

[4]Niekro, Jenkins, Gibson and Blyleven all were league leaders in strikeouts just once.

[5]Replaced Jim Bunning on the top 10 list in 1985. Bunning's departure from it left Johnson as the lone member who collected a significant portion of his career strikeouts—let alone all of them—prior to expansion. What does it mean? A number of things certainly, but not the least of them is that while Johnson's career record lasted 56 years, Ryan's could well fall before the end of the century.

World Series Play: 1977–86

FRANCHISE SUMMARY

Team	League	WS Record through 1986	Last WS	LCS Record through 1986	Last LCS
Oakland	American	3–0	1974	3–3	1981
Pittsburgh	National	5–2	1979	2–4	1979
New York	American	22–11	1981	4–1	1981
Cleveland	American	2–1	1954	—	—
New York	National	2–1	1986	3–0	1986
St. Louis	National	9–5	1985	2–0	1985
Boston	American	5–4	1986	2–0	1986
Cincinnati	National	4–4	1976	4–2	1979
Los Angeles	National	4–4	1981	4–2	1985
Baltimore	American	3–3	1983	5–2	1983
Chicago	American	2–2	1959	0–1	1983
Kansas City	American	1–1	1985	2–4	1985
Detroit	American	4–5	1984	1–1	1984
Philadelphia	National	1–3	1983	2–3	1983
Chicago	National	2–8	1945	0–1	1984
San Francisco	National	0–1	1962	0–1	1971
Minnesota	American	0–1	1965	0–2	1970
Milwaukee	American	0–1	1982	1–0	1982
San Diego	National	0–1	1984	1–0	1984
California	American	—	—	0–3	1986
Atlanta	National	—	—	0–2	1981
Houston	National	—	—	0–2	1986
Montreal	National	—	—	0–1	1981
Toronto	American	—	—	0–1	1985

Yearly Highlights

1977—New York (AL) defeated Los Angeles (NL) 4 games to 2

The Royals for the second year in a row took the Yankees to five games in the LCS before succumbing in the ninth inning of the finale. The Dodgers beat the Phillies 3–1 in the LCS but fell prey in the Series to Mike Torrez's two complete-game wins and Reggie Jackson's three-homer barrage in Game Six. Jackson had five homers and 10 RBIs in the Series.

1978—New York (AL) defeated Los Angeles (NL) 4 games to 2

For the first time all four divisions had repeat winners. Both the Yankees and the Dodgers won their LCSes three games to one, and the Yankees then completed the reprise of the 1977 season by winning the Series in six after losing the opening two games in Los Angeles. Bucky Dent, whose three-run homer sparked the Yankees in their division playoff win over the Red Sox, had 10 hits in the Series, and his Dodgers counterpart at shortstop, Bill Russell, led all players with 11.

1979—Pittsburgh (NL) defeated Baltimore (AL) 4 games to 3

The Orioles held a 3–1 lead in games and had their three mound aces, Mike Flanagan, Jim Palmer and Scott McGregor, ready to apply the clincher. But all three lost, giving the Pirates their second seven-game Series win over Baltimore in the decade. The Orioles beat California 3–1 in the LCS while the Pirates swept Cincinnati.

1980—Philadelphia (NL) defeated Kansas City (AL) 4 games to 2

To win their first world title in their 98-year history, the Phillies beat not only a hot Kansas City team that had knocked off the Yankees three straight in the LCS, but the Astros with a pair of come-from-behind 10th-inning victories in the final two games of the National League LCS. After a disappointing LCS, Mike Schmidt had two homers and seven RBIs in the Series and was outdone only by Amos Otis of the Royals, who led both clubs with 11 hits and a .438 average.

1981—Los Angeles (NL) defeated New York (AL) 4 games to 2

The Dodgers came back from a 2–1 deficit in the LCS to defeat the Expos, then lost the first two Series games. Returning to Los Angeles, they took three straight from the Yankees and then journeyed back to Yankee Stadium and won the closer 9–2 in a fashion that made Yankees owner George Steinbrenner apoplectic and spoiled for him the taste of the Yankees' LCS sweep of Oakland, managed by Billy Martin.

1982—St. Louis (NL) defeated Milwaukee (AL) 4 games to 3

The Brewers became the first team to win an LCS after trailing two games to zip when they took three straight from the Angels at Milwaukee. But in the Series the Brewers had to play the last two games on the road, and the Cardinals won both, led by Keith Hernandez's eight RBIs and Joaquin Andujar's two wins. Mike Caldwell of the Brewers also had two wins and was only one out away, in Game Five, from being the first pitcher since 1977 to complete two games in a Series. To earn the right to meet the Brewers, the Cardinals pasted Atlanta three straight times in the National League LCS.

1983—Baltimore (AL) defeated Philadelphia (NL) 4 games to 1

The Phillies rode Steve Carlton's two wins to a victory over the Dodgers in the LCS, then took the Series opener before the Orioles got untracked. For the Orioles, Cal Ripken hit only .167 in the Series and Gary Roenicke went 0-for-7 after both had murdered White Sox pitchers in the American League LCS.

1984—Detroit (AL) defeated San Diego (NL) 4 games to 1

The Tigers swept the Royals in the LCS and had little trouble in the Series with the Padres as Jack Morris posted two complete-game wins and Alan Trammell hit .450 and knocked in six runs. All the postseason drama occurred in the National League LCS when the Padres took three straight from Chicago after the Cubs were poised to win their first pennant since 1945.

1985—Kansas City (AL) defeated St. Louis (NL) 4 games to 3

The majors changed to a best-four-of-seven format in the LCSes, giving the Royals an opportunity to snatch the AL pennant from the Blue Jays after trailing three games to one. In the Series they likewise fell behind the Cardinals 3–1 but then won three straight to become the first AL expansion team to win a world title. The Cardinals cited umpire Don Denkinger's questionable safe call in Game Six as the reason for their defeat, but their .185 team batting average was a much larger factor. In the LCS, the Cardinals beat the Dodgers 4 games to 2, homers by Jack Clark and switch hitter Ozzie Smith—his first ever left-handed—hanging consecutive defeats on Dodgers reliever Tom Niedenfuer in the final two contests.

1986—New York (NL) defeated Boston (AL) 4 games to 3

After an uneventful regular season in which all four division races were resolved by Labor Day, the Mets beat the Astros four games to two in a National League LCS that was arguably the best-played and most dramatic fall series ever. It culminated in a see-saw 16-inning game—the longest post-season contest in history—which the Mets won 7–6 behind Jesse Orosco, the first relief pitcher to win three games in a championship series. Orosco saved two more contests in the World Series, including the deciding seventh game, but was only one of many Mets heroes in the most remarkable comeback in Series history. Trailing 5–3 with two out in the bottom of the 10th inning of Game 6 and only one strike away from elimination, the Mets rallied for three runs and thereby became the first team on the brink of extinction to overcome so large a deficit in its last turn at bat and then go on to win the Series. The Mets' triumph deprived Boston pitcher Bruce Hurst of the MVP Award—he had already been voted the trophy on the basis of his two Series wins before New York launched its last-ditch comeback—but the Red Sox, although frustrated once again in a bid to claim their first World Championship since 1918, had the satisfaction of staging an equally incredible come-from-behind win in the AL LCS. Down three games to one, Boston trailed the Angels 5–4 in the top of the ninth inning of Game 5 when Red Sox centerfielder Dave Henderson uncorked a two-out, two-strike, two-run homer. The Angels fought back to tie the game in the bottom of the ninth, but lost 7–6 in 11 innings and then were blown out in the final two contests in Boston. Houston starter Mike Scott and Boston second baseman Marty Barrett were the individual pitching and hitting standouts in post-season play, but in the end the Mets superior bullpen, one of the deepest in recent history, was the deciding factor.

WORLD SERIES RECORDS

Batting

Department	Single Series	Career (Minimum 20 games)
Batting Average	.625, Babe Ruth, New York, AL, 1928	.391, Lou Brock, St. Louis, NL
Slugging Average	1.727, Lou Gehrig, New York, AL, 1928	.744 Babe Ruth, New York, AL
Home Runs	5, Reggie Jackson, New York, AL, 1977	18, Mickey Mantle, New York, AL
RBIs	12, Bobby Richardson, New York, AL, 1960	40, Mickey Mantle, New York, AL
Runs	10, Reggie Jackson, New York, AL, 1977	42, Mickey Mantle, New York, AL
Hits	13, Bobby Richardson, New York, AL, 1964 13, Lou Brock, St. Louis, NL, 1968 13, Marty Barrett, Boston, AL, 1986	71, Yogi Berra, New York, AL
Total Bases	25, Reggie Jackson, New York, AL, 1977	123, Mickey Mantle, New York, AL
Stolen Bases	7, Lou Brock, St. Louis, NL, 1967 7, Lou Brock, St. Louis, NL, 1968	14, Lou Brock, St. Louis, NL 14, Eddie Collins, Philadelphia and Chicago, AL

Pitching

Wins	3, achieved by many pitchers, last by Mickey Lolich, Detroit, AL, 1968	10, Whitey Ford, New York, AL
Losses	3, George Frazier, New York, AL, 1968	8, Whitey Ford, New York, AL

Department	Single Series	Career (Minimum 20 games)
Complete Games	3, achieved by many pitchers, last by Mickey Lolich, Detroit, AL, 1968, Bob Gibson, St. Louis, NL, 1968	10, Christy Mathewson, New York, NL
ERA	0.00, Christy Mathewson, New York, NL, 1905 0.00, Waite Hoyt, New York, AL, 1921 (27 innings)	0.83, Harry Brecheen, St. Louis, NL
Saves	3, Roy Face, Pittsburgh, NL, 1960 3, Kent Tekulve, Pittsburgh, NL, 1979	6, Rollie Fingers, Oakland, AL
Shutouts	3, Christy Mathewson, New York, NL, 1905	4, Christy Mathewson, New York, NL
Strikeouts	35, Bob Gibson, St. Louis, NL, 1968	94, Whitey Ford, New York, AL

Lowest Batting Average, Single Series, Minimum 15 at Bats
NL—.000—Dal Maxvill, St. Louis, 1968 (0-for-22)
　　　　　Gil Hodges, Brooklyn, 1952 (0-for-21)
　　　　　Jimmy Sheckard, Chicago, 1906 (0-for-21)
AL—.000—Mike Epstein, Oakland, 1972 (0-for-16)
　　　　　Flea Clifton, Detroit, 1935 (0-for-16)

Lowest Batting Average, Career, Minimum Two World Series and 40 at Bats
AL—.061—Marv Owen, Detroit, 1934, 1935 (3-for-49)
NL—.117—Dal Maxvill, St. Louis, 1964, 1967 and 1968 (7-for-61)

Most World Series Wins By Pitcher without a Loss
6—Lefty Gomez, New York, AL

Most World Series Losses By Pitchers without a Win
4—Don Newcombe, Brooklyn, NL

Most Consecutive World Series Losses by Pitcher
5—Joe Bush, Philadelphia, AL, Boston, AL, New York, AL

Highest World Series ERA by Pitcher, Minimum 20 Innings
8.59—Don Newcombe, Brooklyn, NL

Last Surviving Participant in First World Series
Freddie Parent, Boston, AL, died in 1972. Fred Carrisch, a catcher with Pittsburgh in 1903, lived until 1977 but didn't play in the Series.

First Players to Receive a World Series Share in Five Figures
Members of the 1954 New York Giants ($11,146.90)

First Players to Receive a World Series Share of $20,000
Members of the 1972 Cincinnati Reds ($20,705)

Last Winning Team to Receive a World Series Share of Less Than $20,000
The Reds in 1975, playing in small Fenway Park, got only $19,060.46 per man.

Smallest World Series Purse Shares by Winning Team
In 1918 the Boston Red Sox got only $1,102.51 per man. It was the first year that other first-division teams shared in World Series receipts, plus the players voted to donate 10 percent of the proceeds to war charities—and then briefly went on strike after the fourth game when the crowds at the first three games were disappointingly small.

Largest Crowd to Attend a World Series Game
92,706—Game Five to the 1959 Series, played at the Los Angeles Coliseum

The 10 Most Dramatic Postseason Pitching Achievements
   1. Don Larsen's perfect game in the 1956 World Series.
   2. Ralph Terry's 1–0 victory in Game Seven of the 1962 World Series.
   3. Bob Gibson's five-hit shutout coupled with 17 strikeouts in the opener of the 1968 World Series.
   4. Johnny Podres's 2–0 shutout in Game Seven of the 1955 World Series, giving the Dodgers their only world title while in Brooklyn.
   5. Lew Burdette's second consecutive shutout and third win over the Yankees in the 1957 World Series.
   6. Pete Alexander's strikeout of Tony Lazzeri in the seventh game of the 1926 World Series, followed by two scoreless relief innings.

7. Dave McNally's 1–0 shutout in the last game of the 1966 World Series, completing a string of 33⅔ straight scoreless innings by Orioles pitchers.

8. Allie Reynold's 1–0 two-hit win over Brooklyn in the opener of the 1949 World Series.

9. Catfish Hunter's 3–0 shutout of the free-swinging Orioles in the deciding fifth game of the 1973 American League LCS.

10. Rookie Gene Bearden's 8–3 complete-game win over the Red Sox in Fenway Park, justifying Cleveland manager Lou Boudreau's selection of a frosh pitcher—and a lefty to boot—in the winner-take-all 1948 American League pennant playoff game.

The 10 Most Dramatic Postseason Plate Appearances

1. Bobby Thomson's three-run homer off Ralph Branca of the Dodgers to give the Giants the decisive third game in the 1951 National League pennant playoff series.

2. Bill Mazeroski's 10th-inning home run in the 1960 World Series, giving the Pirates their first championship since 1909.

3. Cookie Lavagetto's double in the 1947 World Series, which broke up Bill Bevens's no-hitter with two outs in the ninth inning and gave the Dodgers the game.

4. Dave Henderson's two-run homer for Boston in the top of the ninth inning of Game 5 of the American League LCS, propelling the Red Sox to a 6–5 lead in the game and spurring them ultimately to the pennant after they were one strike away from being eliminated four games to one by the Angels.

5. Chris Chambliss's ninth-inning home run in the fifth game of the 1976 American League LCS.

6. Willie McCovey's lineout to Bobby Richardson, ending the 1962 World Series.

7. Carlton Fisk's 12th-inning homer to win the sixth game of the 1975 World Series.

8. Bucky Dent's three-run homer off Mike Torrez of the Red Sox in the 1978 American League Eastern Division playoff game.

9. Vic Wertz's 460-foot drive with two runners on, which Willie Mays speared in the eighth inning of the opening game of the 1954 World Series.

10. Earl McNeely's pebble-struck single, which won the 1924 World Series for Washington.

There's an epidemic with 27 million victims. And no visible symptoms.

It's an epidemic of people who can't read.

Believe it or not, 27 million Americans are functionally illiterate, about one adult in five.

The solution to this problem is you... when you join the fight against illiteracy. So call the Coalition for Literacy at toll-free **1-800-228-8813** and volunteer.

Volunteer Against Illiteracy. The only degree you need is a degree of caring.